Mark Twain's
Pudd'nhead Wilson

Mark Twain's
Pudd'nhead Wilson

Race, Conflict, and Culture

Edited by Susan Gillman and
Forrest G. Robinson

DUKE UNIVERSITY PRESS
Durham and London, 1990

Susan Gillman's essay was previously published in the *South Atlantic Quarterly* 87, no. 2 (Spring 1988), © 1988 Duke University Press; a different version appeared as chapter 3 in *Dark Twins: Imposture and Identity in Mark Twain's America*, © 1989, University of Chicago Press. Eric J. Sundquist's essay previously appeared in *Representations* 24 (Fall 1988), © 1988 The Regents of the University of California.

Library of Congress Cataloging-in-Publication Data

Mark Twain's Pudd'nhead Wilson : race, conflict, and culture / edited by Susan Gillman and Forrest G. Robinson.

    p.   cm.

  ISBN 0-8223-1001-5

  1. Twain, Mark, 1835-1910. Pudd'nhead Wilson. 2. Twain, Mark, 1835-1910 – Political and social views. 3. Identity (Psychology) in literature. 4. Slavery and slaves in literature. 5. Social conflict in literature. 6. Race relations in literature. 7. Doubles in literature. I. Gillman, Susan Kay. II. Robinson, Forrest G. (Forrest Glen), 1940– .

PS1317.M27   1990

813'.4 – dc20   89–49753
                                                CIP

Contents

SUSAN GILLMAN AND FORREST G. ROBINSON
Introduction
vii

JAMES M. COX
***Pudd'nhead Wilson* Revisited**
1

FORREST G. ROBINSON
The Sense of Disorder in *Pudd'nhead Wilson*
22

ERIC J. SUNDQUIST
Mark Twain and Homer Plessy
46

MICHAEL ROGIN
Francis Galton and Mark Twain
The Natal Autograph in *Pudd'nhead Wilson*
73

SUSAN GILLMAN
"Sure Identifiers"
Race, Science, and the Law in *Pudd'nhead Wilson*
86

MYRA JEHLEN
The Ties that Bind
Race and Sex in *Pudd'nhead Wilson*
105

CAROLYN PORTER
Roxana's Plot
121

JOHN CARLOS ROWE
Fatal Speculations
Murder, Money, and Manners in *Pudd'nhead Wilson*
137

MICHAEL COWAN
"By Right of the White Election"
Political Theology and Theological Politics
in *Pudd'nhead Wilson*
155

WILSON CAREY MCWILLIAMS
***Pudd'nhead Wilson* on Democratic Governance**
177

GEORGE E. MARCUS
"What did he reckon would become of the other half if he killed his half?"
Doubled, Divided, and Crossed Selves in *Pudd'nhead Wilson;* or, Mark Twain as Cultural Critic in His Own Times and Ours
190

JOHN H. SCHAAR
Some of the Ways of Freedom in *Pudd'nhead Wilson*
211

Notes   229
About the Contributors   255
Index   257

Introduction

Rumors of *Pudd'nhead Wilson* as an "unreadable" novel were not
always greatly exaggerated.[1] What are now regarded as its
leading critical features were once dismissed as the signs of its failure: we read the incoherence in Twain's narrative not as aesthetic
failure but as political symptom, the irruption into this narrative
about mistaken racial identity of materials from the nineteenth-
century political unconscious. Instead of searching for a hidden unifying structure, as did a previous generation of New Critics, the scholars in this volume are after what Myra Jehlen calls "the novel's most
basic and unacknowledged issues." We do thus share the earlier critical passion for detection, although we are not similarly inclined to
dismiss evidence of authorial intention. Most of the essays in this
volume are subtextual studies which seize upon the text's inconsistencies and contradictions as windows on the world of late-nineteenth-century American culture. The collection as a whole seeks to
make the strata of Mark Twain's political unconscious available for
critical scrutiny.

Mark Twain's novel about mistaken identities is manifestly uncertain of its own. The textual history of *Pudd'nhead Wilson* gives
evidence that Twain was unsure whether to regard his errant creation as the farce, *Those Extraordinary Twins*, that first took shape
in his imagination, or to settle instead for the somber tale that later
overtook him. How indeed should we refer to this work, originally
published by the American Publishing Company in 1894 as *The
Tragedy of Pudd'nhead Wilson and the Comedy Those Extraordinary Twins*? Most of the essays in this volume use *Pudd'nhead Wilson* to refer to both texts, thus joining the comedy and tragedy together even more closely than they were in the first American edition.
For most of us, moreover, Twain's ambivalent relationship to his book
points to related ambivalences toward apparently unrelated matters:
race misrecognition, slavery, political cross-dressing, aristocratic liber-

ties, democratic freedoms, and narrative coherence, to name a few. Indeed, that final display of ambivalence – expressing itself in Twain's nervously mocking, interstitial interrogations of his "jack-leg" performance – establishes for one of us that there is a discernible "sense" running through the text's apparently hopeless disorder.

It was precisely *Pudd'nhead Wilson*'s reputation for disorder, and the cultural implications of its relative critical neglect, that inspired the interdisciplinary conference, held in March 1987 at the University of California, Santa Cruz, from which this collection of essays emerged. James Cox's keynote address, with its attention to the centrifugal play of the novel's (and the novelist's) chief contradictions, captured the tone of much that followed. In focusing on the competing tendencies in Twain's character – his fascination with the liberating mechanical technology of print and his bondage as an author to preconscious fantasies, his wish to be free from political tyranny along with his consequent sense of the tyrannies of freedom – Cox correlates the ambivalences at work in Twain's autobiography with the cultural contradictions of the Reconstruction era. Similarly, the essays that follow tend to arise from the perception of divisions in the novel's constructions of race, class, and gender, and in Twain's affiliated attitudes toward political economy and theology, governance, and personal identity. Such thematic variety reflects the disciplinary range of the scholars gathered here (their fields: literary criticism, history, political science, anthropology), and the range of the novel itself, whose fragmentedness appeals to a taste for multiplicity, and invites the kind of interdisciplinary practice on display here. We hasten to add that one critic's rich multiplicity is another's hopeless muddle. Thus the volume closes with a direct challenge to the text's value – as literature, aesthetically defined, or as cultural symptom – and therefore to critical enterprises such as this one.

Mark Twain might have been amused by the expense of so much critical energy on his freakish twin creation. Academic humbug, he might have concluded (our own concluding gesture to the contrary notwithstanding). Still, it is presently our conviction that the time is right for a long, careful look at this vexed but powerful novel. The publication in 1980 of Sidney E. Berger's Norton Critical Edition of *Pudd'nhead Wilson and Those Extraordinary Twins* has provided us with a text that will remain "standard" until the California edition appears. (The Norton Critical Edition is used as the citing text throughout this volume.) At the same time, thanks to the painstaking research of Hershel Parker and others, scholars appreciate more than ever before the so-called "aesthetic anomalies" of the texts and enjoy the opportunity – not exploited by Parker – to make sense of them. Anomalies such as the inconsistently shifting racial characterization of one of the novel's protagonists are evidently geared to the chaotic and confusing sequence – now pretty firmly documented – in which Twain composed and revised the manuscript. This valuable new light on the text's manifestly incomplete aesthetic development forms the occasion, seized upon here, to reformulate the questions conventionally asked of *Pudd'nhead Wilson*, especially about the halting emergence of the dark, enigmatic "tragedy" about racial twins from the "comedy" about Siamese twins.

On a broader critical front, increasing attention to the literary text as social production, and a complementary attentiveness to the textualization of such cultural categories as race, class, and gender make the present moment a particularly auspicious one for an interdisciplinary study of *Pudd'nhead Wilson*. Methodologically most relevant are efforts to situate literary texts in cultural context, and thus to reread them, both as products of the literary marketplace and as agents of cultural and political transformation. This general scholarly trend has as yet unmeasured implications for *Pudd'nhead Wilson*. But one area of exploration that strikes us as particularly promising is bordered by the treatment of race and sexuality in *Pudd'nhead Wilson*: are racial inequalities hereditary or environmental, and how does the novel trace the illicit relationship, central to its plot, between white males and their black female slaves and offspring? These questions are now being recast in the interdisciplinary context of the New Literary and Social History. Recent scholarship has tended fruitfully to pair, rather than to separate, issues of race and sex, in an attempt to articulate the often paradoxical relationships and divergences between figures for racial and sexual identity and difference. A cultural approach to the construction of racial and sexual categories in Mark Twain's novel enables us better to assess received representations of political and social change in the late nineteenth century.

Because its true subject matter is mistaken identity, *Pudd'nhead Wilson* readily lends itself to the meditations on race, class, and gender brought together in this collection. Such a gathering of these now ultra-fashionable categories will undoubtedly appeal to those with a taste for the "new historicism," a term we employ with the understanding that it refers broadly both to a field of study which foregrounds the issues of race, class, and gender, *and* to the production of an alternative cultural realm in which those issues can be addressed adequately. Finally, though, in order to give these issues canonical status, a prior project is enjoined upon us: to demonstrate that this neglected, almost proverbially "secondary" and "problem" text in fact merits the kind of sustained attention generally reserved for "classic" works. The canonical elevation of *Pudd'nhead Wilson*, clearly if implicitly an agenda for several of the critics represented here, is perhaps most forcefully developed when the novel is viewed as a teaching text equal in value to *Huckleberry Finn*.

In advocating *Pudd'nhead Wilson*, we advance the lesson that so-called "lesser" works are often the most telling ones – politically *and* aesthetically telling. Because the novel is itself problematically open-ended, for example, it raises issues in an open-ended way: issues of history and the uses of history, issues of textual authority and of the authority of the American literary canon, issues of race, class and gender. We may go further in this vein to suggest that the status "lesser" is often the sign that a text presents challenges to dominant ideologies. "Lesser," we may find, means vital, critical, central. Thus we offer *Pudd'nhead Wilson* as a case study in contemporary methods of interpreting texts that defy older critical categories. It is a paradigmatic "new text" in that it teaches us how to teach differently.

Bearing the question of teaching in mind, we have organized the essays so that questions are opened and discussed in what appears to be the most useful sequence. Beginning with the keynote address, which is followed by a close look at the compositional history of the text, the essays move outward from late-nineteenth-century ideologies of race and gender, to the analysis of political economy and theology, governance, and personal identity. We offer the rather detailed summaries that follow as an aid to readers with specific topics in mind.

James M. Cox sets the tone for the volume in his free-wheeling "*Pudd'nhead Wilson* Revisited," a series of meditations on the word *race* – meditations which lead him inexorably, even slavishly, he concedes, to a sense of how culturally and morally overloaded a term it is. Cox draws attention to the contradictory dynamics and inertia of American race relations. "Race," he observes, refers at once to the most vigorous of human activities – the race for the Pacific or the arms race – and to the inertial essence of the human species, the races of the human family. In Cox's view, the absolute contradiction of slavery in a free country, of "race" in America, explodes into the myriad divisions of *Pudd'nhead Wilson*, particularly in its opposition between slavery and freedom, an opposition that the novel simultaneously advances and subverts. In recognizing that the first American revolution resulted in freedom from tyranny yet left us with slavery, Mark Twain also saw that the second American revolution brought freedom out of slavery yet left us with the tyranny of freedom, freedom "under the law." In the course of developing his ideas, Cox bears witness to the sense of contradiction that overtook him in his return to a text which he thought he had long since mastered.[2]

Forrest G. Robinson finds in the novel's notable textual confusions a key to what he calls "The Sense of Disorder in *Pudd'nhead Wilson*." Focusing specifically on the discontinuity between the dark central chapters and the "strangely up-beat" conclusion, Robinson argues that the point is precisely the comprehensive blindness of author, book, and reader to the significance of that discontinuity. Rather than confront the full, painful implications of the race-slavery plot, they acquiesce in the tidy solution of the murder mystery. Indeed, the novel's cultural authority lies in this process of evasion, or "bad faith," which enables the retreat to an illusion of resolution where none has occurred. The impulse to address the bitter reality of race-slavery, as it surfaces in the disorderly order of the novel's composition, was evidently in tension with a countering impulse to suppress the same truth. In effect, Robinson concludes, the terms of Twain's truce with bad faith enforced the composition of two stories, one the vehicle of grave cultural analysis, the other a distracting cover. Both stories are "contained" in the published *Pudd'nhead*, forming a pattern of textual doubleness that marks what Robinson sees as a pervasive tendency to acknowledge *and* to deny the tragedy of American race relations.

In his "Mark Twain and Homer Plessy," Eric Sundquist gives historical texture to the explosive doubleness of *Pudd'nhead*, most notably by aligning the trial at the novel's conclusion with the most important civil rights case of its time, *Plessy v. Ferguson* (1896). There is, Sundquist finds, a common legal justification for racism at work in the two cases. The notion of a citizenship rigidly divided along racial lines, as it was constitutionally authorized in the discriminatory "separate but equal" doctrine of *Plessy v. Ferguson*, was at large in a wide variety of social and cultural institutions in the decades before the turn of the century. In its preoccupation with doubling, imitation, and cross-dressing, *Pudd'nhead* is a virtual "allegory" of this dominant trend, not least in its divided sentiments on the sorry spectacle. For if Mark Twain was on one side inclined to subvert the "scientific" category of race, holding it up as a fiction of law and custom, he was also careful to conclude his own fiction with a dramatic reassertion of racial difference. *Pudd'nhead* is thus the literary analogue to a legal system that contrived to re-enslave blacks even as it declared them free, and to the broader historical and cultural context in which that system was embedded.

Turning from the historical drama of Reconstruction, Michael Rogin ("Francis Galton and Mark Twain: The Natal Autograph in *Pudd'nhead Wilson*") gives his attention to the psychodramatics at play in the novel. He begins by observing that in drawing the tragic *Pudd'nhead* out of the farcical *Those Extraordinary Twins*, Mark Twain resolved the far-fetched legal conundrum posed by the inseparable Siamese twins, but at the same time backed into equations of innocence with white, and guilt with black. Having located the novelist at "the center of the deranged, racialist culture" of his time, Rogin develops his case by turning to three of the deeply divided novel's most prominent oppositions. First, taking the rise of *Pudd'nhead* and fall of Tom as his point of departure, and the project of Francis Galton as a major point of comparison, he elaborates on the evolution of the black male stereotype, from the docile child of the antebellum paternal order to the black beast of post-Reconstruction. Second, he reflects on the struggle between *Pudd'nhead*, the male advocate of a sharply defined color line, and Roxana, the female proponent of its collapse. Finally, he turns to the division within Roxana, between the "natural" mother who bears her son into bondage, and the "masquerading" mother who plays with his identity and thereby sets him free.

Susan Gillman's essay, "'Sure Identifiers': Race, Science, and the Law in *Pudd'nhead Wilson*," is clearly akin to Rogin's in its emphasis on the novel's often inadvertently revealing representation of "the social construction of racial identity" in the late nineteenth century. Gillman highlights the text's strange mingling of historical realism with melodrama, arguing that this freak of form is the offspring of the novelist's competing impulses to present and to deny the grave truth of the ongoing crisis in American race relations. Such mixed intentions can be linked to the reality of miscegenation in Southern slave culture, and to the desperate efforts by the master class to mask the truth of that mixing in fictions of white racial purity. But *Pudd'nhead* is most tellingly a barometer to the vexed question of identity construction and social control as it emerged in the wake of abolition. In the novel's dramatization of racial interchangeability, Gillman argues, and in its more oblique preoccupation with permeable sexual boundaries, we catch sight of the culture's tentative address to some of its leading fictions, and, more broadly, to the uncertain foundations of its social knowledge.

In the subtitle to her essay, "The Ties that Bind," Myra Jehlen indicates that she shares Susan Gillman's concern with both "Race and Sex in *Pudd'nhead Wilson*." She construes her major themes historically as ideological fixtures in Mark Twain's America; and, like Gillman, she locates them textually in the novel's conspicuous failures of form. Jehlen draws specific attention to the strange twist by which the novel transforms the initially innocent and wronged Roxana and Tom into the villains of the story. Such lapses in fictional coherence make historical sense as manifestations of the "anxieties aroused by a racist social structure" in which leading elements of identity construction – black and white, male and female, child and adult – are subject to sharply contradictory definitions. Thus in passing from childhood to adulthood, Tom and Chambers proceed from innocence and racial interchangeability into radically different (but equally familiar) stereotypes of the inherently inferior adult black male. In closely related developments, the heroic Roxy, who subverts the system by insisting upon her son's racial equality, later condemns Tom for his trace of black blood, and is finally cast as a guilty slave who threatens the community with chaos. These are the symptoms, Jehlen concludes, of a "stalemate" between an impulse toward social criticism and the conservative incapacity to imagine significant change.

Carolyn Porter shifts the critical focus from David Wilson's plot, with its attention to white male desire and the repressed guilt of the slaveholders, to "Roxana's Plot," the story of resilient, subversive power in "a real black slave mother." If we are to appreciate the anxiety that Roxy arouses, Porter argues, we must abandon the mystified opposition of the black Mammy and the black Jezebel, turning instead to the repressed middle, the potent figure who takes arms against the oppressive establishment. Porter's Roxana is the source, and not merely the agent, of power. In switching the babies, she brings intelligence, courage, and formidable power into subversive alliance against the white patriarchal slave system. In countenancing this Roxana, Mark Twain opened a place in his narrative for the display of the "deep rifts in [his] society's complex and contradictory ideologies." But he had no sooner released this powerful black mother – who takes control of her world and, increasingly, of her story – than he set in motion the repressive David Wilson plot that finally contains her and restores the village to the *status quo ante.*

John Carlos Rowe's essay, "Fatal Speculations: Murder, Money, and Manners in *Pudd'nhead Wilson*," is the first of several to treat institutional issues of political economy, theology, and governance.

Rowe views Dawson's Landing as a point of intersection between an older America and the bustling, aggressive, materialistic society of the post-Civil War era. Yet Mark Twain's sentimental attachment to the mythic rural idyl should not blind us, Rowe insists, to his emphasis (in *Pudd'nhead* and other works) on the continuities between the plantation system and the helpless bondage of labor in the newer urban economics. As *The Gilded Age* makes clear, Mark Twain was aware and critical of the speculative impulse that arose in America after the Civil War. *Pudd'nhead Wilson* extends this analysis by demonstrating that slavery is "not just a provincial agrarian institution but the basis for the speculative economy that would fuel industrial expansion, Manifest Destiny, and laissez-faire capitalism." The slave-owner is thus a speculator par excellence who thrives if he makes sound investments, develops his property, and accurately anticipates trends in the market. Giving ample attention to Mark Twain's disastrous career as a businessman, Rowe elaborates in detail on the implications of economic life in the novel, with a special eye to Pudd'nhead himself, the leader in the new ways of doing business.

In his "By Right of the White Election: Political Theology and Theological Politics in *Pudd'nhead Wilson*," Michael Cowan attends to the complex interplay between politics and theology in Dawson's Landing. He begins with *Those Extraordinary Twins*, observing that the entire political process is cast into uncertainty by Luigi's election to the Board of Aldermen. Here and elsewhere, the meaning of "election" is profoundly ambiguous. There are ironic variations in meaning, for example, in the term's application to slaves and their masters. Cowan goes on to draw out the social and political implications of the marked contrast between the Arminian cast of white religious doctrine, and the strong antinomian strain in black theology, especially as it is interpreted by Roxana. Racial identity, he notes, is Calvinist to the extent that one drop of black blood can "out-vote" a vast majority of white. Cowan goes on to explore the numerous cognate ironies that surface along the uncertain boundaries between the religious and the secular in this novel of rigid if equally (and ironically) uncertain racial categories.

Politics are even more exclusively the concern of Wilson Carey McWilliams in his essay, "*Pudd'nhead Wilson* on Democratic Governance." Observing that the novel is framed by the Jacksonian era in American mass party politics, and that it may be read as a meditation on the ancient question, "Who should rule?" McWilliams approaches the text with an eye to its bearings on American political history, and on democratic ideology. His essay unfolds as a linked series of ruminations, gravitating to the politically paradoxical and subversive in *Pudd'nhead*, and prompted by references to such traditional political thinkers as Plato and Aristotle, Dante, Locke, Franklin, and Jefferson. Their aristocratic pretensions notwithstanding, the F.F.V. leaders of Dawson's Landing are in fact "small-town entrepreneurs" whose authority rests on property, not rank. As a woman and a black, Roxy is challenging testimony to major flaws in the Constitution. And it is a popular delusion that freedom and equality are primary American political values. They take second place, as *Pudd'nhead* shows, to the accumulation of private wealth. But to challenge that delusion directly is probably futile and possibly dangerous. Mark Twain knew this, and thus "elected to write in soft disguises," hoping to beguile his readers – where he could not lead them directly – to reform.

George E. Marcus ("What did he reckon would become of the other half if he killed his half?: Doubled, Divided, and Crossed Selves in *Pudd'nhead Wilson*; or, Mark Twain as Cultural Critic in His Own Times and Ours") moves broadly into the question of personal identity – a question explored in the specific terms of race and gender in earlier essays. According to Marcus, the half-a-dog joke that makes a "pudd'nhead" of David Wilson incorporates key elements of an enduring American cultural critique – namely, that social categories (e.g., race) are constructions, and that the autonomous individual is the leading such category in Western bourgeois culture. *Pudd'nhead* is typical of the late nineteenth century in its containment of an impulse to subvert the category of the autonomous self. The challenge to convention generally features divided, doubled, or crossed selves. *Pudd'nhead* employs all three, though in the crossing of Tom and Chambers it foregrounds the third and most disruptive, where the attempt to keep selves separate is "defeated at every point by the complete merging of both selves in each character simultaneously." Marcus emphasizes that such assaults on the integral self are always contained by hegemonic processes circulating through the novel (Wilson's fingerprinting display, most notably), and much more broadly through the American culture of the time.

In the concluding essay, "Some of the Ways of Freedom in *Pudd'nhead Wilson*," John H. Schaar draws into alignment with the consensus opinion that the novel is a maze of inconsistencies and contradictions (it is "a mess," he declares). But he cannot join the others in viewing the text's manifest shortcomings as usefully telling symptoms, as seams or fissures through which the analyst may penetrate to profitable new insights about Mark Twain's world, and about our own. Rather, inclining toward the position familiarly associated with Hershel Parker, Schaar concludes "that the book is all-but unreadable, that sense cannot be made out of it." It follows that the study of *Pudd'nhead Wilson* is a waste of time. Worse yet, Schaar allows that in lavishing our attention on inferior fictions we draw it away from the real life and the real problems that we share with our neighbors. There are no flattering explanations for this anomalous behavior. Still, because he has agreed to participate, Schaar turns in the body of his essay to the examination of what the novel "can teach about the difficulties of thinking and feeling well and justly" about the related topics of freedom and human social classification. He finds that the book contributes little of value to this discussion.

It hardly diminishes the weight of Schaar's position to record that it did not carry the day at the conference for which these essays were originally written, or to venture that it will do little to dampen the current revival of interest in this flawed child of Mark Twain's imagination. On the other hand, there are undoubtedly readers who will complain that his essay should have been placed first, where it could have done the most good. At the very least, "Some of the Ways of Freedom" will be welcomed as a salutary prod to ever-encroaching complacency, a reminder that in laboring to make sense of Mark Twain's ideological swerves and moral evasions we should be equally attentive to those concealed in our own critical enterprise. It is to be hoped, of course, that the essays in this volume justify themselves by opening new perspectives on the past, and by helping us to make our way forward in the present and future. There are human dividends here, perhaps, that Schaar overlooked. Still, he offers a bracing challenge, not only to our assessment of *Pudd'nhead Wilson*, but also to many of the assumptions at the foundation of the "new historicism" in American letters, with its emphasis on ideology, and its impulse to reshape the canon.

There is no real disagreement, after all, that *Pudd'nhead Wilson* is a "mess." On this there is something approaching consensus. If most of these essays urge canonical status on *Pudd'nhead Wilson*, they do so with a newly sharpened, ironic sense of what it means to be "non-canonical." Let us recall that it was Mark Twain who first expanded upon the novel's grave structural shortcomings. In *Pudd'nhead Wilson* we have a celebrated white male author whose main fictional concerns are the powerless and the excluded, yet who derides himself, in the preface to this novel so occupied with questions of racial and sexual exclusion, as a "jackleg" novelist. He further complicates matters in the preface to *Those Extraordinary Twins*, making a celebrated "confession" of his own putative lack of authorial control over the work that "changed itself from a farce to a tragedy" – an entertaining confession about the vagaries of "original intention" that perhaps unintentionally, but farcically and tragically, has allowed *both* the long search for some hidden, unifying structure in *Pudd'nhead Wilson and* the dismissal of the novel as "patently unreadable."

Our collective critical response to this history is to do what Mark Twain would say is the only thing we can, that is to follow our training slavishly. We are thus imitating our author's own impulse to have it both ways, offering *Pudd'nhead Wilson* as a new classic – a new masterpiece – while emphatically abandoning the notion of the canonical text as culturally transcendent. All of us in this volume have different ideas of how Mark Twain inserted himself into his book, yet none assumes that the novelist was fully the master of the unexampled literary hybrid that he finally produced. Unifying the twelve very different essays in the collection is a critical approach to unfamiliar texts and how to teach them. We begin with the belief that the lack of control all readers sense in *Pudd'nhead Wilson* is a key to the novel's literary and cultural significance. Lack of control for Mark Twain meant freedom from mastery. Or as James Cox would say, Twain left mastery to Henry James, offering himself instead as jack-leg novelist, ever ready to play the irresponsible slave and fool, never able to master the current of plot and pen that enslaved him.[3]

JAMES M. COX

Pudd'nhead Wilson Revisited

O
f all our writers, Mark Twain seems most American, as if he, like race, slavery, and the nation itself were referents that couldn't be deconstructed by language. Of course, a deep irony runs right here. *Mark Twain* is, after all, a pen name, signifying, if it signifies anything, that Mark Twain is all writing and nothing but writing. Then too, slavery itself was a fiction — a fiction of law and custom, as Mark Twain reminds us in, and Evan Carton has reminded us about, *Pudd'nhead Wilson.* Beyond that, this nation was itself a text intruded into history, and a text not even in its "own" language but in the language of the parent nation against which it was rebelling. That leaves race — something different altogether, in that it signifies both the unity and the separation of the human species. As a word in English, the mother tongue yet not the native language of Nature's Nation, *race* refers at once to the most dynamic activity of humanity — as in the race for the Pacific, or the race to arrive on the moon, or the arms race — and most inertial essence of the human species: the races of the human family.

Even such a scansion of the terms reveals how culturally loaded they are. Equally important, they are morally loaded, even overloaded. It is impossible for an American to think about race and slavery without feeling a strong moral charge running like an electric current right through the thought, and running strong enough to color it. These volatile subjects do not admit of pure thought, if there is such a thing. If slavery was an absolute contradiction in a free country, its abolition left the issue of race, with which it had been as inextricably bound as one Siamese twin to another, not dead but vividly living as a moral, social, and legal issue. It took a hundred years after the abolition of slavery to settle the legal issues surrounding race, and there is no end in sight for the moral, psychological, and social issues of race and racism. My figure of race and slavery as Siamese

1

twins is not taken lightly (the fatal pun in that last word, coming so unintentionally to hand, should remind us all of the tyranny of language in all matters and particularly so in this one). George Fredrickson has shown us how inexorably attendant upon antislavery arguments was the complementary desire to remove blacks from the country. That wish had been part of Jefferson's vision for getting rid of slavery; it remained part of Lincoln's vision, and Grant's too — even as late as the 1880s; and it dogs liberal rhetoric to this day — as when we are exhorted to be color blind. A black leader in Atlanta was on the mark when he said that to be color blind is to see only white.

If the Old Republic had freed itself from tyranny by force, the New Union, having freed itself from slavery by force, incorporated antislavery rhetoric into an increasingly imperialist foreign policy forever bent on extending the perimeters of the free world. The expansion, begun as a European vision more of acquisition than of freedom until the arrival of the Puritans with their ideology of religious freedom, eventuated in a vision of freedom sufficiently grand to whelm the Puritan and evangelical extensions of religious freedom: the Enlightenment a loaded term in the context of this discussion. The Enlightenment prevailed because it promised freedom from tyranny — the tyranny of government and the tyranny of religion. In the international competition for North America, it was the English who prevailed, and their language along with them (or did the language prevail and they along with it?). In any event, the country was both conceived in the English Enlightenment and born through it. Yet the enlightened country could not free itself from slavery. Even as the Indians, near extinction, continued to be driven west, black slaves continued to be imported. Jefferson in his *Notes on Virginia* could recognize the sadness of the extinction and feel the fear of the importation, could see that the Indians were being reduced to archaeology even as, in the face of expanding slavery, he could tremble for his country when he reflected that God was just. Removal of the Indians accompanied the consolidation of slavery right up to the eve of Civil War. These were the disconcerting terms of both the white man's and the white philosopher's free country.

Sometimes I want to be guilty about this history; sometimes I am less sure. My grandfather, as near as I can make out, owned three slaves, was a captain in the Confederate army, was wounded at the battle of Gauley Bridge in West Virginia, and was brought home by wagon over almost two hundred miles of rutted roads to live out a semiparaplegic life, yet begot eleven children. I don't know whether

I should be guilty about that, although a colleague once told me that I should. The slaves, freed by both proclamation and war, are buried in the graveyard I can see from my kitchen window. Stones, unmarked and uninscribed – save for one marble slab for Edmund Cox – mark their graves, and could, for all I have been able to discover, mark the graves of early white settlers. I am that close to slavery, which yet seems far away. How much closer it must seem to blacks I find myself imagining, yet cannot know. I mention these facts not so much to reveal them as to provide a transition from the larger context of race, slavery, and America to the author and the text under discussion.

Samuel Clemens lived the first twenty-five years of his life not merely in the Old Republic but in a slave state. He resigned, as he referred to his desertion, from the Confederate army, and so he was both a traitor and a deserter, a capital criminal. Mark Twain was born, as far as we can be sure, in 1863 in Virginia City, Nevada Territory. It was Samuel Clemens's sixth pseudonym, and it stuck. He had tried Thomas Jefferson Snodgrass, Quintus Curtius Snodgrass, Sergeant Fathom, Josh, and W. Epaminondas Adrastus Blab. Thirty years later, he would be writing *Pudd'nhead Wilson*. Forty-seven years and a few months later he would be dead. Samuel Clemens, born in 1835, came in with Halley's Comet and went out with it, as he once promised he would. If he liked the analogy of his own red hair to the fiery hair of the comet, he no doubt liked equally well the fact that, although this comet was predictable, it was nonetheless a far-ranging cosmic traveler. Mark Twain's full success as a writer came with a publisher named Bliss; he went bankrupt investing in a typesetter made by an inventor named Paige; he spent the last years of his life dictating his autobiography to a man named Paine; the stenographer who recorded the dictation was a woman named Lyon. Launched with Bliss, ruined (or so he contended) by Paige, and giving his life to Paine with Lyon as recorder: these are facts that I cannot believe were lost on Mark Twain, and I like to think that he made what he could of them.

The fact of Mark Twain's having dictated his life to Paine should remind us of how much talk had been vital for this writer. Not only had he lectured to audiences almost from the beginning of his career, but he also periodically returned to the platform – was, indeed, to make a round-the-world lecture trip to pay the creditors of his bankrupt machine and publishing enterprises. Talk had, for Mark Twain, a primacy that lay behind writing, and he often felt, or said he felt, that writing could not capture that primacy, as if the voice were the soul of language that was always at the point of being lost in the body of writing. As a lecturer, a performer, Mark Twain sought absolute control of his audiences. Howells, remarking in a letter about Mark Twain's mastery in a Boston performance, observed that "you held the audience in the palm of your hand and tickled it." This desire for complete mastery had its other side. Eagerly as Mark Twain sought control, he was at the same time utterly dependent on the audience, desperately requiring its response. Because he was a humorist, that response was laughter. The response was nothing less than the voice of the other – a vocal yet nonverbal communication not at the end of a performance but all through it, as if the monologue were actually a dialogue. That dialogic relationship with an audience is the drama of the humorist's performance, making it vastly different from a "reading." The audience is from the beginning expecting to be amused, to participate, and to cooperate. More important, the humorist must have the strength to convert the agreeable willingness into a wild and helpless contagion, until the entire audience is literally infected, or, to change the figure, swept up and swept along in the reductive current of helpless laughter. Throughout the performance the humorist maintains a gravity, a deadpan reflecting an almost stupid and unconscious composure – at least he does if he is Mark Twain. His drawl consumes time, slowing both pace and movement, and his hesitation often extends itself into such long pauses that words are poised against silence until silence itself becomes the ultimate compression of humor.

Yet Mark Twain was a writer, his very name a nom de plume, or, as he occasionally and justifiably referred to it, a nom de guerre. Appearing in the middle of Civil War one month after Lincoln's Emancipation Proclamation, the pen name exposed rather than concealed Samuel Clemens and at the same time suggested the possibility of a double identity residing in a single person. Beyond that, it signified Samuel Clemens's past, referring as it did to the steamboat leadsman's call of two fathoms, which in turn referred either to safe or precarious water, depending on whether the steamboat was entering or leaving dangerous shallows. That was not all. Paul Fatout has contended that the name may have been applied to the Samuel Clemens who habitually ordered two drinks on credit at a Virginia City bar. Putting these two origins of the name together, we have an authorial identity rooted first in independence. Not only did it appear at almost the moment the nation declared itself free from slavery, but Samuel Clemens invariably insisted that the steamboat pilot was the most independent man alive. The name was rooted second in drunkenness, which was different but nonetheless a significant type of both slavery and freedom, suggesting as it did both helpless addiction and comic irresponsibility.

These aspects of "Mark Twain" taken together suggest a sense of his identity. He is at once the invention and the author of Samuel Clemens. As invention, he marks both his separation from and identity with the man who had lived almost twenty-eight years not only in a country where slavery was constitutional but also in a part of the country that was defending it, yet he is born in a free country and thus marks the difference between the new union and the Old Republic, between the new law and the old, between north and south. At the same time he is a western humorist at the threshold of heading east, and, as the Wild Humorist from the Pacific Slope, he marks the difference between territory and settlement, between low and high literature, between popular and genteel culture, between humor and high seriousness, between west and east.

If we look at Samuel Clemens in 1892 and 1893, when he was writing *Pudd'nhead Wilson*, he was fifty-seven years old, had lived with Mark Twain for more than half his life, had experienced enormous financial success, yet was facing financial failure in his two major investments: a publishing house in which he was senior partner, and a typesetter in which he was chief investor. Even as he was writing *Pudd'nhead*, he made hurried trips to America from Italy, where he had established a residence in Florence partly to economize his diminishing capital. He had lived the first half of his life without the identity of Mark Twain in a world where slavery was legal, and the second half with Mark Twain in a world where it was abolished. Under the signature—we might say in the handwriting—of Mark Twain he had not only become a world traveler and travel writer, but also had managed a reconstruction of his past that carried him into the world of childhood on the great Mississippi. In *Huckleberry Finn*, he had worked a remarkable conversion of nineteenth-century romanticism into the form of the realistic novel. Locating the poetic myth of childhood upon a raft drifting ever deeper into the slavery of the historically invalidated antebellum South, he made Huck's drifting journey seem a courageous confrontation with the slavery in which he had his historical being. Thus, Huck's "development" is an expression of the historical progress from slavery to freedom. At the same time, the Wordsworthian romantic poetic vision remains very much intact—the vision that childhood's free relation with nature will die into the oppressive conformity of adult society. To negotiate this double vision, Mark Twain (or was it Samuel Clemens?) threw himself out of the book to release Huck Finn's deviant current of language – a vernacular embodying a seemingly clear and realistic Sancho Panza vision of human life charged with a romantic quest for freedom.

Without becoming embroiled in an interpretation or resolution of the double vision in *Huckleberry Finn*, I do want to emphasize how much slavery and freedom are interfused in the novel. Huck and Jim both live in a world of slavery: Huck is free, Jim is a slave. The river, the natural and seemingly free force in the book, making the raft upon its drifting current seem a free place, is yet naturally determined by the law of gravity and is drifting both free boy and slave man deeper into slavery. The current of language seems free, asserting itself against the correct and oppressive rules of civilized or formal adult discourse irrespective of pre- or post-Civil War society. Thus Huck is helplessly rebelling against the law of his own society at the same time that he is violating the rules of genteel propriety. The point to remember here is that he is helpless; he can't help his language and he can't help being for Jim: he is naturally deviant and must then rely on deviousness to help himself. Because he is helplessly, or we could say naturally, against the law of his own society he is consciously a fugitive, even a criminal. His justification of his actions – and he must justify himself because he has internalized both the law of the society as well as his feeling of responsibility to Jim – is animated by a twinned or double conscience that charges him with fear of the slave law on the one hand and with guilt of betraying his friend on the other. This doubled conscience, likened to a "yaller dog," dogs him the deeper he moves downstream, forever threatening the ease and comfort he seeks.

The larger deviousness of *Huckleberry Finn* lies in its relation to an audience in a constitutionally free rather than a slave world. Whereas Huck is a fugitive in the world of slavery, he is the appealing and good-hearted free child to an audience of free secular adults whose moral sense at once approves and is comforted by his involvement in helping a runaway slave. Huck's narrative – written and not spoken – plays upon a secret agreement between writer and reader, the agreement that the white boy's relation of his friendship with and aid to a runaway slave, illegal and disapproved in his own society, will be utterly legal and righteously approved in the free society of Huck's readers. Of all the confidence games played in the book, that act of confidence lies at the heart of Mark Twain's conception of Huck as author of the book. Displacing himself as writer with Huck's "free" and "natural" vernacular, Mark Twain actually divides the will of the book between Huck the writer of a letter signed "Yours truly" and an unnamed, unsignified reader. The letter, not scarlet but black and white, even as it comes across the gulf dividing the historically, legally, and morally invalid slave society from our own legally, morally, and presently constituted world of freedom, is in its language so possessed of a semblance of freedom as to emphasize the *psychological* presence of slavery in a free adult society. As a result of having removed himself from his own fiction, Mark Twain frees his readers, his audience in a free society, to "right" Huck's wrong vision of his actions and provide a positive affirmation over and above Huck's negative relation to the morality of his own society. This inversion is nothing less than the audience's active will, operating not only as a double of the outcast author's inferred intentions but also as a double of Huck's implicit appeal for understanding in all the tight places in which he finds himself.

All this is but an inadequate preface to *Pudd'nhead Wilson*, yet there is one more point to make about the Mark Twain discovered in the Nevada Territory by a Samuel Clemens who went there evading the Civil War and looking for silver. He was not only a product of the new world of American freedom but also a naked embodiment of the capitalist ideology that literally funded the freedom. It was Mark Twain's naked relation to money – to silver – that at once distinguishes and characterizes him among our so-called major writers of the nineteenth century. It is possible, as the criticism of his work in the last hundred years makes evident, to deplore this crucial and vital aspect of his identity. Without simply praising it, I do want to acknowledge the courage involved in Mark Twain's willingness not only to enter, but also to expose his desire to conquer, the marketplace. He sought to be a part of the selling of his writing – sought, in effect, to sell himself; he was to be the trademark, the very brand, of Samuel Clemens's inventions. As a lecturer, he wanted to stand before sold-out houses and sell them on his jokes so that they would be sold. The double of this wish to sell himself was the wish to control the means of production of his work. He had, like Franklin, been a printer, and his desire as a writer was to own not only the company which printed his own work, but also the typesetter which, he rightly recognized, could technologically remove the old laborious task of justifying the right-hand margin. No small part of his motive in writing *Pudd'nhead Wilson* was to save both his publishing house and his typesetter from the panic of 1893. His effort failed.

Pudd'nhead Wilson is not among Mark Twain's best-known works. Of course it is known to specialists, but we shouldn't forget that F. R.

Leavis rescued it from relative oblivion in an old Grove Press edition and wrote an introduction classically misreading the text – at least from the cultural perspective that focuses on race and conflict. There was precious little written on the book when I first approached it in 1955. I emphasize the words *precious little* with a fond nostalgia, since that was a time when an outsetting teacher of American literature could hallucinate the possibility of reading everything written about any American author. Having been brought up a New Critic, I am now beset all around by intertextualism, metatextualism, traces, and tropes, and can only see that if there is a race in trace, as a black colleague pointed out to me, there is a rope in trope. Facing the rush of criticism through phenomenology, new historicism, affectivism, structuralism, reader response criticism, poststructuralism, and all varieties of deconstruction, I feel like Hawthorne, who noted that there comes a time when a person, no longer at home in seeking newer fashions in clothes, settles for being left behind in the old clothes that suit him. Such a person has reached the inertia at the heart of generation, the astonished recognition that he is repeating the life of the fathers. I have even returned to the farm I was raised on and the house I was born in. Yet living so close to that cemetery visible from my kitchen window to the west, death begins to come sufficiently to life to make me run after the new generation to catch whatever life it is casting behind. Still I'm old fashioned enough to want to take texts as I find them. By that I mean I want the published text to take precedence over whatever deletions or changes can be detected in the manuscript. Dismayed by those deletions, changes, and false starts he feels he has discovered, Hershel Parker is pleased to show us a Mark Twain who didn't know what he was doing. Mark Twain had never contended that he knew, and the text of *Pudd'nhead* is a problem because Mark Twain made it a problem in his published text. Whereas in *Huckleberry Finn* he had thrown himself out of the text, threatening anyone who found moral, motive, or plot with punishment, banishment, and execution, in *Pudd'nhead* he keeps himself very much present. He goes so far as to narrate the origins of his conception and to include the wreckage of the first story which had been, he says at the conclusion of his "final remarks" (appended to the text of *Those Extraordinary Twins*), "dug out" of the second story that had in effect grown around it – a literary Caesarean operation.[1] The reader who reads texts and novels linearly "forward" is led from the "tragedy," the second story, through Mark Twain's account of the process of creation, to the "farce," or seed story, that has been so deformed in its removal as to require authorial commentary to fill in lesions and explain discontinuities. Thus the reader's experience pursues Mark Twain's invention from its end to its beginning, from the "finished" tragedy of slavery and detection to the farce of twin freaks. The bound book turns out to be a Siamese-twinned form with Mark Twain's account of the origin providing the ligature between tragedy and farce.

If we proceed along this linear path, we find ourselves moving from the highly plotted, arbitrarily willed tragedy of changelings in a slave society, through the author's account of himself as an incompetent jackleg who lacks mastery of his craft yet remains arbitrary in his decisions, and who, when he doesn't know what to do with characters, drowns them in a well, to the originating so-called suppressed farce about Siamese twins whose single torso forked into two heads with opposed wills. And we move from the Pudd'nhead Wilson who, acting as lawyer-detective defending one of the separated twins in the tragedy, identifies the criminal changeling who has murdered Judge Driscoll, the most honored citizen in the village of Dawson's Landing, and restores the law, the instituted will, of the master-slave society — we move from this Wilson's triumphant victory to the Wilson of *Those Extraordinary Twins*, who, defending the Siamese twins, breaks the will and common-sense law of Justice Robinson by contending that because innocence and guilt reside in a single body, the guilty half cannot be punished without criminally afflicting the innocent. Having broken — or at least paralyzed — the law, Wilson is rewarded by being made mayor. Luigi, the twin who kicked Tom, is elected alderman but cannot take his seat without his brother anymore than he can be seated with him. The matter being once more before the courts, they remain powerless to settle the case, and so the citizens settle it by hanging Luigi. So ends the farce, which has been pushed to the status of a side show (upon the recommendation by one citizen that Luigi be hanged, another says "That's the ticket" [169]). The author of this Siamese-twin novel, in effect saying "Luigi be hanged," appends his "Final Remarks," rehearsing the matter of his ligaturial account of how the characters of Roxy, Tom Driscoll, and Pudd'nhead took over the original story. Having to give them something to do, he says he first provided the action, then reasons for the action, until "the whole show was being run by the new people and in their interest, and the original show was become side-tracked and forgotten."

To proceed from the finished "tragedy" to the suppressed farce is not "to remount the stream of composition" as Henry James said of himself in writing his prefaces for the New York Edition, but to pursue the stream of composition up river to its source. In our end is our beginning. This stream is represented in the form of a will — will

as it bequeaths the narrative into our hands, as it arbitrarily operates between master and slave, as it is socially instituted in the law, as
it documents legitimate property, and as it characterizes the process
of narrative composition. The predominant issue of will is evident
in the very title of the book, *Pudd'nhead Wilson*, fatally reminding
us of Edgar Poe's "William Wilson." Certainly Poe is deeply inscribed
in this book, not only in the name of the titular hero, but also in his
role as amateur detective. William Wilson, Will-I-am Will's Son, was
Poe's anagram for his self-willed narrator whose life of unspeakable
crime had begun with his pursuit of his double, who seemed both
twin and conscience, through all the capitals of Europe before finally
confronting and killing it in Rome. And Poe's detective, C. Auguste
Dupin, in the same self-willed way, actually invents the very crime
he solves. He first reads the narrator's mind in "The Murders in the
Rue Morgue," then reads the account of the insoluble crime in the
newspaper, and finally provides the solution of the crime in the form
of a narrative "deduction" that produces the criminal, as if by presti-
digitation, as the denouement of his account. That isn't all. The
criminal isn't even a criminal, but a sailor whose orangutan aped its
master by trying to shave with a razor, escaped, and killed the women,
uttering in the attack sounds that all witnesses who could hear but
not see the crime attributed to a foreigner. Here was truly an original crime, a crime without a motive that Dupin both invests and
solves. He is even called a double Dupin, possessor of a bipartite soul
at once creative and resolvent. I dwell on Poe, who fell from birth
in Boston into the South, because he is a true forerunner of Mark
Twain, with his recognition that the reader is the double of the author,
that the text is thus the mechanically designed invention relating
them, and that the issue for the modern world will be original crime,
not original sin. The Indo-European root of the word *crime* refers to
a hoarse, rough sound.

But Mark Twain is different from Poe. Poe in his criticism claimed
for the artist a mastery of conscious conception resulting in a narrative architecture of total design. Mark Twain presents himself—
after his finished tragedy—as a helpless slave of an unconscious will,
a writer at the mercy of a narrative current and willful characters
taking their own way. His counterthrust to this unbidden thrust,
especially in this book, is an increasingly arbitrary exercise of plot
machinery. Thrust and counterthrust are in their way an articulation of the master-slave theme of the narrative; they also reflect the
old contradiction in Mark Twain's identity between the wish to maintain absolute control of production and the impulse to be a slave to

a current of language whose law was, as he once said, like a stream that had no law. To be sure, natural streams have two laws, the law of gravity and the law of seeking the path of least resistance. Still, we know what Mark Twain meant by his observation; he saw and sought in helpless obedience to such a narrative current a larger freedom than could be found in laws set forth in the world of literary people and literary art. The profound feeling of freedom in *Huckleberry Finn* arises out of Mark Twain's obedience to just such a narrative current of language and action.

Pudd'nhead Wilson is a different story; neither its form nor substance follows such a current. Instead of following the Mississippi, the action is concentrated in the slave society of Dawson's Landing; instead of pursuing picaresque episode and drift, the form pivots upon dramatic opposition and contradiction; and instead of being thematically anchored to the conflict of a double conscience – social and instinctive – oppressing the narrator and chief actor, *Pudd'nhead Wilson* is confined to the issue of a double will suspended in absolute and contradictory opposition. This double will originates, if we are to believe Mark Twain, in the figure of two-headed Siamese twins who, possessed of diametrically opposed wills and personalities, take turns in controlling their single body.

This symmetrical scheme, rooted in incongruity and deformity, makes a farce of the law, the will of the society, and at the same time drives the narrator to impasse and irresponsibility. Pudd'nhead Wilson, as he functions in what is left of *Those Extraordinary Twins*, explicitly exposes the incapacity of the law to deal with the double will of the twins and implicitly exposes the incongruity of the single or unified will of law to deal with the repressed double will that secretly resides in each individual member of the society. In light of Wilson's anarchic claim that the guilt of one twin cannot be punished without injuring his innocent brother, Justice Robinson, champion of clear and common-sense law, is reduced to a helpless plea to the court and the society: "Look to your homes – look to your property – look to your lives – for you have need!" (154). The town, ignoring the subversion so manifest in Wilson's arguments, applauds his victorious defense of Luigi and proceeds to elect Luigi to the Board of Aldermen. Unable to seat Luigi without including his inseparable brother who was not elected, and confronted once more with courts helpless to decide the case, the citizens of Dawson's Landing elect to hang Luigi.

To turn from this devil-may-care ending of *Those Extraordinary Twins*, which Mark Twain asserts was the original work, to the beginning of *Pudd'nhead Wilson*, which he claims grew around the seed farce, is to see how the conception of the contradictory double will was both transformed and socialized as it was surrounded by the master-slave society of Dawson's Landing. Pudd'nhead Wilson's last name is but an index to the centrality of will in the narrative. Wishing and certainly willing to own half of the invisible barking dog that greets his arrival in the village so that he could kill his half provides the village yokels with the opportunity of bequeathing him the title of Pudd'nhead. His nickname is thus the will of the society.

But the whole issue of will has been introduced and put into play before the actual narrative even begins. In his prefatory "A Whisper to the Reader," Mark Twain, asserting his ignorance of legal matters, tells of having consulted William Hicks on what he calls the law chapters of the book in order to get them right. Having studied law in southwest Missouri thirty-five years earlier and then having come to Florence for his health, Hicks works

in Macaroni and Vermicelli's horse-feed shed which is up the back alley as you turn around the corner out of the Piazza del Duomo just beyond the house where that stone that Dante used to sit on six hundred years ago is let into the wall when he let on to be watching them build Giotto's Campanile and yet always got tired looking as soon as Beatrice passed along on her way to get a chunk of chestnut-cake to defend herself with in case of a Ghibelline outbreak before she got to school, at the same old stand where they sell the same old cake to this day and it is just as light and good as it was then, too, and this is not flattery, far from it. (1)

From this informal and easy reduction of the old master Dante and his heavenly mistress Beatrice to childhood sweethearts on the order of Tom Sawyer and Becky Thatcher, Mark Twain concludes with the following sentence:

Given under my hand this second day of January, 1893, at the Villa Viviani, village of Settignano, three miles back of Florence, on the hills – the same certainly affording the most charming view to be found on this planet, and with it the most dream-like and enchanting sunsets to be found in any planet or even in any solar system – and given, too, in the swell room of the house, with the busts of Cerretani senators and other grandees of this line looking approvingly down upon me as they used to look down upon Dante, and mutely asking me to adopt them into my family, which I do with pleasure, for my remotest ancestors are but spring chickens compared with these robed and stately antiques, and it will be a great and satisfying lift for me, that six hundred years will. (2)

That long sentence, Faulknerean in its unfolding suspension, yet clear Mark Twain in its effortlessness of movement, leads to the very pen name itself, boldly standing as a printed "signature" beneath the prose. To look at this "whisper" is to see the very nature of the twinned or double will of the prose – the formal printed will on the one hand and the moving, informal will on the other, almost drifting through the Florentine dreamlike setting to the swell room of the house where the Cerretani senators are asking to come down into Mark Twain's family – a request that will conversely lift him up. The "Given under my hand" at the beginning of the sentence, even as it echoes the language of a formal will, betrays the underhanded possibilities of this narrative about fingerprints; it also forecasts the end of the sentence which ends with the word *will*.

Then the narrative itself, set in a so-called democratic society retaining a legal fiction authorizing the enslavement of one race by another. Of course that fiction was an enormous social fact in the actual world of Southern slavery; it was made a fiction only by the Civil War, when the fact of democratic freedom was extended to include all persons regardless of race or previous condition of servitude, making the old fact an illegal fiction of the past. Into that invalid past Mark Twain moves his fiction, or, to take his own account of its conception, his fiction moves him. If we do not have to take his word for it, we can do little more than take his words for him. Yet even here his words are double. In the ligaturial account he says that as his tale of the Siamese twins "kept spreading along and spreading along," other people, among them Pudd'nhead and Roxana, intruded themselves and "presently the doings of these two pushed into prominence a young fellow named Tom Driscoll, whose proper place was away in the obscure background" (120). Here Tom Driscoll's emergence into the foreground is presented as a result of the "doings" of Pudd'nhead and Roxana, almost as if they were his parents. These three began "taking things almost entirely into their own hands and working the whole tale as a private venture of their own – a tale which they had nothing at all to do with, by rights" (120).

Yet in the final remarks appended to the conclusion of *Those Extraordinary Twins* the ligaturial account is considerably modified. Here it is Roxy who first wanders into the tale and "had to be furnished with something to do; so she changed the children in the cradle: this necessitated the invention of a reason for it; this in turn resulted in making the children prominent personages – nothing could prevent it, of course. Their career began to take a tragic aspect, and some one had to be brought in to help work the machinery; so Pudd'n-head Wilson was introduced and taken on trial"(169).

In this version characters do not take over. Either their appearance requires invention of work for them (which is the case for Roxy), or the invented work becomes the machinery that in turn requires a new character to run it (the case of Pudd'nhead). As for the author, he begins as an employer who puts the characters to work and ends as the worker who digs out the farçe and leaves the tragedy that is, in effect, his will.

The movement of this will into the slave society involves a separation of the Siamese twins and their subordination to a position of secondary importance in the plot. They are displaced by changelings – two bodies exchanged across the legal barrier separating white from black, master from slave, the active will of master from the passive will of property. Mark Twain's interest in Siamese twins had gone all the way back to the "original" Siamese twins, Chang and Eng Bunker, about whom he had written a humorous sketch as early as 1867 (after their career of being on exhibit, Chang and Eng settled in the village of White Plains, North Carolina, where they owned slaves before the Civil War); his interest in changelings had eventuated in *The Prince and the Pauper*. In his ligaturial account he even mentions that book as having grown in much the same way as did this one. In that book, he had kept the plot as symmetrical as the alliteration of the title. Thus the pauper who has dreamed of being a king becomes the prince by virtue of a change of clothes, while the prince becomes a pauper and experiences the woes of the subjects he was to have ruled (and contends he still does rule). The pauper, on the other hand, learns more and more to play the reality of a would-be king. The plot is resolved when the false prince, at the moment of denying his mother in the coronation procession, realizes that she recognizes him because he characteristically throws his hand, palm outward, before his face in a gesture originating from a moment of childhood fright. Out of the guilt of denying her and the shame of knowing that she has recognized him, he gives back the throne to the legitimate heir, who in turn elevates him to the nobility. Thus the nineteenth-century author's democratic parable is worked out, showing that the illegitimate king, even as he acknowledges his plebian identity, retains the power to give the true king his identity by helping him to remember where the royal seal had been hidden at the time they playfully exchanged identities. Childhood romance set in distant history thus reveals democratic equality at work through an equation at once sentimental and genteel.

Such a sentimental plot could have been possible in the changeling plot of *Pudd'nhead Wilson*. Because slavery had been morally
condemned and legally abolished, it was an inviting field for sentimental melodrama. Indeed, I think that readers to this day, encountering the book for the first time, often bring with them just such
expectations, foreseeing a symmetrical exchange in which the false
heir, given a chance to enter white society, would prove to be good
and either free the false slave in a recognition scene or be freed by him.
But Mark Twain pursues a very different plot line in this book. He
keeps the trappings of melodrama, yet makes the slave who has been
made a master by his mother the villain who sells his free mother – a
slave when she freed him but subsequently freed by the will of her
white master – down the river. That is not all; the mother who, if we
read through to Mark Twain's final remarks, had to be furnished
with something to do, does it by switching the children under the
claim of saving her son from the possibility of being sold down the
river. Yet when she is free, she asks her son to sell her back into slavery as a means of paying off his gambling debts and thereby secur-
ing the blessings of the will of his foster father. As for the false slave,
Chambers, he accepts his slavery without a murmur, as if he had
been born a slave, gradually dropping into his "proper place in the
obscure background." Freed at last by Pudd'nhead's identification of
the false master, he has neither mastery nor freedom in him. Stuck
in the black dialect into which Mark Twain has thrust him, he is
hopelessly out of place in freedom.

That leaves Pudd'nhead. A free man by virtue of being white, yet
not a master by virtue of being a stranger in the village, he is declared a fool and an eccentric by the townspeople and lives an independent existence "on the extreme western verge of the town"(6). By
profession a lawyer, yet without any clients, he pursues his hobby
of collecting fingerprints of all the townspeople, and, in his role of
lawyer and detective, he discovers the true identity of Tom Driscoll,
the invisible dog who has disturbed the peace of Dawson's Landing.
Having identified the man who, at one time or another, is called pup,
cur, low-down hound, and dog, Pudd'nhead is ready to kill him. He
is also ready to take his place in the society as an elected official,
showing no sign of moral judgment against slavery. As exempt from
moral vision as C. Auguste Dupin, he finds full satisfaction in the
theatrics of courtroom drama. Indeed, if we go right to the origin
of things, it has been Pudd'nhead's curiosity about how Roxy tells
the two infants apart that has assured her of the possibility of exchanging them in the first place. In a certain way he, as much as

Cecil Burleigh Essex, is the father of Tom Driscoll, since his observation and Roxy's action are the "doings" that thrust Tom into a position of prominence. He is, in brief, at the conception of the "crime." At the same time, there is a fraternal relation between Pudd'nhead and Tom because both are foster sons of Judge Driscoll; if the Judge has taken his "nephew" into his home after his brother's death, he has also taken Pudd'nhead into the Freethinkers' Society because he recognizes Pudd'nhead's intelligence and admires his calendar entries so much that he shows them to the chief citizens of the village. Rebuffed by their failure to appreciate Pudd'nhead's ironic epigrams, the Judge develops a tender affection for his protege and sole other member of the Freethinkers. These relationships are so implicit as to be repressed; they are what we might call darkly invisible, but they are nonetheless there in this book that deals both explicitly and implicitly with repression. It is not surprising that Henry Nash Smith long ago recognized that Judge Driscoll was the essential father of Tom Driscoll. If his position as Judge has made him the chief custodian of the law, his murder by Tom Driscoll makes him its chief victim.

As hero of the book, Pudd'nhead, after identifying the villain, confidently assumes that the murderer of York Leicester Driscoll (he of the "generous hand") will be hanged. His victory in the courtroom is proof that he has lived down his title of Pudd'nhead, at least in the eyes of the grateful townspeople who decide, in the face of his triumphant detection, that they and not he should be elected as the Pudd'nheads of Dawson's Landing. Pudd'nhead's moral and philosophical judgments, so conspicuously absent in the narrative action, appear in his calendar entries standing above the narratives as epigraphs heading each chapter. They are not against slavery so much as they are a mordant summary of the general human situation. They comprehensively illustrate the folly of human existence, and the ultimate reach of their wisdom is not so much that the institution of slavery was or is evil as it is that all humankind *are* slaves in one way or another – to a God who mismanaged creation, to the idea of property and money, to speculation, or to flattery. In Pudd'nhead's calendar, Adam was not at fault for eating the apple; the mistake was to forbid it instead of the serpent; then Adam would have eaten the serpent. Adam, far from being the original sinner, was the true benefactor of humanity by bringing death into the world. If America was wonderful to find, it would have been more wonderful to miss. The best thing in the world, the true boon, is the Southern watermelon, and had it been in the garden, Eve would never have repented for eating it. The world, in brief, is not and never was a paradise; it is full of fools. April Fool's Day is thus the day disclosing what humans are on the other 364 days of the year. The number of fools killed on July 4 merely confirms that we need more such days because the country has grown so.

It would be too easy to conclude that these observations are misanthropic or even bitter; they are the final product, the last will, of a mind at once detached and undeluded. The wisdom of Twain's years, they are the best that can be said of human experience. As such they are more dry than corrosive, possessing an astringency reflecting the speaker's judgment of himself as much as he judges others. Men are, in a word, Pudd'nheads. It is not that they should die; it's just that, if they only knew, they would and will be better off dead. That recognition is enough to recommend death rather than eternal life to anyone who has had the misfortune to have lived.

The very soul of this wisdom is expressed in the entry heading chapter 10: "All say, 'How hard it is that we have to die'—a strange complaint to come from the mouths of people who have had to live" (44). There is the definition of life. It *has* to be lived; it is the chain of existence itself, is indeed the great chain of being seen through a mordant but not a bitter or cynical eye. As such, life is slavery. This is the ultimate recognition of this book about slavery, and it comes as the conclusion of a man who has achieved success in the society of slavery. It could stand as the wisdom willed from the lawyer who has saved the society. Such wisdom is bound to disconcert people committed to a free society. For us, freedom is the fact and law of history, morality, and society; slavery was precisely the false fact that had to be gotten rid of and rendered into a fiction. The book makes the issue clear at every point; it confidently assumes the complacency with which its audience rests in the fact of its freedom, just as it confidently exploits the audience's assurance that slavery was a monstrous lie. Thus it mocks for the most part the old dead horses of the antebellum South: its honor, its chivalry, its duels, its infatuation with the pretensions of aristocracy, its sentimentality, and its romance. These are the binary absurdities so evident from the complacent perspective of freedom.

The explicit burlesque of the antebellum slave society is but a part of the comprehensive irony of the book. In getting her son out of slavery, Roxy gets more deeply in; in becoming a master, he merely faces the threat of his foster father's withheld will; the slave as master (the false Tom Driscoll) becomes both a tyrant and thief; the master as slave (the false Valet de Chambre) becomes an abject slave.

Beyond that there is the arbitrary plot of the narrative itself. The deepest iron in the irony of this book is the iron plot in which Mark Twain contains the action. Far from being the slave and fool of a narrative current beyond his control, as he claims in his authorial account, Mark Twain visibly rigs every move. His characters, all save Roxy, are locked in the narrowest confines of consciousness and straitened speech. Although Roxy's vernacular allows her an element of poetic and passionate range, it is nonetheless a stereotype of the language of slavery, and Mark Twain as arbitrarily blackens her with it as the slaveholders have arbitrarily made her invisible one-sixteenth black blood outvote the fifteen parts of white blood — as if blood were black or white and not red. He would have us believe, or at least he plays on the belief, that just as social structure determines speech, nurture determines nature; yet his plot settles for the possibility that Tom's one-thirty-second portion of black blood does indeed determine his identity. Certainly that is Roxy's contention in her marvelous confrontation of her son upon learning of his cowardice in the matter of the duel.

Yet Mark Twain's narration leaves an opening — what we might better call a ligature — between the forces of nurture and nature. We are told that the false Tom Driscoll "was a bad baby, from the very beginning of his usurpation"(17), indicating that his badness lies not in his blood but in his transformation into a master. And when Tom learns of his true identity as a Negro and slave, although he is at first shaken to personal foundations by the knowledge, he nonetheless reverts to his old ways because "the main structure of his character was not changed and could not be changed"(45). Although this asserted reversion to "character" can be seen as but a version of genetic determination, the character here referred to is nonetheless grounded in social structure in much the same way that the First Families of Virginia are grounded.

I am not here trying to bring Mark Twain out on one side or the other of the nature-nurture issue. In a real way the narration occupies both sides of the equation, showing that, like master and slave, nature and nurture are Siamese twins in bondage to each other. Yet the resolution of the plot still leaves a disconcerting sense of an imbalance between the two. Part of the imbalance results, as I have noted, from the reader's disappointed expectation on seeing the false Tom Driscoll turn out to be "bad" rather than good upon being freed into his role as master. But the greater part of the imbalance can be attributed to Pudd'nhead Wilson and his fingerprints — what we may call the essential plot machinery of the novel. It is well to recall that, upon gratefully receiving a letter praising Pudd'nhead Wilson as a character, Mark Twain still claimed that he had always thought of Wilson as a piece of machinery. In his authorial accounts, he writes of needing Wilson to run the machinery of the plot. Add to this the fact of Wilson's interest in fingerprints, and we have a figure occupying the margins of science and technology.

Wilson's project of fingerprinting the citizens of Dawson's Landing is the "scientific" extension of his interest in palmistry. It is also related to his advertised occupation of surveying because it involves surveying both the lines of individual and community identity. As for that, Wilson also advertises himself as a conveyancer, and as matters turn out he does indeed transfer titles from one person to another. Wilson's apparent detachment masks the motives of doubt and aggression that are implicitly at play in his unadvertised hobby of fingerprinting. He is not only doubting faces and names of the citizenry; he is also aggressively seeking to locate individual identity before personality and name. It is well known that Mark Twain obtained considerable information about fingerprinting from Sir Francis Galton's book on the subject. What is less well known is that Mark Twain had already used the device of fingerprints ten years earlier in *Life on the Mississippi* as a means of locating a criminal. Even more interesting is the fact that Francis Galton, long before he worked on fingerprints, had made great strides in developing his science of eugenics by studying twins. Galton's aim, as Michael Rogin points out (79), was to establish an aristocracy of talent that would replace the aristocracy of blood. The study of twins, particularly identical twins, enabled him to measure the force of genetic characteristics in relation to the impact of environmental influence. Although much of Galton's work has been superseded and although his Victorian predilections have been exposed, his work on twins is symptomatic of what has followed. Subsequent studies of twins, particularly the most recent and extensive study conducted in the "twin city" of Minneapolis, almost fatally tend to disclose that nature is a more powerful influence than nurture. For all the efforts of social sciences to stress as well as measure the power of nurture, the "hard" sciences find themselves steadily discovering and strengthening the genetic code.

Coming back to Pudd'nhead, his "science" of fingerprinting enables him to "discover" Tom Driscoll and restore the disrupted social order of Dawson's Landing. Utterly free of the social and moral implications of race and slavery, he is rewarded with the power to preside over the restored status quo. That is the "success" he finally secures; his epigrams are the irony above the iron plot dryly mediating the discrepancy between his moral neutrality and his desolating discovery.

That discovery, coming as it does four hundred years after Columbus's discovery of the New World, does not abate the appalling existence of racism and slavery but in effect sustains them – a conclusion leaving us to brood on the function of this detective who has operated the plot machinery of the novel. Mark Twain had, in *A Connecticut Yankee*, invented a character, Hank Morgan, who, representing enlightened nineteenth-century American ideals, had embarked on an imperial effort intended to accelerate the social, political, moral, and technological movement of Arthurian England out of its lethargic state. David Wilson, born in New York state and college-bred, is also a Yankee. Unlike Morgan, who invented the machinery for rushing the fifth century into the nineteenth and finally electrocuted the mailed knights whose very armor provided the ground for receiving his accelerated current, Wilson is the detached and seemingly disinterested scientist using the simplest yet most advanced technology to detect and fix individual identity. At once solitary and marginal, he has no love interest, no romance, but is instead the very instrument for exposing the passage of sexual energy crossing racial lines. He comes not to destroy the society but to occupy, examine, and finally administer it. Mark Twain invents him at a time when the European colonization of Africa is at its apogee. Small wonder that Mark Twain would use Pudd'nhead's calendar entries to head the chapters of *Following the Equator*, the record of his travels through what we now call the third world, published at the moment the United States was to embark on its own full-fledged colonial imperialism.

American imperialism, characterized by uncontrollable arms development and production, has been at the heart of our history in the twentieth century – the American century. Like slavery in the nineteenth century, the dynamic arms race is in effect the institution that we cannot get rid of. No one can really want it, yet it has gone on so long and so much has been invested in it that we are helpless before its power. Treaties and compromises have been attempted; they may regulate, but do not retard, its momentum. Because all this destructive force is generated in the name of freedom, who is to say that we are not slaves to its generation?

I think that Mark Twain, of all our writers, could see that if the first American revolution resulted in freedom from tyranny yet left us with slavery, the second American revolution brought freedom from slavery yet left us with the tyranny of freedom. Such a vision is as disconcerting as the conclusion of *Pudd'nhead Wilson*, a novel that neither we nor Mark Twain would wish to call a masterpiece, that word we use so easily in discussing literature and art. Mark Twain had launched his career by making fun of the Old Masters. Master pilot though he may have been, his humor sought a freedom from mastery. He left Henry James, a true imperialist in the world of art, to be the master while he, the jackleg novelist, seemed always ready to be the irresponsible and maundering slave and fool unable to master the current of plot and pen that enslaved him.

FORREST G. ROBINSON

The Sense of Disorder in
Pudd'nhead Wilson

I want to build a coherent critical argument about *Pudd'nhead
Wilson* on the deeply fractured textual foundation most recently
brought to our attention by Hershel Parker. Parker's plausible reconstruction of the history of the novel's composition at once illumi-
nates and deeply complicates our critical understanding. Directly
and boldly, he challenges us to reread *Pudd'nhead* in light of what
he has revealed. And he goes much further, to insist that all such
attempts to make critical sense of the novel must fail because of the
fundamental incoherence of the text itself. The anomalies and contradictions are so numerous and irreducible, he argues – characters
are hopelessly inconsistent, or they appear "in a story where they
had no business," and entire scenes are "all but meaningless" – that
"the published *Pudd'nhead Wilson* is . . . patently unreadable."[1]

It is essential to our cultural health that we make as much sense
as we can of the stories we tell and retell ourselves, especially when
they touch significantly on matters as prominent and as vexed as
racism and slavery. We must be particularly wary of invitations to
dismiss such stories as meaningless. In fact, and as generations of
American readers have found, there is potent sense in Mark Twain's
seeming nonsense. Few of these readers have been trained literary
scholars. They have not demanded of his books that they conform
to Parker's standards for the "genuine novel" and the "good novel"
where "early scenes prepare for the middle and the later scenes,
where patterns established at the outset are fulfilled in subsequent
pages, where all the aspects really do work together in a transcendent unity."[2] This marked tendency to draw meaning and literary value
into close association with unity is familiar enough, of course, and
it has worked quite well with those tidy, usually rather self-conscious
artists who share it. But there are meanings of great interest to be
found in disunity, in thematic and structural discontinuities, radical

dislocations between "parts," sudden shifts in characterization, and endings that fail to "close" completely.[3] It is to the significant patterning of such breakdowns, such departures from unity, that I will turn in arguing for the deeper sense of *Pudd'nhead*'s disorder.

Mark Twain is surely the most prominent of our groping literary geniuses. His halting habits of composition, and his failures to recognize and consciously control the energy and direction of his work, are well known. His writing, even at its best, is notorious for its resistance to conventional standards of evaluation. As a result, we have learned to account for his creative and cultural authority in spite of, and even in terms of, his alleged defects.[4] Such an approach seems especially appropriate to *Pudd'nhead Wilson*, a novel literally barricaded in authorial acknowledgments that it is without design, a product of unconscious processes, and not to be trusted. Such is Mark Twain's emphatic and unequivocal message in "A Whisper to the Reader," in the remarks prefatory to *Those Extraordinary Twins*, and at numerous points along the way in both narratives. In light of all this, Parker's reiteration of the novel's shortcomings seems rather pointless, save as the occasion for assaults on Mark Twain (who is characterized as lazy, inept, self-deceived, a braggart, and a money-grubbing fraud), and on all the critics (but especially all the New Critics) who have been foolish enough to take Mark Twain seriously.[5]

Still, Parker's textual scholarship is of undoubted value, and there can be little dissent from his assertion that "details about composition and publication are often crucial to any defensible interpretation of works of fiction."[6] The disagreement arises at the point of deciding what to make of such "details." Consider the novel's conclusion, for example. Parker shows that the ending of the published novel was written before most of the Tom and Roxy plot, with the result that the dark thrust of the chapters on slavery is lost sight of in *Pudd'nhead*'s concluding courtroom theatrics. "At no time," Parker insists, "neither in the process of inscription in the manuscript at its fullest form nor in the book, did the ending truly 'close' a unified, carefully structured work of art." Instead, "The immorality of slavery is not a serious issue any more, nor man's inhumanity to man, nor heredity versus training; and Tom's being sold down the river is a throwaway joke."[7]

There can be no serious quarreling with Parker's facts, or with his characterization of the ending of the novel. For all of its apparent right-mindedness, however, this critical turning away recapitulates the very act of suppression that the novel's ending at once commits and dramatizes. If we insist on the strict application of conventional critical assumptions, then we will be blind – as Mark Twain was blind, and, in a sense, as his book is blind – to the terrific significance of the discontinuity between the dark central chapters and the strangely up-beat conclusion. The point here – the meaning – is that comprehensive blindness itself, the failure, ultimately the refusal, to confront the full, painful implications of the Tom and Roxy plot. *Pudd'nhead* dramatizes, quite brilliantly if all unawares, a repeating cultural cycle of address to and evasion of the same dark themes. "The ending is gaudy and thrilling," Parker observes; "it lets the reader close the book dazzled, but it does not bear much thinking about in relation to the rest of the published story."[8] This is precisely, although quite inadvertently, on the mark. It is deeply the function of the "gaudy and thrilling" ending to draw attention away from the novel's tragic drift. The reader is indeed "dazzled," and gratefully if unconsciously so, for he or she has had enough of Roxy and Tom and their hopeless suffering and welcomes the release into happier prospects. Thus the reader joins quite willingly in the evasion that Mark Twain's novel both engages in and "permits." There is discontinuity here, to be sure, but it is hardly meaningless; and if we are able to resist the impulse to dismiss it from further consideration, the ending of *Pudd'n-head*, in its relation to the rest of the published story, will bear as much thinking as we can.

There is no evidence, according to Parker, that Mark Twain was aware of any structural problems in "the big version" of the manuscript – essentially *Pudd'nhead* and *Those Extraordinary Twins* before they were divided – when, in 1893, he urged it upon his publisher, Fred J. Hall. Later on in the same year he separated the Siamese twins and removed them, along with Aunt Patsy and Rowena and others, from the foreground, made a few additional adjustments, and came back confident that this narrative was now "stripped for flight!" He assured Hall that "The whole story is centered on the murder and the trial; from the first chapter the movement is straight ahead without divergence or side-play to the murder and the trial; everything that is done or said or that happens is a preparation for those events. Therefore, 3 people stand up high, from beginning to end, and only 3 – Pudd'nhead, 'Tom' Driscoll and his nigger mother Roxana; none of the others are important, or get in the way of the story or require the reader's attention. Consequently, the scenes and episodes which were the strength of the book formerly are stronger than ever, now."[9]

Quite evidently, Mark Twain was persuaded that he had written a fast-moving murder mystery, and not a penetrating indictment of race-slavery. Most of his readers have been inclined to agree with him. Indeed, it is an important key to the cultural authority of *Pudd'n-head* that it enables the retreat to an illusion of resolution when none has occurred. The author, the reader, and, in its way, the text itself surrender to the impression that the main business of the novel is fully and happily concluded, when in fact it has simply been pushed out of sight and mind.

This process of collusive acquiescence in recapitulating evasions is a phenomenon I have elsewhere described as "bad faith," the deception of self and other in the denial of violations of public ideals of truth and justice.[10] Such departures are most frequently group phenomena, collaborative denials, and bear with them the clear implication that people will sometimes permit or acquiesce in what they cannot approve, so long as their complicity is submerged in a larger, tacit consensus. It is a telling feature of acts of bad faith that they incorporate silent prohibitions against the acknowledgment that they have occurred — denial is itself denied.

My definition of bad faith takes rise from the close analysis of village social dynamics as they are represented in *Tom Sawyer*. I find that Mark Twain's characters are engaged in an elaborate form of social play whose dominant feature is the reciprocal deception of self and other in the denial of departures from leading public values. The term *bad faith* is also applied to the cognate pattern of denial that emerges in Mark Twain's handling of his materials, and that may be observed as well in the audience reception of the book. Thus the cultural dynamics observable in the action of the novel are repeated in the telling and in the response to the tale.

The recapitulating levels of bad faith witnessed in the complex, generally comical, and benign world of *Tom Sawyer* reappear, now in a more pathological form, in *Huckleberry Finn*. Once again, bad faith is everywhere — not only in the behavior of the people in towns along the river, but also in the young hero himself, in his author's management of the story, and in the novel's enduring popular reception. At the root of this pervasive malady is race-slavery, an institution whose maintenance in a Christian democracy requires extraordinary bad-faith denial, and whose existence over time fosters a wide range of kindred deceptions. The culminating episode in this darkly emergent cultural portrait is Tom's famous "evasion," the ostensibly humorous freeing of an already free man. Here as elsewhere in his writing, Mark Twain's approach to the tormented heart of his fictional enterprise intersects with a countering impulse toward distraction. The urge to tell the unbearable truth about Huck and Jim and their world arrives at a culturally revealing impasse with the urge to laugh it all off. This retreat from painful implication is also manifest in the history of the novel's halting composition, and in the enormous appetites for violent distraction among its leading actors. The same may be said for the enduring and widespread reader approval of *Huckleberry Finn*, a response arising out of pleasure that is itself the uncertain issue of acquiescence in Tom's evasion. At all of these levels, then, *Huckleberry Finn* records or prompts a movement toward resolution, never completed, with nightmare. The dark implications of race-slavery press upward against the surface of the narrative, or of consciousness, only to be pressed down, and to rise and fall again and again in a repeating cycle of bad-faith denial.[11]

Viewed against this background, some dimensions of the literary and cultural significance of *Pudd'nhead Wilson* may come to view. Mark Twain was obviously prompted by yet another meditation on "the matter of Hannibal" to explore the devious mechanisms of race-slavery. Just as conspicuously, he was once again incapable of fully acknowledging or resolving the terrible truth that he beheld. Quite characteristically, the really tragic implications of the story began to rise toward the surface only after the narrative, initially conceived and set in motion as comic, was well under way. *Pudd'nhead* is an interesting variation on the usual pattern to the extent that its ostensibly happy ending was firmly in place before the emergent grief was given play. At the same time that it faithfully mirrors its maker's maneuvering to somehow contain the resurgent tragic thrust of his story, *Pudd'nhead* also enables the reader to perform the same bad faith evasion. Given the slightest inclination to skirt the implications of the Tom and Roxy story, the reader is swept up at novel's end by the dramatic conclusion to a tale of mystery and shrewd detection. As Hershel Parker observes: "Since readers know from the next-to-last chapter that Pudd'nhead will at last be fully vindicated, even as far as his dubious hobby is concerned, they bring to the last chapter only delightful suspense over precisely how he will dole out the grand revelation, how high a pitch of excitement he can create before everyone in Dawson's Landing knows what the readers have known all along. In the end Wilson's superior knowledge is publically brought forth in stunningly irrefutable fashion so as to convict a murderer, free a slave, and amaze the whole of the village."[12]

Of course, we must be duly attentive to the novel's final twist — Tom's "pardon" and sale down the river — and to the expressions of discomfort and ironic deflation that it has drawn from some critics. Still, it is surely proper to emphasize that the conclusion draws attention away from the grave irony that it finally reveals. St. Petersburg has it both ways with poor Tom, but that disclosure is ventured briefly, almost in passing, and as a kind of enigmatic addition to an otherwise conventionally happy ending. Thus the conclusion may be said to recapitulate the bad-faith evasion that it reveals, and it invites generally willing readers to join in.

When Mark Twain first sat down to compose *Pudd'nhead Wilson* he had it in mind to elaborate the farcical developments that would follow on the arrival of talented, aristocratic, Italian twins in the sleepy slave community of Dawson's Landing.[13] The story that emerged under his pen is a sometimes humorous narrative involving the inseparable Counts Luigi and Angelo, the infatuated Rowena, her Aunt Patsy, Judge Driscoll, and others. Pudd'nhead Wilson figures in a minor capacity, as does Tom Driscoll, who is introduced as the Judge's nephew, and as Angelo's rival for Rowena's affections. The story features the differences between the twins, a quarrel between Luigi and Tom that leads to a trial, the reaction of the proud Judge Driscoll, who duels with Luigi, Tom's theft of Luigi's dagger, and Pudd'nhead's disclosure of a secret plan for bringing the thief to justice. Most of this turns up in *Those Extraordinary Twins*, but none of it seems to prepare for the abrupt advent of Roxana, Tom's slave mother, who enters the story at this point, apparently from out of nowhere. Quite as abruptly, and equally without evidence of preparation, Tom is revealed to be part black, a changeling, and a heartless villain who sells his mother down the river, kills his uncle for the money to buy her back out of slavery, and is finally brought to justice as the result of Pudd'nhead's dazzling feats of detection. All of this material appears virtually unchanged in the published *Pudd'nhead*.

There is obvious and ample occasion here for the conclusion that the creative process had somehow gone out of control. This was Mark Twain's considered view of the situation. Indeed, he offered *Pudd'nhead* as a leading example of a recurrent development in his writing, when "the original intention (or motif) is apt to get abolished and find itself superseded by a quite different one." Characteristically, a funny story is unaccountably transformed into a grave story (he advances *The Prince and the Pauper* as evidence, but *A Connecticut Yankee* or *Huckleberry Finn* would have served quite as well). *Pudd'nhead* was "a great deal worse" than its predecessors in this regard, because "it was not one story, but two stories tangled together; and they obstructed and interrupted each other at every

turn and created no end of confusion and annoyance. I could not offer the book for publication, for I was afraid it would unseat the
reader's reason, I did not know what was the matter with it, for I
had not noticed as yet, that it was two stories in one. It took me
months to make that discovery."[14]

I take the artist at his word here. For a period of time he perceived
no fundamental discontinuity in his materials, but subsequently he
came to recognize that he had written not one story, "but two stories
tangled together." This is plausible enough, it seems to me, and I ask
merely that we suspend critical judgment long enough to entertain
the possibility that both perspectives on the narrative had their
time and place in the evolution of the novel. His confusion, I suggest, functioned as the reflex of a deeper creative, ultimately cultural, design. Here as elsewhere in *Pudd'nhead Wilson*, it served his
purposes to have things both ways.

Consider the fact that Mark Twain continued to develop the Siamese twins farce cum mystery materials (hereafter called the mystery
plot) long after the abrupt introduction of Roxy and the transformation of Tom (hereafter referred to as the race-slavery plot). The two
stories surfaced on page after page as if they belonged there together. One might speculate that Mark Twain was experimenting
with his narrative, suspending the impulse to resolve the evident
discord in order that the separate strands might play themselves
more fully into view. But this hypothesis will not square with the
fact that Mark Twain later tried to publish the novel with the mystery plot and the race-slavery plot fully intact and side by side in
the pages of his manuscript. In due course I will develop the view
that the two stories are as arguably bound up with each other as
they are demonstrably incompatible. Once again, and quite significantly, it was a matter of having it both ways. At the point of Roxy's
advent it served Mark Twain's purposes to sustain the apparently
incompatible mystery plot because that narrative line had its con-
summation in a benign and thoroughly compelling dramatic conclusion. This is the familiar ending of the published *Pudd'nhead* that
I have aligned with Mark Twain's other distracting, bad faith evasions. In other words, as he released Roxy, fully formed and irresistibly in motion, into his narrative, Mark Twain responded to a simultaneous and countering impulse to contain her, to blunt and obscure
the transforming, profoundly subversive thrust of her story. The
mystery plot admirably answered this need. It filled narrative space
and time, thus diminishing the full force of the race-slavery plot, and
it was the justification for the happily distracting conclusion. Thus

the confusion of having it both ways served as a stay against the painful clarity of Roxy's story, and the savage indictment of white slave culture that it bore with it. This proud, powerful slave forced her way, almost literally against the resistance of her maker's consciousness, into the center of *Pudd'nhead Wilson*; Mark Twain surrendered to her, and to the imperious, deeply subversive creative impulse that she expressed, but only on condition that her story could not, in any conventional sense, be completed.

This line of reasoning from the premise of bad faith gains additional plausibility from its ready application to a second, closely related critical conundrum. We have addressed the question why, having conceived Roxy, Mark Twain didn't abandon the Siamese twins and the egregious Rowena and turn his undivided attention to what so obviously interested him—the forward motion of the race-slavery plot. Alternately, why didn't he go back to the beginning of his manuscript to develop the earlier stages of Roxy's story properly? He resisted the obvious in this second way for the same reason that he resisted it in prolonging the life of the mystery plot—because he was unwilling to give free rein to the unencumbered race-slavery plot. To have returned to the beginning of Roxy's story would have been to risk being completely overtaken by it. Precisely because of its potent autonomy within his imagination, that story spelled trouble; it threatened to carry him, in the sweep of its tragic inevitability, to the very core of what was wrong with his America. He had drifted into the heart of that darkness once before, and he put his feelings about the experience into Huck's mouth. "If I'd a knowed what a trouble it was to make a book," Huck complains, just before lighting out for the Territory, "I wouldn't a tackled it and ain't agoing to no more."[15] Nor was Mark Twain alone in his resistance to a full reckoning with what he knew and felt about race-slavery. As I have argued elsewhere, his tenderness on this score was quite closely attuned to the sensitivities of his audience. *Huckleberry Finn* is our most popular story about race-slavery because it gives us no more of the truth than we can bear.[16] *Pudd'nhead Wilson* is in equally fine adjustment to its readers' tolerances. Had Mark Twain turned from his farcical mystery story to the full, exclusive elaboration of the tragic Roxy, he would have labored in defiance of the strong personal and cultural inclinations that flowed through and defined his creativity.

Mark Twain held fast to the mystery plot and gave it first priority in his writing agenda because that course of action constrained his subversive impulses as they had emerged in the race-slavery plot.

But there is also a sense in which the completion of the mystery plot and the firm installment of its "safe" ending in fact opened the way to the fuller elaboration of Roxy's story. In the published version of *Pudd'nhead*, the final sentences, although potent with ironic suggestion, generally fall on deaf ears. The context, with its unmingled mood of justice achieved, order and confidence restored, is virtually proof against the brief surge of irony. But in the order of composition — the narrative as it found its way into the manuscript — the final sentences are the appropriate and very forceful prologue to the savage indictment of race-slavery that Mark Twain wrote next, and that forms the large bulk of the first ten chapters of the published text. The fully ironic potential of Tom's being sold down the river, which is effectively muffled in the version we all read, is unsheathed when the narrative is read as it was written, and appears as the first in a series of swift, deep thrusts. Roxy's advent marks the first overt indication of Mark Twain's subversive drift. Having conceived his assault, however, he effectively restrained it until the novel's happy ending was fixed. Only then did he give free rein to his insights into the absurd cruelty and hypocrisy and suffering and injustice of American race-slavery. In effect, the terms of his truce with bad faith enforced the composition of two stories, one the vehicle of grave cultural analysis, the other a benign, distracting "cover." Both stories are "contained" in the published *Pudd'nhead*, although the visible, public, bad-faith narrative has effectively anticipated, and thereby served, the pervasive cultural tendency to ignore, or to dismiss as anomalous, the imbedded, subversive race-slavery plot. Thus the reader, capitalizing on the opportunity held out by the published text, enters the cycle of bad faith by recapitulating its most characteristic act of denial.[17]

We can go a step or two further in this line of analysis by giving some attention to the remaining stages in the evolution of *Pudd'n-head Wilson*. The actual composition ended with the completion of the background to the race-slavery plot in chapter 10, a kind of suppressed conclusion to the novel. A similar fate befell the original beginning of *Pudd'nhead Wilson*, most of which was consigned by Mark Twain to the relative obscurity of *Those Extraordinary Twins*. Aptly subtitled "The Suppressed Farce," these chapters derive their humor from the spectacle of the twins before they were divided and installed as principals in the much more serious mystery plot of the published *Pudd'nhead*. The almost embarrassed impatience of Mark Twain's remarks on this material invites the conclusion that it is inferior in literary quality and entirely irrelevant to the drift of the main story. Such comments to the contrary notwithstanding, however, the suppressed chapters in fact appeared in print in the American edition. Evidently enough, it was another instance of having it both ways. Part of Mark Twain wanted to completely excise the farcical first stage in the order of composition; another part resisted. At the root of these contrary urges, as they are manifest in the artist's uncertainty, and in its correlative, the unsuppressed suppression, is bad faith.

Almost from its first page, the ostensibly humorous narrative about the Siamese twins competes for center stage with an emergent, increasingly penetrating commentary on the pervasive duplicity of the society in which it is set. As the story advances, the increasing girth and weight of the social analysis overtakes and threatens to absorb the farce, a familiar general pattern of emergence and displacement in Mark Twain's novels. In this instance, the process involves the close continuity of major themes and images that first appear in a relatively benign comedic frame of reference, only to take on an increasingly grave cast as the narrative progresses. Moreover, and most vitally for present purposes, this process does not terminate with the end of *Those Extraordinary Twins*; quite to the contrary, it continues on an even darker course of development until it ends, in a sense where it begins, in the very painful chapters on the twisted human implications of race-slavery that closed the order of composition. Thus "the suppressed farce" appears as the first step in what may be viewed as an evolving revelation of the intimate connections between race-slavery and bad faith. The impulse to address the painful truth, as it surfaces in the order of the novel's composition, was quite evidently in a state of unresolved tension with the counter impulse, manifest in the published version of the novel, to suppress that same truth. In the outcome the whole story is neither completely told nor completely buried.

When, at the beginning of *Those Extraordinary Twins*, the inseparable Luigi and Angelo first appear at Aunt Patsy Cooper's door, they are described as "a stupefying apparition – a double-headed human creature with four arms, one body, and a single pair of legs!" (124). The twins promptly withdraw to their room, leaving Aunt Patsy and her daughter, Rowena, "conscious of nothing but that prodigy, that uncanny apparition that had come and gone so suddenly – that weird strange thing that was so soft spoken and so gentle of manner, and yet had shaken them up like an earthquake with the shock of its grewsome aspect" (125). Angelo and Luigi are a living affront to settled assumptions about what is "natural." Their assault on the comfortable stability of familiar boundaries culminates in their effortless evasion of the local system of justice, which is reduced to a mockery in its effort to prosecute one of the inseparable pair. In his outraged concluding remarks to the jury, the judge gives voice to the dire implications of the trial's anomalous outcome. "You have set adrift, unadmonished, in this community, two men endowed with an awful and mysterious gift, a hidden and grisly power for evil – a power by which each in his turn may commit crime after crime of the most heinous character, and no man be able to tell which is the guilty or which the innocent party in any case of them all. Look to your homes – look to your property – look to your lives – for you have need!" (154).

Even if we admit, as we must, that the twins are strange, this reaction by the judge is nonetheless extreme, just as the reaction of Aunt Patsy and Rowena, with its apocalyptic overtones, seems to exceed the objective threat to which it responds. The twins are freaks, gross exceptions to ordinary human expectations, who violate rules and boundaries without offering any threat to their legitimacy or stability. Quite evidently, they stir in their hosts an intimation of some grave fault buried deep beneath the rather complacent local equilibrium.

The ostensible comedy of the Siamese twins sends a shudder through Dawson's Landing because it turns on their having it both ways when it comes to ordinary assumptions about individual identity, motivation, and the assignment of legal and moral responsibility. Aunt Patsy and Rowena are stunned, the judge is appalled, and Mark Twain's creativity was galvanized by the twins because their doubleness obliquely mirrors and echoes the bad faith of the dominant social order. Ultimately, of course, their acquittal looks ahead to the punishing irony of Tom Driscoll's immunity to prosecution at the end of the published *Pudd'nhead*. But from the beginning the terrible truth about race-slavery is present as an embryonic glimmering, an emergent, subversive potential in the spectacle of the unnatural pair. The abundant and irresistible evidence here is the content of *Those Extraordinary Twins*. For a page or two Mark Twain gives his attention to what is so conspicuously unnatural in the twins. But before long his attention shifts to what is equally unnatural in the town itself. Everything in Dawson's Landing is characterized by patterns of doubleness that duplicate those to be observed in the twins. Individuals differ from each other in delivering opposed responses to and assessments of the same things. But individuals are also prone to gross internal contradictions. Thus Aunt Patsy moves abruptly from a very negative to a very positive view of Angelo and Luigi. Such differences run parallel to those in the "freaks" in the sense that they are almost always traceable to motives of self-interest. Rowena is inclined to favor the twins because she is desperate for romance. Aunt Patsy takes an initially suspicious view because she is troubled by the idea of two lovers in one — the twins put her in mind of "Sodom and Gomorrah," she says (139) — but once persuaded by the designing Luigi that he and Angelo *are no more twins than you are*" (141), she warms immediately to her prospective son-in-law. The key difference between the twins and their new neighbors is that the newcomers are perfectly conscious of themselves as they maneuver to take full advantage of having things both ways. They are not at all self-deceived in their deceptions. The same cannot be said for the villagers, who contrive to have it both ways without knowing it. Thus what is shameless opportunism in the twins is bad faith in the unself-conscious citizens of Dawson's Landing. This vital difference points to the fact that the Italians are outsiders to the culture of race-slavery, and thus, for all of their cynicism, exempt from the deeper, more destructive doublings of the local bad faith.

The conspicuous but unacknowledged continuity between the doubleness of the twins and the pervasive local duplicity takes its final expression in the election of Angelo and Luigi as representatives of the opposed political parties of Dawson's Landing. Once again, the legal establishment is brought to its knees, but on this occasion the trouble is traceable back through the twins, who are now merely its agents, to an ultimate source in the will of the citizens of Dawson's Landing. Thus confronted with the impossible excess of their own doubleness, the people eclipse the problem — but only at the price of ironically confirming and deepening its influence with them — by lynching one of their newly elected officials. Having it so grossly both ways with their legal system, not to mention its representatives, the townspeople are almost literally hoist by their own petard. But they run no risk of a direct, conscious reckoning with this clearly implied and very severe self-condemnation. For at the same time that the lynching raises the doubleness of the community into plain view, it also serves, in characteristic bad faith, to distract the actors in the rather grave little farce from the manifest significance of their own behavior.

Indeed, it is perfectly clear throughout *Pudd'nhead Wilson* that legitimate public contests between conflicting points of view, whether in the courtroom or in democratic political activities, are always subordinate as trials of justice or the popular will to an impulse to be distracted. Thus when Angelo and Luigi are acquitted, the members of the audience are utterly indifferent to the judge's jeremiad as they crowd "forward to overwhelm the Twins and their counsel with congratulations" (154). Their evident delight in the exciting courtroom drama is obliquely an expression of their deeper gratitude for distraction from their own complicity in the miscarriage of justice they have just witnessed. Here, as in the lynching that so thoroughly reverses the high-sounding legal principles advanced at the twins' acquittal, the audience to the spectacle of doubleness is blithely unaware of the fact that they have gone their victim – or victims – one better in the business of having it both ways.

It is doubly ironic, of course, that the citizens of Dawson's Landing should "distrust and detest" Angelo "because there was such a lack of harmony between his morals, which were confessedly excellent, and his methods of illustrating them, which were distinctly damnable" (168). The charge applies with even greater force to those who level it, and not least because when it suits their purposes they seize upon the same doubleness in the twins as the basis for their approval of Angelo. Such ironies double and redouble upon themselves because the villagers operate on the confident assumption that their world is a binary system in which moral opposites struggle for supremacy, and in which good – thanks to the sway of democracy and Christianity – always triumphs. When challenged, as it is most graphically by the twins, this Manichean scheme is advanced in the name of reason and justice, although in fact it continues to stand only because it is the perfect vehicle, as it is surely the creation, of a culture determined to have it both ways. The necessity for this really profound self-deception, for this righteous blindness, arises out of the fact of race-slavery, an institution that Dawson's Landing does not consider giving up, but whose utter incompatibility with Christian and democratic principles it cannot bear to face. Only against this background of deeply entrenched habits of bad-faith denial does the pervasive doubling and the blind surrender to increasingly ironic moral contradiction make full sense. It is the business of bad faith in *Those Extraordinary Twins*, as it is in *Pudd'nhead Wilson*, to highlight opposition, and to stress the ostensible differences between people and things, that it may enforce or violate those boundaries at will, but without any conscious awareness that it has done so. This habit of blindly having it both ways is present from the beginning of *Those Extraordinary Twins*, and it gathers increasing social weight and tragic implication as it moves, on a clear trajectory, to its climax in the race-slavery plot of *Pudd'nhead Wilson*. Here the insistence on a fixed and rigidly enforced boundary between black and white, which forms the keystone of the entire moral, social, and economic order, stands in stark contradiction to the fact that that same boundary is constantly crossed. The novel is all about how the godforsaken little community manages to violate all of its most carefully guarded social boundaries and moral principles without knowing it.

The strong general line of continuity between *Those Extraordinary Twins* and *Pudd'nhead*, especially as it is manifest in the order of composition, is in fact an aggregate of numerous major strands woven together around the central theme of bad faith. Notions about individual identity, although secure enough in theory, are in fact as unstable and as susceptible to bad-faith manipulation as closely related notions about justice. The unnatural twins, who prompt such freakish reversals in the system of justice, look ahead to what is unnatural in the society that produces Tom, and that resorts to equally extreme distortions of justice in order that it may aquit one half of him, only to condemn the other. Identity, as Luigi tells Angelo, is a social fabrication subject to sudden, quite dramatic transformations (156). The fear of miscegenation, which forms a kind of corollary to the identity theme, stands behind the pervasive fragmentation of families, the general suspicion of children, the general failure to produce them, and the superabundance of single adults in Dawson's Landing. The dread of "unnatural" sexual mixing first appears in Aunt Patsy's evident misgivings about the twins as prospective sons-in-law, only to reappear as a confirmed, if utterly suppressed reality of village life in Roxy, her baby, and all other mulatto members of the "black" community. As an essential element in the evasion of such inconsistencies, there is everywhere a premium on distracting amusement. Most ironically, such retreats from the truth often occur in settings – such as the courtroom in both texts – ostensibly dedicated to its pursuit. From the beginning to the end it is clear that the victims of bad faith are hardly exempt from its influence. Thus the twins readily enter and exploit the social order that finally hangs them, just as Tom and Roxy are, in their different ways, vigorous proponents of the system that destroys their lives.

The continuities between *Those Extraordinary Twins* and *Pudd'nhead* are also evident in the persistence of other non-thematic but no less striking patterns. The pink and scarlet cravats worn by the twins clash so violently that they break "all the laws of taste known to civilization. Nothing more fiendish and irreconcilable than those shrieking and blaspheming colors could have been contrived" (127). Thanks to the spread of an especially vivid breed of geranium, the same combination of colors is to be observed on the cottages in Dawson's Landing. The flowers' "intensely red blossoms accented the prevailing pink tint of the rose-clad house-front like an explosion of flame" (3). The hint of a submerged threat to respectable ways of life, carried over but with subdued implications from the twins outrageous cravats, achieves its fullest, most explicit expression in the "new Sunday gown – a cheap curtain-calico thing, a conflagration of gaudy colors and fantastic figures," and the "blazing red" (13) shawl that Roxy wears when she switches the babies. Images of terrific upheaval and convulsion, clearly cognate with Roxy's "volcanic irruption of infernal splendors" (13), and quite as heavily freighted with implication for the social order, appear first with the twins, the "uncanny apparition" that shakes Aunt Patsy and Rowena "like an earthquake" (125). Aunt Patsy later complains of being "shook up with what we've been through" (126), but her condition is mild enough in its anticipation of the world-shattering revelation that bursts upon poor Tom. The knowledge that he is Roxy's son has the impact of "a gigantic irruption like that of Krakatoa . . . with the accompanying earthquakes, tidal waves and clouds of volcanic dust" (44). Such explosive upheavals, pointing as they do to the perils of bad-faith suppression, link up in an obvious way with the dreams in both narratives, which serve as windows on deeply buried secrets, and with the place of social dogma and unbending authority in containing challenges to the status quo. The subversive wit that surfaces in Mark Twain's language has a similar source.[18] In the aggregate, these lines of continuity give expression to the deep imaginative coherence of the parts of *Pudd'nhead*, from its beginnings in *Those Extraordinary Twins*, through the first conclusion at the end of the published novel, and on to the concealed terminus coiled inside it. Aptly enough, the themes and images that bind the narratives together are largely concerned with submergence and emergence, furtive suppression and subversive return, the repeating bad-faith cycle that circled through Mark Twain's creativity into the significantly divided fabric of his work. Once again, it was the having it both ways that told the tale.

It seems quite unlikely that Mark Twain was ever fully conscious of the submerged coherence of the writing that runs through the scattered "parts" of *Pudd'nhead Wilson*. He meant what he said, I think, when he admitted to having produced "two stories in one" (122). In fact, and as I have suggested more than once, it is entirely consistent with the cultural dynamics of bad faith, as they are evident here and elsewhere in his work, that he should have operated in blindness to his own deepest drift. It is just as appropriate that he should have divided and diverted, and thus effectively denied, the emergent significance of his narrative, without ever recognizing that he had done so, or wondering why. But it needs to be added that Mark Twain was not simply or totally blind to what he was about. To be sure, there are times when this appears to be the case. His impression, lodged in one of the connecting links added to *Those Extraordinary Twins*, that his description of Roxy's "exchange of the children had been flippantly and farcically described in an earlier chapter" (144), is a striking case in point. The same may be said of his sense that "when Roxy wandered into the tale she had to be furnished with something to do; so she changed the children in the cradle; this necessitated the invention of a reason for it" (169), and so on. The impulse that gave rise to Roxy came from beneath consciousness; she surfaced quite against the resistance of bad faith denial, and therefore rather to the puzzlement of her creator. But the same Mark Twain, operating at a different interval in the revolving cycle of bad faith, sneers at the "fiction of law and custom" that makes Roxy and her child slaves, and is pointedly ironic in describing her master as "a fairly humane man, toward slaves and other animals" (9). In fact, he wavered; although strongly inclined to resist the subversive thrust of his material, he was also susceptible to glimpses of his own deeper truth.

As I have already indicated, the tension between the poles of bad faith is discernible in retrospect from the first stages in the composition of *Pudd'nhead*. But the more overt manifestations of the torque in Mark Twain's imagination begin to appear only after the advent of Roxy and the transformation of Tom, when the race-slavery plot joins, and is finally lost in, the concluding bad faith dramatics of the mystery plot. We can catch a glimpse of Mark Twain's address to these enigmatic developments in Pudd'nhead Wilson's approach to the solution of the mystery. When Tom Driscoll presses his thumb against one of the glass slides in Pudd'nhead's quarters, he inadvertently provides the evidence for the solution to the mystery of Judge Driscoll's murder. The attorney reacts violently, "like a person who has been stunned" (103). The sudden revelation of his blindness to the truth, expecially as it has persisted in the very midst of his proud pretensions to scientific rigor, is almost more than he can bear. Once Tom has gone, Pudd'nhead confirms that his departed visitor is in fact the "girl" responsible for the murder. But he comes up short when he discovers that Tom's adult fingerprints, although identical with those taken when he was twelve, don't tally with the ones imprinted when he was an infant. Pudd'nhead is now poised for a shattering insight into the fictions of law and custom at the foundation of the town's leading institution – the same insight that registered quite unconsciously in his initial, seemingly extreme response to Tom's accidental self-incrimination. His brains begin "to clog" under the pressure of what he beholds but cannot consciously grasp, so he surrenders to sleep, and to the clarifying authority of the unconscious. After "a troubled and unrestful hour" (104), he awakens from a dream that opens his eyes to Roxy's switching of the babies.

The dream solution to the mystery is a telling stroke, for it draws attention to the bad faith dynamics of conscious resistance to the powerful, painful truth. During the years when *Pudd'nhead* was written, Mark Twain grew increasingly attentive to the strange doubleness that he experienced in himself, and that he witnessed more generally in the human psyche. Naturally enough, he was taken by *Dr. Jekyll and Mr. Hyde*, although he concluded that Stevenson had drawn "nearer, yes, but not near enough" to the truth that "the two persons in a man are wholly unknown to each other."[19] Appropriately enough, the parts of the self so divided in Mark Twain, and so apparent in Pudd'nhead, do not come fully together in the aftermath of the remarkable dream. Pudd'nhead unfolds the stunning tale as Mark Twain would have – and, in a very literal sense, as Mark Twain did – with great dramatic flair. But the happy collaboration in theatrics is the leading symptom of an incapacity to move past the murder to the much more terrific mysteries of race-slavery, to which the fingerprints and the dream give access, and which Pudd'nhead's initially stunned reaction seems to promise. Quite aptly represented as emergent from beneath consciousness, and briefly glimpsed, the darker truth of Pudd'nhead's dream is overtaken by the frothy poetic justice of his triumph over "hard luck and prejudice" (114).

The final, brief, rather enigmatic trace of the race-slavery plot, which appears in the ironic overthrow of Tom's conviction, is evidence of Mark Twain's wavering in the face of the sharply subversive thrust of his story. There are other examples of this largely unconscious struggle, most of them to be found, not surprisingly, in what constitutes the best example of all – the belatedly composed background to the race-slavery plot. I have already referred to the ironies, quite clearly directed at the slave system, that surface toward the beginning of the now safely "closed" narrative, and that grow more penetrating and more bitter as the race-slavery plot develops in the first ten chapters. If Mark Twain failed to recognize that his surrender to this indictment was conditional on its effective truncation and suppression, he nonetheless left traces of an approach, as tentative and finally incomplete as Pudd'nhead's dream, to the truth of what he was about. On one side, it is remarkable that at the very beginning of his belated elaboration of the race-slavery plot he was careful to insert an account of Pudd'nhead's interest in fingerprints. In at last giving voice to his "tragedy," he was attentive as ever to the background of the distracting mystery story that had, in a sense, already drowned it out. A similar reflex was at work in his decision to suppress two long, bitter passages in which Tom anguishes over the implications of his new estate, and speculates in directly critical and penetrating ways about the brutal paradoxes of the slave system. Once again, the impulse to speak out, even when safely baffled by the larger narrative, is discovered in tension with an urge to deny.[20]

On the other side, there is the enigmatic reference to "Colonel Cecil Burleigh Essex, another F.F.V. of formidable calibre – however, with him we have no concern" (4). As Tom's father, Essex is of intense concern to us, primarily because his identification contradicts in the most dramatic way the "fiction of law and custom" that black and white are easily kept apart, easily distinguished. In fact, Tom is living proof that his father, with most of the respectable men in Dawson's Landing, has it both ways in sexual matters, too. Part of Mark Twain – the part that narrates Tom's birth, but blithely presumes that we will understand, and keep silence, when he neglects to mention a father – joined in this conspiracy of bad faith denial. Another part resisted at least long enough to mention Essex by name, but only to deny in the same voice that he has any significance. This is emphatically not the same thing as simply excluding Tom's father from the narrative. Mark Twain might have done that, with little or no effect on his story or on most of his readers. Instead, in a textbook example of bad faith, he has Tom's father both ways, mentioned and denied, revealed and concealed, all at the same time. This was, in effect, to draw attention to the irresistible declarative urge on the other side of bad faith denial, and to dramatize the deep immersion of the teller in the cultural dynamics of his tale.

Hershel Parker's assault on *Pudd'nhead* leads him to "some questions in basic aesthetics which critics might begin to ponder." I cannot include them all here – there are too many – but I want to offer a representative sampling. "How can the slavery theme . . . inform brief passages or longer units of the book which were written before

Mark Twain introduced those themes into the manuscript (and which were not later revised to contain those themes)? . . . How can passages written as extravagant farce gain profound social significance merely because Mark Twain placed in front of them later-written passages imbued with such significance? . . . How can the same ending close plots as different as those in the full manuscript and the published *Pudd'nhead Wilson*."[21] Obviously, Parker takes it for granted that reasonable answers to these questions, and many others like them, will necessarily work to confirm his comprehensively critical point of view. Quite to the contrary, and as I hope the foregoing argument has demonstrated, I believe that the answers to these questions cast light on the intricate ways and means of Mark Twain's creativity, enhance our understanding of his authority with an enormous American readership, and encourage the continued study of *Pudd'nhead Wilson*.

Parker concludes his commentary by venturing an explanation for what he regards as the almost universal failure of critics to recognize the defects of the novel and the derelictions of the novelist. Drawing on Ralph W. Rader, who in turn draws on the cognitive psychologists, Parker argues that the mind is a "meaning-seeking faculty" which by nature discovers coherence, even when the objective foundation for that discovery is lacking. "It is this order-imposing instinct," he concludes, "(however much it manifests itself in the guise of a mere literary approach such as the New Criticism) which impels readers to celebrate a text containing passages of indubitable interest and power but faked, palmed off as a genuine novel."[22] There is doubtless some value to this general approach, although in Parker's hands it is carried too far in the service of academic sniping, and not nearly far enough in its application to the habits of mind observable in Mark Twain, his characters, and their audience. Mark Twain's epistemology is more complicated and more far-reaching than Parker's. It allows that the mind is a meaning-seeking faculty, but it also dramatizes in a most emphatic way that the pursuit and discovery of meaning is closely geared to the cultural impulse to clear the mind of all that conflicts with a preferred, quite often delusional construction of reality. The human mind is not sometimes found trimming the untidy edges of its pictures of the world; rather, it is constantly engaged in the grossest of evasions and fabrications. Nor is this penchant for fictions the exclusive province of one or another group. Mark Twain's actors are hardly more inclined to self-deception than their audience or their maker. Meaning-seeking is a collaborative cultural enterprise that depends for its success on a broad, ready consensus. Moreover, the elements of ambiguity and downright disorder with which the meaning-seeking faculty must contend are themselves often the manifestation and the product of the unacknowledged will to have it both ways. Thus the complacent discovery and imposition of order in Dawson's Landing, as that activity applies to the social system, the political and legal systems, the regular observance of religious belief, a proud code of honor, the definition of identity in terms of sex, race, family, the giving of names, the very use of the language itself, is carried on in spite of, and indeed quite because of, the conspicuous disorder at once manifest and all but invisible in the slaves who live there, and in the many shades of "black" in their faces.

In his epistemology, then, as in other ways, Parker is ill-prepared to glimpse the coherence of the incoherence that he discovers everywhere in *Pudd'nhead Wilson*. But once his model of human mental activity is replaced with one more nearly in conformity with Mark Twain's, then virtually all of the anomalies that he discovers in the text begin to display a special kind of meaning. It is no longer "adventitious," for example, that the Tom who snatches his hand away because he is afraid of being suspected a thief should, after "Mark Twain had written the passages in which Tom is part-black," draw back because he is afraid of being identified as a slave. The second Tom was there in Mark Twain's imagination from the beginning, inscribed deeply within "the matter of Hannibal," and bound to emerge as the dominant pattern of doubling continued to unfold. The same may be said for the implications that attach themselves to Tom's cowardice after his transformation. Mark Twain's uncertainty about the roles of training and heredity in the formation of "character" is clearly at large in his treatment of Tom from the beginning, and — especially in his hands, and in that fictional setting — clearly loaded from the start with racial implications.[23] Nor is it hopelessly implausible in Tom's characterization that "his obsession with his Negro blood in chapter 10 has already vanished in chapter 11." This apparent anomaly occurs "not by authorial design," Parker declares, "but merely because chapter 11 was written before the ending and chapter 10 after it."[24] But the evident disjunction also illustrates that Tom, like all of the major characters in *Pudd'nhead Wilson*, is an adept at removing from his mind those painful discordancies that conflict with his preferred conception of the world. Once again, having it both ways in the creative process at once anticipates and inadvertently informs, by powerful unconscious design, the identical operations of bad faith dramatized in the tale.

Tom's perfect unwillingness, even incapacity, to face the implications of what he has learned from Roxy underscore what was doubtless Mark Twain's most painfully searching insight into the divided and deceived world that he beheld – at the same time that bad faith denial worked to conceal, and therefore to enable, the cruelty of the white master class, it also served to corrupt the moral lives of its victims and to draw them into unwitting complicity in their own suffering. Thus Roxy is blind – because she cannot possibly bear to see – that in condemning Tom's cowardice she hurls upon her son the whole weight of the master's cruel, self-serving ideology. Without knowing it, she becomes the agent of the prejudice that destroys her life. Nor can she see, as Mark Twain saw, how this blind, tragic complicity works. Roxy's bad faith commences in a moment of fateful choice, when she switches the infants in her care, and thus delivers her child from the life-in-death of being sold down the river. To save her baby, Roxy must take a long step into the heartless, inhumane world of her masters; she must enslave a child to free one, and ruin a life to save one. Although her having it both ways is at least partially redeemed by the extremity of her circumstances, Roxy is no more able to fully accept the cruelty of her act than her masters are able to accept the greater cruelty of theirs. Mark Twain's description of her recoil from implication, from the unbearable significance of her act, is surely the locus classicus for the study of bad faith.

With all her splendid common sense and practical every-day ability, Roxy was a doting fool of a mother. She was this toward her child – and she was also more than this: by the fiction created by herself, he was become her master; the necessity of recognizing this relation outwardly and of perfecting herself in the forms required to express the recognition, had moved her to such diligence and faithfulness in practicing these forms that this exercise soon concreted itself into habit; it became automatic and unconscious; then a natural result followed: deceptions intended solely for others gradually grew practically into self-deceptions as well; the mock reverence became real reverence, the mock obsequiousness real obsequiousness, the mock homage real homage; the little counterfeit rift of separation between imitation-slave and imitation-master widened and widened, and became an abyss, and a very real one – and on one side of it stood Roxy, the dupe of her own deceptions, and on the other stood her child, no longer a usurper to her, but her accepted and recognized master. (19)

On one side, and as Roxy is quite aware, her compliance in consciousness with the outward deception is perhaps essential to success in having it both ways. If her lie is to persuade others, it may be that she must come to believe it herself. But the argument from necessity is demonstrably in bad faith, for it conceals and at the same time advances the deeper, more urgent impulse to self-deception – the incapacity to live in constant, full awareness of the significance of what she has done. In thus yielding to "practical necessity," Roxy retreats from consciousness of the loss of her son, and she spares herself the terrible guilt that she must feel, especially as a slave, for what she has brought upon her master's child. We never see Roxy grieve for the loss of her son; not does she anguish over what she has brought upon the unsuspecting Chambers. She never admits to Tom, or to herself, that his exquisite suffering is to a major extent her responsibility, and there is no evidence of such an admission to poor Chambers. Roxy's having it both ways with the children enforces the bad faith retreat to a "fiction created by herself" that precisely recapitulates the "fiction of law and custom" by which the masters have it both ways with her, and which cruelly enforces her fateful decision. Thus it is the terrible price of her liberating insight and its sequel in action that she become as morally and emotionally dead as her oppressors.

Something of the same thing must be said, finally, for Pudd'nhead himself. He is young, a college-educated lawyer with professional training "in an eastern law school," and he comes from "the interior of the State of New York" (5), the heartland of all varieties of reform in mid-century America, including abolitionism. Mark Twain never says so, but the Pudd'nhead afloat in his imagination must certainly have views about the cruelty of slavery, and about the absurdity of its persistence in America. As we learn in *Those Extraordinary Twins*, he is also possessed of a sharp eye for what is patently ridiculous in Dawson's Landing, but he knows that pointing it out to people "would probably not help them to see it" (159). On the other hand, the well-educated idealist in Pudd'nhead competes with an upwardly mobile young lawyer who is quite ready to sacrifice high principle to the pursuit of self-interest. This is the Pudd'nhead who emerges from the trial in *Those Extraordinary Twins*, a sharp, cynical master of courtroom theatrics and legal technicality who is blithely unconcerned that his victory has its price in a blatant miscarriage of justice. Thus long before Roxy's advent and Tom's transformation Mark Twain had created a character at once acute and sensitive enough to sympathize deeply, even painfully, with their tragic dilemma, but experienced and cynical enough to dismiss such feelings as impractical, unprofitable, and to sweep them aside. The Pudd'nhead who appears in the published novel is simply the continuation of this divided character, this figure fully formed in advance to witness and to prove, but finally to deny, the truth that he came to Dawson's Landing to see. As James M. Cox observes, Pudd'nhead is a "Yankee stranger" who "enters Dawson's Landing, drolly observes the community, taking its fingerprints until he alone can disclose the crime which lies hidden at the heart of the society."[25] He can, perhaps; but of course he doesn't. Instead, he makes drama out of a murder mystery that pleases the crowd, completes his rise to respectability and power, and distracts everyone – himself, Mark Twain, and the audience inside and "outside" the novel – from the deeper wrong that the fingerprints disclose. Thus Pudd'nhead is finally the agent of the degraded, deluded status quo; his act of dramatic disclosure has it both ways in bad faith, and serves finally to conceal "the crime which lies hidden at the heart of society."

But as I have indicated, this doubleness is there in Pudd'nhead from the beginning, and it persists, through various transformations, to the end of the published novel. It takes its most subtle, elusive form in Pudd'nhead's famous remark about the barking dog – a remark that quite accurately mimics, in a knowing, obliquely satirical way, the mechanism of having it both ways, and at the same time results in his removal, by what appears to be forceful ejection, from its field of play. Pudd'nhead knows the town well enough to anticipate what his joke will yield. Thus he contrives to have the pleasure of observing his judges hoist on their own petard. But he knows as well that he will purchase his pleasure at the price of being declared a Pudd'nhead. He pays this price because without quite knowing it he craves the marginality that it confers, the seeming removal from moral complicity in – and from the consciousness of – the wrong that he witnesses in Dawson's Landing. Thus his joke unconsciously recapitulates the bad faith that it consciously ridicules. The same pattern of doubleness figures in the background of Pudd'nhead's calendar, which expresses – what its author seems outwardly to deny, even to himself – that he knows enough about humans and their lives to despise them, and to long for death's oblivion. The conspicuous omission of race-slavery from the topics in the calendar is the surest sign that it is clearly present, in an unconscious way, in Pudd'nhead's bitter misanthropy, his self-contempt, and his deep misgivings about America. He has gone to the dark heart of Dawson's Landing, and returned, so appalled by the swirl of guilt and fear and suffering and hatred that he has seen, and by his own unlooked-for complicity in it, that he has turned away, perhaps on ground of necessity, from consciousness of the transforming spectacle. He is, then, where we find him at the end of *Those Extraordinary Twins*, or at the beginning of the published novel, when he remarks on the dog, or at its conclusion, when he awakens from his brief dream, blind to what it has revealed, and therefore full of energy and optimism and self-assurance, ready at last to assume his rightful place in the local order.[26]

Mark Twain's levitating approval of Pudd'nhead's manipulation of his courtroom audience, like the word "fiction" in his analysis of Roxy's self-deception, is a measure of his immersion as artist and entertainer in the dynamics of bad faith that his story explores. But as these examples also suggest, his mastery of theatrics, like Pudd'n-head's, has its direct corollary in an impulse to distract and deny. Having glimpsed the terrible truth, he could not bear it either, and so, like Roxy, buried it in his own fiction, created at once to express and to conceal the spectacle of cruel injustice that he was compelled to return to again and again because he never told it completely. In sparing the masters their appropriate grief, and in sparing Roxy hers, in banishing Tom's darkest moments from the published novel, and in finally refusing to deal with Chambers's "curious fate" (114), Mark Twain declined, as all of the principal actors in all of his most popular books decline, and as his readers and critics have generally declined, to look deeply or for long at the painful truth about race-slavery that he opened once again to the view. That truth runs so fundamentally and so sharply counter to our proudest, noblest fictions about ourselves that we have witnessed it, as Mark Twain forces us to, only to press it out of sight and mind, as he invites us to, with each culturally obligatory retelling of the tale.

ERIC J. SUNDQUIST

Mark Twain and Homer Plessy

The carnivalesque drama of doubling, twinship, and masquerade that constitutes *Pudd'nhead Wilson* and its freakishly extracted yet intimately conjoined story, *Those Extraordinary Twins,* is likely to remain misread and controversial in estimations of Mark Twain's literary achievement as long as the work's virtual mimicry of America's late-nineteenth-century race crisis is left out of account. Readers have, of course, often found a key to the novel's interpretation in the notorious "fiction of law and custom" that make the "white" slave Roxy legally "black" by allowing one-sixteenth of her blood to "outvote" the rest (8–9).[1] Like so many parodic moments in the book, however, Twain's joke about voting speaks not simply to general anxieties about miscegenation but more particularly to the deliberate campaign to disfranchise blacks and strip them of legal protections that was underway by the early 1890s. Built of the brutal artifice of racial distinctions, both American law and American custom conspired to punish black men and women in the post-Reconstruction years, and Twain's bitter failed fiction, verging on allegory but trapped in unfinished burlesque, has been thought to participate in the black nadir without artistically transcending it or, conversely, without reaching its broader historical implications.

As Hershel Parker and others have demonstrated in detail, Twain's chaotic process of composition and his unconcerned interchange of various manuscript versions make it impossible to place much weight on authorial intention narrowly defined.[2] Yet this hardly leads to the conclusion that Twain's vision had no coherent meaning or that his own comic rationale, contained in the opening of *Those Extraordinary Twins,* reveals nothing of significance about the text's critique of contemporary race theory or Twain's authorial involvement in that critique. Indeed, one might rather argue that the confusion and seeming flaws in the manuscript and the published text, while largely attributable to his haste to produce a book that would ameliorate his financial problems, are also a measure of the social and psychic turmoil that Twain, not least as a liberal Southerner living and working in the North, felt in the post-Reconstruction years. The key phenomena in late-nineteenth-century race relations have just as much place in determining the text's range of implication, its meaning, as do such mechanical factors as compositional sequence and manuscript emendations. Preoccupied with relevant but improperly construed issues of aesthetic unity and verisimilitude, critics have typically missed the primary ways in which *Pudd'nhead Wilson* (1894) and its attached tale of the Italian Siamese twins involves itself in the dilemma over national discrimination against blacks that would reach its authoritative constitutional expression two years later in the Supreme Court ruling in the case of *Plessy v. Ferguson*, while mirroring as well the equally volatile issue of anti-immigrant nativism.

Although the Court's landmark ruling in favor of the doctrine of "separate but equal" was only handed down in 1896, Homer Plessy's case had been pending since January of 1893, after being carried up from the Louisiana Supreme Court to the high court on a writ of error. Despite the manifold thematic and figurative entanglements between *Plessy v. Ferguson* and *Pudd'nhead Wilson*, it is not necessary to argue that Twain had specific knowledge of the case as it came before the Court. It is quite likely for several reasons that he did; but more to the point is the fact that *Plessy* brought to a climax the series of Supreme Court decisions, legislative maneuvers, and developments in sociological theory that had already created the atmosphere in which his wrenching text was composed. The central irony of Homer Plessy's deliberately staged challenge of Louisiana's segregated train car law lay in the fact that he was seven-eighths "white—like Twain's Roxy and her son Tom, he was "black" only by the fictions of law and custom—and his case therefore tied together the radical decline in black civil rights that had occurred since Reconstruction and the fanatical adherence to "one-drop" definitions of negritude that had begun to engulf the South and much of the nation by the mid 1890s. Twain's tale, in which color hallucination, separation and reversal, and the freakish alliance of bodily selves in the twins' story play such critical roles, is a fitting gloss on the nation's rush toward racial extremism in law, in science, and in literature, and its propensity to define equal protection under the Constitution to render the black population invisible or, what was more fantastic, to define color itself not by optical laws but by tendentious genetic theories that reached metaphysically into a lost ancestral world.

Midway into his story, having rather lamely joined his two plots of Tom Driscoll's imposture as a white man and the visit to Dawson's Landing of the Italian twins (no longer Siamese twins except in those textual moments where Twain forgets to disconnect them), Twain offers a scene of minstrel banter between Roxy and her ostensible son Chambers. The latter tells Roxy that Tom, her real son who has now usurped the place of master, is in debt through gambling and likely to be disinherited by his uncle, Judge Driscoll. "Take it back," retorts the furious Roxy, "you misable imitation nigger dat I bore in sorrow en tribbilation." Although it is not the first such scene, this exchange offers the strongest evidence that Roxy, a slave both in body and in mind at this moment in the tale, has trained herself to forget that Chambers is not really her son but rather her rightful master doomed through the machinations of her creation to a life of slavery. More telling, however, is her identifying of him by a doubly ironic phrase, as the "imitation nigger." For Chambers *is* a white man unknowingly imitating a slave. As Tom's virtual white double, he is, as it were, imitation black; and in his speech and actions he, like Roxy, imitates the role of "nigger" defined for him by the white world of enslavement. "If I's imitation, what is you?" Chambers replies, speaking in his own voice and that of Twain his creator. "Bofe of us is imitation *white* – dat's what we is – en pow'full good imitation, too – Yah-yah-yah! – we don't 'mount to noth'n as imitation *niggers*" (35). Or, as George Walker, one of the period's most famous black minstrels, put it in a comment that obviously reached beyond the minstrel stage to define a range of prescribed racial roles, the popular "darky" performances of white minstrels in blackface doomed black actors to what he called the "fatal result" of double imitation: "Nothing seemed more absurd than to see a colored man making himself ridiculous in order to portray himself."[3] Twain both reverses the issue and turns it inside out. Roxy, a black in whiteface, and Chambers, presumed to be a black in whiteface, play minstrel roles as "imitation niggers," Roxy by law and Chambers ironically by means of Roxy's act of rebellion; whereas the legally black Tom passes in whiteface for one of the masters until he is unmasked by Wilson as both murderer and slave, reduced to inventoried property, and sold down the river.

The minstrel show, from which Twain borrowed profusely in constructing *Pudd'nhead Wilson*, forced blacks into humiliating comic roles that had their counterparts in other arenas of national life. In the legal rise of Jim Crow, the South received the blessings of a Northern court; in the cultural rise of Jim Crow, the North adopted Southern plantation ideology. The sections fed imitatively upon one another's racist inclinations, as did the dual erosion of civil rights under federal and state jurisdications that in the aftermath of Reconstruction became increasingly separate and *unequal.* The imitative exchange of identities that the minstrel tradition exploited, at just the historical moment when the nation was engaged in a vast articulation of racism under the disguise of sectional reunion and Old South nostalgia, perpetuated the masquerade of the plantation tradition at the same time it revealed it to be tragedy replayed as farce. The national popularity of minstrel shows in the 1880s and 1890s spilled over into nostalgic depictions of the antebellum South and "darky" characters in magazine fiction, theater, the novel, and the essay, testifying to a widely felt need, spurred by economic and political crises, to resurrect a romantic image of the Old South. At times oblivious to the significant differences among Southern writers, influential Northerners like William Dean Howells enthusiastically promoted the work of such ideologically diverse writers as Joel Chandler Harris, George Washington Cable, and Thomas Nelson Page. Romantic magazine fiction and novels regularly featured mended family ties or the marriage of Northern to Southern mates as a sign of sectional reconciliation. Exploiting this strategy, but in a way manifestly more racist than other Southern romance, Thomas Dixon's saga of the Ku Klux Klan, especially *The Clansman* (1905), was widely popular just after the turn of the century in fiction and on stage, and of course a few years later became the basis for D. W. Griffith's famous film *The Birth of a Nation.* The tremendous success of Dixon's and Griffith's version of American race mythology would have been unthinkable without the legal underpinnings of Jim Crow. As Albion Tourgée noted as early as his well-known 1888 essay on "The South as a Field for Fiction," American fiction and culture were becoming "distinctly Confederate in sympathy."[4]

Without question, *Pudd'nhead Wilson* and *Those Extraordinary Twins* are implicated in the dangerous burden of minstrel humor, and the theme of the plantation masquerade pervades the entire novel in parodic but nonetheless serious forms. For the moment it is enough to say that the immediate challenge for *Pudd'nhead Wilson* was to define the meaning of the phrase "imitation nigger" in late-nineteenth-century America and to suggest, as Twain always did in portraying American race problems, that it is imitation, training, practice, and habit that have created the category of "nigger." While the Supreme Court, along with politicians and social scientists, appealed to abstruse but scientifically resounding categories of "racial instinct" and behavior rooted in the "nature of things," Twain, despite evident traces of "racism" left behind like the undeleted fragments of the conjoined twins' story, subverted the category of instinct and portrayed race as a role—but one that he, an actor of his setting and his age, had great difficulty in throwing off.

Changing "itself from a farce to a tragedy" during his process of composition (as Twain, not quite honestly, explained his method of composition), *Pudd'nhead Wilson* and the story of the twins comically dramatized national policy in which farce and tragedy were indistinguishably conjoined, like black and white in the mulatto body or like the Italian "freak of nature"—separate but equal in name and by law but hardly so in fact (119). The story's endless play on the problems of doubling reflects Twain's own interest in questions of identity, dream selves, and dual personalities, which readers have rightly connected to his partly suppressed fascination with miscegenation and racial doubles.[5] More specifically, it corresponds to an array of dualisms comprising the contemporary American racial trauma: theories of miscegenation and "blood" contamination that polarized the races and divided the mulatto identity; sectionalism and the evident cultural, economic, and legal reunion of North and South that was under way by the 1890s; the conservative drift in constitutional law that created distinct notions of national and state citizenship, with a consequent decay in legal protection of civil rights; and pervading all, the dual layering of antebellum and post-Reconstruction (or Old South and New South) ideologies, the recreation of the dynamics of slavery in new masquerade that Twain adumbrated here, as he had in *Adventures of Huckleberry Finn*, by imposing upon antebellum dramatic action an allegory of the 1880s and 1890s.

By the time of *Pudd'nhead Wilson*, the painful and farcical attempt by Huck and Tom to "set a free nigger free"—as Huck described the charade of Jim's mock liberation into which Twain cast his most penetrating critique of the collapse of Reconstruction ideals—had become a nightmare of tautology. Blacks were free according to the law; but the law, as Twain understood clearly, was more than ever in the process of reenslaving them. Reflective of, if not overtly caused by, growing Northern concern about the freed black population, the sequence of court rulings that prepared the way for the decision of *Plessy* broke down the legal gains blacks had made during Reconstruction largely by giving Southern, states-rights rule precedence over national civil rights protection. The "dual" citizenship that in effect allowed the reconstitution of aspects of chattel slavery in a system of segregation subverted black freedom at the same time that it fired the debate over whether it was environment (the world of social construction) or instinct (the laws of "nature") that created seemingly separate racial characteristics. Both in Twain's novel of racial crisis and in the rising national penchant for Confederate nostalgia, the 1850s and the 1890s, the South and the North, and white and black became freakishly twinned in the failure of freedom. Taking on the voice of corrupted legalism that rules his tale of artificial identity, Twain himself, Southern imposter and pudd'nhead author, stands in mocking yet deadly serious judgment over materials that refused to cohere—materials that, like the destructive constitutional decisions from which they undoubtedly in part borrowed their grim energy, were themselves a "monstrous 'freak,'" a "twin-monster" (169–70) of skewed intentions and betrayed ideals. A full understanding of *Pudd'nhead Wilson* must therefore trace the intricate relationship between Twain's fascination with questions of psychological and racial doubling, and the pervasive dualisms in Jim Crow race theory and the laws of segregation.

When he boarded a Louisiana railroad car in 1892, Homer Adolph Plessy played a deliberate role—the role, as it were, of "imitation nigger." Light enough to pass for white, Plessy had conspired with his cohorts—among them the former black Reconstruction governor and grandfather of author Jean Toomer, P. B. S. Pinchback, and a prominent black New Orleans physician and attorney, Louis A. Martinet—to challenge the state's segregated railroad car law. Enacted in 1890, the law entailed that railway companies carrying passengers within the state "shall provide equal but separate accommodations for the white, and colored, races" by providing separate coaches or by dividing a single coach with a partition "so as to secure separate accommodations." Although plans to contest the Jim Crow law had been formulated almost as soon as it passed the legislature, little headway was made until the Reconstruction judge and literary figure Albion Tourgée, known both for his contentious career as a carpetbagger judge in North Carolina and for his novels of the postwar South, was asked to oversee the legal challenge. Despite Martinet's opposition, Tourgée advised, for reasons that would become apparent but were riddled with irony, that the challenge be made by a mulatto light enough to pass for white. One attempt by a light-skinned black man named Daniel Desdunes failed in its final effect after an interstate railroad was chosen and the state supreme court in the meantime ruled that the commerce clause prohibited Jim Crow regulation of interstate travel. In the second attempt, by Homer

Plessy, an intrastate train was chosen. As soon as he sat down in the whites-only car, Plesy announced himself a Negro to the conductor and was arrested according to prearranged plan. Plessy's argument when his case was brought to trial, predominantly the work of Tourgée, rested in essence on the twin claims, by this time rather familiar, that Jim Crow laws violated the rights and privileges of national citizenship guaranteed by the Fourteenth Amendment and the prohibition of involuntary servitude stated in the Thirteenth Amendment.[6]

Plessy's appeal of the lower court ruling against him to the Louisiana Supreme Court brought forth from Justice Charles Fenner the key ingredients of the eventual United States Supreme Court ruling. Like Justice Henry Billings Brown, who wrote the majority opinion in *Plessy*, Fenner chose the path of anachronism, for his decision was based in one instance on a case decided prior to the enactment of the Thirteenth and Fourteenth amendments, prior, in fact, to the Civil War. Fenner took his language from an 1867 case in which a Pennsylvania Jim Crow railroad regulation was upheld by a court that appealed to racial differences "resulting from nature, law, and custom" and that declared that, "following the order of Divine Providence, human authority ought not compel these widely separated races to intermix." In the antebellum case cited by Fenner and Brown as precedent, Lemuel Shaw, chief justice of the Supreme Court of Massachusetts and Herman Melville's father-in-law, wrote in a decision upholding school segregation in *Roberts v. City of Boston* (1849) that racial "prejudice, if it exists, is not created by law and probably cannot be changed by law." (The plaintiff's attorney, Massachusetts politician and abolitionist Charles Sumner, would be heard from again in postwar civil rights cases.) Two years later, in the famous case of the fugitive slave Thomas Sims, Shaw took on further aspects of Captain Amasa Delano, Melville's satirically portrayed New England commander in "Benito Cereno," and struck a blow for sectionalism and states rights when he ordered Sims returned to the South. Yet by 1855, the year of Melville's enigmatically volcanic story of slave subversion and its repression, the Massachusetts legislature had ignored Shaw's opinion in *Roberts* and outlawed school segregation.[7]

Even so, Fenner and Brown had no trouble in citing the case some four decades later. Indeed, as Fenner pointed out, no paradox was involved so long as one interpreted the Fourteenth Amendment in such a way as to conclude, as "is well settled," that it "created no new rights whatever, but only extended the operation of existing rights and furnished additional protection for such rights." Brown too ignored the Civil War, the Massachusetts legislature, and the civil rights amendments in his eccentric appeal to *Roberts*. In doing so, the Massachusetts-born justice brought to life in the legal world the plantation myth that was then enjoying such a renaissance in the literary world. He likewise doubled the Melvillian irony, as C. Vann Woodward notes, that the opinions of "two sons of Massachusetts . . . should have bridged the gap between the radical equalitarian commitment of 1868 and the reactionary repudiation of that commitment in 1896," while the lone dissenter in *Plessy*, Judge John Marshall Harlan, was a former slaveholding Southerner who "bridged the greater gap between the repudiation of 1896 and the radical rededication of equalitarian idealism" in the 1954 *Brown v. Board of Education* decision. Like Lemuel Shaw, Henry Billings Brown appealed to "established usages, customs and traditions of the people" in his *Plessy* opinion and held that "legislation is powerless to eradicate racial instincts or to abolish distinctions based upon physical differences," that whatever equality is afforded in political and civil rights, "if one race be inferior to the other socially, the constitution of the United States cannot put them upon the same plane." Brown's ruling was perfectly in tune with the leading sociological thought of the day, the essence of which would be summarized in William Graham Sumner's famous dictum that "stateways cannot change folkways." Besides being wrong about the power of legislation, Brown's circular reasoning historically lost sight of the fact that, from the Civil War to the 1890s, some portions of the South had survived without the established customs and usages of Jim Crow. Social equality was rare, of course, but Brown's introduction of the issue was irrelevant to the fact that political equality had been enjoyed by blacks with at least measured success in parts of the South.[8]

The majority opinion in *Plessy*, which Robert Harris has styled "a compound of bad logic, bad history, bad sociology, and bad situtional law" that would rule American civil rights legislation and judgments for the next half century, summed up the degradation of black rights that had occurred over the previous two decades. Like *Pudd'nhead Wilson*, a text obsessively devoted to problems of legal rights, evidence, codes of authority, and the interplay of "natural" and artificial laws, and culminating in a melodramatic burlesque of a trial that sets right subverted racial roles and boundaries, *Plessy v. Ferguson* was at once a mockery of law and an enactment of its rigid adherence to divided, dual realities. What *Plessy* brought to fruition was the long assault on the Fourteenth Amendment that had begun with the *Slaughterhouse Cases* of 1873, in which the Supreme Court first held, in a verdict on the surface not pertaining to black civil rights but in a manner critically destructive of those rights, that the amendment provided "dual" citizenships – national *and* state – and so carefully circumscribed federal protection of rights transcending state oversight as to make national citizenship virtually meaningless. By proposing a reading of the privileges and immunities clause that Loren Miller has designated nothing more than a "judicial fiction," the Court's decision in the *Slaughterhouse Cases* denied that the amendment had been intended – as clearly it had – to protect freedmen from such ignominious regulation as the postwar Black Codes.[9] The *Slaughterhouse* and subsequent cases leading up to *Plessy* reinvoked the notion of duality so crucial to Judge Roger B. Taney's landmark opinion abrogating black citizenship in the *Dred Scott v. Sandford* case (1857), thus – as in Fenner's and Brown's later citation of Lemuel Shaw's verdict in *Roberts* – carrying forward antebellum legal thought into an arena in which it should have had no place.

For the next two decades the struggle continued between a Congress generally intent on furthering the reach of federal law and a conservative Court intent on limiting centralization. Because the curtailment of governmental reach grew out of a complex debate over federalism and applied as well to cases having nothing to do with race, it would be wrong to insist that the court rulings that led to *Plessy* were always mere covers for racist policy. Still, the correspondence between the Court's conservative bent and the national rise in segregationist sentiment allowed states, and individuals or bodies under state jurisdiction, the greatest freedom to legislate and act in patent bad faith on the question of race. For example, *United States v. Reese* (1876), *United States v. Cruikshank* (1876), and *United States v. Harris* (1883) all undermined federal jurisdiction in cases involving Southern mob violence against blacks, in particular those attempting to exercise voting rights. Separating national from state rights, the Court insisted that, while it could prevent a *state* from abridging civil rights, only states themselves could prevent *individuals* from denying blacks their rights. Corresponding to the end of Reconstruction, the establishment of such a federal-state duality had the effect of drawing a stark color line. As Frederick Douglass noted in 1880, "The citizenship granted in the Fourteenth Amendment is practically a mockery, and the right to vote, provided for in the Fifteenth Amendment, is literally stamped out in the face of government."[10]

Most far-reaching and destructive was the Court's overturning of the critical civil rights legislation of 1875 in the *Civil Rights Cases* verdict of 1883. The original sweeping legislation, which governed equal access to accommodations, public conveyances, restaurants, theaters, and the like, had been brought to pass largely through the efforts of the aging Charles Sumner, "so that hereafter in all our legislation there shall be no such word as 'black' or 'white,' but . . . one shall speak only of citizens and of men." The Court's rebuke of Sumner's vision and its extension of racial dualism onto a new plane of significance is evident in the contrasting views represented on the one hand by the majority opinion and on the other by Justice Harlan's lone dissent, which prefigured his role in *Plessy*. The Court (in Justice Joseph Bradley's majority opinion) denied that in finding the federal prohibition of segregation unconstitutional it was "reinventing" slavery. To discover the vestiges of the peculiar institution in acts of "mere discrimination on account of race or color" undertaken by private individuals, Bradley wrote, would be "running the slavery argument into the ground" and unfairly singling out the Negro, not as a "mere citizen" but as "the special favorite of the laws." This resuscitation of the *Dred Scott* view that the Constitution accepted racial distinctions rightly struck Harlan as "subtle and ingenious verbal criticism." In even more forcefully returning power to the states, he argued, the *Civil Rights* verdict ushered in "an era of constitutional law, when the rights of freedom and American citizenship cannot receive from the nation that efficient protection which heretofore was unhesitatingly accorded to slavery and the rights of the master."[11] The Constitution had originally counted the black slave as three-fifths of a person; the Supreme Court now emasculated the amendments that had made blacks whole, once again guaranteeing that the South could number blacks among their population for political representation while reducing them before the law, and at times literally in body, to human fragments.

In defining a dual *constitutional* citizenship that in practice was easily translated into dual *racial* citizenship, the cases leading up to *Plessy* defined the "privileges and immunities" and "equal protection" clauses negatively. That is, the Court consistently denied that anything positive had been added by the process of amendment to the protection of rights already lodged in the state. In the language of Justice Morrison Waite's opinion for the majority in *United States v. Cruikshank* (1876), "The only obligation resting upon the United States is to see that the States do not deny the right [of one citizen against another under the Constitution]. . . . The power of the National Government is limited to the enforcement of this guaranty." In separating national from state rights and declaring that only states themselves could prevent individual citizens from denying blacks their rights – for example, white mobs bent on disfranchisement through intimidation – the Court left equal protection, like Twain's mulatto and even more like his Siamese twins, monstrously lodged in two bodies, neither of which had full responsibility for its legal or moral guarantee. The notion of dual citizenship and the reinvention of slavery exfoliated in *Plessy* into Justice Brown's blunt invention of further distinctions between the law and nature, and between political rights and so-called social rights. The object of the Fourteenth Amendment, in Brown's view, "was undoubtedly to enforce the absolute equality of the two races before the law, but, in the nature of things, it could not have been intended to abolish distinctions based upon color, or to enforce social, as distinguished from political, equality, or a commingling of the two races upon terms unsatisfactory to either."[12] Whatever the intention of Brown's distinction, legal theory and practice alike showed that social and political rights, like the Siamese body, could not be separated without grave risk to both.

Since the Louisiana railroad car statute was not simply a form of private discrimination but rather a state action and thus potentially liable even to the Court's by then weak enforcement of equal protection, the idea of a negative guarantee of rights, with its consequent definition of citizenship as dual, might seem to have been of particular import in the case of *Plessy*. Brown and the majority did not just ignore this fact, however; but, consistent with the evisceration of the Fourteenth Amendment in *Slaughterhouse*, they found it irrelevant to the central issue of *Plessy*, that of "equal" protection. That a state action of segregation was involved in this case in fact became the predicate whereby the Court was able to judge that Homer Plessy's segregation was authorized by the dual citizenship inherent, one could say, in the constitutional "nature of things" and that his treatment was equal under a constitutional Louisiana law. What was clear by 1896, though, was that dual citizenship and negative enforcement of equal protection, even if they were not primarily masks for naked racial discrimination, made it increasingly easy to cover pernicious intent with the cloak of law. *Plessy* was a landmark case not because it drastically altered the direction of legislation and judicial thought but because it concluded the process of transfiguring dual *constitutional* citizenship into dual *racial* citizenship that had unfolded since the end of Reconstruction. The economic and cultural reunion of North and South necessitated political and legal separations that turned the "Negro problem" over to the South, thereby using the South to further what in reality were national inclinations.

After the Supreme Court decision in the *Civil Rights Cases,* one historian has argued, there was throughout the North "not only acquiescence among the white population in the 'Southern Way' of solving the race problem but a tendency to imitate it in practice."[13] As the mob cases of *Harris* and *Cruikshank* had indicated, the essential division was not necessarily that between federal and state jurisdiction but between black and white skin – or rather, black and white "blood."

John Marshall Harlan's famous dissent in *Plessy* built on his view, already articulated in the *Civil Rights Cases,* that federal allowance of discrimination did indeed constitute a "badge of servitude" and a resurrection of "slavery" in the form of the "sinister legislation" states were able to pass.[14] But the meaning of such slavery was more effectively spelled out in Albion Tourgée's brief, which distinguished in antebellum terms between simple chattelism and the black person's "legal condition of subjection to the dominant class, a bondage quite separable from the incident of ownership." As a "defenceless and despised victim of the civil and political society," Tourgée argued, the slave was "in bondage to the whole white race as well as to his owner." Chattelism might be gone, Tourgée concluded, but the Supreme Court decisions culminating in *Plessy* would clearly have reestablished black bondage to the dominant class. Just as Henry Billings Brown recurred to Lemuel Shaw in writing the majority opinion, Harlan echoed the plaintiff's argument advanced by Charles Sumner in the *Roberts* case – that Boston's Jim Crow schools violated central American principles. "We abjure nobility of all kinds," said Sumner, "but here is a nobility of the skin.... We abjure all privileges of birth; but here is a privilege which depends solely on the accident [of] whether an ancestor is black or white."[15] Superimposing 1849 on 1896, the arguments of *Plessy v. Ferguson* recreated caste distinctions that violated American principle, the legacy of the Civil War, and the process of Constitutional amendment. Likewise superimposing the 1840–50s on the 1890s, Twain's Tom Driscoll, a disguised aristocratic master exposed as a slave, echoes Charles Sumner in asking the pertinent question: "Why were niggers *and* whites made? What crime did the uncreated first nigger commit that the curse of birth was decreed for him? And why this awful difference made between white and black?" (44).

Not just the caste division enunciated in *Dred Scott* but the more insidious aspects of slavery itself would reappear under the forms of segregation that began to flourish in the 1890s as the words *white* and *black* acquired newly powerful, separate meanings and "nobility of skin" took on subtleties in some respects more extreme than those regnant in the Old South. In point of fact, the racist underpinnings of the New South, as Twain well knew and dramatized with such fierce passion in *Pudd'nhead Wilson*, required the creation of an Old South myth that in most ways exceeded historical reality. By 1890, the myth received the blessing of the North; the Republican party had given up attempts to break the Democratic "Solid South," and the largely Northern, Republican Supreme Court ruled consistently on the side of the capitalistic development that the New South hoped to attract.[16] In Twain's recreated antebellum world, replete with the gaudy aura of nobility and fabricated genealogies worshipped not only by the white masters but by their black slaves as well, the code of Southern gentlemen appears to be at odds with or to despise recourse to law. In the New South, however, the code and the law were approaching identity to the extent that the code was based on racial or genealogical purity, and mob pressure dictated the legal suppression of black political rights. The aristocratic code of the Old South, part of the stage machinery of *Pudd'nhead Wilson*, was central to the "fiction" created by the New South, not least because it imagined a time when the question of black legal rights had been virtually meaningless. In the new order, white supremacy "outvoted" black rights at the polls and in the courts until, in *Williams v. Mississippi* (1898), the first state disfranchisement case to come before the Supreme Court, the legal definition of duality gave a free hand to individual and communal racism. Confronted with Mississippi's 1890 suffrage law, which excluded various convicted criminals, required a poll tax, and finally demanded that the prospective voter read and interpret a section of the state constitution – an act clearly liable to official abuse – the Court replied that such codes did not deny equal protection or, "on their face, discriminate between the white and Negro races." Specifically, Justice Joseph McKenna wrote, it was not shown that the administration of such laws "was evil but only that evil was possible under them."[17]

At the same time, blackness outvoted whiteness in the blood, and "one-drop" ideology drove mulattoes toward blacks – or, in the case of those who were light enough to pass, toward a masked existence among whites. Lynching peaked in the early 1890s, as Twain was writing, and national campaigns against it were sparked by Ida B. Wells's powerful 1892 editorials on lynching for the *Memphis Free Speech* and the *New York Age*, reprinted as a pamphlet entitled *Southern Horror: Lynch Law in All Its Phases*. Revived schemes for the deportation of blacks to colonies in Africa or Latin America were further evidence of the white desire for separation. Fears of increased black criminality and degeneration created the paradoxical situation in which racist exclusion and black alienation fed imitatively upon one another, creating – as Twain a few years later would write of lynching – a "mania, a fashion; a fashion which will spread wider and wider, year by year, covering state after state, as with an advancing disease." In Twain's imagined world of *Pudd'nhead Wilson*, the power of imitative behavior can, as in Roxy's case, destroy the slave's awareness of her own oppression or her recognition that her son has been transformed by her own hand into her abusive master; in the "United States of Lyncherdom," as Twain called it, the power of imitation can define roles of black submission, roles of black segregation, and ultimately roles of black destruction. The imitative behavior that spread disfranchisement laws to state after state during and after the 1890s, and decimated black economic and social rights in the process, thus gave to lynching a figurative dimension that made it all the more virulent. As Joel Williamson has argued, "One could lynch just as effectively by genteel means as crudely by rope and faggott. Negroes could be lynched by account books. And they could be lynched by written history," so as to open "the way for an honorable reunion of North and South."[18] The rewriting of Confederate myth and Reconstruction fact gives the "fiction" of race relations special meaning in the 1890s, and it is this "lynching" that Twain's novel comes close to joining in its indulgence in the darkest satire on Southern life and American racial practice since Tourgée's 1879 novel of Reconstruction, *A Fool's Errand*.

When Tourgée went before the Supreme Court to argue the case of *Plessy v. Ferguson*, an observer remarked in the *Washington Post* that he was on "another fool's errand." The allusion to Tourgée's novel rightly foresaw that the arguments of his brief for Plessy were as doomed as his previous hopes for racial harmony in Reconstruction North Carolina, where he served as a superior court judge from 1869 to 1879. A man of principle but decidedly an outsider (perhaps even a pudd'nhead to the locals), Tourgée in retrospect styled his idealistic venture the dream of a foolish man – but the kind of man who is "both fool and genius, – a fool all his life and a genius after his death, or a fool to one century and a genius to the next, or a fool at home and a prodigy abroad."[19] The implications of their fiction were only approximately allied, but Twain and Tourgée nevertheless played the fool with dead seriousness on the issue of race, Twain not least because the role of his main fool, attorney David Wilson, was so clearly entangled in the performance of Mark Twain the author.

Even though Twain had long been fascinated by the combination of farce and brutality latent in legal systems, the sequence of critical civil rights rulings after Reconstruction must have been crucial to his novel's mad ridicule of laws, evidence, courts, and trials, all failing in their primary duty to bring about justice, much as Tourgée discovered that the weight of military occupation and legal proscription could not properly restore order or create true justice during Reconstruction.

Even though he did not perhaps deserve the description of genius or of hero, the history of the legal battle for black civil rights culminating in *Brown v. Board of Education* would recognize not Albion Tourgée but John Marshall Harlan as the "fool" half a century ahead of his time. Still, it is Tourgée's arguments that bear most precisely on the legal and racial figurings of *Pudd'nhead Wilson*. His attempt to drum up national support for the case with a vigorous newspaper campaign primarily in the North and through the efforts of the National Civil Rights Association (or NCRA, which he had established in 1891, with George Washington Cable among others on its executive board) met with strong and immediate early success. Given Twain's relationship with Cable, strained though it was by the early 1890s, and given too his general interest in the promotion of black rights, it is probable that Twain was well acquainted with Tourgée, his writings, and his civil rights efforts. Disagreement among various race leaders over tactics, conservative attacks, and Southern physical intimidation of blacks undermined the organization, however, and by the time *Plessy* was heard the NCRA hardly existed; the atmosphere of race hatred had heightened, not abated; as Tourgée had hoped; and his errand before the court seemed more foolish than ever. Nevertheless, Tourgée's arguments were of great, if sometimes ironic, importance. In addition to detailing the mechanisms by which Jim Crow reconstituted the essence of slavery – the slave being in "bondage" to the entire white race, not just the property of a single owner – Tourgée turned the property argument on its head (and explicated his choice of a very light mulatto like Homer Plessy) by insisting that the Louisiana segregation law had deprived Plessy of his property, which in this instance was vested in his "reputation of being white." "Indeed," Tourgée asked, is whiteness "not the most valuable sort of property, being the master-key that unlocks the golden door of opportunity?" Apparently hoping to fool the property-minded judges into recognizing an element of color that would destroy Jim Crow by rendering it chaotic, Tourgée opened himself to the irony that such an argument would in reality protect only those who could pass – the mulatto elite – and define equal protection just as restrictively and negatively as the Court already had, only locating it at a different mark on the color line. Whatever its merit in protecting the rights of at least the mulatto elite, the brevity of this portion of his argument suggests that Tourgée had, by 1896, recognized its foolishness. Even so, it underlined the hallucinatory character of the Jim Crow laws that were ushered in by *Plessy,* which over the next half a century would reach such extremity that Tourgée's further speculations on the color line were not in the least foolish: "Why not require all colored people to walk on one side of the street and the whites on the other? Why may [the state] not require every white man's house to be painted white and every colored man's black?" As Tourgée saw, there was no logical end to such discriminations, and Brown's reply that they must be "reasonable" was nothing to the point. The primary question, in Tourgée's view, was "not as to the *equality* of the privileges enjoyed, but *the right of the State to label one citizen as white and another as colored.*" In holding indeed that "a single drop of African blood is sufficient to color a whole ocean of Caucasian whiteness" – to *outvote* it – the Supreme Court called Tourgée's bluff and exposed the nadir of the new segregationism.[20]

It was in this climate that Twain wrote and against this particular legal backdrop that his tale of miscegenation, doubling, and legal fictions of color, ownership, and identity must be read. For in their opposition to radical racists, liberal politicians were likewise compelled toward fantasy or, in any event, toward significant accommodation of racism. A good example would be Cable's controversial essay written in reply to the *Civil Rights Cases* of 1883, "The Freedman's Case in Equity," which Cable delivered regularly on the lecture circuit with Twain and published in the *Century Magazine* in 1885 before including it that same year in his volume *The Silent South.* Driven from the South because of the power of his message in favor of black political rights and against segregation, Cable nonetheless paradoxically pointed out that his essay did not touch the domain of social privileges, that "social equality is a fool's dream," and he intimated that the real risk of miscegenation now resided not among Negroes but among those in the mulatto elite who might successfully mix with the white population. Before professional jealousy spoiled their friendship, Twain and Cable discussed the problem of miscegenation and the threat of black supremacy in the South, the tempestuous issues that underlay the foolish dream of social equality and soon found release in Twain's fiction.[21]

Cable's lectures and essays on behalf of blacks brought forth not only the scorn of the radical South but also the advocacy of Jim Crow by reunion-minded Northerners. As tolerance of any signs of equality "evaporated in a passion for racial purity," Williamson has written, an obsession with "invisible blackness" put mulattoes – indeed, anyone suspected to be of tainted ancestry – at risk not in the South alone. Like Homer Plessy, moreover, mulattoes found themselves increasingly in the peculiar position outlined by Charles Dudley Warner, Twain's former novelistic collaborator, who wrote sympathetically of the relative racial harmony that existed in mid-1880s New Orleans despite the city's inconsistent mix of segregation customs and regulations. Yet because "society cannot be made or unmade by legislation," Warner noted, in anticipation of Justices Fenner and Brown, the "instinct in both races against mixture of blood" had better be heeded by blacks as well as whites, for it is "they who will see that there is no escape from the equivocal position in which those nearly white in appearance find themselves except by a rigid separation of the races."[22]

Warner's lecture was delivered at the Cotton Centennial Exposition of 1885, one of numerous expositions in the 1880s and 1890s jointly sponsored by North and South to promote sectional reconciliation and Southern industrialization, and it therefore signals a common intellectual subcurrent in the drive toward reunion. The most prominent crusader who crossed the Mason-Dixon line in the other direction was Henry W. Grady, the editor of the *Atlanta Constitution*, whose appearances before Northern audiences and whose posthumous volume *The New South* (1890) trumpeted Dixie's vision of racial and sectional harmony through segregation and Northern investment. Like Cable and Warner, Grady similarly appealed to barely latent Northern fears of miscegenation and increasing black population, and he maintained, somewhat incoherently, that there was in both whites and blacks a natural aversion to mixing that had been broken down by mulattoes. Falling just between the critical years of *Pudd'nhead Wilson* and *Plessy v. Ferguson*, what might now be considered the most revealing instance of the spread of the segregationist thesis occurred in Booker T. Washington's famous 1895 address to the Atlanta Cotton States and International Exposition: "In all things that are purely social we can be as separate as the fingers, yet one as the hand in all things essential to mutual progress."[23] Within a contemporary atmosphere charged by physiological race theory, Washington's metaphor of the hand neatly balanced cooperation and segregation by appealing to an image of separate but equal brotherhood composed of both social and natural law. In *Pudd'nhead Wilson* fingerprints paradoxically demonstrate Tom's inviolable individuality and the fact that he belongs to a group scorned for racial identity alone; and Tom, recognizing that "a man's own hand is his deadliest enemy" and "keeps a record of the deepest and fatalest secrets of his life," hides his palm from David Wilson to keep the "black-magic stranger" (52) from reading therein the sign of his guilt as well, it seems, as the sign of his invisible color. Indeed, Francis Galton, the father of Pudd'nhead Wilson's "black-magic" science and author of *Finger Prints* (1892), speculated – incorrectly – that supposed signs of differing racial characterisics such as intelligence would appear in the prints themselves. What is more, Galton went on to achieve his greatest renown as a promoter of eugenics, which advocated the progressive breeding of a better society and which in the American climate of the early twentieth century automatically took the form of nativist theories of protection against the threat of race suicide through miscegenation and immigration.[24] It is possible that Twain, following Galton, harbored the suspicion that racial characteristics could be detected in fingerprints. But his use of the metaphor of the revealing hand in *Pudd'nhead Wilson* seems rather to mock the theory that segregation was rooted in organic laws susceptible to proof by the new scientific and sociological study of heredity. In addition, his anachronistic introduction of fingerprinting science into an antebellum story served to enforce the critique of post-Reconstruction appeals to antebellum legal findings and race ideologies, the means for "reinventing" slavery as rigid segregation. Washington's similar metaphor, while with careful calculation defining the social construct of a biracial society as organic, nevertheless demonstrated the power of those appeals in its acceptance of segregation as a necessity for political harmony and economic progress.

Segregation into dual halves of society, as in dual standings before the law, left blacks and whites in significant ways more divided than they had been during slavery, with blacks, as Tourgée argued, again in bondage to a dominant white class. "Equal" and "separate" were twinned by law but in reality arranged in a hierarchy. Likewise, the widening gulf between colors swallowed into an abyss those whose very bodies were marked by the violation of racial barriers. Escape from what Warner rightly called the "equivocation" of the mulatto's dual status lay not in identity or unity but in segregation, not in "equal" but in "separate" existence as it came to be defined by mob rule and by courts of law. Thus, when Pudd'nhead Wilson translates mob opinion into the rule of law at the conclusion of Twain's novel, he simultaneously reveals the hidden "nigger," the white man with black blood, and moves to the apex of the townspeople's values. Recasting his joking irony about the halves of an "invisible dog" into the final revelation of racial law, Wilson reverses the "election" and "verdict" that early on voted him a fool and carries out his original threat against that dog – to kill his half (5-6). Exposed at last as the "miserable dog" (103) to which he has been compared by Roxy, Wilson, and even himself throughout the novel, Tom is condemned for the crime of murder but punished for the crime of being black when he is sold down the river as part of the estate's inventory. And his other half, Chambers, like the innocent but nonetheless dead half of the hanged freak in *Those Extraordinary Twins*, is "killed" as well by being thrust into a ruling class to which he cannot by habit belong.

The fear of "mongrelization" that pervaded radical rhetoric about miscegenation imputed bestiality to blacks but suggested also that, in their rise toward political or social equity with whites, blacks were at best able only to "imitate" the requisite manners and intelligence of civilized society. Playing on the imitation of "forms" and "habit" that Twain said could be concreted into "automatic," "unconscious," and "natural" behavior (19), stock minstrel scenes and racist literature denied the priority of environment in forming character and satirized black pretensions to manners, learning, or political sophistication. Twain's inquiry into imitation as a component of character reaches no very satisfactory judgment about the ratio between instinct and training in the case of Tom Driscoll; but just as imitation defined the era's promotion of racist sterotypes and its proliferation of legal sanctions against "black blood," so the imitation of white manners by blacks underscored the legal drive to prevent any true imitation of white rights. The danger that imitation might actually lead to the acquisition of political and social graces or to economic gains became uncanny in the figure of the mulatto: was he "white," or did he, like Tom Driscoll, adopt a pattern of imitative behavior that suppressed the "'nigger' in him" (45)? The mulatto concentrated the problem of racial doubling insofar as he could be said to imitate or parody, but not to own, the property of whiteness. The *de jure* dual citizenship that made for *de facto* racial dualism left the mulatto a "freak" of natural law, while the spread of segregationist thought and policy made the light mulatto an uncanny reminder that blackness both *was* and *was not* visible and whiteness both *was* and *was not* a form of property with legal significance.

The theme of imitation, which circulates through *Pudd'nhead Wilson* so as to define patterns of behavior, violence, and judicial practice, is lodged most provocatively in the thematic dialogue between the Italian "freaks" and their Jim Crow counterparts, Roxy and Tom, the "imitation niggers." The "two stories tangled together," producing "no end of confusion and annoyance," Twain would claim in comic defense of his flawed tales, until the "doings" of Pudd'nhead and Roxy "pushed up into prominence" the character of Tom and the three of them took over a "tale which they had nothing at all to do with, by rights." The result was the notorious "literary Caesarean operation" by which Twain separated his two stories, pulling the freak story "out by the roots" and thus himself giving twin birth to the freak tale and to its racial double (119–20). The figure of the maternal body unites Twain and Roxy in the "doings" that produce both Tom – Roxy's son by the shadowy, off-stage aristocratic figure, Colonel Cecil Burleigh Essex – and Tom's story, a fantasy union in which Twain recapitulates the sins of the white fathers within the authorial body of the black mothers. Becoming (black) mother as well as (white) father to his illegitimate mulatto heir, Twain brings to the surface of consciousness apprehensions he had once intimated in his well-known response to William Dean Howells's review of *Roughing It*. "I am as uplifted and reassured by it," Twain wrote Howells, "as a mother who has given birth to a white baby when she was awfully afraid it was going to be a mulatto." Drawing perhaps on his recorded dream fantasies about black female sexuality, Twain's authorial imitation of master-slave miscegenation lodges in his own body the sexual and racial doubleness at the heart of his story, and it provides a double connection – a Siamese linkage – to the two imperfectly separated tales, illuminating the double imitation in which Tom and Roxy themselves are engaged as actors in the stage play of Twain's social critique. In Roxy and Tom is centered the paradox of alienation and imitation. They strive to, and physically *do,* imitate the white masters, Tom by actually becoming one – to such an extent, in fact, that he is willing to sell Roxy *down* river to raise money for his debts. But the subtleties of the color line render them all the more different for being nearly the same in their possession of the property of whiteness. Like the ironic outsider, Pudd'nhead Wilson, who in his first encounter with the townspeople appears an "uncanny" spectacle (5), and even more like the "uncanny apparition" of the Siamese twins (125), the imitation niggers literally embody a violation of the "laws" of nature and call forth the uncanny fright that Freud assigned to the double: "something which ought to have remained hidden but has come to light."[25] Tom's blackness, like Tom's very existence as a character, is revealed by Twain's participation in the "tragedy" of miscegenation, by his willingness to incarnate in his act of writing the coupling of slave and master while at the same time standing judicially, ironically detached in the role of his foolish hero, Pudd'nhead Wilson.

When Tom is brought to light at the conclusion of the novel, his whiteface disguise is removed and his blackness revealed. Although Twain in his original manuscript had allowed Tom to realize, when Roxy reveals his identity, that the "nigger" in him was not genetic but the Lamarckian result of "decades and generations of insult and outrage," whereas his *white* blood" was "debased by the brutalizing effects of a long-drawn heredity of slave-owning" (191), such rational meditation is inexplicably deleted from *Pudd'nhead Wilson*, where all that can come to light is the hidden mark of blackness, the "nigger" in Tom. As the "imitation nigger" that Tom becomes as the slave Roxy's son, he is a parody of himself and of those "blaspheming colors" sported by the Siamese dandies (127). Like the freak, the mulatto was held by some social theorists to be an unnatural hybrid, destined to die out through a failure of reproduction – a perversion of the organic development toward higher, more pure racial forms – while to others he represented the most potent contaminating danger to those forms. The mulatto in effect became the scapegoat for contemporary Confederate apologists, the master's conjunction of property and reproduction; but he also therefore symbolized the "enslavement" of the white race to its past sins, an enslavement Twain's authorial involvement in the process of miscegenation self-consciously doubled. This relationship of dependence and servility, rewritten in the aftermath of Reconstruction to imitate, if not re-create, antebellum slavery, is also what Twain dramatizes in the figure of the twins. In one of the shreds of their Siamese form left unrevised in *Pudd'nhead Wilson* Twain designates their sideshow exploitation in Europe as "slavery" (28). In the twins' story itself Angelo finds normal men to be "monstrosities" and "deformities," and their separateness an "unsocial and uncanny construction," but he still desires "that he and his brother might become segregated from each other" (136–37). The farcical exchanges of control over their body between Angelo and Luigi mimics both the mulatto's dilemma and the South's. In *Pudd'nhead Wilson*, the twins are separated (the liberal segregationist solution), but in *Those Extraordinary Twins* they are hanged (the radical racist solution).

Twain's twins were Italian, and he modeled them to some extent on the Tocci brothers, late nineteenth-century Siamese twins who like Angelo and Luigi had two heads and four arms but only two legs.

Yet he drew as well for the *meaning* of the twins for his novel on his 1868 comic sketch about the famous Chang and Eng, "Personal Habits of the Siamese Twins." In Twain's postwar imagination the twins became a mock replica of sectional strife: Eng fought on the Union side and Chang on the Confederate; they took each other prisoner and were exchanged for one another as prisoners by an army court. Their marriages and drinking are subject to Twain's comic eye, as in *Those Extraordinary Twins,* and although he fails to mention that Chang and Eng were also slaveowners, the irony of that fact had obviously become far more suggestive by the 1890s when the uncanny spectacle of the freak came back into his writing.[26] By then, the twins' bodily servility pointed not just to the conjoined intimacy of white and black but also to the uncanny resurgence of antebellum manners and social theory in late nineteenth-century life, the freakish doubling of reactionary myth in contemporary postures. The fratricidal conflict that Twain turned into burlesque in 1868 had by 1894 become organized along racial lines, with South and North increasingly allied against the black man—tied to him as though by physiology (as in many cases he was) yet anxious to be cleanly separated. The explicit return of latent Civil War models of fratricidal intimacy to Twain's consciousness, along with the authorial embodiment of miscegenation itself, paralleled the uncanny doubling in race law whereby the courts, as in *Plessy,* appealed to antebellum case law that should have been long dead and buried but now returned from repression to "reinvent" slavery under new legal sanction.

Chang and Eng were Twain's original model for the figure of twinship that yokes the extraordinary twins to Tom and Chambers or to Tom as mulatto, but the more physiologically apt Tocci brothers were an even better model. In addition, the fact that Angelo and Luigi are Italian is far from insignificant. In anti-immigrationist thought of the 1880s and 1890s Italians were widely thought, on the basis of their "color," their reputed criminal activities, and their comparatively low standard of living, to be among the most degraded of immigrants, and their willingness to mix with blacks brought forth excited nativist charges that new immigrants would further "mongrelize" America's racial stock. The Italian twins' blurring of the color line has an even more specific force in *Pudd'nhead Wilson.* Besides satirizing the aura of nobility and culture that surrounds the gentleman twins, Twain also capitalized on the common sterotype of Italians as criminals especially adept in the use of knives and prone to impassioned violence and vengeful assassination. The climax of such anti-Italian feeling, in fact, came in New Orleans just the year before

Homer Plessy set out to test the segregated train car law. When a jury failed to convict a group of Italians on trial in 1891 for the murder of a New Orleans police superintendent, supposedly because of his efforts to bring Mafia members to justice, a rioting mob of several thousand attacked the prison and lynched eleven of the suspects. The case created a national sensation, with the prosecution complaining that it was impossible to get convictions against the Mafia because of their strict code of honor, while politicians and periodicals lined up to defend or attack the mob's makeshift execution of the "assassins" and the atmosphere of lawlessness and "bloody duels" that some said had made it possible. Most importantly, the lynchings ignited a diplomatic crisis when Secretary of State James Blaine refused to grant redress to the families of the victims, some of whom were Italian citizens, or guarantee the indictment of the mob (President Harrison finally offered redress some months later). The administration's logical but unsatisfactory contention was that the controversy came about because of the Italian government's inability to understand the "dual nature of our government" – that is, its division into federal and state jurisdiction. The incident grew briefly into a serious war scare and, as John Higham notes, dramatized the entire question of immigration "as nothing had dramatized it since the Haymarket Affair."[27]

The government's appeal to the notion of "dual" citizenship of course made the Italians liable to state oversight in the same way that the Supreme Court had said blacks like Homer Plessy were liable to state, not federal, laws for their protection. The incident demonstrates, moreover, the fact that lynching in the 1890s was not reserved for blacks alone but had spread like an epidemic across many racial lines. By the same token, however, the fervor of anti-immigrant thought that was crystallized in New Orleans showed that there was no paradox involved when the most radical of Southern racists, such as South Carolina's Benjamin Tillman, turned out over the course of the decade to be outspoken anti-imperialists. Fearing further contamination by alien peoples, they sought the expulsion of blacks from America, or at least their political and economic suppression, rather than greater "paternal" responsibilities for the colored races of the world. Neither anti-imperialist arguments nor anti-immigrationist arguments achieved ascendency in the 1890s, but the New Orleans Mafia lynchings and the subsequent national outburst of militant patriotism had an important effect on the process of reunion between North and South that would reach its peak in the Spanish-American War at the close of the century. In dramatic demonstrations of loyalty, Union and Confederate veterans' groups pledged cooperation against the Italian enemy if war should come. Journalists and politicians alike called for sectional unity in the face of the seeming threat from abroad and the purported fifth-column danger within. The lynchings and their aftermath gave South and North a further opportunity for reunion — again over what was perceived to be the criminality of "lower" races.[28]

Writing most of *Pudd'nhead Wilson* and its appended burlesque at his villa in Italy or on trips back and forth to the United States, Twain might be imagined to have deliberately cultivated the dead-pan voice of his protagonist and the detached irony evident in his opening "Whisper to the Reader," with its bogus rhetoric of authentically rendered courtroom scenes and legal language, and its absurd mockery of antique cultural traditions. Such ironic distance on the problems of American race relations and the New South is certainly present in the tale, but it is inconceivable that Twain was not impressed by the Italo-American crisis and the light it cast on the blurring of the color line caused by non-Anglo immigrant races. The Italian twins, in their Siamese version, define the conjunction of black and white that Twain located in the bodies of Roxy and Tom. As immigrant figures they simultaneously bridge the gaps between white and black, and between North and South, further segregating one pair while unifying the other.

The rhetoric of ironic distance with which Twain opens *Pudd'nhead Wilson* must be taken as his defense against direct implication in the emotional pain of the tale, a disguise, like Tom's color, that covers a latent and incriminating truth that will be revealed at the end of the tale. Provisionally separated from America (and his own personal financial troubles), Twain nevertheless came back in his foreign twins to just the problem his own black changeling would pose when he revised his novel and lodged the problem of doubling not in the now separated twins but in the now "Negro" Tom and his slave Chambers. Angelo and Luigi, both of them charged with the crime of kicking Tom Driscoll when only one is guilty, are exonerated in confusion by a court that refuses to "imitate other courts"; but when their paralyzing double election to the board of aldermen cannot be resolved by court after court, the citizens lynch "one" of the twins (149, 169). Lynching, that is, takes the place of or approximates the justice of the courts. Twain, as we have seen, would later claim that lynching thrives on imitative behavior, something his novel had already shown to apply to the whole range of human attitudes and actions, including his authorship, and something the

Supreme Court cases that laid the groundwork for his satire had shown to be key to its own decisions, as one after another the civil rights cases destroyed the gains of Reconstruction by mimicking antebellum law and carefully dividing black from white.

"Imitation is the bane of courts," remarks the judge in *Those Extraordinary Twins* before condemning the hung jury for failing to convict Angelo-Luigi and thus setting free a being with "a hidden and grisly power for evil," by which crime after crime may be committed with no way to separate the guilty one from the innocent (153–54). In *Pudd'nhead Wilson* it is the Siamese-like secret mulatto Tom who, disguised in blackface and a woman's clothing, commits undetected crimes (93–94). His ultimate crime, the murder of the judge, is committed with the knife of the Italian twins against a man whom Twain had originally thought to cast as Tom's actual father and whom he loosely modeled on his own father, John Marshall Clemens, both a slaveholder and a sometime judge, his name, like that of John Marshall Harlan, an echo of past heroic justice. Judge Driscoll, in any case, is the book's symbolic father in his relationship to Tom, Chambers, and Roxy, as well as in his upholding of the *code duello* and the laws of aristocratic prerogative. Despite Twain's own suppression of evidence, as it were, the murder thus follows a logic of revenge. In James Cox's words, Tom becomes "the avenging agent who carries back across the color line the repressed guilt that has gathered at the heart of slavery." More than that, he carries the antebellum world into the post-Reconstruction world in yet another way. In playing out the parricidal rebellion of the black slave against his master-father – or, if his disguise as a woman or his role as Roxy's son is taken into account, as the slave avenging the master's sexual abuse – Tom fuses the Old South and the New by dramatizing the reversal in meaning miscegenation underwent after emancipation. Between 1865 and 1890 the fact of slaveholding miscegenation by white masters and the fear of black slave rebellion were together transformed into the specter of black crime and contamination – the Negro as mongrel or "beast."[29] The imitation white Tom, now like a minstrel performer masquerading in the disguise that parodies his hidden slave status, becomes in effect the mulatto killer of contemporary race theory. In blackface and women's clothing, however, his part includes the maternal authorial disguise adopted by Twain himself, divided as ever between exposing Tom as a "nigger" and participating in his revenge against the aristocratic Southern fathers. Twain's double participation in the plot of his novel thus imitates the Siamese-like entanglement he attributes to his characters. Separate but equal, his twin, paradoxical inclinations toward black vengeance and racist suppression must lie at the heart of his novel's flawed form as well as its dangerously comic representation of Reconstruction's tragic failure.

Tom's crime with the knife momentarily implicates the Italians, already considered "assassins" because of his slander of them. As in late-nineteenth-century America, however, it is the black man who is found to be most liable to criminal guilt. Twain leaves unsettled the question of whether it is the "nigger" in Tom that leads to the killing, though as allegory it can be read no other way. Likewise, Tom's traits of laziness, criminality, and cowardice, which Roxy herself ascribes to his hidden race, may be a sign either of aristocratic degeneration or of blackness as defined by the radical thesis and the minstrel sterotype. But the stereotype itself is enforced by a disturbing negative imitation in the scene where Tom's newly acquired eastern mannerisms are burlesqued by a black bell ringer: the black man plays the minstrel to mock the white man who, secretly black, is playing a mannered role that he does not yet know to be a role (24). When Twain adds to this Tom's knowledge of his blackness and his blackface disguise during the murder, his inquiry into imitation reaches a crisis, for Tom's worst traits, like his "color" – or like the guilt of the Italian twins before the jury – can be traced neither to birth nor to training alone, neither to black nor to white. As Twain says of Tom's remorse over his "uncle's" killing, "He was playing a part, but it was not all a part" (99).

Tom's identity belongs neither to his whiteness nor to his blackness; and the novel, like the law of the land in Jim Crow America, leaves him unprotected, stranded between dual worlds of jurisdiction neither of which is responsible for his acts or for his rights. The hero of the novel has no trouble convicting Tom – convicting him both of murder and of pretending to be a white man. Tom's sale down the river indicates which is the worse crime, or at any rate demonstrates that the murder follows from the masquerade. The value of Tom's whiteness as a kind of "property" does him no more good than it did Homer Plessy; the court recognizes only his blackness, in which property is not self-possession or identity but a sign of the rights of others. Consciously tying his own flawed art to the courtroom theatrics of David Wilson, Twain engaged in a ghostly reduction of the world of the novel to a stage play of parodic codes and habits in which the law dressed as one more player, and in his identification with Wilson Twain admitted his complicity in restoring to order the plantation myth subverted by Roxy's act and Tom's role.

The road to reunion of North and South required both the reinvention of the Confederate myth in the cultural domain and the reactionary readings of constitutional law carried out by legislatures and the Supreme Court. In his reply to Cable's "The Freedman's Case in Equity," the popular Southern writer Thomas Nelson Page had argued, at just the time Twain was writing *Pudd'nhead Wilson*, that in the encroaching struggle against a rising Negro population, "The only thing that stands today between the people of the North and the negro is the people of the South."[30] Page's plea for state rights and Southern control of the "Negro problem" met with increasing favor in the North during the 1890s. It needed and received the assent and support of figures like Pudd'nhead Wilson, who can be read both as an outsider to the South and, ultimately, as its most admired representative, the one who most embodies its cherished codes and racial values. Taken "on trial" (169) by Twain as a "fool" who exposes the town's pretensions and failure of ironic insight, Wilson, it might be said, matures into an eloquent spokesman for Jim Crow. If Tom Driscoll was his Homer Plessy, Twain's pudd'nhead representative of the law was no Albion Tourgée or John Marshall Harlan but rather the rising voice of segregation. Convicting the black man of imposture as a white gentleman, Wilson's miraculous revelation of Tom's identity restores the community's subverted aristocratic order, much as the overturning of Reconstruction and its accompanying civil rights legislation restored an antebellum racial hierarchy in the new dress of Jim Crow. Crossing geographical as well as chronological boundaries, Wilson is the sign of sectional reunion in law and in culture. His voice of irony, not unlike Twain's own deadpan voice, modulates from critique to accommodation. Both separated from and yet intimately tied to the story whose conclusion he creates, Pudd'nhead-Twain freakishly twins in himself both the racist inclinations bred in him since birth and the countering condemnations of racism that are the better part of his conscience. In Twain's novel, fiction and law imitate one another, and the greatest challenge, in the end, is to separate "racism" from its parodic critique.

MICHAEL ROGIN

Francis Galton and Mark Twain

The Natal Autograph in *Pudd'nhead Wilson*

Pudd'nhead Wilson, denied the chance to practice law during his first twenty years in Dawson's Landing, finally wins two cases. His victories occur in two different stories, however, one in *Pudd'n-head Wilson* and the other in *Those Extraordinary Twins*. The Siamese twin Luigi kicks Tom Driscoll in the farce about the twins, but Pudd'nhead exonerates Luigi because "his identity is so merged in his brother's" that the jury cannot find him guilty without punishing Angelo as well. Pudd'nhead's victory in the twin's trial defeats justice and outrages the presiding judge for the inability to separate guilt from innocence will set loose a "grisly power for evil" on the world.[1]

Pudd'nhead Wilson outwits the law in the farcical trial; in the tragic trial he enforces it. When Mark Twain "pulled the twins apart and made two individuals of them,"[2] he enabled Pudd'nhead to establish the guilt of one child born on the same day as his innocent changeling. The victimized judge in the farce becomes the deceived and murdered Judge Driscoll in the tragedy, and now Pudd'nhead catches the killer.

When Mark Twain pulled apart his twins to separate the guilty from the innocent, he produced a book about race – a fact that undercuts the notion (advanced, for example, by Henry Nash Smith) that the two natures in one body have moved from the twins to Tom Driscoll. Tom sustains a double, tragic consciousness only for the briefest moment after he discovers his true identity (44–46). The mulatto son contains two races, not two natures. White on the outside, he is black on the inside, and although his upbringing as a master in slave society may be responsible for some of his bad qualities, Tom hardly resembles the all-white scions of the First Families of Virginia. He exhibits instead the stereotypical defects of the slaves. Mark Twain conceived Tom as a coward and thief before he invented

73

Tom's mulatto mother to account for Tom's character. Turning Tom into a mulatto did not transform a farcical reprobate into a tragic victim. Rather, blackening Tom made his "one drop of Negro blood" (the Swedish title of the novel) into the sign of and explanation for his guilt. That is not just what Roxana, Tom's mother, says; it is what the novel says. Tom is guilty because he is black; he is guilty from birth, from his mother's birth and from her mother's before her. Whatever the meaning of a taint traced through the maternal line, Tom is irredeemably guilty. He is no tragic mulatto, innocent victim of the slave society that practiced, but condemned the fruits of, miscegenation. Models existed for a tale of the tragic mulatto; Twain himself had sketched such a story, but Tom Driscoll is not its protagonist. When Mark Twain introduced race into his tale about twins, he separated the guilty from the innocent by making the guilty black.[3]

But that fact, from which genteel criticism of *Pudd'nhead Wilson* flees, only begins to comprehend the novel. In naturalizing race by reducing it to blood, Mark Twain brings us to the center of the deranged, racialist culture that trapped him. An uncontaminated stance of superior, moral condemnation would have produced merely a tract. Like *Billy Budd,* another claustrophobic late work written at the same time, *Pudd'nhead Wilson* was taken over by characters on whom its author had not planned. These new characters transformed simple stories (one comic, the other nostalgic) into revelations of the horror of the American 1890s (one as the power of blackness, the other as iron cage). And in both cases the story's force resides not in the author's detached judgment against the world depicted, but in his participation in such a world.[4]

Tom Driscoll is one of the characters who invade *Pudd'nhead Wilson*; Valet de Chambre, Tom's changeling double, is another. I have suggested that the inseparable Angelo and Luigi are replaced not by an internally divided Tom, but by the division between the guilty Tom and the innocent Chambers. That doubled opposition between Tom and Chambers, however, fails to organize the new story. First, although the twins' separation allows the guilty to be punished, it does not save the innocent. Because Chambers was raised as a slave, he lacks the capacity to be free. If heredity dooms Tom, environment dooms Chambers, and far from indicating Mark Twain's incoherence on the relative influences of heredity and environment (as some critics think), the doom that the changelings share points to a blackness that covers the novel as a whole.

Chambers, however, is not a novelistically sufficient bearer of that blackness – the second reason why the Tom-Chambers split does not account for *Pudd'nhead* — because he largely disappears from the tale. Mark Twain recognized that neither Tom alone nor Tom and Chambers had taken over his story. "I have pulled the twins apart," he wrote when he finished *Pudd'nhead*, but he did not go on to describe Chambers and Tom. He continued instead, "3 people stand up high, from beginning to end, and only 3 — Pudd'nhead, 'Tom' Driscoll and his nigger mother Roxana."[5] Beneath the division between Tom and Chambers, Twain suggests, lies the next lower layer, the opposition between the guilty black who masquerades as white and the detective-scientist who exposes him. But there is a deeper layer still, for Twain also wrote that the "doings" of "a stranger named Pudd'nhead Wilson, and a woman named Roxana . . . pushed up into prominence a young fellow named Tom Driscoll."[6] Tom in that family romance points to the opposition between the "stranger" and the "nigger mother" who, together, produced him. We first examine the split between the changeling born in February 1830 and the stranger who came to Dawson's Landing that very same month (5), then turn to the opposition between Pudd'nhead and Roxana, and finally consider the deepest opposition of all, that within Roxana that implicates Mark Twain.

Tom is on top for the first part of *Pudd'nhead Wilson* because his true color is hidden from the town; Pudd'nhead, the town blind to his talents, is on the bottom. The two men change places through the one's exposure of the other.[7] The exposure of Tom must be distinguished, however, from the exposure of slavery that also runs through the novel. To understand that separation of race from slavery, which produced the Tom-Pudd'nhead split, we must turn to two dominant themes in the political culture of the 1890s.

The first was the closing of the frontier, which the Bureau of the Census proclaimed in 1890 and which Frederick Jackson Turner made famous three years later. Turner's essay, written the same year as *Pudd'nhead Wilson*, announced the disappearance of the territory to which Huck could escape. The end of the frontier turned *Pudd'nhead*, as Leslie Fiedler saw long ago, into a Southern rather than a Western[8] — no raft, no river, no place outside society for interracial idyll, no principle of pleasure. In *Huckleberry Finn*, the bond between Huck and Jim condemned slavery, to be sure, but slavery also enabled it, and there is an affection for Clemens's boyhood world totally absent from *Pudd'nhead Wilson*. Mark Twain retained sympathy for the slave South when he wrote *Huckleberry Finn*, for slavery was conjoined with a freedom outside itself — the geographic space of nature, the imaginative space of boyhood. In *Pudd'nhead*

Wilson, forced back into small-town slave society, "Pudd'nhead, 'Tom' Driscoll and his nigger mother" are trapped as Huck, Tom Sawyer, and Nigger Jim are not.

Thus *Pudd'nhead* contains a more bitter condemnation of slavery than does *Huckleberry Finn,* but slavery was defeated before either novel was written, and a new system of racial subordination was taking its place. *Pudd'nhead* thus embodies a paradox: slavery is dead but inescapable. Familiar to psychoanalytic criticism, that paradox caught not just Mark Twain but the South as a whole. The trap of the dead planter father, as we shall see, "weighed like a nightmare on the brain of the living" in the political unconscious.[9] In the increasingly crazed political consciousness, however, living blacks signified the legacy of slavery. And the response to freed blacks generated the second theme that marks *Pudd'nhead Wilson,* the separation of race from slavery and the obsession with the black savage.

A new system of racial radicalism, as Joel Williamson has labeled it, came to dominate the South as Mark Twain was writing *Pudd'nhead Wilson.* Antebellum racial conservatism, which continued to hold sway during Reconstruction, had a place for blacks, the children in an organic paternal order. *Huckleberry Finn* subversively fulfilled that organicism, as the interracial bond develops in escape from slavery and as the child slave becomes a nurturing mother. Tom's torture of Roxana, by contrast, mocks the organic familial tie, and that is because Tom is not the black child of conservative thought but the black beast of racial radicalism. The shift from West to South wiped out the space for interracial male idyll and forced a confrontation with interracial heterosexuality.[10]

Freed from slavery's civilizing restraints, according to the racial radicals, the Negro regressed to bestiality. Two linked forms of sexual menace obsessed racial radicals. The first was the specter of the black rapist, a fantasy that generated the all-too-real lynchings that swept the South between 1889 and 1915. Lynchings were concentrated in the West before 1889, and most victims were white men. In the 1890s, the practice shifted from the West to the South, as if to mark the closing of the frontier, and the overwhelming number of targets were black. The number of lynchings reached a high of 156 in 1892, the year Mark Twain began *Those Extraordinary Twins.*[11] Unlike *The Leopard's Spots* and *The Clansman,* Thomas Dixon's best-selling racist fantasies of ten years later, *Pudd'nhead Wilson* avoids lynching and rape. (Luigi is lynched in the farce, not Tom in the tragedy; the tragedy plays with sexual aggression, the comedy does not.) *Pudd'nhead*'s subject instead is the second staple of racial radicalism, the fear of miscegenation. That fear, contained by the slave structure that protected whites from the consequences and reversals of actual black-white miscegenation, erupted in racial radical fantasies. As Dixon wrote in *The Leopard's Spots,* "One drop of blood makes a Negro. It kinks the hair, flattens the nose, thickens the lip, puts out the light of intellect, and lights the fire of brutal passions." Dixon wished for visible signs of black guilt that *Pudd'nhead Wilson* refused to grant, for in spite of his guilty drop of Negro blood, Tom Driscoll passes as white.[12]

The black rapist and mulatto in radical fantasies inverted the real character of interracial assault. These fantasized figures shifted the guilt from white plantation fathers to powerless black men and the victimization from black women to white. Lynchings punished black men for the interracial sexual aggression for which white men were responsible. *Pudd'nhead Wilson,* by contrast, seems to return the blame for miscegenation to its origin. Judge Driscoll, to be sure, is neither Tom's father as Mark Twain had originally planned nor his master. Nor did Mark Twain follow through on his notes for the novel and have Tom search out his father to kill him. But the shadowy F.F.V. double of Judge Driscoll who fathers Tom, and Tom's master, the Judge's brother, are both clearly stand-ins for the Judge. Tom's father and his master die the same day (43); absent from the novel, they leave behind as their representative Judge Driscoll, whom Tom kills. Perhaps, having modeled Judged Driscoll on his own F.F.V. father, Judge Clemens, Mark Twain did not want to give the judge a mulatto son. *Pudd'nhead Wilson* points nonetheless to parricide as revenge for miscegenation.[13]

In distancing Tom from Judge Driscoll, however, Mark Twain does more than substitute one guilty father for another. By presenting Judge Driscoll sympathetically, blackening Tom's character, and making Tom a quasi-parricide, Mark Twain turns Tom from the victim of miscegenation into its guilty sign. *Pudd'nhead* punishes Tom for the exposure of the father, the exposure he embodies. The novel therefore repeats the biblical curse of slavery, wherein Ham is condemned to be a "servant of servants" for seeing his father naked. Tom feels "the curse of Ham" upon him because Ham in American racial genealogy is the father of slaves.[14] The sexuality of the naked father imprisons the son who makes it visible. As a sign of the sexual guilt of the fathers, Tom absolves them, a transfer of guilt from white father to black son that goes back to the beginning of slavery. But in the 1890s there was an additional shift that decisively moved the South's interracial complex from slave society to black nature.

Tom is a sign not just of the sins of the fathers, but of their defeat. Hysteria about the black rapist characterized neither slavery, whose social order kept blacks in their place, nor Reconstruction, when whites feared political uprisings not sexual assaults. The guilty sexual black emerged only with the twin defeats of the fathers, first in the Civil War and then in their complicity, even after the end of Reconstruction, in encouraging Northern political and economic penetration of the South. In Joel Williamson's formulation, Southern white men might not be able to protect the South from the North, but they could protect white women from black men.[15] The white woman is missing from *Pudd'nhead Wilson*, to be sure, but the father is present and defeated, outwitted before he is killed. His murder, although set before the Civil War, marks the definitive defeat of planter paternalism, the replacement of the guilty but powerful slave-owning father by the black parricide, and the emergence out of slavery's overthrow of the black monster.

The defeated fathers, whether Mr. Justice Robinson in the twins' trial or Judge Driscoll in *Pudd'nhead Wilson*, cannot restore justice and order. Pudd'nhead, who outwits the fathers in *Those Extraordinary Twins*, does their work in the book that bears his name.[16] In avenging the dead father, however, Pudd'nhead takes his place as neither Tom the false claimant nor the real blood son, Chambers, is able to do. That triumph ushers in a new social order. Judge Driscoll's power derived from property, human property, and their desire for and status as property trapped Chambers and Tom.[17] Pudd'nhead's authority comes not from the ownership of property, but from human capital in the modern sense; he has invested in acquiring not other human beings, but a professional skill. Both Judge Driscoll and Pudd'nhead are lawyers, but whereas the former relies on persuasion, which can make things seem different than they are, the latter possesses a science. Pudd'nhead tells the guilty from the innocent, against racial and sexual disguise (for Tom dresses as a girl to rob his victims), through his mastery of the science of fingerprints. Francis Galton's *Finger Prints,* published the year Mark Twain began *Those Extraordinary Twins*, gave Twain the method for catching the parricide who had taken over his book. "Let no one despise the ridges [on fingers]," wrote Galton, the father of eugenics, "for they are in some respects the most important of all anthropological data."[18]

By comparing sets of fingerprints taken at different times, Pudd'nhead exposes the black murderer who possessed the identity of his white changeling double. Because fingerprints establish individual rather than racial difference, however, their use in *Pudd'nhead Wilson* may seem fortuitous. It is not. "The general aspect of the Negro print stikes me as characteristic," wrote Galton. "They give an idea of greater simplicity." But although "the impressions from Negroes betray the general clumsiness of their fingers," Galton admitted, "their patterns are not so far as I can find, different from those of others." Galton's hope that his science of fingerprints would connect individuals to race was disappointed. Nonetheless, fingerprinting was part of his scientific project to establish hereditary variation in talent and character, a project that took a racial turn in America.[19]

Galton's aim was to investigate the origins of "natural ability," to give "the more suitable races or strains of blood a better chance of prevailing speedily over the less suitable." Although he believed that some races were inferior to others, like other Europeans Galton used eugenics primarily to support class rather than racial hierarchy. Eugenics became a scientific theory of racial inferiority in the United States. Eugenicists developed the IQ test; Americans used it to prove black inferiority. The state-arranged marriages Galton favored to promote the survival of the fittest became anti-miscegenation laws in America.[20]

Twins were crucial for eugenicists, as they are in Mark Twain's twin texts. Fingerprints established that Luigi was not Angelo in *Pudd'nhead* so that "his fellow-twin could never personate him and deceive you" (108–9). The more important purpose of fingerprints, distinguishing Tom from Chambers, was to make inheritance inescapable. Galton proposed using twins for that purpose because the life histories of identical twins reared apart would show that heredity overcame environment. Because Twain could not separate his Siamese twins for that purpose, he substituted changelings. In work that has been exposed as fraudulent, the Englishman Cyril Burt claimed to have confirmed Galton's hypotheses by studying fifty-three sets of identical twins. The American Arthur Jensen has used Galton's theories, IQ test results, and Burt's faked twin studies to argue for black inferiority.[21]

Galton's claim to find hereditary talent in families of "natural ability" may seem to honor the fathers. But Galton rejected the aristocracies of title and wealth in favor of an aristocracy of talent. He was, after all, knighted Sir Francis Galton for his accomplishments, not his origins. Galton, like Pudd'nhead, achieved success through scientific method. He was ideologist for the new, professional middle class that he exemplified. The farcical outcome of Pudd'nhead's scientific method, which makes Tom property again, masks a different result in the time the novel was written. Pudd'nhead sustains slavery in the novel, but paternal planters and F.F.V.s, who assigned blacks a place as working slave children, were being replaced by the scientific racism that made blacks degenerate, superfluous, and disposable. Blood, which once signified noble family alliances, pointed now to the racial body. "The concern with genealogy became a prescription with heredity," in Michel Foucault's words, as "the health of the [bourgeois] organism" substituted for "the antiquity of [aristocratic] ancestry." By the 1920s the South had buried the race question, and eugenics was triumphant in America. The First Families of Virginia had given way to Fitter Family Contests in which families competed to prove the superiority of their blood lines. The first such contest was held in 1920 in Topeka, Kansas, at the Kansas Free Fair – the F.F.C.s had replaced the F.F.V.s.[22]

Fingerprints provided a foolproof way of establishing individual difference. "Every human being carries with him from his cradle to his grave certain physical marks which do not change their character," Pudd'nhead explains. "These marks are his signature." "Duplicates" of an individual's height and form exist, but "his physiological autograph . . . cannot be counterfeited . . . – there is no duplicate of it among the swarming populations of the globe!" (108). Fingerprints defeat masquerade, disguise, doubling, and counterfeit identity; they identify the true and unique individual "character." That victory for Pudd'nhead Wilson is a defeat for Francis Galton and Mark Twain.

Fingerprint patterns "almost beyond change" for Galton[23] establish blood beyond change for Mark Twain. Fingerprints fail by succeeding for both authors, but they do so in opposite ways. Fingerprints defeat Galton because they cannot establish racial and characterological difference; they defeat Mark Twain because they can.

Galton could not connect fingerprints to anything either inherited or significant in human character. He acknowledged "great expectations, that have been falsified, namely their use in indicating Race and Temperament." Galton wanted to join fingerprinting to eugenics, but the two sciences were sundered irretrievably because of the human insignificance of the science of individual difference. Palmistry, unlike fingerprinting, joined the physical properties of an individual's hands to his or her character and fate, but Galton dismissed palmistry as pseudoscience. Although Pudd'nhead uses palmistry to tell the twins' history, his success is left over from the farcical story and irrelevant to the racial tragedy. The science that matters in *Pudd'nhead* identifies a unique individual "character" racially fixed at birth, a character that makes no moral sense and that individuals are powerless to change. The insistence on racial categories, exposed by fingerprints and invisible to the naked eye, destroys the world of individual meaning and self-making that it was designed to preserve.[24]

Pudd'nhead Wilson fails to grasp the pyrrhic nature of his victory. That understanding appears instead in the split between Pudd'nhead the detective, who solves the crime and becomes mayor of Dawson's Landing, and the man who is author of Pudd'nhead's calendar. The former reinstates slavery and racial difference; the latter sees what Pudd'nhead's victory means. Pudd'nhead the character kills his half of the dog (the "cur" who refuses to fight a duel, the "low-down hound" who sells his mother down the river, the "miserable dog" that Pudd'n-head convicts) and preserves the other (Chambers) half. Pudd'nhead the author sees that such an exposure of guilt contaminates everything. Hence the famous calendar heading, "Columbus Day," for the Conclusion: "October 12, the Discovery. It was wonderful to find America, but it would have been more wonderful to miss it" (113). James Cox calls *Pudd'nhead Wilson's New Calendar* an "extended inversion" of the maxims in *Poor Richard's Almanac* because the calendar turns success into failure.[25]

Fingerprints discover secret guilt. As Susan Gillman writes, "Tom's fate threatens that the hidden taint of black blood could be disclosed in any white person."[26] Fingerprints establish racial difference, however, only where that binary opposition already exists, so that the difference between two individuals will be the difference of black and white. Chambers, necessary to prove Tom black, is the instrument by which Pudd'nhead at once establishes the opposition between Tom and Chambers and displaces it by that between Tom and himself. That opposition, in turn, opens up Pudd'nhead's self-division between the character who rises from the exposure of racial difference and the author who sees the meaning of such success. But Pudd'n-head's dependence on racial difference exposes a deeper opposition still, that between individual difference and indiscriminate duplication; between black-and-white and mulatto; between Pudd'nhead Wilson and the "nigger mother, Roxana." Tom falls and Pudd'nhead rises in the story, but Roxana and not Tom begins the book in control. Her hidden, in-control self engenders chaos, however, and Pudd'nhead restores order by acquiring her power.[27]

"Columbus Day" introduces the final chapter of *Pudd'nhead Wilson*. The chapter in which Tom's exposure actually occurs begins with a different maxim:

Even the clearest and most perfect circumstantial evidence is likely to be at fault, after all, and therefore ought to be received with great caution. Take the case of any pencil, sharpened by any woman; if you have witnesses, you will find she did it with a knife; but if you take simply the aspect of the pencil, you will say she did it with her teeth. (99)

This calendar entry is not simply black and ironic like the others, but vengeful as well, and its target is "any woman." It points to the clumsiness of Roxana's effort at improving the life chances of her son, the marks she has left behind that Pudd'nhead will expose. A woman who seems to have had a pencil between her teeth but has actually had it under her knife, whose pencil-sharpenings look like teeth-marks, introduces Pudd'nhead's discovery of the marks that identify Tom.

Roxana transforms *Those Extraordinary Twins* when she forces her way into the farce. She appears when Angelo begins to court Rowena, the white innocent whose head is full of Scott.[28] Because Angelo cannot romance Rowena without the presence of his dark half, Luigi, *Those Extraordinary Twins* calls for sexual jokes at Rowena's expense. Mark Twain's "censor," Olivia Clemens, whom he also called his "Human Angel" during their courtship,[29] forbade such sexual play and so the romance between Roxana and Tom replaces that between Rowena and Angelo. The "'nigger'" in Tom (45) makes him shy of Rowena in her brief appearance in *Pudd'nhead*; the dark twin attached to Angelo would not have been so retiring.

Roxana's displacement of Rowena turns farce into tragedy. The white mother dies giving birth in *Pudd'nhead,* leaving only a black mother to nurse both the black infant and the white. The absent white mother underlines the contrast between Roxana and Rowena as one of sexual and not simply racial difference. That contrast is not between white mother and black whore, but between white virgin and sexualized black mother. Rowena's romance was to have been with Angelo; Roxana's is with her son.

Roxana loves Tom so much that she gives him up. The cult of domesticity honored self-sacrificing mothers; Roxana is its exemplar. Maternal blood proves stronger than domestic ideal, not because Roxana backslides, but because her natal tie contaminates Tom at birth and is exposed by Pudd'nhead Wilson. The revelation of Tom's "natal autograph" reconnects the son to his mother, and Tom's maternal entrapment is Pudd'nhead's liberation. Fiedler calls Tom that part of Mark Twain who failed his mother's plea on his father's deathbed, "Only promise me to be a better boy. Promise me not to break my heart," pleads the bad boy exposed by Pudd'nhead.[30] But although Tom's persecution of Roxana mocks the bond of mother-love, Pudd'nhead is the ultimate victor over it.

Roxana traces her descent from African, Indian, and white American nobility. Her concern with genealogy mocks the F.F.V.s. Nonetheless, if she triumphs, black becomes white, mulattoes take over, and the son with a drop of nigger blood becomes the father who sleeps with white women. Her victory would vindicate the mothers who, given the racial division of sexual labor under slavery, carry the taint of blackness in America. Pudd'nhead displaces the white fathers to preserve their cultural myth. He rescues personal, masculine identity, against the maternal-mulatto confusion by fixing it in binary, racial opposition.

Where does Mark Twain stand in the competition between Pudd'nhead and Roxana? As a young Virginia City, Nevada, newspaper editor, Mark Twain had anonymously reported that the proceeds of a Carson City ladies' fancy-dress ball were being "sent to aid a Miscegenation Society in the East." When a rival editor accused Mark Twain of slandering white women, he challenged the editor to a duel, and the two men exchanged insults until Twain left the Nevada Territory abruptly without fighting.[31] Miscegenation was the fruit of the fathers' hidden connection to black women; dueling was their public defense of the white female honor that the connection to black women at once protected (from sex) and betrayed. Young Mark Twain was encountering the identity elements – miscegenation, fancy dress, and the flight from dueling – that would later give birth to Tom Driscoll.

Tom was the unacknowledged son of Judge Driscoll/Clemens, Samuel Clemens's twin and dark double. Mark Twain bridged the gulf between white boy and black boy, but that bridge was collapsing in the 1890s; Twain's dark side had lost its playful aspect and had become demonic. Samuel Clemens had grown up under slavery. As Mark Twain lost his belief in the pleasure contained in that slave childhood, his black identification became a torture and not an escape. William Dean Howells's favorable review of *Roughing It,* Mark Twain had commented in 1872, made him feel like "a mother who has given birth to a white baby when she was awfully afraid it was going to be a mulatto."[32] Racial cross-fertilization was no longer a joke when it produced Tom Driscoll.

Sometime in the 1890s, perhaps earlier, Mark Twain dreamed his famous dream of uncompleted seduction; in the dream, a black woman sold him a "mushy, apple pie" and made him "a disgusting proposition." When she offered him the spoon from her mouth with which to eat the pie, "my stomach rose – there everything vanished."[33] The dream unites food and sex at their black, maternal source, waking up Mark Twain. The opposition in the dream between black mother and white man appears in *Pudd'nhead,* where the one has a sexual stake in ending racial difference, the other in preserving it.

So Mark Twain, by "a kind of literary Caesarean operation," as he wrote, "pulled one of the stories out by the roots, and left the other one." He pulled out the child story, as Cox has said – Luigi/Angelo and Rowena – and left "the nigger mother Roxana."[34] Even a "jackleg" writer was expert enough to bring forth a child by Caesarean, as the natural mother cannot. Pudd'nhead triumphs over that mother in her story, the mother-story that remains, because mother-love is no match for professional skill. The Southern professional man nurtured and sexually cared for by a black woman (if we merge Clemens the child, Mark Twain the author, and the character, Pudd'nhead Wilson) takes his revenge.

But if *Pudd'nhead* reveals Mark Twain's growing trouble with blackness, he has not simply chosen Pudd'nhead in the contest with Roxana. The undisguised acceptance of mulattoes would end binary racial doubling, either through the identification of mulattoes as a separate racial class, neither black nor white, or through the disappearance of the system of racial classification altogether. The former characterized the West Indies during Mark Twain's lifetime, the latter (as the peopling of America by mulattoes) would be Ike McCaslin's nightmare in William Faulkner's *Go Down, Moses.* But no one in *Pudd'nhead Wilson* can imagine the opposition between a system of binary racial classification and its absence, much less stand for the latter. Rather, Pudd'nhead and Roxana support two different modes of racial doubling, the one exposed, fixed and inexorable, the other mutable and disguised.

That opposition divides Roxana herself, who is not simply bifurcated from Pudd'nhead but is also internally split between the natural mother inexorably tied to her son and the masquerading mother who plays with identity to free him from her. In that latter guise, Roxana represents American blacks whose natal autographs labeled them slaves, disguising their actual identities, and who responded with masks to create what space they had for protection and play. As masquerader, Roxana is an artist parallel to Pudd'nhead the scientist. Tom and his mother before him think that they can dress up and disguise identity; Pudd'nhead defeats Roxana and ends their masquerade. His fingerprints establish an identity fixed from birth against a fluid identity constructed in storytelling and play. But the identity Pudd'nhead exposes allies him with the natal mother; together they imprison the son in his inescapable, racial natal bond. Play with counterfeit identity, however, defined Mark Twain. By establishing indisputable racial difference, the fingerprints that imprison blacks cut off Sam Clemens from his connection to blackness and end Mark Twain's ability to play. Blackness becomes something no longer to be taken on and off, escaped and disguised; it is inevitably, disastrously present. As Cox writes, Pudd'nhead Wilson is "Mark Twain's repression of himself."[35]

The absence of evidence, James Cox tells one story to show, proves the veracity of a Mark Twain tall tale: "The only truth that can be told is one which reveals rather than conceals the fact that it is a lie."[36] Pudd'nhead's palm readings may be that sort of truth; his fingerprints are not. *Pudd'nhead Wilson,* with its changelings and fingerprints, is a tall tale whose irrefutable evidence brings Mark Twain's American fiction to an end.

Mark Twain's Caesarean points, therefore, not to the power of the script doctor but to the power of the mother. The script doctor gives birth to *Those Extraordinary Twins* in the metaphor; the doctor simply extracts the story that got in Roxana's way. It was the "mulatto" not the "white baby" that mattered. If we see Mark Twain neither as the script doctor nor as at one with his "piece of machinery" (as he called *Pudd'nhead*),[37] but rather as the author presiding over the book as a whole—the calendar and Roxana as well as the trial—then Mark Twain has shown what Pudd'nhead's revenge on the black mother means and what it costs. The farce was dangerous because it promoted identity confusion and evaded adult responsibility. But the mother story, scientifically reducing identity to natal autograph, establishes a fixed racial character against the power of play. The mother story exposes a far greater "grisly power for evil" than that unleashed in the extracted child who drew Mark Twain back to its mother.

SUSAN GILLMAN

"Sure Identifiers"

Race, Science, and the Law in *Pudd'nhead Wilson*

A book is the writer's secret life, the dark twin of a man.
—WILLIAM FAULKNER, *Mosquitoes*

Soon after *Pudd'nhead Wilson* was published in late November 1894, the well-known contemporary critic and novelist, Hjalmar Hjorth Boyesen, reviewed the novel with the kind of qualified praise it has received ever since. Puzzled particularly by Mark Twain's "stock" treatment of the highly charged issue of race relations, Boyesen struck a typically bemused tone at this "novel of the ante-bellum days in Missouri, rather melodramatic in plot." "If anybody but Mark Twain had undertaken to tell that kind of story," the review begins, going on to list the elements of "that kind of story":

with exchanges of infants in the cradle, a hero with negro taint in his blood substituted for the legitimate white heir, midnight encounters in a haunted house between the false heir and his colored mother, murder by the villain of his supposed uncle and benefactor, accusation of an innocent foreigner, and final sensational acquittal and general unraveling of the tangled skein — if, I say, anybody else had had the hardihood to utilize afresh this venerable stage machinery of fiction, we should have been tempted to class his work with such cheap stuff as that of . . . the dime novelists. But Mark Twain, somehow, has lifted it all into the region of literature.

Part of the "somehow," Boyesen suggests, is a certain historical verisimilitude in *Pudd'nhead Wilson* — the "credible and authentic" local atmosphere — that makes us "swallow the melodrama without a qualm — exchange of heirs, haunted house, murder, and all — and scarcely dream that we have been duped until we wake up with a start at the end of the last chapter."[1]

Readers since Boyesen have continued to invoke similar terms. Like him, many have felt "duped" by *Pudd'nhead Wilson's* "tangle" of the "authentic" and the "melodramatic," the historical texture em-

86

bedded in (and sometimes suppressed by) the most conventional of sensation plots. So many difficult questions about the social construction of racial identity surface partially in the narrative, only to be arbitrarily closed off by the formulaic clarity of the conclusion to the murder/detective plot, where there seems to be no room for racial loose ends. Even the history of the composition of the manuscript bears out this reading, given that the text which began as a farcical literary sideshow about Siamese twins became entangled with a racial "tragedy" of the antebellum South. As Hershel Parker points out, the manuscript in the Morgan Library, consisting of both the Siamese twins story and the race/murder plot, raises questions primarily about race and how Mark Twain represented – and avoided – racial issues in the process of composition and revision. After conceiving of the idea of switched racial identities, for example, roughly about midway during the composition process, why did Mark Twain proceed to write – and then cut out – much new and explicit material on Tom Driscoll's agonizing discovery of his racial patrimony?[2]

This is at once a textual, social, and ethical problem: although readers recognize race relations as *Pudd'nhead Wilson*'s central problematic, the novel has tended to generate inward-looking readings that remain for the most part confined within the terms of the text itself.[3] Rather, I would argue, Mark Twain's tangled textual skein must be anchored in, and perhaps unraveled by, the context of the cultural circumstances that produced it. Both *Pudd'nhead Wilson* and *Those Extraordinary Twins* condense what may strike us now as an incongruous combination of fads, vocabularies, and concepts, all of which were then part of the debates over whether and how biological differences determine the natural capacities of racial groups. *Those Extraordinary Twins*, for example, was based on the Tocci brothers, the Italian (rather than Siamese) twins whom Mark Twain had seen on exhibit in 1891, and was also inspired by the power of the cultural mythology that arose around Siamese twins at the time.[4] *Pudd'nhead Wilson* drew similarly on popular culture, incorporating fictional forms (the detective plot, the changeling plot), and most important, historical circumstance. The novel's satire of racial classification by fractions of blood mirrors problems in American race relations during both the antebellum period in which the novel is set and the 1890s when it was written.

In this sense, Twain's novel implicitly reminds readers that racial codes regulating miscegenation and classifying mixed-race offspring did not disappear after Emancipation but instead were reenacted or reaffirmed, with even more rigorous definitions of whiteness, during the nineties, when antiblack repression took multiple forms, legal and extralegal.[5] *Pudd'nhead Wilson* was serialized in *Century Magazine* in the middle of a decade that saw not only an epidemic of lynchings but also the beginnings of newly enacted Jim Crow laws defining the "Negro's place" in a segregated society, laws paralleled in the political sphere by a variety of voting restrictions to disenfranchise most blacks. The novel may thus speak even more pointedly to the growing racism of its own era of the 1890s than to the race slavery abolished thirty years earlier. At the very least, the connection between the times of the book's setting and of its writing acknowledges silently an unwelcome tie between race slavery of the past and racism in the present, just as the link between *Pudd'nhead Wilson* and *Those Extraordinary Twins* acknowledges an unspoken kinship between those defined as other, freakish, monstrous, whether Siamese twin or mulatto.

The farce, however, makes a mockery of the Siamese twins' grotesque attachment, whereas the tragedy, obsessed with genealogy, race, and miscegenation, offers a critique of an American historical actuality. But as Boyesen suggests, *Pudd'nhead Wilson* similarly combines the authentic with the sensational and the melodramatic, a textual combination almost as grotesque and freakish as the narrative of the Siamese twins. From the beginning the novel offsets an implicitly historical and contextualized sensibility with a conventionalized, melodramatic mode. Precise details of time and place frame the first chapter. It is 1830. "The scene of this chronicle is the town of Dawson's Landing, on the Missouri side of the Mississippi, half a day's journey, per steamboat, below St. Louis." Such detail had framed the manuscript from its inception, although it originally started with the arrival of the Siamese twins and was dated "about 1850." After the addition of the race plot, Twain rewrote the first chapters, incorporating the history of the exchange of the babies in their cradles, and set back the date twenty years so that the two children would be twenty-two around 1850.

The original date may have had no particular significance, but recast in the setting of a "chronicle" of "a slave-holding town" (a phrase added only during revison), 1850 becomes a memorable year and the Mississippi River locale a special place. The census of 1850 counted mulattoes for the first time. In that year, in Kentucky and Missouri, there was one mulatto slave for every six black slaves. And in that year, Joel Williamson comments, "the slave frontier was the trans-Mississippi South, and it was also preeminently the area of mulatto slavery"; he concludes that "where slavery was strongest and getting stronger, it was also becoming whiter." One further paradoxical result of this racial mixing became apparent in the "new intensity of white racial exclusiveness" during the 1850s.[6]

These multiple historical contradictions are not exactly articulated in *Pudd'nhead Wilson* but rather registered, I would argue, as confusingly and as obliquely and as inconsistently as Williamson's account of their historical manifestations indicates. That is, he shows how Southern whites enabled themselves, ironically through increasingly stringent color consciousness, to deny the apparently undeniable presence of increasing racial intermixture. With a similarly tortuous combination of denial based on acknowledgment, the two chapters of Twain's novel immediately following our chronological and geographic introduction to Dawson's Landing turn away from the historical context of the "chronicle," and instead plunge us into the narrative world of popular fiction (the Pudd'nhead Wilson/fingerprint plot and the Roxana/changeling plot). By thus submerging history in melodrama, or by uneasily combining these two modes, the novel participates in a strategy of presenting and yet denying its own historical and racial context. The ironic result: *Pudd'nhead Wilson* pushes us back to the cultural context that is missing. This book is Twain's own "dark twin" – a mirror, we will see, of what has been repressed both in his culture and his own perception.

At the center of the novel is a problem of knowledge (social, scientific, legal) epitomized by the institution of race slavery. Committed to maintaining the differences between racial groups as a means of distinguishing the slave from the free, American slavery spawned, and then tolerated, the anomaly Twain calls the "pure-white slave": the mulatto who, appearing no different racially from his free white relatives, creates a pressing need for the many preposterous social and legal fictions of slave society. Partly a novel of detection and discovery, *Pudd'nhead Wilson* exposes a number of these fictions in the course of exposing a murderer. The murder plot culminates by satirizing the legal fiction that a slave is both property (an extension of the master's will) and nonproperty (in that he can be tried for very willful, antisocial acts, such as murder).[7] In addition, the novel's obsession with genealogy makes us aware of another social fiction, what George Fredrickson calls the "official dedication to maintaining a *fictive* 'race purity' for whites.[8] From the very beginning in which Roxana, trading literally on the babies' interchangeability, switches the two in their cradles, the novel detects a central ambiguity suppressed in law, if not custom, by slave society: if not by color or other unalterable physiological differences, how can we differentiate individuals and groups? How do we know who is master and who is slave, who is to be held accountable under the law and who is not? Finally, with the unsettling trial at the end, the novel asks, how sound is the basis of that knowledge? How do we know what we know is true?

More than any other characters in the novel, Roxana and her son Tom trigger this epistemological confusion through their multiple interchanges of race and sex. Not only does she engineer the switch of the babies, but also – as with her son's numerous racial and sexual disguises – she puts on blackface and male clothing, in her case, ironically, in order to escape from slavery. Particularly when mother and son assume both racial and sexual disguises, they enact the tangle of fact and fiction through which identity is constituted in this world. Each taking on aspects of the other's gender, they act out a mingling of boundaries which stands for the mingling of blood denied by this biracial society through its policies of racial classification. The infamous formula that makes Roxana – "to all intents and purposes as white as anybody" – a black slave is only a fraction: "the one-sixteenth of her which was black out-voted the other fifteen parts and made her a negro."[9] And what enforces this illogical arithmetic other than the socially sanctioned contract summed up by the verb "out-voted"? The verb reminds us that these measurements measure ideologically produced differences between the races. Roxana's racial identity is socially created, "a fiction of law and custom," but a fiction shored up and made to look like fact through the pseudo-mathematics of blood lines. For Twain the apparent precision implied by minute fractional divisions (one-sixteenth, one thirty-second) only underscores their disjunction from reality. All that counts racially in Dawson's Landing are two categories: black and white.

Mark Twain's representation of racial identity as a system of deceptive mathematics has historical precedent in the unique "descent rule" that has been the principle basis of racial classification in the United States. According to this ancestry rule, all descendants of mixed unions are classed with their black ancestors. The resulting two-category system (such as Twain depicts) originated in efforts, mandated by state legislation since the colonial era, to restrict interracial marriage and to determine the status of mixed offspring; by the time of the Civil War, in order to facilitate enforcement of anti-miscegenation laws, more precise definitions were formulated as to what proportion of black ancestry placed an individual on the other side of the color line. The usual antebellum rule for determining who was what was one-fourth or one-eighth, meaning that those with such proportions of black "blood" – anyone with a black or mulatto ancestor within the previous two or three generations – must be classified as black. This "statutory homogenization of all persons with Negro ancestry," as Winthrop Jordan calls it, was peculiar to slavery as it developed in the continental United States. Not even in South Africa, Fredrickson notes, "despite the triumph of white supremacy and segregationism," has such a "rigorous ancestry principle been used to determine who is white and who is not."[10]

The rigor of the American two-category system can be judged by common linguistic usage. Other than the term *mulatto* (which was indistinguishable from *Negro* for legal purposes), no terminology existed in the United States with which to recognize varying degrees of intermixed "blood," or to define a hierarchy of legal status derived from those shades of distinction. Elsewhere, studies of comparative race relations show, racially mixed offspring ("half-castes" or "half-white") have usually been acknowledged as an intermediate group in systems of racial stratification with varying degrees of fluidity between white, "colored," and black. Such acknowledgment was reflected in the development of terminology to distinguish various racial mixtures. In Latin America and the British West Indies, for example, racially mixed offspring were labeled according to fractions of "blood": *mulatto* meant one-half white; *sambo*, one-fourth white; *quadroon*, three-fourths white; and *mestizo*, seven-eighths white.[11]

Twain's minute fractions mock the genetic absurdity of this way of quantifying the genetic makeup. But however theoretically and genetically untenable, this complex linguistic machinery established a fact of social practice: miscegenation was a publicly accepted, almost institutionalized practice in some New World slave societies, whereas the absence of analogous terms in the United States suggests that racially mixed offspring simply were not officially acknowledged.[12] The reasons for such denial may be summed up in the language of a pioneering Virginia statute of 1691 that banned, for the first time in the colonies, all forms of interracial marriage. The legislation's stated purpose was "the prevention of that abominable mixture and spurious issue."[13] The essential word is "mixture." Mulattoes blurred the clear separation between the races essential to American race slavery, and miscegenation was thus perceived as a threat to a biracial society. Particularly threatening to this two-part order were the "free persons of color," most of whom were mulattoes. "We should have but two classes," declared one grand jury deliberating the expulsion of the "free colored" from South Carolina in the late

1850s, "the Master and the slave, and no intermediate class can be other than immensely mischievous to our peculiar institution."[14] The grand jury testimony verges on acknowledging the contradiction that this "intermediate" group – an "abominable mixture," neither white nor black, slave nor free – violates the logic of the institution that produced it and therefore must be suppressed.

If, as a result, the mulatto was legally erased, deprived of any status under the law, the problem of race mixture itself was not altogether suppressed in contemporary political, scientific, and religious writing. A widespread proslavery argument of the 1850s drew on current knowledge of heredity to theorize that the offspring of miscegenation would be an unnatural type, the mixture of races adapted to very different geographic regions, and hence unable to procreate beyond two or three generations. The eventual result of race mixture was inevitably sterility, according to another "scientific" argument offering "proof" in the sterility of an animal hybrid, the mule – an analogy linguistically enforced in the word *mulatto*, borrowed from the Spanish and derived from the Latin *mulus*. Scientific justification was not the only authority appealed to in antimiscegenation writing. Immediately after the war, miscegenation became for some the essential sin against God that caused the South to lose. Defeat "is the judgment of the Almighty," wrote one low-country Carolina planter in 1868, "because the human and brute blood have mingled to the degree it has in the slave states. Was it not so in the French and British Islands and see what has become of them."[15]

The widespread revulsion against race mixture expressed in all of the above writings – the Virginia statute, the grand jury testimony, the scientific arguments on hybridism, and the planter's religious argument – help to explain both why and how the fiction of race purity was maintained in the face of so much evidence to the contrary. As Jordan puts this contradiction: "by classifying the mulatto as a Negro [the white slaveowner] was in effect denying that intermixture had occurred at all."[16] When Mark Twain, later in the 1890s, framed racial identity in *Pudd'nhead Wilson* as an issue of acknowledgment and denial, both for himself as an author and for southern society, he was thus openly articulating the *sub rosa* judgment of many of his contemporaries.

Indeed, once slavery was abolished the question of the color line, and its impact on the representation of race relations, became, if anything, all the more pressing. For many white southerners, George Washington Cable pointed out in 1885, looming in the passage of the

Fourteenth and Fifteenth Amendments and the freedman's participation in Reconstruction governments was the "huge bugbear of Social Equality": equality meant the "social intermingling of the two races," with its "monstrous" suggestion of "admixture of the two bloods" and "the utter confusion of race and corruption of society."[17] What Jordan calls the "peculiar bifurcation" of American racial categorization represented, then, for Twain and others, even more than purely a legal effort to control the results of interracial sex. The restrictive policy attempted broadly to control "black" encroachments on "white" identity, to fix racial identity as an absolute quantity with clear boundaries rather than on a continuum of gradations, one shading into another. Fears expressed about "amalgamation," an antebellum term equivalent to miscegenation, corroborate what I will show to be Twain's association of race mixture with the destruction of basic assumptions about identity – not only racial, but also social and even sexual identity.

One traveler in the antebellum South singled out what he called the "bugbear of 'amalgamation.'" The traveler's journal noted that even the reform-minded Lyman Beecher was "so far jaundiced" that he supported African colonization, because "he considered it a salutary preventive of that amalgamation, which would confound the two races and obliterate the traces of their distinction." Similar arguments, bent on maintaining these "irresistible" "natural" differences, were advanced from colonial days through the Emancipation Proclamation by other, even more eminent advocates of black emancipation and colonization. In 1781 Thomas Jefferson asked in *Notes on the State of Virginia*, "Will not a lover of natural history, then, one who views the gradations in all the races of animals with the eye of philosophy, excuse an effort to keep those in the department of man as distinct as nature has formed them?" Jefferson's argument against race mixture was reiterated in 1862, when Abraham Lincoln addressed a small group of black leaders in the White House on the subject of returning all American blacks to Africa. "You and we are different races," he said. "We have between us a broader difference than exists between any other two races."[18]

Both Jefferson and Lincoln were articulating a general fear of amalgamation shared both by those who advocated some form of black emancipation and by the anti-abolitionist "gentlemen of property and standing" in antebellum America. For the latter, especially, Leonard L. Richards asserts, amalgamation was personally and intimately threatening: it tapped the "fear of assimilation, of being 'mulattoized,' of losing one's sense of identity." For such men, tied to family, class, community, and position, race mixture went beyond a threat to race purity: it was a harbinger of "the breakdown of distinctions among white men, the blurring of social divisions, and the general levelling process that they saw enveloping ante-bellum America"; it was a first step to becoming "cogs in a mass society."[19] For Southern women of the same class, such as Mary Boykin Chesnut, amalgamation also threatened a more private, familial order, as a well-known 1861 entry in Chesnut's diary suggests:

Like the patriarchs of old, our men live all in one house with their wives and their concubines; and the mulattoes one sees in every family partly resemble the white children. Any lady is ready to tell you who is the father of all the mulatto children in everybody's household but her own. Those, she seems to think, drop from the clouds.[20]

For both men and women, proslavery apologists, abolitionists, and reform-minded anti-abolitionists alike, the issues of race mixture and interracial sexual relations struck at the heart of basic assumptions about the individual's place in home and society.

The "stock" changeling formula in *Pudd'nhead Wilson*, then, altered by Twain so that "twinned" black and white babies are exchanged in their cradles, acts out an interchangeability between the races that resonates with anxieties of the 1890s as well as of the antebellum years. Just so, the end of the Civil War and Reconstruction were characterized by optimism and even by radical thinking on race relations that gave way in the eighties and nineties to something old, something new. The law, once used to regulate the peculiar institution of slavery, now underwrote the far more broad-reaching ideology of white supremacy in state laws regulating relations between the races and establishing rigid lines of segregation. By the beginning of the twentieth century, for example, laws against intermarriage were passed in all but one of the seventeen states that had made up the slave South in 1861, and as recently as 1930, twenty-nine of the forty-eight states made intermarriage illegal. At the same time, for purposes of racial identification, the color line was more stringently and narrowly defined. As late as 1970, for example, in Louisiana the legal fraction defining blackness was still one thirty-second "Negro blood." Fredrickson argues that "most southern states were operating in accordance with what amounted to a 'one-drop rule,' meaning in effect that a person with any known degree of black ancestry was legally considered a Negro and subject to the full disabilities associated with segregation and disfranchisement."[21]

Such heightened awareness of what George Washington Cable

called "the Negro Question" characterized the years during which Twain wrote *Pudd'nhead Wilson*. The new race laws and the accompanying cultural conversation about the South's "race problem" articulated for Mark Twain, in concrete social and political terms, a longstanding problem: the connection between the maintenance of social control and the construction of identity. During this period (extending roughly from the late 1880s through the 1890s), the debate over race relations brought to the fore two bodies of contemporary knowledge — one legal and one scientific — that asserted the feasibility of drawing sharp racial, sexual, or social lines around groups of human beings, thereby ensuring the divisions many believed necessary to social stability. For Twain the possibility of such certainty as held out by the law and by the science of heredity was as deeply attractive as it was illusory and destructive. These contradictions finally collide in the conclusion of *Pudd'nhead Wilson*, when lawyer/detective/scientist David Wilson puts to the legal test the science of fingerprinting — a method of differentiating "each man from all the rest of the human species," according to the geneticist Francis Galton, "to an extent far beyond the capacity of human imagination."[22]

Alone among Mark Twain's fictional detectives, most of whom, he once commented, "extravagantly burlesque the detective business — if it *is* possible to burlesque that business extravagantly," David Wilson is genuinely adept at the procedures of detection and proof.[23] His chosen profession, the law, depends upon this skill, but since his fatal half-dog joke prevents him from practicing law in Dawson's Landing, his ratiocinative powers reveal themselves in more eccentric ways. Wilson's eccentricity as well as his outsider status remind us that he was created in the image of Sherlock Holmes, one of Twain's several forays in exploiting the comtemporary market for detective fiction. Conan Doyle's Holmes had been a best-selling phenomenon in America ever since the first Sherlock Holmes story, *A Study in Scarlet*, appeared in *Beeton's Christmas Annual* (1887). An alienated intellectual, Holmes had popular appeal in part because he stood out from the institutionalized police detectives of the Pinkerton series or the Beadle dime novels. Holmes's "passion for definite and exact knowledge," for example, sometimes isolates him even from the devoted Watson, who criticizes the detective's intellect in *A Study in Scarlet* as "a little too scientific . . . approach[ing] to cold-bloodedness."[24] In creating his own detective, Twain picks up on the somewhat alienating ratiocinative powers of Conan Doyle's popular character: Tom Driscoll snidely sings Wilson's praises as the "great scientist running to seed here in this village."[25] In *Pudd'n-head Wilson*, as in popular detective fiction, one condition of intellectual power is isolation from the community, which, like Dawson's Landing, both fears and needs its scientists.

Mark Twain also appropriated from popular fiction the equation between seeing and deductive power, perhaps most memorably expressed in the insignia of the Pinkerton agency, which bore an open human eye with the motto "We Never Sleep" beneath it. Sherlock Holmes's power, too, is notably ocular; his special vision enables him to deduce biographical facts from ordinarily unnoticed details. Wilson's superior intellect also expresses itself through superior visual observation. Both his hobbies of reading palms and collecting fingerprints demonstrate a type of Holmesian second sight, for they emphasize the reading and interpreting of signs that are, to the interpreter, visible traces of the past in the present. In this fascination with ocular proof, Twain draws upon the popular caricature of the detective with magnifying glass, bending over what seems like invisible matter, collecting all possible facts because even trivial details may prove to signify.

When a whole elaborate plot may be thus untangled by discovering one essential fact, we have abandoned the problematic nature of causation in the real world of masters and slaves, where victim and victimizer both are bound together by the institutional effects of slavery. No such entanglements can remain in the secure universe of the detective story, where fixed laws give meaning to particular events, and, through the detective's knowledge, random events are ultimately arranged into one coherent line of causality from the murderer to the deed.

The characters in Twain's novel react to the deductive powers of the detective with much the same combination of awe and skepticism that Twain himself sometimes expressed toward the writer's omniscient eye. Indeed, we know, he went so far as putatively to reject his own authorial omniscience in the preface that connects *Pudd'nhead Wilson* to *Those Extraordinary Twins* (the Siamese twin tale "changed itself from a farce to a tragedy while I was going along with it" and other, new characters began "taking things almost entirely into their own hands and working the whole tale as a private venture of their own," leaving Twain with not one "but two stories tangled together"). And of David Wilson's own interpretive abilities, Tom Driscoll mocks, "Dave's just an all-around genius, . . . a prophet with the kind of honor that prophets generally get at home – for here they don't give shucks for his scientifics. . . ."[26] If Twain's detective, like the self-professed "jack-leg" novelist himself, is less a prophet than a disturber of the peace, and if his "electrifying revelations" at the end of the novel are more disruptive than restorative, then what judgment are we to make of his solution to the mystery of a murderer's identity? More particularly, what are we to make of *how* rather than *what* he knows: along with the murderer, what is on trial in the courtroom conclusion is Wilson's method of deducing identity, his "scientifics," the fingerprinting system.

In this case, the author shares his character's passion for scientifics, for while writing *Pudd'nhead Wilson* in 1892, Clemens "devoured," as he put it, Francis Galton's *Finger Prints*, just published that year. In part his enthusiasm came from the novelty, and hence, he thought, salability of this material; "the finger-prints in this one is virgin ground," he assured his publisher Fred Hall, "absolutely *fresh*, and mighty curious and interesting to everybody."[27] But in larger part Clemens was fascinated by both the scientific findings and the credentials of the eminent geneticist (and cousin of Charles Darwin) Galton. Recalling in 1897 how he had relied on Galton's book while writing *Pudd'nhead Wilson* in 1892, he wrote in a letter: "The fingermark system of identification . . . has been quite thoroughly & scientifically examined by Mr. Galt [*sic*], & I kept myself within the bounds of his ascertained facts."[28] Chief among the facts on which the plot turns is Galton's demonstration that fingerprints can establish the identity of the same person at any stage of his life, between babyhood and old age (and for some time after his death, Galton adds), as well as differentiate between twins ("It would be totally impossible to fail to distinguish between the fingerprints of twins, who in other respects appeared exactly alike").[29]

Even more provocative for Clemens, I would argue, than these particular "ascertained facts" was Galton's broad and spirited endorsement of the wide-ranging potential of fingerprinting as a method of "personal identification." Not only would the prints be of value in identifying criminals, Galton points out, but also in ferreting out the less willful kind of imposture that had long fascinated Mark Twain: the possibility "of a harmless person being arrested by mistake for another man," for example, "and being in sore straits to give satisfactory proof of the error."[30] "Let no one despise the ridges on account of their smallness," Galton urges a possibly skeptical readership.

They have the unique merit of retaining all their peculiarities unchanged throughout life, and afford in consequence an incomparably surer criterion of identity than any other bodily feature. . . . To fix the human personality, to give to each human being an identity, an individuality that can be depended upon with certainty, lasting, unchangeable, always recognisable and easily adduced, this appears to be in the largest sense the aim of the new method.[31]

Apparently persuaded as much by Galton's impassioned tone as by his facts, Mark Twain puts all of these claims to the test in the dramatic courtroom conclusion of *Pudd'nhead Wilson*. When Wilson unveils his theory of who murdered Judge Driscoll and presents the evidence that proves its soundness, he also implicitly tries the case for what Twain learned from his research in Galton's *Finger Prints*. This "mysterious and marvelous natal autograph," Wilson argues, constitutes virtually perfect proof of identity:

Every human being carries with him from his cradle to his grave certain physical marks which do not change their character, and by which he can always be identified. . . . This autograph cannot be counterfeited, nor can he disguise it or hide it away, nor can it become illegible by the wear and the mutations of time.[32]

Like Galton's, Wilson's tone becomes more impassioned, his parallel clauses building in length and intensity, as he moves beyond the data to contemplate the potential of what he calls these "sure identifiers." Fingerprints, in Galton's terms, reliable means of "Personal Identification," render deception through impersonation or accident impossible by enabling each individual to be absolutely differentiated from the rest of the species. Wilson waxes eloquent about this method, building suspense in the courtroom audience by defining what the method is not. This signature is not a person's height, "for duplicates of that exist; it is not his form, for duplicates of that exist, also, whereas this signature is each man's very own – there is no duplicate of it among the swarming populations of the globe!" Even identical twins, Wilson pointedly concludes, "carry from birth to death a sure identifier in this mysterious and marvelous natal autograph. That once known to you, his fellow-twin could never personate him and deceive you."[33]

At this point in the argument, Wilson pauses and, as Mark Twain the performer used to "play with the pause," theatrically lets his brief silence "perfect its spell upon the house," before putting on his final display, submitting himself to an actual, on-the-spot test of his claims. While his back is turned, he asks several members of the jury, whose fingerprints he has collected over the years and so knows well, to make their prints on a glass window in the courtroom, where the two accused twins will also make their marks. This experimental procedure, as he requests, is repeated twice on different panes, for as he puts it, "a person might happen on the right marks by pure guess-work, *once,* therefore I wish to be tested twice." The reader is almost as gratified as the courtroom audience when Wilson correctly identifies the various prints ("This certainly approaches the miraculous!" says "the Bench"). But the source of our gratification is different from theirs. For us, the only real suspense in the novel has been waiting not for the identity of the murderer (which we've known all along) but for the moment when Wilson would discover that he has the means to prove it. And that moment finally arrives in the suitably theatrical trial, which opens in chapter 20 with this rather ominous entry from "Pudd'nhead Wilson's Calendar": "Even the clearest and most perfect circumstantial evidence is likely to be at fault, after all, and therefore ought to be received with great caution."[34]

How, then, ought we to receive the evidence of the fingerprints? What do those "sure identifiers" actually reveal? Wilson, no longer the flamboyant rhetorician but the dispassionate man of science, now draws on the ostensibly neutral, value-free variables of science and the syllogistic structure of logical reasoning to complete his presentation of the evidence. The fingerprints tell us first, he argues, using the impersonal notation preferred by Galton, that "A was put into B's cradle in the nursery." "In the majority of cases," Galton remarks, "the mere question would be, Is the man A the same person as B, or is he not? And of that question the fingermarks would give unerring proof."[35] In the case Twain creates, things are not quite so clear. What happens next, Wilson explains, is that "B was transferred to the kitchen, and became a negro and a slave – but within a quarter of an hour he will stand before you white and free!"[36]

Neither the triumphant tone nor the burst of applause from the audience nor the aura of logical deduction and absolute clarity disguises the fact that Wilson's conclusion, though strictly "the truth," is also illogical and arbitrary, almost more confusing than clarifying. Fingerprints appear to be the one measure of unique, noncontingent individual identity, but are in practice relational indices that must be read in and against the context of other sets of prints. Yet in spite of the methodologically essential social context, the fingerprints tell us nothing socially, as opposed to physiologically, significant about either A or B as individuals, much less about the lives of "Chambers" or "Tom." What they prove, in fact, is that one can be interchangeably "white and free" and "a negro and a slave." In this way Twain thus out-Galtons Galton. Galton finally had to admit that fingerprints do not reveal racial grouping or characteristics; he acknowledged "great expectations, that have been falsified, namely their use in indicating Race and Temperament."[37] Rather than stopping at this point, Twain goes even further than Galton, showing that though fingerprints do, indeed, establish racial difference, those categories are not biologically fixed but rather culturally determined. Knowing, then, that Tom, considered white, was born black and enslaved and is once again so constituted does nothing to fulfill Galton's promise that fingerprinting will "fix the human personality" and "give to each human being an identity, an individuality." Instead, like any other "natural" index of the self — race or gender, for example — fingerprints point toward the culture that appropriates nature as the basis of socially constructed identities.

Rather than leading to any stable, independent determinant of identity, then, the fingerprints focus attention on the social context that authorizes their use in the science of "personal identification." That social context most explicitly enters the novel during the sentencing phase of the trial, the moment in the courtroom when the social voice speaks most directly to reaffirm its values and to reestablish the order disturbed by the crime. In Twain's case, though, the sentence accomplishes no such righting to order. Although the murderer, now defined as "the false heir," makes "a full confession" and is "sentenced to imprisonment for life," the creditors of his ultimate victim, not Judge Driscoll but "the Percy Driscoll estate," argue that "a complication" has ensued. Building much the same structure of logical reasoning as Wilson does, they establish first that "the false heir" should have been "inventoried . . . with the rest of the property" at the time of its owner's death; that he was thus "lawfully their property"; and furthermore, "that if he had been delivered up to them in the first place, they would have sold him and he could not have murdered Judge Driscoll." Hard on the heels of this stunning conjecture, in a triumphant burst of illogic, comes the conclusion to both the creditors' argument and to the novel.

therefore it was not he that had really committed the murder, the guilt lay with the erroneous inventory. Everybody saw that there was reason in this. Everybody granted that if "Tom" were white and free it would be unquestionably right to punish him — it would be no loss to anybody; but to shut up a valuable slave for life — that was quite another matter.

As soon as the Governor understood the case, he pardoned Tom at once, and the creditors sold him down the river.[38]

The author and his reader see a different "reason" in this. If "Tom" or Tom or "the false heir" (the proliferation of names seeming to replace human substance with linguistic form) is pardoned only to be sold down the river, we reason, then words like "pardon" and "punish" (and "reason") have lost their meaning in Dawson's Landing, a society where an "erroneous inventory" can first assume the human burden of guilt and then, logically, escape human punishment. By the same agreed-upon fiction, a "valuable slave" is defined as chattel, not to be held accountable for human antisocial acts, and therefore even the law must obey the rules of logic and conclude of the murderer that "it was not he that had really committed the murder." But because only whites have the "unquestionable right" to punishment under the law, it also follows that in this case a valuable slave – will-less chattel – must be "pardoned" for a crime he could not by definition have committed. Finally, if the guilty party is the "erroneous inventory," then all of Southern society is implicated in the crime because it participates in and oversees the slave system that requires such inventories. The trial thus bears witness to the anguished tangle of contradictions surrounding the slave system, and, further, to the strange fact that while these contradictions expose themselves in the legal and linguistic fictions of slave society, they also keep that world from falling apart under their weight.

To thus discover that the criminal in a detective story is not one individual but an entire society is to disrupt the premise of narrative order and social justice upon which the form is based. Fomenting such disruption, Twain in 1893 appraised "the whole story" a success, "centered on the murder and the trial; from the first chapter the movement is straight ahead without divergence or side-play to the murder and the trial."[39] Such a narrative invokes expectations of the ritual confrontation between law and criminality that concludes most detective fiction with the restoration of order. Rather than coming to a schematic resolution, though, the conclusion of *Pudd'nhead Wilson* initiates polarities between innocence and guilt, slave and free man, loss and profit, punishment and pardon, only to expose them finally as "fictions of law and custom." Similarly, the changeling plot does not culminate in the conventional discovery of the child's noble birth, a discovery which ordinarily vindicates the noble behavior he has exhibited from the beginning as it restores class lines and fulfills the audience's desire for order, both narrative and social.

Pudd'nhead Wilson deliberately denies such wish fulfillment. Through the detective plot that its author so admired, the novel arouses the reader's craving to discover, the desire to turn the act of reading—palms, fingerprints, or texts—into a means of discovery and resolution of apparently impenetrable mysteries. But if Twain's detective acts out the author's desire that human knowledge could so accurately systematize the world, the character also oversees the author's deconstruction of his own fantasy. Wilson's classification system helps him to discover the false Tom (or "Tom"), but in exposing a "white" man as a "black" slave, it also exposes the whole society that created, but does not acknowledge, its own nemesis. Whether one calls this a discovery of America's "own secret self" (Leslie Fiedler) or of "the repressed guilt which has gathered at the heart of slavery" (James Cox), such a discovery makes knowledge more of a threat than a deliverance.[40] Tom's fate threatens that the hidden taint of black blood could be disclosed in any white person, tapping the dread that all "secret murderers are said to feel when the accuser says 'Thou art the man!'"[41] The craving to discover has reversed itself into fear of exposure.

Thus Pudd'nhead Wilson's Calendar entry for the final chapter reads ironically, "October 12, the Discovery. It was wonderful to find America, but it would have been more wonderful to miss it."[42] For a murder mystery, in which the murderer's identity has been known from the very beginning, to close with a problematic discovery (is to confirm the earlier hint that *how* we know has replaced *what* we know as the object of inquiry. When the novel ends, its various scientific and legal bodies of knowledge—definitive means of identification and differentiation—result in no certainty at all.

More disturbingly, the contortions that the law goes through at the last moment to reverse or undo itself in Mark Twain's courtroom—the guilty party, once white and free, identified as a slave, defined as property, and pardoned—are analogous to the process of legal reversal enacted after Reconstruction. In a series of state laws and Supreme Court cases, the "freedmen" saw their legal rights reduced, eroded, and eventually nullified by the law. The process that once outlawed slavery in the late 1860s legalized segregation in the 1870s and 1880s, culminating most explicitly two years after the publication of *Pudd'nhead Wilson* in the "separate but equal" doctrine of the 1896 Supreme Court case, *Plessy v. Ferguson*.[43] The novel confirms in an American context what Twain's later anti-imperialist essays would conclude globally: that in spite of the Fourteenth and Fifteenth Amendments, the law had not only failed to solve the "Negro Question," but worse still had been positively enlisted in the service of reconstituting white supremacy, both in the United States and abroad. That many of the world's "civilized," "Christian" powers were, under the banner of imperialism, justifying the colonizing of Kipling's "lesser breeds without the law" meant for Twain a double defeat. Thereafter neither the law, which permitted and enforced the farce of "separate but equal," nor science, which shored up racism with theories of "natural" degeneration, would hold out any promise of addressing America's most pressing social problem.

But as well as casting doubt on these hallowed bodies of knowledge, two great allies of late-nineteenth-century American civilization, the novel also implicates the author's own omniscience and control over his text. Mark Twain's Preface, we remember, brings his own intentionality under suspicion, deriding himself as the author of a tale that "changed itself from a farce to a tragedy" while it was also "spreading itself into a book." Perhaps what he most rejected was how both stories resist the project of definitively separating the innocent from the guilty in social, racial, and sexual terms. Neither the farcical issue of the Siamese twins' singular/plural duality, nor the tragic issue of black/white division is ever resolved. The trials – a total of three in the two works – fail to ascertain individual responsibility in the face of necessity (either the twins' physical bond or the biological, social, and economic ties of slavery). And finally, the specific methods of identification through readings of the body (skin color, fingerprints) also fail, in Galton's terms, to "fix the human personality, to give to each human being an identity, an individuality."

Instead of a "true self" and clear standards of verification, what Mark Twain discovered in his own fiction was the constructed and artificial character of essential social measures of identity – measures that, as the history of race relations demonstrates, we nevertheless totally depend upon. The novel, therefore, also exposes even as it exemplifies the mechanisms by which we persuade ourselves that the constructed is the real. For without such constructs, or when they are momentarily inverted, the conclusion to *Pudd'nhead Wilson* suggests, the individual may find himself permanently displaced, nowhere socially recognizable. The "real heir," we remember, ends without a proper name or place or self, while the "false heir" disappears, pardoned and sold down the river. Mark Twain himself ends with his sense of authorial omniscience shaken, the writer still bound, the preface to the farce admits, by and to the unintentional disclosures of his own writing. Not even in the world of his own making could he imagine liberation under the law or discover a secure basis for knowledge of self and other. Like Aunt Patsy Cooper in *Those Extraordinary Twins*, Twain came increasingly to doubt whether he could "know — absolutely *know,* independently of anything [others] have told [him]" even that "reality" exists. Following *Pudd'nhead Wilson*, Twain's last major set of writings becomes obsessed with the question, "how do we know what we know is not a fiction or a dream?" The tendency in the thoroughly grounded, deeply historical *Pudd'nhead Wilson* to question conventional boundaries of racial identity expands in the dream tales into challenging the borders of reality itself.

MYRA JEHLEN

The Ties that Bind

Race and Sex in *Pudd'nhead Wilson*

L iterary fictions can no more transcend history than can real persons. Although certainly not universally acknowledged, in the current criticism this truth has replaced the former truth that literature is a thing apart. Once banned from the interpretation of books for violating the integrity of the imagination, considerations of race and sex (and of class) have entered into even the most formalist readings.[1] Race and sex are now found organic to problems of organic form. As a result, those problems have become vastly more complicated than when a literary work was thought to invent its own sufficient language, for then the task of the critic, although complex, was also simple, it was to show how everything within the text worked together, taking coherence as given. A poem or story was a puzzle for which the critic could be sure that he or she had all the pieces and that they dovetailed.

Neither assurance is any longer available; one cannot be certain a work seen as engaged in history is internally coherent, nor that the issues it treats finally hang together. This development is not altogether congenial to literary critics, who mean to analyze works, not to dismantle them. But if we take literature's link to history seriously, we will have to admit that it renders literature contingent, like history itself. My case in point is *Pudd'nhead Wilson*, the writing of which posed problems that were made impossible to resolve by the history of racial and sexual thinking in America. The ideologies of race and sex that Mark Twain contended with in this novel were finally not controllable through literary form. They tripped the characters and tangled the plot. *Pudd'nhead Wilson* exemplifies the tragedy of the imagination, a literary kind that, ironically, only a historical criticism can fully appreciate.

Pudd'nhead Wilson builds its plot upon a plot. The subversive schemer is a young slave mother named Roxana (Roxy), who is thrown into panic one day by her master's casual threat to sell some of his slaves downriver into the inferno of the Deep South. Reasoning that if he can sell these, he can as readily sell her baby, she first determines to kill herself and the child rather than lose it to the slave market. Then she finds another way. Being not only a mother but the Mammy of her master's child, she simply switches the infants, who look so much alike that no one suspects the exchange. In contrast to their perfect resemblance as babies, the two boys grow up totally unlike. The black child taking the white's name of Tom (for Thomas à Becket Driscoll), becomes a treacherous, cowardly thief; the white child, assuming the black name, Valet de Chambre (Chambers), is gentle, loyal, honest, and brave. Tom's path of petty crime leads eventually to murder, and his victim is his putative uncle and guardian, the much-loved benevolent Judge Driscoll. A pair of visiting foreign twins are wrongly accused of the crime and are about to be convicted when Pudd'nhead Wilson, a local sage in the tradition of shrewd Ben Franklin, uncovers the real murderer who is, coincidentally, the real black. The amiable foreigners are vindicated, the real white man is freed from his erroneous bondage and restored to his estate, and the murderer is punished. He is not hanged because — not being really a gentleman but a slave — he has to be punished as a slave: he is sold downriver into the Deep South.

Twain starts off simply enough with a farce whose characters' opportunistic prevarications expose established lies. The lie Roxy exposes when she successfully replaces her master's child with her own is that racial difference is inherent. As the ground for slavery, this racism is unambiguously false, its inversion of human truth dramatized in Roxy's dilemma: she can jump in the river with her baby or live in daily peril of its being sold down the river. Given those alternatives, her stratagem appears righteous and even fair despite its concomitant enslavement of the white baby. Without condoning this but simply by focusing on Roxy and her child, the story enlists the reader wholly on their side since the failure of the scheme can mean only the sale of mother and child, no doubt separately, or their common death.

But then things take an odd turn, which in fact will culminate in an about-face, the reversal ultimately going so far as to transform the exposure of Roxy and her son into a happy ending that rights wrongs, rewards the good, punishes the bad, and restores order all around. When, at an eleventh hour, Pudd'nhead Wilson unmasks Tom and justice is done, the reader is actually relieved and gratified. If by this intervention the story does not exactly celebrate the return of the escaped slave to bondage or his sale to the demons of tidewater plantations, neither does it regret these events. Roxy's broken spirit and the double defeat of her maternal hopes are pitiable sights to be sure, but there is a consolation prize. In *Pudd'nhead Wilson*'s finally rectified moral economy, Roxy's punishment is quite moderate. Not only are the legal authorities of the town of Dawson's Landing forbearing, but also "The young fellow upon whom she had inflicted twenty-three years of slavery continued [the pension she had been receiving from Tom]."[2] Exemplary generosity, to be sure, but also a startling turnaround. Roxy, who once was so helplessly enslaved that her only recourse was suicide, is now being represented as herself an enslaver. Adding insult to injury, the pension her victim bestows upon her makes her appear still more culpable. Roxy and her baby exit as the villains of a story they entered as the innocently wronged.

Twain recognized that this about-face required explanation. One reason Tom turned out so badly and Chambers so well, the narrator suggests, is because they were brought up in opposite ways. "Tom got all the petting, Chambers got none. . . ." The result was that "Tom was 'fractious,' as Roxy called it, and overbearing, Chambers was meek and docile" (18–19). Slavery is made to counter racism here much the way it does in *Uncle Tom's Cabin* and not to any better effect except that the black man made Christ-like by his sufferings is really white, so that in the absence of real blacks similarly affected the case is not fully made. All that these distortions of character argue is the evil of human bondage, not the equality of master and slave, and even less so when we know that the master is a member of the slave race. For Stowe, countering racism was incidental, indeed she had only a limited interest in doing so, up to the point of establishing the humanity of the slaves in order to argue her central case, which was against slavery. But this is not Twain's situation when he published *Pudd'nhead Wilson* in 1894, thirty-two years after Emancipation. In fact, his novel and its story of the baby exchange has little to do with slavery: the plot does not follow Chambers the white slave in order to depict the horrors of his condition, but Tom the black master and the crimes he has all his freedom to perpetrate. In appropriate contrast to *Uncle Tom's Cabin*, *Pudd'nhead Wilson* is only peripherally concerned with the atrocities of the slave system. Although Chambers is sadly disadvantaged by his years of servitude, his debility has too little force to motivate the novel, nothing much comes from it or is expected to. On the contrary, everything comes from Tom's ascension to power, all of it bad.

Nothing in the original premise of the story predicts this sad development, so the obvious question is, Why does Tom, the former slave, turn out so villainous and dangerous a master? The most congenial explanation—that Tom has been fatally corrupted by his translation into the class of oppressors—omits too much of the story to serve. Twain offers it only half-heartedly, presenting the true white planters as a decent lot, often absurd in their chivalric poses and inadequate to their ruling tasks, but on the whole men of integrity, faithful to their "only religion," which is "to be a gentleman . . . without stain or blemish." Even their slaveowning seems less evil than careless. The description of Pembroke Howard as "a fine, brave, majestic creature, a gentleman according to the nicest requirements of the Virginian rule. . . ." (4) mingles affection with mockery, and although his dash is balderdash, there are worse things—Tom for example. His sale of Roxy treacherously and symbolically downriver is transcendingly evil, branding him an unnatural son and a denatured man. To underline the exceptional quality of his betrayal, Twain shows Tom prepared to sell his mother twice over, for when she escapes and seeks his help against pursuing slave-hunters, only her threat to repay him in kind prevents him from turning her over.

It is more than a little perverse that the two characters who actually traffick in slavery are both black. Percy Driscoll's threat to sell his misbehaving slaves is the novel's original sin responsible for Roxy's desperate deed. But having the sale itself take place offstage and specifying that, unlike Tom, the judge only sells to his relatively humane neighbors and not to the Simon Legrees of the Deep South, attenuates our sense of the planter's guilt. On the contrary, the story pointedly reports Tom's plan to sell his boyhood companion Chambers, a plan foiled by Judge Driscoll, who buys Chambers to safeguard the family honor: "for public sentiment did not approve of that way of treating family servants for light cause or for no cause" (22). Tom's corrupting environment, therefore, does not explain why the disguised black is both more deeply and differently corrupted than his fellow slaveowners, a development that is the more startling because it reverses the initial expectations of virtue inspired by his first appearance as a hapless babe.[3]

But if no explanation emerges directly from the novel, consider its historical context. The year of its publication, 1894, was the eve of McKinley's election and a period of accelerating racism marked by the bloody spread of Jim Crow. The formative experience of *Pudd'nhead Wilson*'s era was the defeat of Reconstruction, not the end of slavery. In that context the story of the replacement of a white baby by a black has a local urgency we may miss at this distance. And its progress from a good thing to a bad as the black boy grows up to murder the town patriarch who is his uncle and to rob, cheat, and generally despoil the whole village, as well as plunge his mother into a worse state than she had been in before, makes as much sense in history as it fails to make in the story.

In the story, Tom's villainy appears only arbitrary. As much as Twain justifies Roxy's revolution by appealing to the transcendent motive of maternal love, making her insurrection finally inevitable and in no way a sign even of inherent rebelliousness, he damns Tom from the start as "a bad baby, from the very beginning of his usurpation" (17). So the good black is a woman; the bad, a man. The good woman, complicated enough within herself to act badly while remaining herself good, is black; the bad man, lacking interiority and simply expressing a given identification that is barely an identity, is also black. With this formula, *Pudd'nhead Wilson* emerges as a remarkable exploration of the anxieties aroused by a racist social structure, as a literary locus classicus of one modern (in its integration of individualist concepts of identity) paradigm of race, and perhaps most strikingly, as the exposition of the relation between the racial paradigm of race and a modern paradigm of gender. The conjunction of race and sex is more often pictured as an intersection but here it is an interaction. Moreover, this interaction does not simply join, but combines, race and sex so that in certain pairings they are more stringently limiting than when taken separately.

When Twain associates the black race with the female sex, he represents racism in the uncontroversially repugnant form of slavery. Roxy's force and shrewdness work to disprove stereotypes of servility. Her sovereignty over the children extends naturally to the story of which she is a sort of author. She achieves the highest status available to a fictional character when she and the narrator are the only ones who know what is going on and can truly identify the participants. The white baby's mother is dead, and his own father fails to recognize him. Roxy alone knows who he is – and what. Further, the way she knows this bears its own anti-racist implications; because both babies have flaxen curls and blue eyes, her discrimination can have nothing to do with physical characteristics. Thus as she identifies, them, in her own image, *who* Tom and Chambers are is entirely independent of *what* they are. They embody the American ideal of individualism, the belief that a man is what he makes of himself, which is potentially anything he determines.

Consonant with this liberal view, *Pudd'nhead Wilson* initially defines black character in universal traits as benign as Roxy herself. If Roxy at times falls prey to the lure of unattended objects, "Was she bad?" Twain muses. "Was she worse than the general run of her race? No. They had an unfair show in the battle of life, and they held it no sin to take military advantage of the enemy – in a small way." He insists, "in a small way, but not in a large one" (11). Even as Twain writes this, Roxy takes the very large military advantage of exchanging the infants. But the petty thievery, in this case not even her own, that has called down the wrath of her master and thus precipitated this ultimate transgression was a very small crime. If Roxy's pilfering turns to pillage, the novel suggests that this is not her fault, hardly even her doing, but that of a criminal society that monstrously deforms not only marginally guilty relations, but also purely innocent ones.

The night of the exchange, Percy Driscoll, whose threat to punish theft by selling the thief has raised for Roxana the specter of her child's own commodity status, sleeps the sleep of the just. By contrasting her master's smug oblivion to her anguished wakefulness, through which she becomes for this moment the story's consciousness, Twain condones and even endorses her crime. The novel continues to side with her when it is not Roxy but Percy Driscoll who enforces the children's inequality, permitting the ostensibly white boy to abuse the child whom he fails to recognize as his son (19). In this representation of the political economy of slavery in terms of the family, the author's voice speaks against the regnant patriarchy, espouses the oppressed, and applauds subversion. Fathers in Mark Twain are not a nice lot, and boys are frequently abused. A black woman enslaved by white men is the natural ally of white boys. Would that all boys had mothers like Roxy!

Tom's becoming a man, however, rearranges this scheme radically. His passage into manhood, marked by his return from Yale, seems to start the story over. At Yale he has been a desultory student but has acquired a number of grown-up ways that pose unprecedented grown-up problems. His indifferent intellect has prevented any deeper penetration, but Tom has acquired the superficies of elite culture, its dainty dress, and its mannered ways. The local youth naturally scorn such refinements, but when they set a deformed black bellringer dressed in parodic elegance to follow Tom about, the young popinjay is debunked more profoundly than anyone in the story suspects. And it is unclear just what is being satirized: is it simply foppish pretension, or rather some special absurdity of black foppery? Because the characters are unaware that their parody of Tom possesses this additional dimension, it becomes a joke shared by the narrator and the reader, a joke with a new target.

Twain had already mocked black dress when he described a despairing Roxy adorning herself for her suicide. Her ribbons and feathers, her wondrously gaudy dress, certainly reflect on her race, but the butt of the joke is not race as such. Being black is not given as ridiculous, although blacks may behave ridiculously. In the later episode being black is itself absurd: the private joke we share with the narrator is the very fact of Tom's negritude, that while pretending to be a high-falutin' gentleman, he is really a "Negro." Here, the novel begins its turnaround from the initial view implicit in the identical babies, that human beings are potentially the same to the final dramatization in the Judge's murder, of black duplicity and violence as inherent racial traits.

Tom's grown-up inferiorities in fact make his spoiled childhood irrelevant. He cannot have acquired his fear of duelling, for instance, from being raised a Southern gentleman. While his overexcited peers in the Dawson's Landing peerage fall to arms at the least imagined slight, Tom turns tail at the first sign of a fight. This is only one of a constellation of traits that define Tom as a different sort of beau ideal, the very type of the upstart Negro of post-Reconstruction plantation fiction: cowardly, absurdly pretentious, lazy and irresponsible, a petty thief but potentially a murderer. Born the generic, universal baby, Tom has grown into a very particular sort of man, unlike both his white and his black fellows; on the white side, he is not capable of being a master, and on the black, he has been dangerously loosed from the bonds that keep other black men in check.

I want to stress the next point because it is central to the racial/sexual paradigm developed in *Pudd'nhead Wilson*. The white man who has taken Tom's place might have been expected, in the context of the novel's increasingly essentialist view of race, also to manifest an essential nature. He does not. "Meek and docile" in adaptation to his powerless state, Chambers yet does not become a white man fatally misplaced among blacks, as Tom is a black man fatally misplaced among whites. This asymmetry embodies that of racial typing that applies only to the inferior race. The superior race, when defining itself in the terms of modern individualism, claims not a better type, but the general norm — universality or the ability to be any type and all of them.

Unhappily for Chambers, however, universality imparts only potential, a capacity to become rather than an already defined (therefore limited) being. That is, what characterizes the norm embodied in the superior race, instead of a particular set of traits, is universal potential. Such potential realizes itself in relation to environment: ironically, the white "Chambers" is far more vulnerable to the shaping force of the exchange, for had Tom remained a slave he would have unfolded into essentially the same man, although a crucially less powerful one and for that reason a less harmful one. So Chambers, unlike Tom, adapts to his sad situation and is shaped by it. In one important respect his adaptation represents one of the novel's most basic if unacknowledged issues. As I suggested earlier, in Roxy, Twain endorses a black woman's subversion of the white patriarchy, whereas in Tom, he rejects a black man's takeover. The fate of Chambers begins to explain why Twain distinguished so sharply between mother and son by revealing the stake in his relation to the latter.

That stake is manhood. Through Tom's usurpation, the white community of Dawson's Landing risks losing its manhood. A black woman exercising the authority of motherhood in a white society may call in question the domestic ideology of white womanhood. In *Pudd'nhead Wilson* this domestic ideology means the genteel sentimentalism of aunts and widows. Had it been only a question of Roxy's passing off her child as the child of a white lady, the baby switch would have been a disturbing but limited affair. But the far more encompassing event of a black man occupying the place of a white man, wielding the same power, usurping (Twain's repeated term) the authority of white fatherhood connotes a global reversal that, instead of emancipating the iconoclastic boy who typically articulates Twain's abhorrence of genteel culture, literally emasculates him. The subversion in Tom's usurpation of white identity turns Chambers into a woman, for femininization is the lasting result of that unfortunate man's slave upbringing. Once a black slave, he can never take his place among his real peers: "The poor fellow could not endure the terrors of the white man's parlor, and felt at home and at peace nowhere but in the kitchen" (114). Note that Chambers's loss of manhood is clearly regrettable only because he is white. A black man may be improved by the attenuations of femininity, as is the case elsewhere with Twain's motherly Jim. One stereotype of the black man threatens violence and uncontrollable sex. The other has him contemptibly effeminate. Black men are seen simultaneously as excessively male and insufficiently masculine. Inextricably entangled in these ideological contradictions, Tom is incoherently both. Although his final act is a stabbing, earlier in the story, disguised as a woman, he robs houses. The witnesses who fail to recognize in a dress the man they know as a white gentleman are actually seeing the real Tom, who thus shows himself one way and another not a real man.

By the logic of the different *kind* of identity that real men develop, a black mother can be the ally of rebellious boys, but a black father would rob them of their very selves as heirs to the mantle of universal (white) manhood. We stand with Roxy when she defies the social order to save her boy-child. But when this child grows up, he embodies a revolution which has displaced the erstwhile ruling children, usurping their manhood. Once this implication has been realized by the story's unfolding, even the benignity of Roxy's crime seems retrospectively less certain. On the last page of the novel, the story finally represents the exchange not as freeing the black child, but as enslaving the white.

That ending was implicit all along in the slave situation, which stipulated that the only way to free Tom was to enslave Chambers. This unhappy reciprocity, however, was not manifest in the story so long as it focused on mothers and children. The maternal economy is a welfare state. Its central concern is not production but distribution, and even when it is unfair, it has primarily to do with giving, allocating privileges and goods among the more or less undifferentiated members of a group who seek more not from each other but from the mother/state. But production, not distribution, was the chief care of the market-capitalist economy of the United States in the late nineteenth century; and in that context, distribution was a matter of competitive acquisition.

Much has been written about the relation of these two economies that in some respects confront and in others complement each other.[4] The peculiar slant of *Pudd'nhead Wilson* comes from presenting them not, as usual, synchronically, as simultaneous dimensions of one society, but diachronically, the market economy following the maternal. Thus sequentially related, with each one in its time defining the fictional universe, their contradictions emerge more sharply, along with the way that the hierarchy of family and state, private and public, gives the market the last word. It certainly has the last word in *Pudd'nhead Wilson*, as we will see. Although a mother may take something from one child and give it to another who needs it more but not deprive the former, in an economy in which personally recuperable profit is the bottom line, taking away and giving must show up on the ledger ultimately. And when self-sufficient individuals—men and fathers—possess unequal amounts of power or wealth, reallocation, however equitable, does mean deprivation: one gets only by taking away from another. At the point at which the story of Tom and Chambers leaves the nursery and enters the market-place, Tom, who as a baby was the innocent and even rightful recipient of the freedom he unjustly lacked, becomes a usurper; Chambers is seen to have been robbed.

The maternal and market economies which in their turn dominate the plot of *Pudd'nhead Wilson* do coexist to a degree. Although the story starts out in Roxy's control, the market wields overwhelming force from the first because the power of whites to sell blacks to other whites inspires the exchange of the babies. But at this point, even though in Roxy's world slavery functions as a harsh necessity that will ultimately deprive her of all power, the market as such is not yet the primary setting. Indeed, when this necessity first manifests itself, she resists successfully, temporarily returning her world to its prior order and keeping both babies. All through their infancy and childhood she administers her welfare system, taking care of both of them as fairly as she can under the circumstances despite the fact that her own child is in the master position and would be favored if she were fully to implement the unfairness of the slave system. When Tom is no longer a mother's child but his own man, however, he takes over the fictive universe and administers it his way. Because he is a man, whatever the quality of his administration, it participates directly in the patriarchal economy and in this new context the baby exchange realizes its meaning in the trade of Chambers's white manhood for Tom's black impotence, and vice versa.

Because the asymmetries of race and of sex are parallel, Roxy's innate character as a mother is congruent with her innate nature as a black woman. Paradoxically, even ironically, this very limit permits Twain to endow her as a character with a considerable degree of transcendence, the way that Flaubert, for example, endows Emma with much of his own sense of self without ever questioning the non-transcendence of female selfhood as such.[5] Roxy, a black woman, actually approaches individualist selfhood while her son is denied it altogether and is depicted as capable of achieving self-creative powers only by the outright usurpation of whiteness. On the other side, Chambers's failure to achieve manhood, in dramatizing the transcendence of white identity which defines itself by going beyond nature, also points up a terrible vulnerability that springs from the very quality that makes white men superior. To be capable of making oneself and one's world is a very fine thing, but that ability has its price. The price of white men's power of self-creation is the risk of failing not only to achieve but also to be, whereas women (as such though not always as fictional characters) and blacks are essentially and thus invulnerably what and as they are born. And this inequality of vulnerability counterbalances racial inequality, coming first, in the ideological and psychological universe of *Pudd'nhead Wilson*, to equate the plights of blacks and whites then finally to make blacks appear stronger, or at least more threatening.

An essentialist identity requires, for the good of the community, more social control; it is too little vulnerable to be allowed as much freedom as identities that carry their own constraints in their vulnerability. It is generally recognized that the ratio of self-making to being determines the status of modern individuals, so that the more a man is his own author the higher he ranks and the more authority he wields. The converse is less often articulated, that an essentialist identity not only brands the socially inferior but also necessitates their submission. In one scene of *Pudd'nhead Wilson* this logic almost begins to justify slavery.

In this scene, Chambers has just revealed to Roxy that her errant son is a dissolute gambler who at the moment owes the huge sum of $200. Roxy is stunned: "'Two – hund'd – dollahs! . . . Sakes alive, it's mos' enough to buy a tollable good second-hand nigger wid.'" Now the irony, indeed the wit, here lies in the fact that the $200 Tom has gambled away are $200 *he* would fetch, being himself "a tollable good second-hand nigger." But the possibility of buying and selling human beings, which up until this point has implied such intolerable violations of natural law as the separation of mothers and children, has become, astonishingly, a way to measure and *preserve* genuine value: Tom's worthlessness as a white man is measured by his gambling away his worth as a slave. Lest we not grasp this point fully, Twain spells it out in the ensuing dialogue. Chambers's report that Tom has been disinherited for his scandalous conduct infuriates Roxy, who accuses her supposed son of lying, calling him a "misable imitation nigger." Chambers retorts, "'If I's imitation, what is you? Bofe of us is imitation *white* – dat's what we is – en pow'full good imitation, too . . . we don't 'mount to noth'n as imitation *niggers*'"(35). But Chambers *is* an "imitation nigger," being really white. He is also really honest and good, as he shows by openly declaring his purported blackness, unlike the true blacks in the story who lie about race. Once again the reader of *Pudd'nhead Wilson* understands a scene by knowing better than the characters and the better knowledge is the reality, the truth, of race.

The preceding scene plays directly to the concealed switch of Tom and Chambers and exactly negates its original thrust that whites and blacks can be exchanged because in *fact* blacks can be essentially white – read: universally human. Now on the contrary, the exchangeability of physically resembling blacks with whites represents the way apparent likeness can mask real and profoundly different beings. Initially, clothing and social status were seen as hiding real human resemblance. These same superficial differences have come to mask real difference, and the bodily likeness of Tom and Chambers that first expressed their common humanity now renders their total opposition invisible. People may *appear* equal, it says, but they are really not.

What matters in this scene is the real difference between Tom and Chambers while what had mattered about them at the start was their real likeness. Coincidentally in the same episode, Roxy herself sadly dwindles as the narrator ascribes her anger at Chambers for reporting Tom's disinheritance to her fear of losing "an occasional dollar from Tom's pocket" (35). This is a disaster she will not contemplate, the narrator laughs. But earlier, Roxy defined herself in relation to a larger disaster, not the loss of a dollar but the sale of her baby. And when two pages later Tom actually does refuse his mother a dollar, the novel's shift of perspective is complete: where the injustice of racial inequality was first measured by the violation of Roxy's natural motherhood, now inequality will be justified by the spectacle of the emancipated and empowered Tom's unnatural sonhood. Roxy's subsequent threat to expose him articulates his falseness; the "truth" about Tom is that he is false, that he is not who he is or should be. Henceforth the story of *Pudd'nhead Wilson* is not about interchangeable babies irrationally and unjustly rendered master and slave, but about a black man who has taken a white man's place. Roxy herself, who first identified Tom as a universal baby – who revealed him as "white" as any baby – now dubs him a "nigger."

The first name she had bestowed on her child was the name of a servant, Valet de Chambre. The fine sound of it appealed to her, Twain explained, although she had no notion what it meant. But we do, and when we first laugh at it we do so out of affectionate condescension. When later Roxy exchanges this name for that of a lord, Thomas à Becket, we begin to see that both names have their serious implications: they project a spurious identity that yet determines what each man becomes. In the end, however, we find that we have been wrong twice, first when we took the names lightly, but second when we took them as seriously damaging misnomers. Valet de Chambre was all along the correct identification of a man born a servant and for a time dangerously misnamed a master.

Thus Roxy's final renaming of Tom does not merely exchange one name for another, but redefines the very nature of his identity. When she called her son Tom and thereby made him the equal of whites, it was on the ground that in himself he was indistinguishable from whites. Scrutinizing his golden babyhood dressed in white finery, she marveled: "'Now who would b'lieve clo'es could do de like o'dat? Dog my cats if it ain't all *I* kin do to tell t'other fum which, let alone his pappy'" (14). When babies are fledgling individuals, one as good as another in anticipation of each one's self-making, pappys cannot tell one from another, for indeed paternity is irrelevant. But when racial nature enters into identity, paternity becomes all-important.

Roxy announces Tom's blackness to him by saying "'You ain't no more kin to old Marse Driscoll den I is!'" With this she claims him— "'you's my *son*'" (41)—but the ground of this claim is a renunciation. Even as she demands that he recognize her maternal authority— "'You can't call me *Roxy*, same as if you was my equal. Chillen don't speak to dey mammies like dat. You'll call me Ma or mammy, dat's what you'll call me . . .'" (42)—she abdicates the transcendent authority that earlier enabled her to name *him* into an identity she had more than borne: created. Henceforth he may call her "Ma or mammy" and accede to her orders, but for both this will ratify subjection, in fact servitude. Even the reclamation of this maternal authority is limited, bounded by the surrounding patriarchy. "'You'll call me Ma or mammy,'" Roxy storms, "'leastways when dey ain't nobody aroun.'" For him to recognize her as his mother in public, of course, would reveal his real identity as a slave, whereupon Roxy would lose him to the authority of his father, and to the paternal authority of the slave system. Roxy had been able on her own to make Tom white, when she was in charge and nature and race were in abeyance, but making him black requires her to invoke white patriarchal authority.

Through a master irony the revelation of his real white father seals Tom's status as a black son: a chastened Tom surrenders to his new status by asking timidly, "'Ma, would you mind telling me who was my father?'" (43). The final link connecting Tom to his mother— identifying him as a slave—is her knowledge, her ability to call on the name of a white man. And through the medium of Roxy's pride as she tells him that his father was "'de highest quality in dis whole town—Ole Virginny stock, Fust Famblies'" (43), the authority of Cunnel Cecil Burleigh Essex parodically but surely reaches forward from that past all-generating moment when he could command Roxy to bear his son, to declare that son now a black slave. "'Dey ain't another nigger in dis town dat's as high-bawn as you is,'" she ends, proferring an identity that is the fatal opposite of the one she had conferred on him at the start of the story. "'Jes' you hold yo' head up as high as you want to — you has de right, en dat I kin swah'" (43).

One sign of Roxy's demotion to the status of just another fond mother is that she is wrong about this: Tom has neither the right nor the capacity to hold up his head. Despite his excellent white descent, he is simply not of cavalier mettle. And on the occasion when he runs away from a challenge to duel, Roxy herself sadly draws the inevitable conclusion: not even his superior white siring can redeem his fatal flaw: "'It's de nigger in you, dat's what it is. Thirty-one parts o'you is white, en on'y one part nigger, en dat po' little one part is yo' *soul*. 'Tain't wuth savin'; 'tain't wuth totin' out on a shovel en tho'in in de gutter. You has disgraced yo' birth. What would yo' pa think o' you? It's enough to make him turn in his grave'" (70).

Roxy's racism is comically undercut certainly, but in the service of what alternative view? We are the more at a loss for a proper liberal riposte in that Roxy's parting shot travels directly to the end of the novel and its definitive return of Tom to the now unproblematical status of "nigger." "'Ain't nigger enough in him to show in his finger-nails,'" she mutters, "'en dat takes mightly little — yit dey's enough to paint his soul'" (70). It was because of his white, thus raceless or race-transcendent fingernails that she had been able to raise him to the status of master. But now it turns out that his fingernails did not accurately represent the case. Rather, as all discover, his identity lies in his fingerprints, and no one transcends his fingerprints.

Wilson's resort to fingerprints to establish Tom's true identity solves more than the judge's murder. It provides a more encompassing resolution of the novel as a whole, for his astounding revelation restores both racial and sexual order. Indeed, in that any satisfactory ending would require that the truth be revealed and, because only Roxy could reveal it, it is not easy to imagine how else Twain could have ended his story. For Roxy to solve the mystery would not constitute an ending, not so much because her confession would be dramatically unlikely as, on the contrary, because by identifying Tom and Chambers accurately she would reassert precisely the power to identify that has so badly compromised Dawson's Landing. For Roxy to name her son and his white counterpart a second time would confirm her authority, thus perpetuating the racial dilemma of *Pudd'nhead Wilson*. Reconstruction would continue.

In Pudd'nhead Wilson, however, Twain finds an alternative truth-teller. Male to a fault in his entire self-sufficiency, Wilson counters, then surpasses, Roxy's authority: to the babies' identical fingernails which enabled Roxy to declare them identical, Wilson opposes finger-prints representing the apotheosis of difference, uniqueness. Now, fingerprints are not racially but individually distributed. Therefore they cannot testify to Tom's racial nature but only to his personal character. Nonetheless, in the courtroom scene, Wilson invokes the telltale fingerprints categorically, to rule out categories of persons in order to identify the individual miscreant as himself the represen-tative of a category.

Wilson, who represents the category of authoritative white men commanding both law and language, begins by announcing this authority to the community: "'I will tell you.'" This is what he tells them: "'For a purpose unknown to us, but probably a selfish one, somebody changed those children in the cradle'" (112). So far is the story from casting doubt on any aspect of this emerging elucidation, its miraculous verity is reinforced when the narration turns briefly to Roxy portrayed thinking pathetically that "Pudd'nhead Wilson could do wonderful things, no doubt, but he couldn't do impossible ones," and that therefore her secret is safe. But what is impossible to her is as nothing to Wilson. Having named the exact time of the exchange (thus returning to the crime's origin to master it whole) and having identified the perpetrator, he continues in the irrefutable idiom of scientific formulas: "'A was put into B's cradle in the nur-sery; B was transferred to the kitchen, and became a negro and a slave . . . but within a quarter of an hour he will stand before you white and free!'" He controls time and place. "'From seven months onward until now, A has still been a usurper, and in my finger-records he bears B's name.'" And now the coup de grace: "'The mur-derer of your friend and mine—York Driscoll, of the generous hand and the kindly spirit—sits among you. Valet de Chambre, negro and slave.'" Roxy's response is poignantly telling. Before the miracle of white masculine omniscience, she can only pray: "'De Lord have mercy on me, po' miserable sinner dat I is!'" (112–13).

Wilson's godlike authority has appropriated the story, raveling the order of the white community as he unravels the case. In the pro-cess the story has also been rewritten, however, with a new begin-ning that brushes Roxy's motive aside with the casual conclusion that whatever this motive was, it was selfish (in context a stun-ningly ironic term that the text leaves uninflected) and redrawing its characters and issues in stark blacks and whites.

And what about Pudd'nhead himself? The instrument of resolution, what is his relation to the order he restores? First, although he wields the authority of the white patriarchy, he is not himself a father but a bachelor, a lone, even an outcast figure whose own authority the village has only this moment recognized and then only because of his trick with the fingerprints. For himself, although he rescues the established order, he is acutely and at times bitterly aware that those who administer it are not often worthy of their power. The joke that earns him the nickname "Pudd'nhead" has turned out more serious than it seemed. On his first day in town, Wilson became a fool in the eyes of his neighbors when he declared that he wished he owned half a loudly barking dog so he might kill his half. Now he has saved half a dog, while the other half dies. There is nothing joyous in restoring the status quo of Dawson's Landing. Twain may have been reluctant to see black men acquire the power of whites and may have viewed their bid for a share of power as outright usurpation. He did not vindicate white society. This is a familiar dilemma in his work generally which frequently ends, as does *Pudd'nhead Wilson*, in a stalemate between radical criticism and an implicit conservatism expressed in the refusal or the inability, when it comes to it, to imagine significant change. The stalemate here seems particularly frustrating: change must be defeated, yet nothing of the established way of life appears worth preserving.

The depth of *Pudd'nhead Wilson*'s concluding depression may gauge the sounding it takes of perhaps the most profoundly embedded images in the American mind, the images of race and sex. Separately but especially interacting, these images sometimes not only activate the imagination, but they also disable it, trapping it as Mark Twain seems to have been by the impossible adjuncts of racial equality and white authority, of maternal justice and patriarchal right. When in the end the rule of the white fathers is reestablished by the fiat of law, there is no rejoicing. Pudd'nhead Wilson himself is an outcast and a failure. Playing out his private charades alone in his study, he represents the writer as outcast and failure. If he also represents the writer as lawgiver and defends the system he hates, even against its victims who threaten it by trying to lift their oppression, this is not a productive paradox but a paralyzing contradiction. Pudd'nhead Wilson, expressing his author's own anguish, would really have liked to kill his half of the dog but was afraid finally of leaving the house unguarded.

CAROLYN PORTER

Roxana's Plot

Many critics of *Pudd'nhead Wilson* have agreed on the extraordinary power of Roxana as a character, while others have at-
tended more to her problematic behavior, such as the radical changes
in her demeanor, her white supremacist attitudes, and her capacity
for both cruelty and tenderness, and have offered a variety of explanations either to defend or to attack Twain's portrayal. The critical
response shows a marked tendency, however, to use her sexuality to
account for both Roxana's power and the problems she raises as a
character.[1] For example, in the most compelling and nuanced analysis
of the novel as a whole, James M. Cox calls Roxana "the primary
force in the world she serves" and underscores that force as "sexual."
He traces a circuit of power in the novel's plot structure originating
in the white, male lust of the Southern slaveholder. What "explains
Roxana's power," according to Cox, is the "submerged lust" of the
white male, whose "passion" is transferred "from the white wives to
the slave mistresses." Roxana serves as the repository of "the guilt
of their repressed desires," so that "their guilt is objectified in her
repression." Her son, Tom Driscoll, thus becomes "the avenging agent
who carries back across the color line the repressed guilt which has
gathered at the heart of slavery." Therefore, Tom's assassination of
his foster father, Judge Driscoll, is the thematic center of the plot,
and his "murder suggests the anarchy which the white society has
by its own action released upon itself." As Cox tracks the trans-
mission of guilt and desire *from* the white male *through* the black
female and *back onto* the white male, he also tracks power from
its "origin" in the white, male "lust out of which [Tom] was created"
down to Roxana, who is only the "immediate source" of Tom's "dark
force." If "the power of those who rule has been transferred to those
who serve," its origin remains marked at the site of the white, male
father, and its final restoration is secured by the "dark comedy" of
Pudd'nhead Wilson's ascent to the position of authority left vacant
by Judge Driscoll's death. The oedipal pattern, in which white males

hold, lose, and then regain power, is fulfilled by David Wilson's story, which is itself plotted along a circuit of power originating with and returning to the white male. "Having precipitated the crisis," Cox notes, David Wilson concludes the plot he has himself "set in motion by his own idle remark to Roxy" when he unveils Tom Driscoll as both black and a parricide.

It is this dual status, of course, which makes Wilson's plot resolution a case of "disjunctive irony." He exposes the killer in the community's midst, but by the same act he exposes that community's "secret history" of miscegenation. Thus the indictment of the society implicit in Wilson's exposure of Tom Driscoll as "black" is finally deflected and its threat recontained by the restoration to the status quo it effects by convicting him as a killer. Accordingly, both Wilson and his plot are "repressive," serving to recontain and deny the "erotic motive" buried in the adultery which is the "primal action . . . from which the entire plot originates."[2]

I have rehearsed Cox's argument at such length because it seems to me that he delivers the definitive analysis of the novel's plot, insofar as it can be understood to originate in the white, male desire, repression, and guilt of the Southern slaveholding class, and to culminate in the simultaneous exposure and repression of that origin. He delivers as well a definitive diagnosis of the novel's flaws as a product of that same repression operating through the plot machinery centered in *Pudd'nhead Wilson*. Within the terms of his argument, both the analysis and the diagnosis are wholly persuasive. Yet those terms themselves are grounded in an essentially Freudian framework marked by oedipal struggle and a focus on repressed male sexual desire that is significantly limited and limiting in its treatment of Roxana. Such a framework accounts splendidly for David Wilson's plot as a repressive mechanism, but it cannot finally account for the fact to which Cox himself testifies when he says that "Only Roxana has the power to create drama and to become the primary force in the world she serves."[3]

Such a statement underscores every reader's sense that Roxana generates a good deal of the energy that moves the often creaky machinery of the novel forward. If we focus on Roxana as "primary force," even as a kind of prime mover of events in the world she serves, then the repressive function that Cox accurately attributes to *Pudd'nhead Wilson*'s plot looks rather different. What makes that plot's censorship visible becomes less a matter of its success at repressing Roxana's sexuality than its *failure* wholly to recontain the disruptive force of what amounts to another plot – Roxana's plot.

In order to account for Roxana's resilient power, which suffers repeated deflection and suppression only to return in new guises and disguises, we need to attend to her status as mother. "Mother" is to be understood here not as a "natural" but as a social identity defined in Roxana's case by a set of particular legal, social, and cultural codes that make the slave mother at once antebellum America's most tragic victim and potentially one of its most powerful subversive agents.

No doubt the axiomatic problem of the Southern black woman stereotyped as "Jezebel" (to borrow the label used by the historian Deborah White) plays a critical role in Roxana's troubled creation, but the critical focus on her sexuality has obscured her status as mother and underestimated the force of the anxieties unleashed in both Twain and his readers by a figure who is both sexual and maternal. The opposition Jezebel/Mammy in the antebellum South repressed a great deal of social and psychic conflict and confusion among the white slaveowning classes. As with the analogous oppositional stereotypes of the black man as rapist/Uncle Tom, an ideologically secured psychic defense operates to force the Other into two contradictory, interdependent, and equally mystified positions. Such either/or stereotypes only point to the excluded middle that they repress.

This region has been, of course, partly colonized by literary convention as the site of the "tragic mulatta" who signals and represses at once the fact that slave women were sexual objects of desire in the eyes of their white masters. And clearly, Roxana's status as a mulatta is crucial to Twain's story. But in order to assess what makes it crucial, we need to see it within the context that Hortense Spillers has described. For Spillers, the mulatta is a figure of containment for white culture; what in reality threatens exposure – the physical evidence of miscegenation – is culturally recontained by a defensive sign deployed as an "alibi, an excuse for . . . otherness," as Spillers calls it. A term that "designates a disguise, covers up . . . the social and political reality of the dreaded African presence," *mulatta* or *mulatto* serves as a "semantic marker" that "exists *for others* – and a particular male other," according to Spillers. As a mulatta, Roxana certainly exposes the "covert tradition" of miscegenation, but her serial ordeal as a mulatta *mother* intent on saving her son exposes much more. Typically, the mulatto is a son or daughter who undergoes a crisis upon discovering a black or mulatto mother. Roxana is – first and last – that mother. Indeed, her status as a mulatta is established only to be immediately refocused by her status as a slave mother.[4]

Roxana is introduced as a set of contradictions: she sounds black, but looks white; "majestic" in "form and stature," fair-complexioned, she has a "heavy suit of fine soft hair," but it is "concealed" by a "checkered handkerchief"; "sassy" among her black friends, she is "meek and humble" among whites. These contradictions result from that "fiction of law and custom" that officially resolves them by dictating that "the one-sixteenth of her which was black out-voted the other fifteen parts and made her a negro." Thus Roxana's invisibly "mixed blood" matters not at all to her cultural, social, or legal identity. What matters – as Twain immediately reports – is that "she was a slave, and salable as such," and her child "too, was a slave."[5] In short, Roxana's white appearance is a plot device in the story of a slave mother and her child. Indeed, it is the central plot device, a tragic equivalent to "those extraordinary twins" in the "suppressed farce" that Mark Twain said he "pulled out by the roots" from the mother-text of *Pudd'nhead Wilson* (119). But it is her son's mulatto status, more than Roxana's, which invites Twain's brief exploration of the plight of the "tragic mulatto" faced suddenly with news of a black mother.

By attending, then, to Roxana as the slave mother, we can gain access to that blurred, confused, and anxiety-producing region of the excluded middle repressed by the binary, Jezebel/Mammy (a space of contradiction too often sutured over in white culture by the figure of the tragic mulatto). What comes into and out of focus in Twain's portrayal of Roxana is a region where mothers are sexual, slaves are powerful, and women are temporarily out of (and thus in) control. Roxana's agenda as a protagonist is set by her status as a slave mother, but in pursuing that agenda, she exposes not only the falseness of the Mammy/Jezebel opposition, but also the inadequacy of either "Mammy" *or* "Jezebel" to contain or represent the slave woman. The partitioning of sexuality from motherhood that is implicit in much of the critical response to Roxy is undermined in the novel itself, and thus such critical analysis cannot account fully for either Roxana's power or her problematic behavior. Indeed, that partitioning is a defense against what Twain was unable entirely to defend against – a slave mother wielding a subversive power in ways that threaten both narrative and social control.

From this viewpoint, *Pudd'nhead Wilson*'s coherence is undermined not by the dissociation of Roxana's character from a plot that operates to repress her sexuality, but rather by a struggle between the unsuccessfully suppressed slave mother's story and the story of the white fathers whose oedipally grounded plot Cox makes so lucid. In other words, *Pudd'nhead Wilson* is the scene of conflict between a repressive paternal plot and a subversive maternal one.

Before exploring Roxana's plot, I should make clear the severe limits within which its subversive power emerges. Roxana's remarkable series of strategems to save her son do not, finally, succeed. No matter how powerfully Roxana wields the forces she learns to appropriate from the white patriarchy, her son is finally sold down the river. The plot I wish to foreground here is one that only emerges temporarily, in what might be called the artificially induced gap between the white slaveowning patriarchy's *threat* of such a sale, and its final enforcement of that threat twenty-three years later. Roxana's "plot" exposes contradictions in the white, slaveowning patriarchy, signaling a potentially explosive negative power to thwart and undermine its rule, but her plot has no power to *alter* that rule itself, and more pointedly, it has no power to deflect that rule's crushing force on the slave mother's bond with her child.

In Roxana's plot, the primal action is not adultery, but childbirth. The first event recorded in this plot is also the first event recorded in the novel; in chapter 1, after describing Dawson's Landing and its "chief" citizens, Twain reports of Percy Driscoll, "on the first of February, 1830, two boy babes were born in his house; one to him, the other to one of his slave girls, Roxana by name" (5). But it is not until Roxana switches these two "boy babes" that her plot proper gets under way. No doubt, she acts in response to a threat from above, the threat of her son being sold down the river. However, it is worth noting that the threat is not immediate; she is not guilty of the recent petty theft to which her fellow slaves have confessed and for which they, not she or her child, are going to be sold. Her master's act, in other words, is technically what starts the plot rolling, but only technically. It is Roxana's ability to understand the threat posed by this incident that leads to her radical response.

It is also worth noting how radical a response it is. Provided with motive and opportunity, she is also endowed with the courage to commit an act so violent in its implicit threat to her society that it is unthinkable, and so invisible. The children's striking resemblance, and their white appearance, coupled with the fact that no one can tell the difference between them save Roxana, provide opportunity only. The threat of her child's ultimate loss provides motive only. What we can easily fail to notice is that Roxana's act requires a will so strong, and a calculating mind so acute, that it can conceive of a "plot" so "beyond the pale" that it cannot even strictly be called criminal. The law cannot forbid it because the law cannot imagine it. When the "law" in the shape of Pudd'nhead Wilson, detective man-qué, is finally forced to imagine it, the discovery requires the modern "scientifics" of fingerprinting, and even with this tactical aid, Wilson remains thoroughly befuddled until the very last moment.

The mainspring of Roxana's plot lies in the implications of the exchange with which it begins. When Roxana switches the children, she commits two subversive acts: she reduces the real Tom to slavery, and she creates a new "Tom" by renaming her son. As Evan Carton has pursuasively argued, "her attempt to save one twin by dooming the other reiterates the structure and the illusion of the society it challenges." What Carton calls the "paradoxical imitative character of her enterprise" indeed haunts it from the outset, but it does so in ways that subvert as well as reiterate the white slaveholding patriarchy.[6]

This dimension of Roxana's endeavor comes into view if we attend first to her son's translation from slavery to freedom and the terms on which the novel invites us to understand it. Roxana acts to save her own son from a fate not only worse than death, but also functionally equivalent to it. From beginning to end, the novel enforces this equivalence between death and being sold down the river. When she conceives her plan, at the story's outset, Roxana is on the way to drowning both herself and her child to save the latter from being sold down the river. At the story's end, Tom is saved from life imprisonment by being restored to his status as property and sold down the river. As Richard Chase, among others, has noted, "down the river" serves as the novel's version of hell, and throughout the story, it is clear that there is little difference between death and slavery in the Deep South.[7]

As Orlando Patterson has argued, part of what makes slavery a form of "social death" is its status as a commutation of an actual death sentence.[8] The slave "lives" under the continuous threat of a death to which she or he is nonetheless socially condemned. Because the slave can always, in principle, be killed by the master, the slave's life is always conditional on that master's consent that he or she live. In *Pudd'nhead Wilson*, this condition is foregrounded when Roxana perceives the threat posed by Percy Driscoll's decision to *refrain* from selling her fellow slaves down the river *this time*. She understands that her very life, and that of her son, is permanently conditional – a commuted death sentence that can always be revoked at the master's will. For the slave, what this means is that survival depends upon remaining alienable. Roxana's fellow slaves express heartfelt gratitude at being sold, but not sold down the river. In terms of the novel's identification of death with being sold down the river, they preserve their lives by remaining alienable. This logic is pervasive. Percy Driscoll's treatment of his slaves is echoed at the end of the novel: "As soon as the Governor understood the case, he pardoned Tom at once, and the creditors sold him down the river" (115). The novel closes as it opens, with a pardon followed by a sale.

In this light, Roxana's opening gambit needs to be understood not only as a reiteration of the white patriarchy's structural inequality, but also as a specific imitation of the white master's power to enforce that inequality in the form of social death. Comprehending her permanently alienable status as itself predicated on a threat of death permanently in force, Roxana first seizes power over her life and that of her child by deciding to end them both. She then finds a way of commuting this double death sentence when she conceives her design to "save" her son. She thereby institutionalizes a power over her son that imitates the slaveholder's dominant position as commutator of a death sentence that he can always revoke. But if Roxana seizes the power to commute the metaphoric death sentence of being sold down the river, she clearly still lacks the power to enforce that threat.

This is hardly surprising. After all, no matter how violently subversive Roxana's secret act is, it remains — and *must* remain, to have its immediately intended effect — secret.[9] Further, Roxana remains a slave. What is surprising is that twenty-three years later she is able to enforce the threat implicit in her deed, to exploit its actual consequences in terms that, for a while, at least, transform her imitation of the master's power into an active appropriation of it.

In order to understand this turnabout, it is necessary to explore the relation of killing to selling in the slave economy of social death as it operates in this novel, so as to see — what Patterson fails to see — how the slave mother is specifically positioned in and by that economy.

The complexity of the analogy between killing and selling is revealed by the novel's technically flawed ending. As everyone has noticed, in order to sell Tom down the river at the end, and thus restore him to his status quo ante, Twain must "forget" that Tom's double, Chambers, has already been sold and Percy Driscoll's estate thereby credited with the money Judge Driscoll paid for him. Because there is one slave whose exchange value is already accounted for, in this view, the sale of a second under the same name is redundant — a gratuitous addition made necessary by Twain's desire to underscore what George Spangler aptly calls a "parable of property."[10]

Yet what counts as contradiction on the surface of Twain's plot is quite consistent with the rules of property and exchange as they operate in Roxana's plot, where the economy's operation is experienced by the slave. Here, the condition of alienability is definitive, as Roxy demonstrates when she allows Tom to sell her back into slavery. Legally, she may be "free," but actually, she can always be sold and resold. In this economy, the same person can clearly be sold twice, that is, for a double profit. All that is necessary is that the person be designated "black." In Roxana's case, as she notes, it is her speech that identifies her as black despite her white skin. In Tom's case, it is finally his fingerprint that identifies him as black, despite his white speech *and* his white skin. But in both cases, all that is required for a person to be placed on the sale block, to be alienable, is proof of a specific racial identity. What makes Tom's sale at the end possible as well as logical, then, is an extension of the principle of the slave's alienability in terms of his or her name, or more accurately, the lack of one.

The real anomaly of Tom's sale lies deeper – in the perception that two bodies have been sold under the same name. From the slave's perspective as always-alienable property, once his racial identity is proven, "Tom" has no identity at all as a person. This is clear from the fact that he loses his patronymic surname. As Roxy tells him "you ain't *got* no fambly name, becaze niggers don't *have* 'em" (41). If racial identity is "a fiction of law and custom" and thus manipulable by and subordinate to capital, so is the identity that depends upon, and is represented by the "name of the father." Once reduced to nameless property, that is, two bodies can occupy the same alienable identity. This point is, in fact, demonstrated at the book's outset by Roxy's exchange of the babies and helps to explain why the exchange lacks symmetry. If Roxana "saves" her son from sale, she simultaneously places her master's son, potentially, on the sale block, an exchange that does not free anyone. Because the legally defined distinction between "free" and "slave" seems so absolute, it is easy to assume that Roxana's original exchange of the free Tom and the enslaved Chambers operates on a one-to-one ratio. If one is free, the other is a slave, and vice versa. But this ratio holds no more firmly within the economic system than it does within the racist society. If both children in the end become niggers, the one legally and the other culturally, this outcome is consistent with the contaminating force of a system of property and exchange value that replicates the contamination of nigger blood. Once a slave, always a slave. Once a nigger, always a nigger – even to the fifth generation in Tom's case. In other words, the exchange of A for B, as David Wilson later refers to the original Tom and Chambers, is no simple act of turning A into B and B into A so that the two can be returned to their original condition by a legal decision. Instead, it turns the free Tom (A) into the slave Chambers (B) and yet, despite Roxana's continual efforts, B ultimately reverts to B. Tom's reversion to the status of alienable property is always, from the moment of his un-naming, a potential threat.

In short, the symbolic form that the threat takes for Tom is the erasure of his surname. Without that name, he is subject to the slave's condition, in which death is either exchanged for alienability or else accepted as the only alternative to it. It is the lack of the name that accords a paternally founded identity that matters here. Accordingly, the exchange of the names, "Tom" and "Chambers," which designates a one-to-one exchange of two identities for each other, is functionally a chimera and is irrelevant in a system in which all that matters is the presence or absence of "Driscoll." This point is underscored by the striking contrast between what is at stake in Wilson's loss of "David" for "Pudd'nhead" and what is at stake for either Tom or Chambers in the loss or gain of "Driscoll."

Roxana's power to erase that name provides her with the leverage to appropriate and turn the white master's power against him. She has, of course, exercised this power over the real Tom Driscoll at the outset. But in blackmailing her son, she threatens to repeat her own initial erasure of "Driscoll" from the real Tom's name by un-naming the false Tom. The power she calls upon here enables her to complete the imitation of the white master by enforcing the threat of death he wields, and this power emerges as a result of her status as a slave mother as dictated by the antebellum slave code.

Because this code observed the Roman rule of matrilineal descent, in which the child follows the "condition" of the mother, no matter what the father's status, a slave mother, in giving birth, delivered her child into slavery. It is this rule, among other unwritten laws, that Roxana subverts when she inserts her son into the patrilineal, and patriarchal, system, in which he becomes the "heir of the house" (15). In one sense, this is a re-insertion because her son's father is a member in good standing of the white master class to which Roxana, in effect, returns her son. As a changeling, Tom thereby temporarily escapes his maternal legacy of slavery and social death and eventually devotes his attention to retaining his paternal legacy of a surname and the property accompanying it. But (in this context at least) the fate of the newly enslaved Chambers, whose name has been erased, designates the hidden power that eventually displays itself in Roxana's aggression against the white patriarchy. A crack in the patriarchy is opened to view on the site of the slave mother's body as the locus of miscegenation, a gap that opens because of the patriarchy's legal recognition of the slave mother as the source of her child's *lack* of identity. If in giving birth, the slave mother condemns her child to social death and the status of always-alienable property, that birth blots out the father and thereby condemns the child to an always-alienable condition marked by a lack of surname. Thus, within the slave family, the slave child is automatically made into property, and the slave father is automatically rendered legally impotent. The body of the slave mother, meanwhile, is the putatively passive conduit that the white master uses to castrate the slave father and appropriate the slave child as always-alienable property.

That, in any case, is how the system was supposed to function. But as the work of social historians – not to mention black women novelists – has abundantly demonstrated, slave mothers *and* fathers actively and often effectively combated the corrosive effects of this system on the slave family. (Despite which, the discussion of the "Black Matriarchy" and its sins never seems to stop.) Roxana's is neither a stereotypical nor a real slave family, but her case can perhaps help reveal the flaw in a system predicated on the slave mother's passivity. In Roxana's blackmail plot, we find that mother appropriating as power the negation of the father enacted by the son's birth. What makes this possible is also what makes it radically subversive: the father is a white master (as, in this case, is the son, at least on the face of it). But this subversive power exercised in succession over two "white" sons (one, "real", one "false"), in revenge for "two centuries of unatoned insult and outrage" (39), is blighted by the subtext of horror that emerges in the fate of two "black" sons, and the condition of the mother that fate exposes. It is difficult, as well as painful, to separate these two sides of Roxana's plot, but it is necessary to do so in order to grasp the plot's implications.

If in her initial switching of the children, Roxana erased the real Tom's paternal identity, she returns twenty-three years later, recognizing her power to erase that of the false Tom. If we translate real/false to "white/black" or master's son/slave's son, she has already, of course dealt this blow, sub rosa, against the master's son. Having given birth to her son, Roxana saved him from the fate his birth decreed. By appropriating the matrilineal descent rule, she suspended its negative power in regard to her son; at the same time, she exercised that power over the master's son. If she can blot out one father, she can blot out another. But now, the negative power implicit in the slave mother's position becomes explicit, as the repressed returns literally with a vengeance. Roxana has recognized her power not only to erase the name of the father by identifying her son, but also to threaten with death the white master who is her son by exposing him as her son. The slave mother's power to negate paternal identity, both disclosed and suspended at the moment Roxanna exchanged the babies, is now unleashed and aimed not only at Tom, but also through him at the white patriarchy, against which Roxana turns the same threat on which its power relies.

More specifically, until Roxana's return, all that Tom has to lose is his inheritance. After her return, and her revelation of his origins, he stands to lose his name and, symbolically, his life as well. By exploiting his fear of the first loss, Roxana is able to make good her threat of the second. And by exploiting his fear of the second, she is able to siphon a livelihood from the Judge's coffers. She thereby wreaks her revenge *on* Tom for mistreating her, and *through* him, on the white masters whose crimes she wants to avenge. Tom's life now depends upon providing for her survival, as befits the slave's relation to his master. Of course, because Roxana's extorted funds depend upon Tom's retaining his legacy, and thus upon his remaining in the judge's good graces, they both remain subject to the white master. Yet *within* this patriarchal system, Roxana has opened a rift that enables her revenge, and through Tom, she creates havoc in Dawson's Landing.

The whole show, of course, is a bluff. Roxana cannot prove that she is her son's mother. Like all bluffs, hers can work only by not being called, but that it works for so long is testimony not only to Roxana's shrewdness as a "blackmail" artist whose manipulation of Tom makes him seem almost smart on occasion, but also to the obliviousness of the white masters whose social structure she subverts. That it works for so long testifies particularly to the remarkable blindness of David Wilson; Roxana knows Wilson to be her chief adversary from the start, but it takes him forever to see her as his.

Indeed, all the white fathers lack personal force, to put it mildly. Essex ("Tom's" real father) is – significantly – no more than a name. Percy Driscoll, his next "father," dies bankrupt, his finances having apparently gone into decline soon after his own son's birth. As for Judge Driscoll, his central identity lies in his reputation as a gentleman. He can swing elections, but he is too "infatuated" with Tom to exercise any genuine authority over him (93). The story of how Chambers acquires the name "Tom Driscoll's nigger pappy" suggests that effective paternal power might reside in the vacant position of the black father, were the "black" son allowed to become a father, that is, possess a name. This incident also foreshadows the relation between

Tom and the Judge. Like the Judge, who keeps believing Tom despite Tom's repeated failure to make good on any of his promises to reform, Chambers believes Tom when he says he is drowning and thus "unfortunately"—as Twain says—saves his life. Tom then stabs Chambers, and when that fails to kill him, Tom tries to have Chambers sold down the river. When Judge Driscoll buys Chambers in order to "prevent" this "scandal," he ironically "saves" his brother's real son from the death that such sale implies. When the white patriarchs act in this novel, they act blindly. Further, the Judge's primary means of eliciting our respect is his friendship with David Wilson, the "true son" who finally names his "father's" killer and assumes his "rightful" position of authority in Dawson's Landing.

But Wilson, if we bracket his calendar, *is* a pudd'nhead. His intelligence is proven, and his ascenscion to authority vindicated in the end, but only after what amounts to Twain's extended humiliation of him as a detective who is remarkably dull-witted when it comes to reading his evidence. Most noteworthy is his persistent and blundering confusion over the identity of the "young woman" in Tom's room, "where properly no young woman belonged," and his search for this "mysterious" girl's fingerprints, despite his faith that a "gentleman" like the Judge "could have no quarrels with girls" (97). Roxana, certainly, has a "quarrel" with the class represented by the Judge, and in light of this fact, Wilson's "pudd'nheadedness" reflects the white masters' blindness to the violent power of the black woman in its midst. Tom wears his mother's clothes to disguise his movements as a thief and to cover his getaway as a murderer, and so Pudd'nhead Wilson pursues the clue of the mysterious woman in black. But what is a red herring on the novel's surface points to a vital truth at its center: Roxana, as a "black" woman, has turned Tom into her instrument for revenge. Figuratively, the knife that Tom uses to kill the Judge is an extension of the knife Roxana holds on Tom when she forces him to accompany her home in St. Louis. That none of the appointed authorities of Dawson's Landing imagine this is hardly surprising. That Wilson fails to see it suggests that the superior intelligence that Dawson's Landing has marginalized all those years may be somewhat overrated.

Aggressive and shrewd, the Roxana who deceives Wilson and rules Tom, advising him in his thievery while forcing him to "behave" more effectively than any of his fathers, ought to present a gratifying spectacle, not least because with Tom as her agent, running in and out of houses and dressed in her clothes, Roxana has everyone in Dawson's Landing thoroughly baffled and confused. But as any reader of *Pudd'nhead Wilson* can attest, gratification is hardly the word for our responses to this novel. To account for this, we need to attend to the other side of the slave mother's unique position as the locus of negation. Roxana's status as "imitation white" provides the precondition for her campaign of vengeance, a campaign that exposes a critical gap in the slave economy of social death, a gap that opens precisely on the site of the mulatto mother. What enables her attack on the white patriarchy is that she can turn the power inscribed on the slave mother's body – the power to negate the slave father – back on the white father. But this radical displacement entails the alienation of that father's "white" son as well, a fact that serves Roxana's purpose only insofar as Tom is that "white" son. But of course, "Tom" is not Percy Driscoll's "white" son. He is Roxana's "black" son.

Consequently, what looms up behind Roxana's vengeful subversion of the white fathers is the fundamental and unchanging horror of the condition that motivates it – the slave child's "natal alienation" from his mother, and her foredoomed loss of him. In the excruciating chapter 4, for example, in which Twain describes Tom's childhood culminating in "an abyss of separation" between Roxana and "her boy," the abyss in question is not simply that which opens as the master-slave relationship overtakes and destroys the mother-child bond. Several ideologically charged and contradictory codes (e.g., the black Mammy and her white charge and the white mother's love of her child) circulate through the story told in this chapter, but none wholly deflect the horror of the situation they both describe and obscure – that of the slave mother condemned to the loss of her child. Beneath the confusions of real/false and white/black lies the distinction "my son"/"his son," and the erasure of two white fathers' names entails the destruction of two "black" sons' lives. Satirizing the Southern ideology that exalted the Mammy's devotion to her white owner's children as well as theirs to her, Twain displays Roxana as full of "impotent rage" at Tom, and Tom as an irredeemable little bully to her. Twain includes a hilarious account of Tom as a "bad baby" that must have rung as true to the mothers of Twain's day as it does to those of ours, but the humor is corroded throughout by the racist implications it inevitably fosters. Likewise, when he appeals to the white culture's sanctification of the mother, Twain both satirizes this ideology, calling Roxana a "doting fool of a mother," whose son becomes her "master, and her deity," and yet invokes its cultural force by depicting Roxana's fall "from the sublime height of motherhood to the somber deeps of unmodified slavery," as Tom's "chattel" and "dog." What makes this chapter so painful to read is what both destabilizes Roxana as a character and generates the entire novel's radically disjunctive tone. In appealing to such codes to tell the story of a black mother's alienation from a "white" son become a "master," Twain's chapter exacerbates the horror of the slave mother's plight as not only the victim, but also the reproducer of social death. What is represented explicitly as a double-bind blocking the immediate avenues of revenge implicitly refers us to the violently severed bond between slave mother and child.

That is, because she is "imitation-white," as Chambers tells her, Roxana can subvert the matrilineal rule of descent, but only at the cost of losing her son entirely. By disowning him, she makes him free but no longer hers. Once the maternal bond to him is worn thin by his mistreatment of her, she is faced with the fact that to "own" Tom as hers, even if she could prove her claim, would make him a slave, subject to being sold down the river – the very fate from which she had set out to save him. But, as we have seen, Roxana finds a way out of this impasse; by threatening to "own" him before the Judge, Roxana can bring vengeance on him as well as on the white masters. What she cannot do is "save" her son, for the dilemma she faces with regard to her "white" son – to own him is to make him a slave – uncannily reiterates precisely the slave mother's constitutive double-bind: to give birth is to inflict social death. In other words, to give life to her child is to condemn him to death: it is this contradiction – so brilliantly explored in Toni Morrison's *Beloved* – which reveals what the economy of social death that Patterson describes entails for the slave mother. And it is this logic which Roxana's plot both resists and horribly confirms. If to blot out one father means that you can blot out the other, the same negativity entails that any child you have you must lose. From the opening moment when she decides to drown her child, to the closing one in which he is sold down the river, death is the slave mother's predetermined legacy that Roxana tries to, but finally cannot, abort. The choice she confronts at the outset, between seeing her son sold away or killing him herself, in retrospect collapses; from her position, death is not merely the equivalent of being sold down the river, but identical to it.[11]

From this vantage point, the space of the narrative opened up between Percy Driscoll's threat of sale and his creditors' final enforcement of that threat twenty-three years later may be figured as a space pried open between the jaws of a vise. In a sense, what keeps those jaws from closing for so long is the continual substitution of alienability for death that Roxana negotiates. For example, Chambers becomes alienable so Tom can "live"; Roxana sells herself back into slavery to save Tom; and Tom must find the money to buy Roxana back in order to save his life. Because the white slaveowning masters continue to buy and sell, and the "inventory" remains intact, they remain blindly aloof from the feverish strategems we observe going forward around them. Like Percy Driscoll, as a class they are too concerned with their speculations to notice any substitutions in the specific bodies that are the vehicles of their capital. Recall that no matter how much Roxana's second owner may admire her, he is quite satisfied to be reimbursed for her loss. From the white slaveowning class's viewpoint, the slave's life *is,* quite literally, his or her alienability as property so that the "erroneous inventory" held responsible for the judge's murder is corrected to everyone's satisfaction by Tom's final sale down the river. But from Roxana's viewpoint, that sale is her son's death, snapping the vise shut forever.

Roxana's plot, then, drives in two directions at once. Most explicitly, it operates to subvert the white patriarchy. The plot device of an "imitation white" slave mother focused Roxana as a slave mother of 1850 through the lens of the 1890s, with its "one-drop" rules, its lynchings, Jim Crow laws, and *Plessy v. Ferguson* two years away. Roxana's power to erase the name of the father thus emerged and enabled Twain to assault, humiliate, and expose the white Southern gentleman, to attack virulently the slave society he had ruled and the racist society he had bequeathed and still ruled. Thus, Cox is quite right to identify the novel's target as the white Southern patriarchy. What needs to be added is that it is the matrilineal rule of descent reinscribed on the mulatto mother that makes Roxana such a powerful weapon in Twain's arsenal. The negating power that the white patriarchy has invested in the body of the slave mother backfires here. If the white fathers have used the slave mother to erase the name of the black father, Roxana turns this negating power back onto the white fathers. Insofar as it is a matter of revenge against the white fathers, then, Roxana's subversive power is appreciable. But insofar as it is a matter of sons rather than fathers, her plot backfires on Roxana herself. If what the slave code termed "the condition of the mother" enables Roxana to blot out the white father, it also compels her to blot out the "black" son – *her* son, for whose sake she had acted in the first place.

On the one hand, Roxana's plot foregrounds the radical difference in the fates of the two sons in order to drive home the moral idiocy of that "fiction of law and custom" that enforces the color line. But on the other, it also exposes the similarity in their fates; for the slave mother, that is, both fates are "killing." The slave mother's constitutive double-bind is thus explosively revealed, but corrosively recontained by the *Pudd'nhead Wilson* plot. This, I believe, is why Roxana as a character is thoroughly contradictory in herself – and destabilizing to the entire novel.

It is not only Roxana's sexual force that must be repressed. Nor is it only a question of Pudd'nhead Wilson finally bringing down the curtain on Roxana's career as an "imitation" master. Most fundamentally, what gives Roxana's plot its radical and disruptive force lies in the contradiction at its heart – a contradiction we can imagine Twain violently warding off even as it looms up more powerfully all along – the contradiction between a power to negate, but one unleashed from within – and brutally reinforced as – the slave mother's negated position. This contradiction might account for, although by no means redeem, the well-known moments in the novel that provoke a kind of moral vertigo in the reader, such as Roxana's appeal to "white folks'" example to justify her exchange of the babies, her infamous genealogy speech, or the scene in which she excoriates Tom for his cowardice and blames the nigger in him. Such an account would require another essay, but I could suggest how we might proceed. For me, one of the worst among many moments in *Pudd'nhead Wilson* comes in the courtroom scene, when Roxana cries out, "De Lord have mercy on me, po' misable sinner dat I is!" and the clock strikes twelve. In some nightmarish version of Cinderella, Roxana is reduced to the rags of a racial stereotype. And rather than a prince, she finds in Twain a stern judge who condemns her in the final chapter as the recipient of a pension from "the young fellow upon whom she had inflicted twenty-three years of slavery" (114).

There is no way to read this and other comparable passages without succumbing to a kind of ethical nausea. But there may be a way to account for such passages by suggesting that the aggression Roxana's plot unleashes in Twain's text is driven out of control by the horror that provokes it, so that Twain gives in to the temptation to turn that aggression against Roxana herself. As black women in this country have always known and have testified repeatedly, this would not be the first or the last time that the black mother got blamed.

JOHN CARLOS ROWE

Fatal Speculations

Murder, Money, and Manners in *Pudd'nhead Wilson*

"You can't do much with 'em," interrupted Col. Sellers. "They are a speculating race, sir, disinclined to work for white folks without security, planning how to live only by working for themselves. Idle, sir, there's my garden just a ruin of weeds. Nothing practical in 'em."

"There is some truth in your observation, Colonel, but you must educate them."

"You educate the niggro and you make him more speculating than he was before. If he won't stick to any industry except for himself now, what will he do then?"

"But, Colonel, the negro when educated will be more able to make his speculations fruitful."—CHARLES DUDLEY WARNER AND MARK TWAIN, *The Gilded Age* (1873)

It is good to begin life poor; it is good to begin life rich—these are wholesome, but to begin it poor and *prospectively* rich! The man who has not experienced it cannot imagine the curse of it.—*Mark Twain's Autobiography*

In the "Conclusion" of *Pudd'nhead Wilson*, Tom Driscoll is sentenced to "imprisonment for life," only to be claimed as the legal property of the creditors of the Percy Driscoll estate, who had been able to recover only "sixty per cent" of the indebtedness of the estate at the time of Percy's death in the fall of 1845. The final two paragraphs of this uncanny novel constitute Twain's most withering satire of slavery as a legal and economic institution. Claiming that "'Tom' was lawfully their property and had been so for eight years," the creditors claim that his imprisonment would deprive them further of their property and any return they might expect from its "investment." Their arguments go well beyond, however, Twain's customary satire of the obvious absurdity involved in defining a human being as chattel. The creditors argue successfully that the violation of their rights occasioned by the mystery of Tom's origins is the real cause of the murder of Judge Driscoll: "[I]f he had been delivered up to them in the first place, they would have sold him and he could not have murdered Judge Driscoll, therefore it was not he that had really committed the murder, the guilt lay with the erroneous inventory. Everybody saw that there was reason in this."[1] The absurd attribution of a murder to an "erroneous inventory" is understood conventionally as Twain's satire of an antebellum legal system that in its worst moment would throw out Dred Scott's suit for liberty on the grounds that as a slave he had none of the legal rights of a U.S. citizen. Indeed, the conflict between property rights and civil rights is such a common theme in Twain's writings that this final turn in the already labyrinthine legalities of *Pudd'nhead Wilson* seems merely to underscore a familiar issue.

Yet by 1894, the surreal legal and existential situation of the antebellum slave must have seemed an increasingly anachronistic issue for the contemporary reader, even if the social and economic fates of black Americans were recognized by many to be as hard as ever.[2] Twain's historical romances, as I think such works as *Huckleberry Finn, Pudd'nhead Wilson, A Connecticut Yankee,* and *The Prince and the Pauper* deserve to be called, employ historical distance to suggest how little the contemporary reader's society has progressed from the serfdom of either medieval England or antebellum America. In each of these works, Twain suggests that apparent – and often very dramatic – social changes merely have reinstated rigid social and class hierarchies; hints and foreshadowings of how such social transformations will effectively repeat the past quite often are incorporated in the dramatic action of the historical romance. Thus the fate of Jim at the end of *Huckleberry Finn* – a freed black man with nowhere to go – or that of the educated and freed black man ("a p'fessor in a college") scoffed by Pap Finn (in chapter 6) foreshadow accurately the plight of emancipated blacks under Reconstruction.[3] More obviously, the technological marvels that Hank Morgan brings to Arthurian England merely intensify the violent power struggles of the ruling class. In *Pudd'nhead Wilson,* the arbitrariness and irrationality of the law will survive the Civil War and Emancipation without substantial reform.

Despite the thematic continuities Twain may establish between the preindustrial societies in which his historical romances are set and modern, industrial America of the Gilded Age, he often subscribes to his own special "history" of an America divided strategically by the Civil War. The rural, settled, slow-paced Midwest of "Old Times on the Mississippi" is forever changed by the railroads, land development, and westward expansion that accompanied – both as causes and effects – the political upheaval of the Civil War. I need not quote here those familiar passages from *Life on the Mississippi* in which Twain contrasts the romance of the steamboat and the near-transcendentalist qualities of its pilots with the brute realism of the railroad and the aggressive enterprise of its agents. Even when charged with the sins of the slave scheme, frontier Missouri often assumes the guise of a more "innocent" and manageable world than the openly corrupt cities of post-Civil War, industrial America. Within this mythology, then, slavery is a cruel institution of rural America, whose passing is replaced by the more insidious forms of social and economic domination that would be faced by the immigrant, the emancipated black, and virtually any man or woman with only the means of honest labor. In this context Twain serves well those myth critics who would maintain a sharp distinction between rural and industrial economies in America and thus, of course, the distinction between their social values.

Despite Twain's understandable sentimentality about an older, rural America, works like *The Gilded Age* and *Pudd'nhead Wilson* suggest that the sources of modern, postbellum, industrial corruption are to be found in rural America. A vigorous, albeit equivocal, even hypocritical satirist of modern technology, Twain understands slavery itself as not just a provincial agrarian institution, but the basis for the speculative economy that would fuel industrial expansion, Manifest Destiny, and laissez-faire capitalism. The slave is, after all, the ultimate "speculation," insofar as the buyer invests a relatively small amount of money – for purchase and maintenance – in hopes of watching that capital grow into the accumulated labor power of a healthy, long-lived slave. And insofar as the slave may be bred to multiply the owner's wealth, the speculation promises an enormous and virtually endless return for a very modest investment. All of this is accomplished by virtually no labor invested on the part of the owner, whose claim to a high return on his or her venture capital must be based on the risks that he or she is willing to run: the unpredictable losses that may be occasioned by mistreatment, illness, flight, or infertility of the slaves. In short, the slaveowner stakes claim to authority on "business acumen," the ability to tell a "good" property from a "bad," in virtually the same manner that a speculator stakes a claim by *predicting* how a particular property will rise or fall in the marketplace. Slaveowners commonly counted their slaves as capital assets, but the market value of such assets depended upon speculation regarding future productivity of both crops and children. Indeed, such speculations might well be improved by development, much as land speculators attempted to improve a particular property by subdivision, cultivation, or even the improvement of natural features (dredging rivers, draining marshes, clearing forests). One of the motives behind the taboo against miscegenation, other than the obvious motive of maintaining clear distinctions between rulers and ruled, may well have been the fear that publicity regarding "mixed progeny" might jeopardize the legal standing of the slave as chattel. Owners mated with their slave women not merely for their perverse pleasure, but with the hope of producing assets, of increasing the promise of their original investments.

In *The Gilded Age,* Warner and Twain represent virtually every aspect of the post-Civil War American business and social life as infected with the disease of speculation. Colonel Beriah Sellers was immensely popular with nineteenth-century readers, thanks to the gaudy splendor of his speculative rhetoric. A darling of contemporary theatergoers, Colonel Sellers inflates everything from turnips and water to his own name: "When we first came here [Washington, D.C.], I was *Mr.* Sellers, and *Major* Sellers, and *Captain* Sellers, but nobody could get it right, somehow; but the minute our bill went through the House, I was *Colonel* Sellers every time. And nobody could do enough for me; and whatever I said was wonderful. . . . Yes, sir, to-morrow it will be General, let me congratulate you, sir; General, you've done a great work, sir, – you've done a great work for the niggro; Gentlemen, allow me the honor to introduce my friend General Sellers, the humane friend of the niggro."[4] In *The Gilded Age,* parents have more children than they can care for, husbands are bigamists, and people speculate in the most unexpected futures: social reputation, political speeches,. congressional votes, literature, genius, the imagination, a university.

The very notion of "speculation" in *The Gilded Age* is expanded from mere investment in the future of a marketable commodity to include the venture of psychic, social, or financial capital in something that has only a potential future value. The value of such speculation depends, of course, on the inverse proportion of investment to return: the less work, money, or human energy committed to a project, the greater its potential value. In the place of hard work and capital, the speculator spends *words* profligately on the projects – in brochures, speeches, conversation. Words, it would seem, especially those that require no thought (*conventional* words), are *free.* Speculation in postbellum America is criticized by Warner and Twain quite simply because it *discourages* honest labor and increasingly alienates economic and moral *value* from labor. Great fortunes are made and lost overnight, as Colonel Sellers never tires of telling his disciples; steady, dedicated labor seems sheer folly in an economy in which the value of a manufactured item or agricultural product might change dramatically as a consequence of market conditions fueled by unpredictable speculators. To refuse to play the speculative game is merely to become a victim of the system; most of the honest laborers in *The Gilded Age* lose their earnings to some boss whose speculative scheme fails, or are cheated of their wages by the real bosses, the accountants.[5] To play the game puts one in precisely the situation of the gambler, who has only an illusory authority over an intentionally arbitrary system.

The town of Dawson's Landing in *Pudd'nhead Wilson* begins as a sleepy "slave-holding town, with a rich slave-worked grain and pork country back of it. . . . It was fifty years old, and was growing slowly – very slowly, in fact, but it was still growing" (4). Twain describes a town in 1830 (Tom and Chambers are born on February 1, 1830) that is, like most of his fictional Missouri towns, virtually indistinguishable from Hannibal or a host of other riverfront towns at the eastern edge of the American frontier. By 1853, however, Dawson's Landing has elected a mayor, incorporating itself as Hannibal had done in 1845, and otherwise shows signs of adapting to the economic ferment that helped Jacksonian America enter the modern industrial age. Like St. Petersburg in *Huckleberry Finn* or Hawkeye, where Colonel Sellers has his "mansion" in *The Gilded Age,* Dawson's Landing is Twain's touchstone for the changes coming to rural, agrarian, slaveholding America.

The "transitional" quality of Dawson's Landing during the twenty-three years covered by the narrative drama is often noted, but primarily to indicate how modern America brings into relief the antiquated values of antebellum feudalism. Twain provides certain details, however, that make *Pudd'nhead Wilson* a commentary on the shared economics of slavery and the new speculative economy that would carry us through the Civil War into the Gilded Age. When read in light of these economic details, David Wilson becomes an even more problematic character than he has been for previous critics because it is Wilson who helps adjust the law to this new economy, vindicates the murdered Judge Driscoll and his venerable descent from the First Families of Virginia, and lends scientific credibility to speculations in commodities as diverse as dogs, mothers, babies, slaves, signatures, fingerprints, and birthrights.

Critics often forget Percy Driscoll, younger brother of Judge Driscoll, actual father of Chambers and assumed father of Tom. This neglect is hardly surprising because Percy Driscoll's funeral is announced at the end of chapter 4; his role seems primarily to provide the means for Twain to help Roxy cover the tracks of her deception in switching the infants. Percy appears to be little more than a guywire in the general stage machinery of the drama. In customary fashion,

Twain quickly makes Tom an orphan, whose adoption by his uncle and aunt helps emphasize his marginal familial status. In general, the unnatural bonds between children and nominal parents (aunts and uncles are customary) in Twain's fiction remind us that parent-child relations in such an artificial society are more conventional than natural. For example, in *Huckleberry Finn*, parents repeatedly are exposed as inadequate for the most elementary tasks of child-rearing, as Huck's stories of abandoned, mistreated, and orphaned children attest.[6]

In *Pudd'nhead Wilson*, the distance between parents and children is made even more explicit. Raised by slaves, ignored by their white parents, the children of slaveowners have more in common with the slaves than with their own parents. Given the long history of unacknowledged miscegenation, slaves like Roxy may be as little as "one-sixteenth black," so that her own child is "thirty-one parts white," even though he remains "by a fiction of law and custom a negro" (9). In view of such circumstances, it is hardly surprising that Percy Driscoll might have difficulty telling his own child apart from Roxy's, but Twain adds that Percy is also easily tricked because he has little familiarity with his own child. Describing Roxy's child, Twain notes: "He had blue eyes and flaxen curls, like his white comrade, but even the father of the white child was able to tell the children apart – little as he had commerce with them – by their clothes: for the white babe wore ruffled soft muslin and a coral necklace, while the other wore merely a coarse tow-linen shirt which barely reached to its knees, and no jewelry" (9).

It is common enough to comment that the only difference between these two children is their dress, signifying class in the perfectly conventional manner so likely to be satirized by Twain. Yet, two other observations are worth making. First, the close resemblance between Tom and Chambers, especially in a novel so obsessed with twins and doubles, encourages us to think at this early stage in the narrative that they share the same father. This expectation is only partially frustrated by Roxy's confession to Tom that his father was Colonel Cecil Burleigh Essex, another F.F.V. in Dawson's Landing. By chapter 9, when Roxy tells Tom who his father was, we are not likely to trust much of what Roxy says; indeed, the pride with which she tells Tom suggests at least delusions of grandeur if not outright deception on her part. Percy Driscoll and Colonel Cecil Burleigh Essex die conveniently in the same season and paragraph: "There were two grand funerals in Dawson's Landing that fall – the fall of 1845. One was that of Colonel Cecil Burleigh Essex, the other that of Percy Driscoll" (22).

The only other mention of the Colonel is made in Twain's introduction of the chief citizens of Dawson's Landing in chapter 1: "Then there was Colonel Cecil Burleigh Essex, another F.F.V. of formidable calibre – however, with him we have no concern" (4). This mysterious character often has troubled critics. Why introduce him, if he is to play no other role in the narrative than to provide the "name" of Tom's white father? And why dismiss him so hastily, if the entire plot depends on family origins? On the other hand, his name, title, and convenient death in the same season as Percy Driscoll's provide Roxy with an excellent means of protecting herself. If we assume that Tom is the natural son of Percy Driscoll and Roxy, then we might conclude that Tom would have less to fear were Roxy to expose his true identity to Judge Driscoll. Mindful of the scandal such miscegenation in his own family might cause, Judge Driscoll would be likely to reach a settlement with Tom, albeit hardly one comparable to the inheritance that Tom expects from his uncle. On the other hand, exposed as the bastard child of Cecil Burleigh Essex and Roxy, Tom could expect little from Judge Driscoll other than prompt sale down the river.

Assuming that Tom is at least possibly the illegitimate son of Percy Driscoll, we may also suggest that he is but one part of Percy's general speculations. The younger brother of Judge Driscoll has little "commerce" with his only surviving heir, leaving him to the care of Roxy, not only because Mrs. Percy Driscoll dies "within the week" of the child's birth, but also because "Mr. Driscoll soon absorbed himself in his speculations" and left Roxy "to her own devices" with the children (5). Percy Driscoll's financial speculations have a central part to play in the plot, even though they are mentioned so early in the narrative as to be forgotten by the end. Roxy's plan to switch the babies is motivated principally by the fear inspired by her master's threat to sell all his slaves "down the river," unless the one who has stolen a "small sum of money" confesses to the theft (9). As Twain points out, "all were guilty but Roxana," and Twain goes on to explain the unwritten custom by which Southern servants were entitled to take small items – generally food or supplies – without punishment. Such informal servants' "rights" (sometimes called "smouching rights") are still in effect in the South, so Percy Driscoll's anger over that missing money seems extreme, if not indecorous. It is possible that his anxiety reflects the urgent circumstances of his own finances. Once Roxy has switched the babies, she is saved from the risk of the master's close attention to such domestic matters by his preoccupation with business: "For one of his speculations was in jeopardy, and his mind was so occupied that he hardly saw the children when he looked at them, and all Roxy had to do was to get them both into a gale of laughter when he came about them; then their faces were mainly cavities exposing gums . . ." (16). Further problems with this speculation force Percy and Judge Driscoll to leave Dawson's Landing for seven weeks, further assuring the success of Roxy's deception: "Within a few days the fate of the speculation became so dubious that Mr. Percy went away with his brother the Judge to see what could be done with it. It was a land speculation, as usual, and it had gotten complicated with a lawsuit. The men were gone seven weeks. Before they got back Roxy paid her visit to Wilson and was satisfied" (16). By the time he dies in 1845, "Percy Driscoll had worn himself out in trying to save his great speculative landed estate, and had died without succeeding. He was hardly in his grave before the boom collapsed and left his hitherto envied young devil of an heir a pauper" (22).

Percy Driscoll's speculations in real estate recall, of course, John Clemens's "bequest" to his family of a hundred thousand acres in the Knobs of Tennessee (for which he paid $400), as well as his financial failure in Hannibal. The legendary "Tennessee land," with its fabled natural resources and excellent location, haunted the Clemens family for many years after the father's death. It is the same land that Squire Hawkins buys at the beginning of *The Gilded Age* and becomes the focus of the plot in Warner's and Twain's ruthless satire of the speculative economy of postbellum America. Twain's mother and his brother, Orion, floated any number of grandiose schemes on the promise of that Tennessee land, most of which was sold off in small parcels over the years to meet the family's urgent needs. In *The Gilded Age*, the Hawkins's land in the Knobs of East Tennessee becomes the center of an elaborate congressional swindle engineered by two of the Hawkins's children, Colonel Sellers, and Senator Dilworthy. The Senator sponsors a bill for the government purchase of the land as the site for the "Knobs Industrial University," which would be "open to all persons without distinction of sex, color or religion," and whose principal purpose would be the educational emancipation of black men and women (*GA*, 311, 312). That this colossal swindle "trades" on public sentiments for the improvement of the educational and economic opportunities of emancipated blacks in postbellum America is obvious enough; that slaves and freed blacks share the common fate of being commodities in speculative America is only slightly less obvious.

What finally caused Judge Clemens's financial ruin remains somewhat unclear, although Twain refers in his *Autobiography* and the sketch, "The Villagers," to the debt on which Ira Stout defaulted and which Judge Clemens had co-signed as guarantor. Dixon Wecter notes that there is no surviving record of any default by Stout that also involved Judge Clemens.[7] Nevertheless, one of the several subplots of *The Gilded Age* concerns the romance between Philip Sterling and Ruth Bolton, whose father, despite being a Quaker and a lawyer, is ruined several times by his friend, Bigler, who repeatedly talks him into providing surety for Bigler's many speculative schemes.

Judge Clemens's financial plight was so extreme by 1841 that he and Jane had to sell their interest in their home and lot; in the same period, "the Clemenses parted with their slave girl Jennie, . . . whom the Judge had once whipped, but who had served as 'mammy' to Sam and the other young children."[8] This was the same domestic slave that Twain recalls his father selling to his business associate, Beebe, who subsequently sold her down the river. In "The Villagers," Twain writes: "Was seen years later, ch[ambermaid] on a steamboat. Cried and lamented."[9] At least in some sense, Roxy, Percy Driscoll, and Judge Driscoll have biographical origins in Twain's recollections of his personal family circumstances in Florida and Hannibal, Missouri, in the 1830s and 1840s, just as the "Tennessee Land" and various speculative schemes in *The Gilded Age* explicitly satirize his father's cursed bequest to his family.[10]

Besides Ira Stout's financial irresponsibility, what most likely wrecked Judge Clemens's speculations in vacant land and "rental properties along Hill and Main" in Hannibal was the ten-year depression that followed the Panic of 1837. Most of the speculative ferment in the United States in the 1830s was sparked by the promise of the vast frontier, so that speculators invested heavily in canal projects, early rail and other transportation ventures, as well as in land that would be in the path of westward expansion. Andrew Jackson attempted to control land speculation by issuing the "Specie Circular" of 1836, which required "specie payment for public land." The economic consequences of this act were declining prices for land, pressures on banks holding government funds, and subsequent bank failures in many states.[11] Missouri was still primarily an undeveloped part of the frontier in 1837, and it consequently suffered less than eastern states committed to ambitious canal and railroad developments. Even so, the Panic of 1837 and the depression that followed it had national consequences, severest for those who had staked their fortunes to speculative enterprises. The Panic of 1837 falls precisely between the births of Tom and Chambers in 1830 and the death of Percy Driscoll, who is ruined by his land speculation, in 1845.

Roxy's switching of the babies is itself a "speculative" venture, a "gamble" against the chances of being discovered and thus sold down the river for her sins. What prompts her rebellious action is the master's threat to sell all his slaves down the river, a threat that we have suggested may well be caused more by his own financial reverses than mere arbitrariness. Roxy's "venture" with such modest human "capital" is little more than an imitation of what white masters did with their black commodities under slavery, risking that the black child will grow to become a valuable property from a relatively small investment. Virtually "born" (born *again*?) of this speculative enterprise, which like most of Roxy's actions imitate white men's behavior, Tom would seem to have the proper background for a gambler.

Twain is careful to tell us, however, that Tom learns to gamble at Yale; he wants the reader to be certain not to associate Tom's vices with the black portion of his heredity. His gambling is his "inheritance" from his white father, whether "Cecil Burleigh Essex" or Percy Driscoll. Land speculation and gambling go hand-in-hand, of course, and the western folk myth of the Mississippi gambler has its origins in the gamblers and speculators who did business on the steamboats that were so crucial to the commercial development of Missouri from 1820 to 1865.[12] Tom's gambling is part of his effort to play the role of the Southern aristocrat with disposable income and leisure time, but it also associates him with the new economy fueled by speculators and get-rich-quick artists from Eastern urban centers of banking and finance. That Tom should learn to gamble at Yale should not surprise readers of *The Gilded Age,* in which the two most naive speculators, Philip Sterling and Henry Brierly, were classmates at Yale. Henry's first words are, "'Oh, it's easy enough to make a fortune,'" and he sends them both on the road to ruin by vaguely asking Philip, "'Well, why don't you go into something? You'll never dig it out of the Astor Library'" (*GA*, 95). As a couple of eastern swells, Philip and Henry epitomize "the young American," to whom "the paths to fortune are innumerable and all open; there is invitation in the air and success in all his wide horizon" (*GA*, 95). Although Warner and Twain make their own capital out of Senator Dilworthy's fraudulent scheme for the "Knobs Technical University," they repeatedly compare its innovative technical curriculum with models in Switzerland and Germany. Indeed, part of the cleverness of the plan for this university is that it *does* propose the sort of educational institution that Twain and Warner would consider enlightened. By contrast, the liberal arts education offered at nineteenth-century Yale would seem to encourage nothing other than the vague expectations and romantic ideals of young fops like Henry Brierly and Philip Sterling, each of whom learns ultimately the hard realities of this speculative economy.[13] Like Percy Driscoll's land speculation, Tom's gambling jeopardizes his estate and thus the Driscolls' social authority. All of Tom's criminal actions are designed to cover his debts and thus assure his inheritance from Judge Driscoll. The child of speculating parents and of a speculative era and region, Tom fulfills that destiny by repeating in his own character the economic "failures" that punctuated the American economy from the Panic of 1837 to the Panics of 1873 and 1893.

Indeed, *Pudd'nhead Wilson* was written on the verge of the Panic of 1893 (and rewritten and proofread during the Panic), which was the final blow to Twain's publishing company, Webster and Company, and his dreams for the commercial success of the Paige Typesetter. Twain returned from Europe in the middle of the Panic, and he "couldn't borrow a penny."[14] Everything that he and Warner had predicted in *The Gilded Age* had come to pass with a vengeance, so it is hardly surprising that the legal servitude of the black in antebellum America should be confused so brilliantly with the economic servitude of Tom to the speculative interests of the new age. In debt for $80,000 as a consequence of the failure of Webster and Company and the Paige Typesetter, Twain would work his way back to solvency only by repeating his father's own "honorable" payment of "a hundred cents on the dollar" of the debts he had collected half a century earlier.[15] As familiar as the story of Twain's business failure and moral triumph may be, its relevance to the economic themes in *Pudd'nhead Wilson* remains untold. That he *did* follow his father's example reveals more than just Twain's integrity; that repetition may well have suggested to him the perverse continuity between antebellum and postbellum America. The gulf separating "Old Times on the Mississippi" from the new, progressive America must have appeared much narrower than it once had seemed to Twain. Writing his early drafts of *Pudd'nhead Wilson* in Italy, where he had "exiled" himself and his family to try to "economize," Twain responded to the Panic of 1893 as if it were some perverse fate sent specifically to punish him. The agrarian institution of slavery had been replaced by the urban servitude of those victimized by a speculative economy. The fact that Twain was no mere innocent victim, but himself an active figure in the very speculative enterprises that Warner and he had so viciously criticized in the year of the last major American panic – the Panic of 1873 – must have weighed heavily upon the writer's conscience. In this regard, Tom Driscoll and Percy Driscoll might be read allegorically as versions of Mark Twain and Judge John Clemens.[16]

Such an autobiographical allegory, however, is less interesting than the more general consequences of a narrative designed to reflect the continuity between an older slavery and the new slavery of urban economics. Tom and Percy are not the only characters affected by this speculative economy. Freed in Percy Driscoll's will, Roxy works for eight years (1845–53) on a Mississippi steamboat, saving her money to provide herself with a modest income when she is too infirm (at forty-three!) to work any longer: "She had lived a steady life, and had banked four dollars every month in New Orleans as a provision for her old age. She said in the start that she 'put shoes on one bar'footed nigger to tromple on her with,' and that one mistake like that was enough: she would be independent of the human race thenceforth forevermore if hard work and economy could accomplish it" (33). As every reader will recall, she bids goodbye to her "comrades on the Grand Mogul," only to discover that the "bank had gone smash and carried her four hundred dollars with it" (33). Had Roxy's modest savings remained safely in that New Orleans bank to pay her a poor return in interest as retirement income, she never would have returned to beg and threaten her natural son, Tom. Without the support of Roxy's intelligence and rage, Tom undoubtedly would have even more quickly caused his own financial ruin. Nevertheless, it is unlikely that he would have murdered his uncle or had his curious origins exposed. Quite obviously, both Roxy's vengeful authority and the rage inspired in Tom by her revelation of his black origins fuel his subsequent crimes in *Pudd'nhead Wilson.*[17] Giving quite so much weight to the economic "deus ex machina" of this New Orleans bank failure would, of course, be excessive were it not that *Pudd'nhead Wilson* incorporates so many equally "minor" details regarding speculation, each of which has a significant effect on the plot.

Critics have often noticed that Roxy's character, as powerfully vengeful as it becomes in the narrative, is nonetheless governed consistently by the values of the white ruling class. Roxy's pride regarding Tom's high birth, her attendance at the duel between Judge Driscoll and Luigi, her hard work and economy while a chambermaid on the *Grand Mogul,* and her maternal sentiments for Tom – all of these somewhat questionable "virtues" identify her self-reliance as well as her criminal potential with white values. Writing in a period when white America addressed the "negro question" by calling in various ways for the religious, educational, and economic "reformation" of the emancipated black, Twain ruthlessly satirizes the ways in which the black who would follow the customs of white America would end up victimized yet again, trapped in a new economic servitude that would continue to our own day. The freed black would share with the European immigrant and the naive young white American the fantastic promise of speculative, expanding America, only to become the agent of the same old thieving powers of the eastern bankers and urban tycoons.

Percy Driscoll dies in 1845, the year in which John L. O'Sullivan "coined the phrase Manifest Destiny . . . to promote the annexation of Texas."[18] As Michael Rogin reminds us, Manifest Destiny became the rallying cry of a short-lived group sponsored by O'Sullivan, "Young America," which "was militantly expansionist and Anglophobic," as well as in favor of "universal democracy, equality, and the overthrow of European kings."[19] In *Pudd'nhead Wilson*, the political enthusiasms of groups like "Young America" are satirized by the anti-temperance "Sons of Liberty," whose only rallying cry seems to be a drinking song. Even so, the liberal movements that supported Manifest Destiny and opposed slavery often claimed that the encouragement of Northern industrial interests in the course of westward expansion might provide the "answer" to slavery. Abolitionists knew that mere "emancipation" by law would hardly solve the problem of American blacks born and raised in slavery. New land and ambitious speculative ventures, including the railroads that would open the frontier, were often promoted on humanitarian grounds as promising employment and opportunity for freed slaves and other oppressed minorities. Roxy's hard-earned $400 is a small measure of the economic promise that Manifest Destiny might offer the freed slave; its loss in the bank's failure is Twain's satire of the economic realities that would disillusion freed blacks as well as European immigrants with the economic "promise" of American expansionism.

Roxy, Tom, and Percy are not the only speculators in *Pudd'nhead Wilson*. David Wilson, "a young fellow of Scotch parentage . . . had wandered to this remote region from his birthplace in the interior State of New York, to seek his fortune. He was twenty-five years old, college-bred, and had finished a post-college course in an eastern law school a couple of years before" (5). Like Philip Sterling in *The Gilded Age*, David Wilson lacks the obvious trappings of the fortune hunter; Philip's friend, Henry Brierly, for example, spends others' money on hotel rooms and fancy dinners with virtual abandon. Brierly is a youthful Colonel Sellers, whereas Sterling and Wilson have the modest qualities and potential virtues of the honest laborers Twain admires. Even so, both Sterling and Wilson are lured to the frontier of Missouri by the promise of "fortune." It is only as a consequence of Wilson's apparently casual remark about the dog that he is condemned to hang out a shingle and try the practice of law, then the more modest professions of surveying and accounting.[20] Even so, all of the three professions Wilson attempts to practice in Dawson's Landing are dependent upon the speculative economy of the region. Like the Kentuckians who came to Missouri in the 1820s and 1830s with capital and slaves, David Wilson, who is from New York State, "had a trifle of money when he arrived, and he bought a small house on the extreme western verge of the town"(6). That this "small house" is next door to Judge Driscoll's house suggests that Wilson's "trifle of money" is somewhat greater than Twain leads us to believe. Arriving in Dawson's Landing to profit from the modest development boom of the years following the admission of Missouri to the Union in 1821, Wilson virtually announces himself as a speculator and fortune-hunter in his "deadly remark": "'I wish I owned half of that dog'" (5). Only a fool or a speculator would think in terms of "half-interest" in a dog, and the townfolks' judgment of Wilson's certain folly reflects their reliance on the customs of an older, landed economy.

Unable to practice law on account of this foolish remark, Wilson does occasional surveying and accounting, occupying his "rich abundance of idle time" with the "universe of ideas," notably his experiments in palmistry (7). In *The Gilded Age,* Colonel Sellers always has some new "invention" under way, ranging from eyedrops to stoves. Scientific experimentation and speculation go hand-in-hand for Twain, whose own experiences with the Paige Typesetter and fascination with inventions of all sorts are notorious features of his biography. Although Twain respected inventiveness and the technology it promoted, he had good reason to be suspicious of the inflated expectations that the "scientific spirit" brought to America. Wilson and Judge Driscoll are both "free-thinkers," by which we assume they are mild agnostics, but "free thinking" in general is mercilessly indicted in *The Gilded Age* as one of the sources for the unchecked speculative "instinct" (as Twain and Warner call it) in modern industrial America.

David Wilson and Tom Driscoll are frequently contrasted by critics, who follow Twain's own lead in calling attention to Wilson's "rise" at the expense of Tom's "fall." Because Wilson attracts our sympathies with the satiric humor of his "calendar" and his generally marginal status in Dawson's Landing, modern readers have been quick to associate him with Twain's own views. Thus George Spangler suggests that Tom's greed anticipates the rampant materialism of the Gilded Age, whereas Wilson's "disinterestedness and immaterialism" are tokens of an alternative that we ought to associate with Twain's ideal.[21] Such interpretations have always foundered on the simple fact that David Wilson uses his experiments in fingerprinting not merely to "solve" the murder of Judge Driscoll and save the innocent Luigi from hanging, but that these same experiments are given legal status in a case that allows the townspeople to attribute such criminality to Tom's black heredity. David Wilson's "triumph," as the new mayor of the newly chartered city of Dawson's Landing, as courtroom lawyer and expert witness, even as amateur sleuth, is perhaps the most perverse heroic conclusion in modern literature.

Tom twice associates Wilson's forensic work with his fingerprints as "his palace-window decorations," and Wilson himself declares in court that he knows these "signatures . . . as well as the bank cashier knows the autograph of his oldest customer" (105, 109–10). Wilson's idle "speculation" in "paw prints" clearly assumes more than just *economic* value by the time he has solved the crime; his scientific "knowledge" of the origins and identity of any man so recorded is comparable to that of the absolute authorities of the European monarch or the American judge. In the speculative economy of the Gilded Age, no one's "identity" will be subject to the customary tests—the property, social habits and company, and local history that had given a man "reputation" and thus "identity" in older, small-town America. In this new world of changeable roles, ever-new "schemes," and both geographical and social mobility, men and women will be known only in their styles and fashions. Only a Colonel Sellers, whose "absolute" is paradoxically his infinitely malleable rhetoric (his only enduring "capital"), will have a "character," but the word will thus assume its idiomatic meaning: "Oh, *what a character!*"

At the dawn of such an era, Wilson's idle speculation in fingerprints, an avocation that is until the trial apparently useless, becomes the capital of the law, the scientific "basis" for judging human actions and relating those actions to larger sociohistorical forces. When Tom murders the Judge, Tom is disguised as a black man (he has blackened his face with charcoal); when he flees the scene, he is disguised as a girl. These masks are the "proper" murderers, who take their revenge against the master who has stolen both the black man's liberty and exploited the sex of both white and black women. These exploited "halves" of the slave, especially as they are prompted by the justifiable rage of Roxy, are the avenging angels of Tom's apparently individual and "criminal" act. It is worth noting at this point that Twain's literary style enables us to make such connections between individual "characters" and their socially symbolic acts in ways that are distinctly different from the "writing" of David Wilson's dramatic pantographs. Wilson introduces a "scientific" measurement of personality that extends the commodification of human beings under slavery to the general economy of America. Aware of the writer's complicity in the corruptions of the new economy (Philip Sterling, for example, initially wants to be a writer), Twain is at some pains to distinguish his own "tale-tale telling" from the inflated rhetoric of Colonel Sellers or the courtroom histrionics of David Wilson.

A reasonable objection to this argument is that Wilson does indeed save Luigi from conviction for Judge Driscoll's murder, but the fact that Luigi is held legally responsible for this murder depends upon another of the many hypocrisies of Dawson's Landing. We must remember that while Wilson runs for mayor, the Italian twins are running for aldermanic seats. Judge Driscoll and Tom are reconciled as father and son during the campaign by virtue of their "election labors" to defeat the twins. What Twain calls twice their "hard work" includes spending "money ... to persuade voters" and the Judge's "closing speech of the campaign," which is notable for the inflated rhetoric by which it offers a "character assassination" of the twins. Previously associated with the new speculative economy only in the help he gives his brother, the Judge is in this context directly linked with what Warner and Twain consider two of the most insidious effects of the "speculative instinct": exaggerated, romantic rhetoric (hyperbole) and vote-buying.[22] Having "scoffed at them as adventurers, mountebanks, side-show riff-raff, dime-museum freaks," the Judge closes by claiming that "the reward offered for the lost knife was humbug and buncombe, and that its owner would know where to find it whenever he should have the occasion *to assassinate somebody*" (83). The Judge's accusation invokes the *code duello* of the region, and it is the *Judge* who refuses Count Luigi's challenge, declining "to fight with an assassin – 'that is . . . in the field of honor'" (92). Wilson then explains the significance of the Judge's refusal to Count Luigi: "The unwritten law of this region requires you to kill Judge Driscoll on sight, and he and the community will expect that attention at your hands – though of course your own death by his bullet will answer every purpose. Look out for him! Are you heeled – that is, fixed?" (93). Nothing could be stranger, of course, than the newly elected mayor explaining the murderous intent of the town's judge to his intended victim! But even granting the absurdity of this "unwritten law of the region" and the circumstances of its narration, we are bound to wonder why Luigi is at risk for his life in the trial from which Wilson nominally "saves" him. Given the circumstances of such an "unwritten law," Luigi certainly has the reasonable argument of "self-defense," whether Tom's criminality is revealed or not.

Unfortunately, Twain provides no explicit motivation for Wilson's defense of Luigi other than his immediate perception that "neither of the Twins" made the marks on the knife handle (97). The motives for Wilson's triumphant revelation of Tom's identity in the courtroom, however, have often been interpreted as part of Wilson's bid for legitimacy with the townspeople of Dawson's Landing. Until his murder, Judge Driscoll was Wilson's protector and guarantor of his rights in town. In fact, the Judge's paternal concern for Wilson, this aspiring lawyer – perversely doubles the Judge's relation to his stepson and nephew, Tom. Without this surrogate father, Wilson must legitimate his new role as mayor, which he does not only by assuming legal authority in the courtroom but also by "saving" Luigi. Luigi is, of course, no more saved by Wilson than Jim is saved by Tom and Huck at the end of *Huckleberry Finn*, but the irony of this salvation is that it causes Luigi and Angelo to "weary of Western adventure" and return "straightway . . . to Europe" (114). Although Wilson and the twins run for different civic positions, Twain announces the results of the election in terms that suggest syntactically their competition: "Wilson was elected, the twins were defeated – crushed, in fact, and left forlorn and substantially friendless" (84). That the Judge would suspect these two foreigners of being charlatans, all the while being surrounded by a society based on fraud – whether that of slavery or the new speculative economy – fits perfectly Twain's satiric purposes. The fact that Wilson's hard work – the first he performs in the narrative – in saving Luigi, revealing Tom as a slave, and turning the hapless Chambers into a white heir helps restore order in this small community remains far more troublesome.

For Wilson is no "mysterious stranger" sent to Dawson's Landing to reveal its own unconscious lie. What Wilson helps accomplish is hardly that familiar "disturbance" in Twain's other small towns that provokes some searching re-examination of their social values and contracts. Wilson proves himself to be not only a "proper" gentleman but also a leader, who will carry this town into its urban era in the wake of the new economics that would sweep America in the course of the Civil War and its aftermath. In this sense, Wilson is the appropriate heir to the arbitrary authority represented by Judge Driscoll and the F.F.V.s. Wilson is the "accountant," who helps make possible the correct "accounting" of Percy Driscoll's mortgaged and speculative estate. Wilson's palmistry is a new "science" of human accounting that promises the effective translation of the chattel of slavery into the commodity of labor manipulated by the urban speculator. Roxy, that wily imitator of the white man's slickest tricks, convinces her son to sell her down the river on the basis of a *forged bill of sale*. Tom's *signature* turns Roxy back into a saleable commodity. Wilson melodramatically concludes his courtroom speech by commanding: "Valet de Chambre, negro and slave—falsely called Thomas à Becket Driscoll—make upon the window the finger-prints that will hang you!" (112). For a second time, then, Tom's "signature" turns a human being into capital, which will in fact circulate by way of Percy Driscoll's creditors. Tom's forgery of his signature on his mother's bill of sale is, of course, doubly forged. Every signature of ownership on a slave deed must be a base forgery for Twain. Industrial, speculative America would transform that "forged ownership" into the capital *naturally* authorized by the very body of its workers. In America of the Gilded Age, there will be yet other forgeries by means of which the fact of slavery will be transformed into the broken promises and elusive opportunities that would become the wages of the freed black and European immigrant. The "profit" earned from such a speculative accounting as David Wilson's is neither property nor cash; like the antebellum slaveowner, David Wilson plays for power and authority. The last we hear from Colonel Sellers in *The Gilded Age,* he is embarking on yet a new and even more vainglorious venture than any before it: "'I've seen enough to show me where my mistake was. The law is what I was born for. I shall begin the study of the law. . . . There's worlds of money in it! whole worlds of money! . . . Climb, and climb, and climb—and wind up on the S*u*preme bench. . . . A made man for all time and eternity!" (*GA*, 426). In the character of David Wilson, Colonel Sellers finds at last the profession and personality to which the speculator is born: philosopher, scientist, humorist, detective, lawyer, and mayor—America's Renaissance Man.

What, then, of "Pudd'nhead Wilson's Calendar" with its evocations of Twain's familiar skepticism and irony? The aphorisms still serve the purposes of Twain's general satire of Dawson's Landing, its slave-holding values, and the modern economy that it is entering. As David Wilson's "scratchings," such social and human criticism have become merely the "decorations" of a popular calendar, witty "saws" like the wisecrack about that dog. That his own skepticism and social criticism would become merely the "idle" pastimes of "freethinking" hypocrites like Judge Driscoll and David Wilson may well be Twain's deepest fear—and one realized in part in our postmodern economy, whose stock in trade may be the wisecrack.

MICHAEL COWAN

"By Right of the White Election"

Political Theology and Theological Politics
in *Pudd'nhead Wilson*

I n many obvious respects, *Pudd'nhead Wilson* is, like most of Twain's
earlier fiction, a relentlessly secular work. It places most of its
explicit attention on the historically constituted institutions, processes, and beliefs characteristic of Dawson's Landing, and it examines
the features of social and cultural life primarily from a perspective
that focuses on human agency and natural process in the workings
of this world. Even the religious institutions and beliefs of Dawson's
Landing are treated most apparently as socially constructed phenomena, reflections of human desires and impulses more than of God's
ways. In some respects, in fact, the community's dominant religious
beliefs seem so completely subservient to the dominant political,
economic, and social values that, if they cannot be conveniently used
to justify those values, they are brushed aside or brought into line.
As the narrator laconically observes in chapter 12, if the "unwritten
laws" of honor held by a "gentleman" of the First Families of Virginia
"required certain things of him which his religion might forbid: then
his religion must yield . . ." (58).[1]

But this seeming reduction of the role of religious belief and speculation is only part of the story of a narrative that seems of mixed
minds about nearly everything it touches. For one thing, even when
a servant of class and caste interests, an element of both dominant
and countervailing ideology, religious discourse often offers the inhabitants of Dawson's Landing inspiriting rhetoric for their social and
political maneuverings. In fact, to the extent that serious ideological
conflicts manifest themselves in this community, they are likely to
do so partly in the garb of "theological" conflicts – conflicts sometimes
marked by the inhabitants, but even more often by the narrator
himself. Several versions of a "Christian" God compete for the atten-

tion of both the inhabitants and readers of *Pudd'nhead Wilson* and its severed relative, *Those Extraordinary Twins,* and those competing versions both reflect, as symptoms of, and serve as discursive weapons for the central secular interests in Dawson's Landing. At the same time, such versions offer competing perspectives on those secular dynamics. Put too simply, the narratives, particularly when taken collectively, offer in fragmentary, provisional form what we might call a politics of theological discourse, or a theological politics, one related complexly to the racial politics of *Pudd'nhead Wilson* and to the general political and legal processes and assumptions of *Those Extraordinary Twins.* Each theological version is utopian in that it offers not only an image of ideal social and political relationships, expressed as a vision of heavenly citizenship, but also an image of political legitimacy personified in a Deity who both confers citizenship and governs with the consent of those so honored. The theological politics, in other words, involve competing political theologies. At stake are conflicting answers to two distinct but related questions, questions with both secular and religious implications: Who can be elected? and Who can be saved? And cutting across these questions is another: If secular faith is not to be based on religious faith, what *can* it be based on?

Responding to the theological implications he finds in the narrative, Stanley Brodwin has usefully argued that, in its deterministic and pessimistic cast, *Pudd'nhead Wilson* is "a theological study of man's nature whose intrinsic pattern is modeled on the myth of the fall of man. Temptation, pride, banishment, and damnation, dramatized in biblical terms, provide the key to the novel's meaning. . . ."[2] Brodwin contends that the novel gains artistic and philosophical coherence through its "two linked tragedies," one concerned with the moral "fall of America" as a result of slavery, the other with "the more significant and unifying theme of original sin" that lies behind the account of the specifically American tragedy.[3] As stimulating as is Brodwin's thesis, the relationship between his two tragedies – the moral/secular and the theological – is more problematic than he suggests. Rather than congruent, their implications may, in at least some respects, work at cross-purposes. More than many of Twain's books, *Pudd'nhead Wilson* raises more unresolvable questions than it answers. To what extent can it be seen basically, as Brodwin argues, as a theological allegory that uses slavery and racism as types? To what extent, as many critics have argued, can the novel be more appropriately treated as a secular sociopolitical drama in which religious discourse either obfuscates or rationalizes secular interests? To what extent is religious faith – either hopeful or bleak – treated as a delusion? To what extent does *Pudd'nhead Wilson* anticipate the dark religious determinism and nihilism of Twain's later years? To what extent do its theological resonances add rhetorical weight to the drama? Contribute to its ironies? Fuel its sympathies? In offering hints of all these possibilities, especially when taken in conjunction with *Those Extraordinary Twins*, *Pudd'nhead Wilson* seems plausibly readable as a transitional agnostic work of an imaginative but troubled free-thinker who leaves in the text the traces of an improvisational meditation that focuses less on the ultimate truth value of any particular secular or theological interpretations of this world than on their ambiguous relationship and on the problematic consequences of human belief in any particular interpretation. The narrative both is tempted to choose sides – to take its half of the dog and "kill" the other half – and at the same time resists that temptation. As John Carlos Rowe has argued to slightly different purposes, *"Pudd'nhead Wilson* achieves its greatness by virtue of its strategic dissonance, its refusal to resolve its issues."[4] If for the sake of the drama alone, it sets against each other the fragments of several competing belief structures and watches their struggle play itself out to inconclusive if rather bleak results.

One useful pathway into this struggle is along the trope of translation. In numerous ways, the plots and structures of *Pudd'nhead Wilson* and *Those Extraordinary Twins* work by means of a series of literal and figurative translations, or transformations of an object or text from one discursive context to another. In a community in which physical bodies, whether those of slaves, of Angelo and Luigi, or those that Wilson fingerprints, are such major legal and cultural texts, it comes as no surprise that the central energizing translation of *Pudd'nhead Wilson,* for example, involves Roxy's exchange of two babies. But words are also undergoing constant, if often-unmarked, exchange between various discursive contexts in each narrative. Their translation from one discourse to another is rarely neutral or merely literal: moved from context to context, they are changed and in turn change their contexts. In these two narratives, they are affected by and in turn affect both the politics of body and the politics of soul. One way of getting at this dynamic is to consider the multiple, crossover functions of two terms: "elect" and "save."

Along with courtroom trials, elections consume a considerable amount of the publicly oriented time and energy of the inhabitants of *Pudd'nhead Wilson* and *Those Extraordinary Twins.* These two activities are, in fact, often closely linked. While the courtroom scenes of both narratives have often been the subject of critical attention, however, elective processes in each have come under somewhat less scrutiny. It should come as no surprise, of course, that in a small, antebellum, relatively (although quite unevenly) "democratic" Missouri community of the sort that might have been observed by a Tocqueville or a Dickens (or their Italian twin stand-ins), political contests provide one of the dominant stable features of the town's annual public life-cycle – help establish the beat of its social rhythms. The major such election in both narratives, spanning several chapters in each, involves David Wilson's charter election run for mayor and Angelo and Luigi Capello's try for alderman. But elections are to some degree or another bound up with most other major institutions in Dawson's Landing, and in ways that make their function and meaning not entirely self-evident. If the process of being "elected" to membership in these institutions seems often casual, the assumptions underlying the process come close to the very heart of the way in which the community sees individual status to be achieved and community welfare to be preserved. As Twain said in 1906, "If we would learn what the human race really *is* at bottom, we need only observe it in election times."[5]

Embedded in the officially "democratic" notion of election in Dawson's Landing are significant, if muted, tensions. On the one hand, for example, elections are officially manifestions of a convenanted society of "free" individuals, and in at least two senses. First, an individual freely chooses to stand for membership in some body (slavery being a painfully obvious exception), but volunteering is often not sufficient grounds by itself for membership. Such membership also, typically, requires an invitation or election by the body's existing members. The relationship between elected and elector is reciprocal, each confirming in the electoral process the free agency of the other. On the other hand, that process is founded on subtly coercive elements. In chapter 11 of *Pudd'nhead Wilson*, Luigi and Angelo are elected to the town's "rum party," the perhaps-appropriately-named Sons of Liberty (54–55). The Sons then discover that Angelo is a teetotaler and "opposed to our creed" and therefore "desires that we reconsider the vote by which he was elected." However, "according to the by-laws," that reconsideration has to be carried over to "the next regular meeting" for action (55). The protocols of the electoral process cannot be lightly ignored without calling the legitimizing basis of the organization itself into question. Perhaps significantly, this second meeting never takes place, at least within the space of the text. Angelo's "temporary membership" thus in effect becomes an ongoing membership. He has been elected to a society in whose creed he does not believe but, in a formal textual sense, cannot escape.[6]

What is true for the Sons of "Liberty" is true for the society as a whole. One (at least, free white men) can (as the twins do) relatively easily take out citizenship papers and be fairly readily accepted, and even welcomed, by the community – become the beneficiaries, so to speak, of a "white election." But the community may require a price for that citizenship and a price for trying to renounce it. That price reflects the election's function not merely as a rite of individual status elevation (or reversal) but, as Victor Turner and others suggest, as a ritual of communal self-identification and self-authorization. Elections are a key element in the process by which Dawson's Landing legitimates not only its leaders and members but also itself, and points to and enacts its own moral authority as a polity.

Elections and the (to a certain extent unconscious) political and cultural assumptions that underlie them are so significant to the town, in fact, that they contribute key tropes and symbols to other aspects of the town's existence. Some of these figurative uses stay relatively close to the actual facts of the town's electoral processes as social and political events. Such an election occurs in the very first chapter when David Wilson, on his first day in the village, makes his comments about "an invisible dog" and "stood elected" as a pudd'nhead by the "group of citizens" who hear his remark (5–6). (That the electoral process is characteristically related to the juristic process is suggested by the other tropes with which the narrator inscribes Pudd'nhead's election: "That first day's *verdict* [my italics] made him a fool, and he was not able to get it set aside, or even modified" [6].) The electoral metaphor comes full circle in the concluding chapter of the novel, in the wake of Wilson's spectacular courtroom drama and victory, as "troop after troop" of citizens fall over each other in their eagerness to pay homage to his now "marvelous" and "golden" "sentences" (the latter term suggesting not only his calendar aphorisms but the judgments he utters both in and outside the courtroom):

And as each of these roaring gangs of enthusiasts marched away, some remorseful member of it was quite sure to raise his voice and say –

"And this is the man the likes of us have called a pudd'nhead for more than twenty years. He has resigned from that position, friends."

"Yes, but it isn't vacant – we're elected." (114)

It is not at all clear that the speakers fully recognize in their own playful comments the implication that the communal office of pudd'nhead is filled less by free choice than by communal necessity: by the need for a margin that helps define center, a nonauthority that helps define legitimate authority. But, as the casual ease with which they use the image may suggest, elections and their attendant processes and institutions are so pervasive in Dawson's Landing that, for all the conscious attention the town's inhabitants focus on them, they are also in many respects taken for granted. Their existence is assumed as a part of the natural rather than constructed reality of the town. The implicit as well as explicit values assumed to be manifest in and furthered by elections are seen by the townspeople and their leaders as self-evident. They cannot imagine a world without elections, and they cannot imagine electoral processes and outcomes that violate cherished official tenets of community life. The narrative, in contrast, manifests both explicitly and implicitly an engagement with electoral problematics and ironies, both in the practice and in the conception of election.

A number of elements of these problematics are articulated more fully in *Those Extraordinary Twins* than in *Pudd'nhead Wilson*. Given the town's social and symbolic structure in which "election" and "judgment" are characteristically, if ambiguously, intertwined, it is not surprising to find the major voting contests in *Those Extraordinary Twins* tied to another important political event that is itself a kind of contest – the trial of Luigi and Angelo for "their" kicking of Tom. The trial seems at least as much a quest for jury members' votes as it is a search for truth or justice. Wilson's success in defending the twin(s) leads to his nomination as mayor. But the kicking of Tom also prompts another event, Luigi's duel with Judge Driscoll, that in turn leads to the twins' own political elevation. Luigi fights the Judge courageously until the stroke of Saturday midnight, when his Siamese twin, Angelo, a principled pacifist, takes over control of the brothers' shared legs, and flees from the duel:

By nine o'clock the town was humming with the news of the midnight duel, and there were but two opinions about it: one, that Luigi's pluck in the field was most praiseworthy and Angelo's flight most scandalous; the other, that Angelo's courage in flying the field for conscience's sake was as fine and creditable as was Luigi's in holding the field in the face of the bullets. The one opinion was held by half of the town, the other one was maintained by the other half. The division was clean and exact, and it made two parties, an Angelo party and a Luigi party. The twins had suddenly become popular idols along with Pudd'nhead Wilson, and haloed with a glory as intense as his. The children talked the duel all the way to Sunday-school, their elders talked it all the way to church, the choir discussed it behind their red curtain, it usurped the place of pious thought in the "nigger gallery." (164–65)

In some respects the episode can be seen as both a generative model of the community's central political process and as a sign of the power of its civil religion, one that makes haloed saints of its political heroes and finds no incongruity in bringing these secular saints into the discourse of its religious institutions. In fact, the terms of religious and civil discourse can be translated in both directions. If politics takes on aspects of secular theology in Dawson's Landing, theology can also offer competing models for its politics.

A "real" election, for Dawson's Landing, depends on division – a divided dog, if you will: a division that the election itself is then intended to resolve. (We note that Wilson's unopposed nomination for mayor is characterized as "unprecedented.") The division, of course, is often not merely between men or groups but between ideas, and the contest over who is the best man is often fought in terms of who represents the best principle. Thus, far from "merely representing Whigism, which was a matter of no consequence to him," Angelo becomes "the chosen and admired champion of every clique that had a pet reform of any sort or kind at heart" (167). These differences in principles are typically treated by the contestants and their supporters not merely as differences but as oppositions. At least in their campaign rhetoric, both sides of the community seem to want (if not unambivalently) the election to result in a clear, unambiguous victory for their principles, and defining those principles oppositionally is a partial means to this end.

But just as Dawson's Landing does not get such clarity in the kicking trial, so it does not get it in the election. In fact, Twain satirizes the difficulty in separating principles by literalizing the difficulty in separating men:

But as the canvass went on, troubles began to spring up all around – troubles for the twins, and through them for all the parties and segments and fractions of parties. Whenever Luigi had possession of the legs, he carried Angelo to balls, rum shops, Sons of Liberty parades, horse races, campaign riots, and everywhere else that could damage him with his party and the church; and when it was Angelo's week he carried Luigi diligently to all manner of moral and religious gatherings, doing his best to regain the ground he had lost before. As a result of these double performances, there was a storm blowing all the time, an ever rising storm too – a storm of frantic criticism of the twins, and rage over their extravagant, incomprehensible conduct. (167)

It seems not implausible to suggest that, in making a farce of the twins' "incomprehensible" conduct, Twain is satirizing one of the basic assumptions that lie behind at least the discourse of the election process itself: the assumption of clear division.

But if the assumptions governing the process are suspect, the results of that process must inevitably be suspect. If the principles contested over in an election are – as manifested in the candidates – in fact intermixed and hence ambiguous, how can one determine what principle (or who) has really been elected? Thus, Luigi cannot be sworn in with the other new city officers:

> There was a complication in his case. His election was conceded, but he could not sit in the board of aldermen without his brother, and his brother could not sit there because he was not a member. There seemed to be no way out of the difficulty but to carry the matter into the courts . . . . In the meantime the city government had been at a standstill, because without Luigi there was a tie in the board of aldermen, whereas with him the liquor interest . . . would have one majority. But the court decided that Angelo could not sit in the board with him . . . and at the same time forbade the board to deny admission to Luigi, a fairly and legally chosen alderman. . . . As a result, the city government not only stood still, with its hands tied, but everything it was created to protect and care for went a steady gait toward rack and ruin. (168–69)

The narrator notes laconically that "at last the people came to their senses" and deal with their problem by hanging Luigi – the event on which the narrative ends. But if the farcical mode of the conclusion reaches for our wry smiles, we may also find ourselves, upon further reflection, confronted by the ironic realization that the hanging of Luigi does not really solve Dawson's Landing's election problem. If the board of aldermen is in effect "hung" without him – evenly split and hence incapacitated – his removal will still leave the board split and the town government and even, by extension, the town welfare still in peril. That is, hanging Luigi has perpetuated the town's political crisis. The crisis of his legitimacy as an elected official – a crisis created by the fact that he unavoidably brings something considered illegitimate with him – becomes also a crisis of the legitimacy of the town's political structure itself. Perhaps the town can resolve that crisis by calling a new election upon Luigi's death. But the narrator does not allow (or think of) that resolution. Rather, he abruptly ends the narrative, leaving the town's political legitimacy, at least for the attentive reader, still in question – a particularly traumatic state of affairs, one would imagine, for the newly chartered city: unable to exercise in its very founding the power it claims as not only the consequence but the source of its charter.

We thus have something of a conundrum. On the one hand, elections are a critical part of the stabilizing process by means of which Dawson's Landing anchors its sense of reality and legitimacy. On the other hand, since elections by their very nature introduce contingency into the community – a sense of something "up for grabs," not to be taken for granted – they have the potential to be a destabilizing force. As stabilizing processes, elections both *acknowledge* the virtue of and *confer* virtue and authority on those elected and, at the same time, reciprocally confirm the legitimacy or "naturalness" of the election process itself and of the community that has elected them. On the surface, David Wilson's election as mayor seems of this sort. But, in *Those Extraordinary Twins*, at least, this mutual legitimation must rest not on concrete history – the experience of a completely successful election – but on unproven faith: faith that the contingent, destabilizing element is merely provisional and will give way to and in fact serve the sense of community continuity and legitimacy, and faith that, in the final count, elections really do confer and confirm legitimate merit. In the traumatic case of Luigi, election works only if the community – and the reader – is willing to overlook, or "kill," certain troubling aspects of the secular election experience and to appeal, if implicitly, to an extralegal, extratextual, or even extrasecular source of legitimation and meaning.

Twain's interest in the conflicts between various notions of election and in the ambiguities embedded within the notion of election itself is also manifest in *Pudd'nhead Wilson*, but here he not only approaches the theme more indirectly but also with a larger arsenal of implication. Although the charter election for mayor and aldermen appears again, it is not developed with the same rhetorical energy that it is in *Those Extraordinary Twins*, nor with the same specificity. In *Pudd'nhead Wilson*, the twins are not given party affiliations, but simply asked, vaguely, "to stand for seats in the forthcoming aldermanic board" (74). Whereas Luigi defeats Angelo in *Those Extraordinary Twins*, the emphasis in *Pudd'nhead Wilson* is on the anguish of their collective defeat: "The brothers withdrew entirely from society, and nursed their humiliation in privacy. They avoided the people, and went out for exercise only late at night, when the streets were deserted" (84). Their withdrawal from a daytime world of public election parallels a similar movement in the narrative toward an often-implicit exploration of certain more private and darker resonances in the notion of election. One small sign of this exploration is the metaphorical use of election to suggest the social construction of identity that reflects Dawson's Landing's dominant racist ideology: "To all intents and purposes Roxy was as white as anybody, but the one sixteenth of her which was black outvoted the other fifteen parts and made her a negro" (8–9). In general terms, the narrator's use of the electoral metaphor is a quiet reminder that, as in *Those Extraordinary Twins,* many of this community's conventional divisions and distinctions need for their legitimation, as do the community's leaders, the sense of having been "freely elected." More obviously, the metaphor can be seen primarily as an ironic commentary on the undemocratic basis of racial categorization, a world in which all votes are not equal. In a further irony, in fact, it is *"white"* voters who have designated "black blood" to count more heavily than "white blood" in the "identification" of individuals. Most crucially, the white electorate – that is, those whom the community defines as white – bases its legitimating and self-legitimating vote on the basis of its faith that it can read from things seen (often skin color; if not skin color, then speech, dress, or behavior) the essential black and white qualities of things unseen. Of all the bases of this faith, whether seen as rationalization or rationale, the most significant in this narrative are those embedded in religious discourse. But, as I will argue, slaves and ex-slaves also draw on religious discourse for their own purposes, as the narrator does for his. In often-muted and fragmentary ways, the three parties are engaged in battles that are both secular and theological. It is in *Pudd'nhead Wilson* more than in any other of Twain's novels that the charged division of black and white is linked to such terms as "elect" and "save" in a way that forces a striking if inconclusive confrontation of the intersection between the seeming ways of humankind and the possible ways of God.

One useful way of getting at this intersection is to consider the often-discussed episode in chapter 2 in which Percy Driscoll, frustrated in his effort to discover which of his four house slaves has stolen a small amount of money from him, presents them with a dire threat:

"I give you one minute . . . if at the end of that time you have not confessed, I will not only sell all four of you, *but –* I will sell you DOWN THE RIVER!"
It was equivalent to condemning them to hell! (12)

The implications of this passage and those that surround it may be more complicated than appear at first glance. Various cultural historians have pointed to the fact that, in a Bible-reading antebellum society, the notion of being sold down the river could readily be seen, by slaves and abolitionists alike, as equivalent to going metaphorically to a kind of physical and social hell, as embodied in the extremes of the slave system in the lower South. Certainly Harriet Beecher Stowe was suggesting this metaphorical connection in pressing Uncle Tom toward the dark golgatha of Simon Legree's Louisiana plantation, to face an avatar of the Devil. The drawable, if problematic, parallel between Huck Finn's worries about "going to hell" and his and Jim's ineluctable slide down the Mississippi suggest the force of this metaphorical correspondence in Twain's own work. In the episode noted above, Twain not merely introduces but also extends the analogy:

> It was equivalent to condemning them to hell! No Missouri negro doubted this. Roxy reeled in her tracks and the colour vanished out of her face; the others dropped to their knees as if they had been shot; tears gushed from their eyes, their supplicating hands went up, and three answers came in the one instant:
> "I done it!"
> "I done it!"
> "I done it! – have mercy marster – Lord have mercy on us po' niggers!"
> "Very good," said the master, putting up his watch, "I will sell you *here* though you don't deserve it. You ought to be sold down the river."
> The culprits flung themselves prone, in an ecstasy of gratitude, and kissed his feet, declaring that they would never forget his goodness and never cease to pray for him as long as they lived. They were sincere, for like a god he had stretched forth his mighty hand and closed the gates of hell against them. (12)

Most obviously, the passage on one hand brings acid satire to bear on a hegemonic slaveholding system that analogically allows a smug slaveholder to play a secular version of a Calvinistic God over his slaves. What we also need to account more for, however, is the narrator's emphasis on the slaves' ecstatically "sincere" and effusively expressed "gratitude" for Driscoll's "mercy." It is perfectly plausible to argue, of course, that, in addition to their genuine relief at having been spared a terrifying earthly fate, they are simply reacting strategically to someone who has absolute political and economic control over their physical well-being. They know well enough, as much as it pains them to perform it, the sort of groveling behavior and ego-stroking that will save their skins. Nevertheless, the rhetoric of the passage implicitly points to another model for their behavior. The drop to the knees, gushing tears, and "supplicating" hands have probably been learned at slaves' revival meetings. Whatever their private rage or fear as they plead with their secular master to save their bodies, they are also quite used to supplicating a higher Master on behalf of their souls.

The slaves may well hold their religious beliefs with some degree of sincerity, and those beliefs may well reflect more than a simple hegemonic cooption by the self-serving theology of the slaveholder. There may very well be in their beliefs, in fact, some elements that are potentially subversive of the slaveholder's cosmological claims to legitimacy and authority. Such a potential becomes clearer in the improvisational meditations of Roxy, the most imaginative and artistic of the slaves – the one who, by a coincidence that may be more than coincidence, is saved from the earthly downriver hell as a *result* of her religious faith:

> She was horrified to think how near she had come to being guilty herself; she had been saved in the nick of time by a revival in the coloured Methodist Church a fortnight before, at which time and place she "got religion." The very next day after that gracious experience, while her change of style was fresh upon her and she was vain of her purified condition, her master left a couple of dollars lying unprotected on his desk, and she happened upon that temptation when she was polishing around with a dust-rag. She looked at the money awhile with a steadily-rising resentment, then she burst out with –
>
> "Dad blame dat revival, I wisht it had 'a' be'n put off till to-morrow!"
>
> Then she covered the tempter with a book, and another member of the kitchen cabinet got it. She made this sacrifice as a matter of religious etiquette; as a thing necessary just now, but by no means to be wrested into a precedent; no, a week or two would limber up her piety, then she would be rational again . . . . (10–11)

Roxy may look at her religious beliefs as an "irrational" nuisance in the realm of moral values – much as the narrator of "The Facts Concerning the Recent Carnival of Crime in Connecticut" views his conscience – but her traumatic experience with Driscoll certainly gives her plausible grounds for giving credence to the efficacy of religious faith. That she acknowledges the stark limits to the *earthly* efficacy of such faith is manifest in her initial decision to drown her child and herself. She takes little stock in the probability of secular "salvation" for slaves or black people. But equally strikingly, she never wavers in her faith in the possibility for the salvation of their souls. Realizing that killing Driscoll "wouldn't save" her child "fum goin' down de river," she tells her sleeping child that "yo' po' mammy's got to kill you to save you . . . " (13). The Jordan of revival preachers' sermons and the notion of death as a passage to a heaven of joy are clearly on her mind as she consoles her child: "we gwine to jump in de river, den de troubles o' dis worl' is all over – dey don't sell po' niggers down the river over *yonder*" (13). As is signed by her double-directioned use of "save" and her conflation of the Mississippi and the Jordan rivers, Roxy, for all her seemingly naive literalism with regard to Biblical language, is engaged in a crucial act of translation. She is planning to do something that makes sense to her in theological at least as much as in secular terms. If a "fiction" from a secular standpoint, it is a fiction that empowers her toward independent action. Such notions prompt her to dress herself in "her new Sunday gown" and to prepare her son for death by dressing him in baby Tom's "snowy" baby-gowns – that is, to dress him not merely in the conventional garb of the angels and heavenly hosts but a garb that, in its whiteness, serves as a visible type of a saved soul. And it is this sincerely motivated act of "dressing for heaven" – of preparing herself to enter the society of God – that in turn leads Roxy to what surely must appear to her, given the context, as a divinely granted revelation: "Now a strange light dawned in her eyes" (14). It is only now that the secular implications of "saved" – the possibility that her child's body can be rescued and kept from harm in *this* life – enter Roxy's consciousness again, its secular resonances still mixed with the religious connotations: "oh, thank de good Lord in heaven, you's saved, you's saved! – dey ain't no man kin ever sell mammy's po' little honey down de river now!" (15).

I stress the sincerity of Roxy's religious faith because I believe we misread her child-switching, as have many critics, if we see it as motivated merely by secular ends, and her justification of that act as mere rationalization. Roxy's awareness of the secular possibilities of turning her son "white" – of making his "snowy" appearance become his public identity – comes only after, and as a result of, her making her son "white" for *religious* ends: marking him as electable, or in fact already elected, to membership in a heavenly society. It is important to understand her faith if we are to make adequate sense of the after-the-switch "theological" justification she offers to herself, as she translates into her own immediate situation the works of "dat ole nigger preacher." But that justification and its implications for both Roxy and the narrative as a whole cannot be sufficiently grasped unless we pay attention to the general context of religious discourse available to the inhabitants of Dawson's Landing. Roxy's justification must be seen as improvisational political theology that becomes a contender in the community's theological politics, a politics that pits not only "free-thinkers" against the faithful but, more profoundly if more covertly, blacks against whites. In complex ways, if ways often more implicit than explicit in the narrative, the religious discourse of Dawson's Landing, the concern over the state of souls, is deeply implicated in the community's battle for bodies—not only the battle over who can control whose body, but over what bodies are eligible for election as full members of the community and over who is a legitimate elector. The slaveholding structure not only uses religion as an ideological tool to justify its power and status but also sees in its power and status an index of the truth of its religious convictions. The slaves, in contrast, not only use religion to justify whatever physical resistance, however limited, they can make to that dominant structure but also posit a spiritual society that serves as radical critique and alternative social model to the dominant structure.[7]

At first glance, the differences between white and black religious dicourse in Dawson's Landing seem slight. Most of the town's Protestant residents, products of the Second Great Awakening, seem to officially and publicly profess some version, from milder to more severe, of the Calvinistic conviction that human beings are naturally fallen and need God's freely given grace to wash their sins away and draw them into the company of His elect.[8] God must elect the sinner despite the sinner's undeserving state. The electorate is an electorate of One, not a majority rule. Further, the rhetorical stress on humans' deserving of eternal punishment, or separation from the heavenly society of God, had potential elitist implications that might not be altogether lost on the status-conscious members of the community. In *Tom Sawyer*, Tom must endure a minister's "prosy . . . argument that dealt in limitless fire and brimstone and thinned the predestined elect down to a company so small as to be hardly worth the saving." Such ministers undoubtedly are also preaching in Dawson's Landing.

If ceremonially sceptical of the power of human effort in the matter of salvation, however, most white residents seem to have drifted in daily practice toward more optimistic Arminian notions that "right living" is not merely a duty owed God, whether one is saved or not, but a way of giving one's own salvation a helpful nudge along the right path—a demonstration of obedience to the Great Elector that may in fact incline Him to extend election one's way.[9] In practice, if not in theory, Arminianism tended toward a conflation of the community's dominant moral codes—and in particular its emphasis on acceptable social conduct—with "faithful" behavior. When Miss Watson tells Huck Finn that "*she* was going to live so as to go to the good place," she is of course taking an Arminian line. If ordinary white citizens of Dawson's Landing take such a line, it is even less strange that the community's white leaders find in their own secular success and authority an Arminian sign of their true identity and legitimate destiny. If their way of life is not merely a blessing by God but a just confirmation of that life's merits, a challenge to that life — for example, slaves' stealing of their property — is, they must believe, a challenge to God. Well can Percy Driscoll, in his deluded pride of self-making, see himself as acting as God's agent in threatening to send his disloyal servants to hell.

Even white free-thinkers like David Wilson hold views at least parallel to, and perhaps even indirectly founded upon, the dominant religious views of the community. As various critics have noted, Wilson's calendar offers in general a portrait of humans as pathetic, fallen creatures — a portrait that, for all its comic and satiric touches, has unmistakable Calvinistic resonances. If there is any major variation to a Calvinistic stance, however, it is not in the calendar's stress on humans as helpless, but in its suggestion that God may not be an omnipotent Being but a blunderer who gives mistaken orders and botches His creations. Rather than the Puritan view of human accidents as God's laws, Wilson's calendar suggests a universe in which God's accidents become human laws.

Such an iconoclastic theological perspective is of course in deep tension with the seemingly Arminian outcome of Wilson as a finite character in the narrative. Wilson's plotted behavior and motives seem on the surface less Jonathan Edward's, Michael Wigglesworth's, or even John Winthrop's than Benjamin Franklin's, the self-made "collector" who invests in "truths" (whether aphorisms or fingerprints), who "capitalizes" on that investment in order to gain community standing and the ability to play agent of eternal as well as social law, and who accepts that concluding standing and authority as a justly earned consequence of his own freely chosen actions. His white election at the conclusion of both *Pudd'nhead Wilson* and *Those Extraordinary Twins* — one of the few events those two severed works have in common — would thus seem a secular demonstration that salvation can be earned by and visibly manifest in independent action and free thinking. In some respects, in electing Wilson mayor, the white community of Dawson's Landing is electing Arminianism as the justifying principle of its own legitimacy. It is celebrating itself as a covenanted community whose blessings it has actually earned: a community beatified by the rectitude of its institutions and moral values, a community in which all whites can be elected.

Such a white communal self-election requires that the community kill out of its consciousness, as Wilson hides his calendar, and as Twain buries in *Those Extraordinary Twins*, the dark possibility expressed by the most religiously earnest white character in either narrative, a character described by Twain in a chapter headnote as a man who "was always seeking truth" (143). If Wilson's free-thinking can lead him, in the privacy of his calender, to what, in Calvinistic terms, would be seen as a relatively mild emphasis on humans as mainly fools, it is Angelo, the relentless seeker of religious truth, who nurses in private a conviction even closer to the heart of Calvinism: "To him, in the privacy of his secret thoughts, all other men were monsters, deformities . . ." (137). It is conceivably significant that such secret convictions seem expressible only by someone who, like his darker brother, has been a slave (28).

In *Pudd'nhead Wilson*, this black and ironically "Angelic" viewpoint is held most forcefully not by the white community but by the slave community, and articulated primarily through Roxy. In some respects, both slaves and slaveholders in Dawson's Landing are bound by a common evangelical, democratically tending Protestantism whose common strands the slaveholders cannot fully acknowledge lest it compromise their own legitimacy. Whatever whites may believe about their slaves, the slaves themselves believe in their own capacity to save their souls if not their bodies. Lawrence Levine has argued that "the religious revivals which swept large numbers of slaves into the Christian fold in the late eighteenth and early nineteenth centuries . . . were based on a practical and implied, if not invariably theological or overt, Arminianism: God would save all who believed in Him; Salvation was there for all to take hold of if they would."[10] The slaves are able to imagine a heavenly society in which they will be full citizens, "respectable" members. As Roxy tells her son, while dressing him up for his legitimate heavenly part: "De angels is gwine to 'mire you jist as much as dey does yo' mammy. Ain't gwine to have 'em putt'n' dey han's up 'fo' dey eyes en sayin' to David en Goliah en dem yuther prophets, 'Dat chile is dress' too indelicate fo' dis place'" (14). As with white Arminianism, such evangelical convictions tend to link election and human agency, salvation and moral behavior. Thus, after being "saved" and "getting religion" at a Methodist revival meeting, Roxy refrains from stealing her master's money as a matter of "religious etiquette" (10–11). Whatever its hopeful aspects when applied to themselves, however, slaves can also turn Arminianism against the slaveholder. If one can save oneself through good works, one can damn oneself through bad works. It is a religious and not merely a moral vision that slaves appeal to in attacking slaveholders for their acts of oppression, for the prideful attempt to play god over other humans. They are able to sever conventional white morality from spiritual election and, in so doing, convict slaveholders in a court that is higher than the one in which Wilson achieves his secular victory. In a guerilla warfare that is part of a theological politics, they transform the conventional meaning of "black" and "white" deeds:

They had an unfair show in the battle of life, and they held it no sin to take military advantage of the enemy – in a small way; in a small way, but not in a large one. They would smouch provisions from the pantry . . . or any other property of light value; and so far were they from considering such reprisals sinful, that they would go to church and shout and pray their loudest and sincerest with their plunder in their pockets. . . . The humane negro prowler . . . [was] perfectly sure that in taking [a] trifle from the man who daily robbed him of an inestimable treasure – his liberty – he was not committing any sin that God would remember against him in the Last Great Day. (11–12)

If slaves can have faith that they can be saved, they can also imagine that it will be the white devil who, in the ultimate Courtroom, will be sent down river.

It is in fact this imaginative ability to use the white people's religion against them, to imagine a God who is an agent not only of "black" justice but also of black vengeance, that leads the artistic Roxy in her fateful switching of children to a rationale that, far from Arminian, draws instead on an opposed theological perspective closer to a traditional Calvinism: "It was dat ole nigger preacher dat tole it . . . . He said dey ain't nobody kin save his own self – can't do it by faith, can't do it by works, can't do it no way at all. Free grace is de *on'y* way, en dat don't come fum nobody but jis' de Lord; en *he* kin give it to anybody he please, saint or sinner – *he* don't kyer. He do jis' as he's a mineter. He s'lect out anybody dat suit him, en put another one in his place, en make de fust one happy for ever en leave t'other one to burn wid Satan" (15).

Although most critics tend to see this passage as Roxy's rationalization of her own self-interested actions, I believe it equally plausible, as I have suggested previously, to argue that she genuinely sees herself at this moment as merely an agent of God's own mysterious power to impose both free grace and damnation.[11] Just as slaves can use Arminianism not only for their own interest and against the slaveholders', so Roxy can make similar use of frontier Calvinism. Even if God is all-powerful and humans absolutely helpless, He can save helpless slaves and damn ruling white men as easily as the other way around.

But the language of the passage, whatever its basis in the nineteenth-century version of conventional Calvinist discourse, has even a more radical potential – a potential for which, two centuries earlier, John Winthrop was to expel Anne Hutchinson from his covenanted community. In Roxy's stress not only on the absolute power of God and the absolute helplessness of humans but also on the absolute unreliability of external earthly signs (the appearance of being either "saint or sinner") as an index to salvation or damnation, she is (if unconsciously, as Twain himself may be) drawing upon the legacy of another rebellious, socially and politically subversive woman, Anne Hutchinson. Not merely the Puritanism of Winthrop's "covenant of grace," Roxy's improvisational theology, at least at this moment, is closer to the "heresy" of Antinomianism.[12] Roxy's own subversiveness lies not merely in translating two bodies between contexts but in justifying it on the basis of a theology that would make nonsense out of all secular moral distinctions, cast radical doubts on any necessary relationship between grace and appearance, between justification and sanctification. However briefly, then, this passage raises the possibility of seeing *Pudd'nhead Wilson* not merely as an ironic playing out of the competition of black and white versions of Arminianism or even of conventional nineteenth-century religious and secular faiths but as the battlefield for two dark forms of "free" or heretical thinking: one embedded in the nominally scientific determinism of Wilson's appeal, through his fingerprinting, to natural laws of his fingerprinting; the other embedded in Roxy's momentary vision of the radical arbitrariness of experience – a vision not far from the suggestions in Wilson's calendar that human history is a series of cosmic mistakes, the product of a blundering rather than omniscient Creator. If *Pudd'nhead Wilson,* as Forrest Robinson and others have powerfully argued, demonstrates the deep immorality of both slavery and racist rationalizations of slavery only, in "bad faith," to repress that demonstration,[13] it also raises, more darkly, the possibility that, from certain cosmological perspectives, all moral distinctions are arbitrary. If the slaves' own theology can offer a vision of slaveholding as not merely immoral but sinful – not merely a crime against humankind but a rebellion against God's commandments – and thus serve them as a counterhegemonic weapon against slaveholders' complacent sense of themselves as elected and legitimate, the bleakest implications of the improvisational meditations of the narrative's two artists, Roxy and Wilson, cast doubts on human ability to really know what is sinful.

These deep, if inchoately expressed, theological ambivalences of the narrative are reflected in part in the codes embedded in the discourse not only of the novel's characters but also of its narrator. If inconsistently, the narrative not only attacks racist constructions of the *secular* meanings of white and black – points to the unreliability of physiognomy or socially constructed definitions of white and black behavior as guides to the complexities of individual identity – but also uses the color conventions of the white community's racist theology against that very community. There may be a racist dimension to the color symbolism of Protestantism that finds sinfulness as black and sanctity as white. There may be even further racist ironies in the homologies between the secular notion that, in the social construction of identity, one drop of "black" blood, can "out-vote" a human-ful of "white" blood, and the conventional Calvinist construction of the human soul that stresses that even one "black" drop of sinfulness can outweigh all one's good deeds and impulses unless contravened by God's power and mercy – that sinner can always outvote saint without the intervention of God's election. But it is perfectly possible for Twain – a man capable of dressing in white while warming his pen in hell – to cast an ironic eye on the convention itself. Roxy may attack her son for his cowardly lack of a sense of honor by using standard racial coding in a way that conceivably suggests Calvinist underpinnings: "It's de nigger in you, dat's what it is. Thirty-one parts o' you is white, en on'ly one part nigger, en dat po' little one part is yo' *soul.* Tain't wuth savin'; tain't wuth totin' out on a shovel en tho'in' in de gutter" (70). But she also posits in virtually the same breath a dark and honorable ancestry for Tom and herself – dark parents who, ironically, are also the parents of America's white founders: "En it ain't on'y jist Essex blood dat's in you, not by a long sight – 'deed it ain't! My great-great-great-gran'father en yo' great-great-great-great-gran'father was ole Cap'n John Smith, de highest blood dat Ole Virginny every turned out; en *his* great-great-gran'mother or somers along back dah, was Pocahontas de Injun queen, en her husban' was a nigger king outen Africa – en yit here you is, a slinkin' outen a duel en disgracin' our whole line like a ornery low-down hound! Yes, it's de nigger in you!" (70).

It is hard to know whether it is Roxy's improvisational haste or the narrator's that causes her to use "nigger" in such diametrically opposite ways. Whatever the intention, the effect is to make "nigger" implicitly synonymous with the human race as a whole, in both its morally light and dark aspects. If the "nigger king outen Africa" can be considered by Tom, in another context, in a narrowly racial sense (when he first learns he is part "nigger," "He said to himself that the curse of Ham was upon him" [45]), in other spots the narrative suggests another even earlier and more comprehensive avatar of that African ancestor. At one point, attacking Tom's cowardice, Wilson calls him a "degenerate remnant of an honorable line!" (63). Strictly speaking, Wilson is referring to Tom's white American ancestry. But the narrative itself is pointing symbolically to a much longer human line, one that, like Roxy's, leads back through all the human "races" in their divisions to the "founding family" of the human race itself. Whatever the significance of the numerous references to Adam and Eve in Wilson's calendar, it is certainly tempting to see Tom, as Brodwin does, as the most degenerate descendant of the long tragic line extending from them to him — a living continuant of his primal ancestors' fall from grace. In fact, one might even see in his dissolute life a typological recapitulation of many of the major morally and spiritually dark waystations in that history: the jealous persecution of a brother (the Cain-Abel story retold in his relationship with Chambers), the stealing of a brother's legacy, the worship of a golden calf, the murder of a patriarch, and — in selling his mother "down de river" — the Judas-like betrayal of a loving savior. As Roxy makes explicit, "You could be Judas to yo' own mother to save yo' wuthless hide!" (90). From a dark Arminian perspective, Tom's own actions have shrunk his soul to what the narrator calls "his small soul" (85) — a soul finally good for nothing, as his mother suggests, but to be cast into the gutter. From this perspective, his being sold down the river in the last "sentence" of the narrative is a typologically just conclusion. It is what every "black" soul finally deserves. At the same time, "Tom" is translated by the dominant community from moral and religious into even more relentlessly secular terms: from criminal and sinner to property. Ironically, he is "saved" for his highest and best economic use. Certainly such a classification seems to represent the Last Judgment of the Dawson's Landing powers-that-be, including Wilson the elected.

Whether it represents the last judgment of the narrative itself is less certain. Roxy's concluding meditations may well lead in directions that veer away from the narrative's easy resolution. Upon Tom's earthly defeat, and hers, she falls back on what throughout the novel has been one of the few constants in her life: "In her church and its affairs she found her only solace" (114). When Tom is convicted, Roxy instinctively assumes the attitude of prayer — "flung herself upon her knees" — and cries, "De Lord have mercy on me, po' misable sinner dat I is!" (113). If a dark theology, it at least offers her "black" soul as well as her defeated body a small ray of hope in an unknowable and arbitrary God who can still elect either earthly sinner or saint.[14] Looked at with the troubled eye of a faith that has not yet denied its Antinomian tendencies, the fate of her son — and of herself — must seem less a sign of rational earthly justice than another dark reminder that earthly pain is simply a manifestation of God's inscrutable ways, and of humans' helplessness until He elects them. Until that great election, in which the sole voter is the great Judge who will also preside over the Final Judgment, no individual, no matter what their earthly success and no matter how responsible their moral behavior, can ever know for certain whether he or she is heading downriver. In such a spiritual universe, even a Pudd'nhead Wilson's own election may be in doubt, whatever his earthly victories.

Nothing in the concluding narrative necessarily contradicts Roxy's dark theology; nor does it affirm that theology. It simply juxtaposes to it Wilson's final calendar entry, which also remains ambiguously aloof from the chapter it heads and even from the possibly optatively Arminian implications of Wilson's own election and trial victory. The calendar's conclusion is gnomic, not clarifying: "It was wonderful to find America, but it would have been more wonderful to miss it" (113). With the dual sense of both secular and spiritual possibility resonating in the appeal to wonder, we might be forgiven for finding ourselves reminded of the narrator's suggestion in another "down-river" tale, Melville's *Confidence-Man*, that "something further may follow of this masquerade."

The masquerade has in fact traced its ambiguous and uncertain course from the very opening of the novel, in its (perhaps) deceptively mild pastoral evocation of Dawson's Landing:

In 1830 it was a snug little collection of modest one and two-story frame dwellings whose white-washed exteriors were almost concealed from sight by climbing tangles of rose-vines, honeysuckles, and morning-glories. Each of these pretty homes had a garden in front fenced with white palings and opulently stocked with hollyhocks, marigolds, touch-me-nots, prince's feathers, and other old-fashioned flowers; while on the window-sills of the houses stood wooden boxes . . . in which grew a breed of geranium whose spread of intensely red blossoms accented the prevailing pink tint of the rose-clad house-front like an explosion of flame. (3)

Viewed from the angle of a benignly Arminian theology, one might catch here in the details and tone many hints of a secular Eden that may in fact be a sanctified sign of a higher justified state, a living manifestation of beatitude. But in the color-coded culture of Dawson's Landing, and of Twain's late-nineteenth-century America, it is hard not to find complications in this description of a seemingly innocent, beatific, and abundantly creative garden. The garden, after all, both surrounds "white-washed exteriors" and is in turn fenced by "white palings." It is indeed a white world that has been seemingly blessed in Dawson's Landing, subject to the sort of "white election" to which Emily Dickinson was to give a very personal meaning. And yet that election, certainly in its secular, social version, seems to have been achieved – or perhaps luckily and even undeservedly inherited – at a terrible human price: built on the scars and bones of a socially damned race that is constantly being sold down the river; a "race" that, nevertheless, in its own creative energy, brings "color" to this world – including the drama that Roxy's religiously inspired child-switching launches. When Roxy prepares to commit suicide in chapter 3 she puts on her "new Sunday gown," "a conflagration of gaudy colors and fantastic figures" that cloaks her in a "volcanic irruption of infernal splendors" (13). One is tempted to remember the "intensely red blossoms" that clad Dawson's Landing's white exteriors "like an explosion of flame." And one may be tempted to speculate that this community may be caught in more flames than one, depending on whether one's angle of vision is relentlessly secular, hopefully or darkly Arminian, Calvinist, Antinomian, or agnostically provisional. Whether the flames do or do not offer a type or warning of moral or spiritual destruction, the possibility with which Twain would fuel many of his later fictions and essays, in *Pudd'nhead Wilson* they suggest at the least that the artist needs flames to fan, and that theological politics are a powerful fan.

WILSON CAREY McWILLIAMS

Pudd'nhead Wilson
on Democratic Governance

Courts and hustings are the stage for much of the tumult in Pudd'nhead Wilson, but politics is also present behind the scenes and in the design of the story itself. Framed by years which define an era in American party politics, Pudd'nhead Wilson begins in 1830, just before Jackson's first election and the birth of mass parties, and ends in 1853 with the triumph of the Democrats. The Virginians, children of the founding generation, yield to the "new men"; Pudd'nhead Wilson is, apparently, a complete chapter in the democratization of political life.[1]

Twain's readers, however, know that Nemesis is in the wings: within a year, the Kansas-Nebraska Act will shatter the victorious Democracy, along with the "second American party system."[2] The Democrats' flaw is their inability to deal with slavery as a matter of principle; like David Wilson, their mayoral candidate in Dawson's Landing, the Democrats are capable only of pragmatic accommodations which mend the fabric of slave society. In this sense, Pudd'nhead Wilson speaks to the limits of party politics, enunciating the fairly obvious truth that a party cannot correct fundamental defects of the whole of which it is a part.[3] Of course, the story also has much more to say: the shortcomings of party point to the need for statecraft, and, as Robert Regan argues, Pudd'nhead Wilson is a sustained reflection on the ancient question, "Who should rule?"[4]

In the simpler politics of Dawson's Landing, rule and political motivation appear in relatively pure form. Small-town government offers only limited possibilities for material gain and no hope for grand designs.[5] Power in Dawson's Landing, modest at best, derives from wealth, not office. Ruling is more magisterial than imperial, manifested in judging rather than commanding, and political office ordinarily is sought as a badge of dignity or a source of honor.

Citizens in Dawson's Landing, consequently, are asked to choose a republican nobility, and their judgment is relatively unclouded by extrinsicalities. The voters' interests are not involved in any immediate or important way, and the only ostensible political issue in Twain's story turns on attitudes toward drink – and even that standard is relaxed, by the drinkers at least, out of good fellowship and in recognition of personal character (55–56).

Implicitly, the homey politics of Dawson's Landing reflects the ancient doctrine that rule is an ordering according to some virtue or excellence, a first principle thought to epitomize the best life. Democratic elections are evaluations of *qualities*: a self-governing people elects the models held up for its emulation. In deciding who should rule, the citizens of Dawson's Landing are asking, Who deserves honor?, and hence, What is honorable? At the most fundamental level, democratic governance involves an inquiry into the nature of nobility.[6]

Our national text on republican nobility is the letter to John Adams in which Jefferson declares his belief in a "natural aristocracy," and *Pudd'nhead Wilson* amounts to a critical response to Jefferson's argument.[7] Jefferson maintains that human rule originally derived from "bodily powers," especially physical strength. Gunpowder, however, has put "missile death" into the hands of the weak as well as the strong. Strength of body has been lowered to the level of the social graces; like "beauty, good humor, politeness and other accomplishments," it is now no more than an "auxiliary ground of distinction." The aristocracy of body, then, is natural, but its importance is historically relative, declining with the advance of civilization. By contrast, artificial aristocracy, based on wealth or birth, is the child of civil society because it rests solely on custom and convention. Natural aristocracy in the enduring sense, on the other hand, is founded on "virtue and talents" and is intended by nature "for the instruction, the trusts and the government of society." The best regime, Jefferson contends, provides for the separation of rulers from their counterfeits, the "pseudo-*aristoi*" of convention and body, a task which Jefferson holds is best left to citizens and elections.

But Jefferson's historical argument, with its claim that civilization reduces the importance of "bodily powers," ought to have called into question the two distinctions of body embedded in the American founding, the inequalities of race and gender. For prudential reasons, the Framers gave slavery a place in the Constitution, but they did not believe it could be justified philosophically. They did, however, harbor at least the suspicion that race establishes a natural hierarchy, and they do not seem seriously to have questioned the inferior status of women.[8] In *Pudd'nhead Wilson*, Twain does not stop with Jefferson's categories, although his critique explores each of them; he goes on to search out flaws in the foundations of American political society.

Rulers at the outset of the story, the F.F.V.s aspire to be thought an aristocracy of birth, and the Virginians do have a courtliness which sets them apart from their fellows. However, their pretense of high-born gentility is as thin as their Elizabethan names are pretentious. In fact, the Virginians are small-town entrepreneurs, somewhat ashamedly avaricious for the property which is the real foundation of their position. Percy Driscoll is a speculator, worn out by the effort to save his property; the Judge is killed when "wearied" by a late night spent at "work upon his finances" (22,94). Confronted with European aristocrats, the Judge reveals himself to be a booster, pitifully vain about the petty "splendors" of Dawson's Landing and his own small honors. In politics, the Judge does not hesitate to use bribery and innuendo, and intellectually, while the Judge's free-thinking ties him to the deism of the founding generation, he is as dogmatic as his Presbyterian friend, Howard (31, 58, 79, 83). The F.F.V.s are genteel Babbitts, Whiggery personified, paladins of the bourgeoisie.

The Virginians' real claim to aristocracy rests on their code of honor, their appeal to the ideal of courage. Upholding mannered force, the F.F.V.s are a residuum of Jefferson's aristocracy of strength. In an important sense, they are still people in the state of nature, clinging to natural freedom and self-enforced law, not natural rulers but pre-political individualists. Nominally servants of the law, Judge Driscoll and Pembroke Howard disdain it for themselves, ranking personal honor above law and religion alike.[9]

Driscoll and Howard, born about 1790, are heirs to the Framers' doctrines — especially, given their pride in Virginia, to Jefferson's teaching — and their code reflects the logic of that inheritance.[10] In liberal theory, government and law are restraints to which one submits in order to control others, always to be minimized for oneself. Liberty, the Framers' first principle, deprecates and undermines the government of laws, their great achievement.[11] Freedom erodes form: in that sense, Tom Driscoll is a debased but natural child of his own rearing and the Framers' theory.[12]

The code of the Virginians elevates them above craven and vulgar materialists, but at bottom it is unworthy. Chapter 12, which discusses the codes, is the most clearly sermonic discourse in *Pudd'nhead Wilson*: the body of the chapter is patently an illustration of the text from the Calendar, which defines bravery as the virtue of fleas. Courage requires "mastery of fear," and similarly, presumes knowledge of what is to be feared. The code of the F.F.V.s, however, has no such philosophic grounding; it rests on a parochialism which makes Virginia – and implicitly, Virginians – the center of creation, an individualist's granfalloon.[13]

Unlike the F.F.V.s, Angelo and Luigi Cappello, born to "the old Florentine nobility," are conventional aristocrats in Jefferson's classification (27).[14] Virtually identical in body, they differ in religion, in politicality, and in attitudes toward drink and duelling; their dissimilar personalities underline the artificiality of rank based on birth and blood (48, 54, 143–44). And yet, in addition to "charm of manner and easy and polished bearing," the twins have a substantial political virtue: they are generously considerate of others. Faced with Judge Driscoll's self-preoccupied local pride, the twins "admired his admiration," respecting Driscoll's dignity and his patriotism even though they could not share his evaluation of his own and Dawson's Landing's glories (31).

Noblesse oblige, but in this case it does so with little or no apparent condescension, possibly because the humbling experience of "slavery" – the need to earn a living by being exhibited – has taught the Cappellos to distinguish between social appearances and human realities (28). Those who are born to rule, if they learn what it is to be ruled, have evident political advantages over those who are merely born free. Yet even at its best, the aristocracy of convention must take second place to natural nobility: the twins are nominated for aldermen, but David Wilson runs for mayor.

Wilson, born in 1805, is a child of Jefferson's era, a "new man," undistinguished by birth or wealth, who eventually passes Jefferson's test for natural aristocrats by winning the suffrages of his fellow citizens.[15] Wilson's career, however, also allows Twain to criticize the Enlightenment's idea of politics, especially for its rejection of the distinction between theory and practice, its deprecation of the limitations of the political.[16]

First, Wilson's very success helps to indicate the shortcomings of Jefferson's confidence in popular judgment. The public in Dawson's Landing does not come to appreciate Wilson's theoretical wisdom about human nature. Rather, the community's esteem derives from the striking "effect" Wilson produces in the courtroom, his ability to present evidence to the eyes, not his insight into things unseen. Public perception rarely goes behind the appearances, and in important ways, political culture and convention define what is seen. Politics, in the ordinary course of things, takes place in the Cave.

This is as it must be. In *Those Extraordinary Twins*, the twins' physiological peculiarity does not entirely obscure the fact that Wilson's courtroom defense (143-53) rests on a philosophic truth: action is an imperfect guide to intention and identity; what we *do*, so often the result of fortune and circumstance, does not reveal who we *are*.[17] In heaven, Captain Stormfield discovered, Shakespeare ranks below a Tennessee tailor and an Afghan horse-doctor, both of whom would have written greater poetry than the Bard, but were born to circumstances which discouraged their talents. Heavenly justice is perfect, and what is due to an individual is determined by who he or she is, not by what he or she has done.[18] Yet, as Judge Robinson points out in *Those Extraordinary Twins*, no civilized—in fact, no earthly—community can operate on that basis. Here below, human identity involves an element of mystery, and political societies must hold us responsible for our conduct and rank us according to our achievements. Political rule is at best an imperfect justice, bound up with the approximations of convention.[19]

Nevertheless, nature violated will be revenged. The tension between appearance and reality, praxis and truth, is a standing threat, more or less severe, to the order of civil society. Sooner or later, the fabric of convention will tear under the strain. It is a vital part of political rule to accommodate practice to nature, ordinarily by patching the cloak of conventionality—although sometimes, a more radical reweaving is required.[20]

A natural aristocrat, consequently, must be an outsider as well as an insider, informed by the theorist's suspicion of appearance and appreciation of the ironies of civil life. Political rule presumes an element of sympathetic disdain for convention and its proprieties, a theoretical disrespect for respectability. In the ancient wisdom the best ruler is also the best thief.[21]

Pudd'nhead Wilson sets the tragedy in motion because he sees, speculatively, behind the babies' clothing, detecting what has escaped the white citizens of Dawson's Landing, that Tom and Chambers are practically indistinguishable.[22] This theoretical perception that the appearances are deceptive encourages Roxy to violate the community's fundamental distinction between white and black. Yet in the end it is also Wilson's theoretical qualities which lead him to restore the community's order.

His merely practical reasoning is an impediment in at least two ways. First, Wilson represses his inarticulate and speculative suspicion that Tom may be the murderer. And second, Wilson's practical problem is solved when he is confronted, by accident, with the evidence that Tom committed the crime. It is his theoretical impulse that leads him to examine *all* of Tom's fingerprints – carrying things back to their origins, seeking a complete natural history – and thence, via a dream, to the discovery that the babies had been exchanged. Wilson's discovery reestablished the proprieties, demonstrating that the crime had not been committed by a gentleman, but by a "negro and slave." He provided Dawson's Landing with a new, scientific basis for the view that identity is based on "blood," for fingerprints, although subtle and ordinarily invisible, still offer a definition of the self based on the body and the appearances.

However, Wilson also changed the old order, giving it a jog in the direction of nature. His solution turns on the subversive principle that those who appear to be slaves may in fact be free, and that it may be the nominally free who are slaves.[23] That hint of new truth, more than any technical ingenuity, places Wilson among the aristocrats of nature.

Comparing Wilson to Benjamin Franklin reinforces this dimension of Twain's teaching. *Pudd'nhead Wilson's Calendar* is *Poor Richard's Almanac* in reverse: where Franklin's maxims promise success, Wilson's are more apt to reveal that success is sham.[24] Nevertheless, both Franklin and Wilson begin as ambitious new men – Wilson's first words tell us to "get the trick" – and eventually make their fortunes.[25]

In Wilson's case, of course, success is delayed because the failure of his joke causes him to be regarded as a fool. As Jay Hubbell observes, however, the joke is hoary small-town humor which oldsters in Dawson's Landing would surely have understood.[26] Their response to Wilson may, in fact, amount to putting him in his place. Twain spoke of Franklin's "unseemly endeavor to make himself conspicuous when he entered Philadelphia," and Wilson begins in a similarly bumptious manner. Franklin got away with his forwardness; Twain contrives to have Wilson rebuked and excluded, leaving him – unlike Franklin – the school of detachment.[27]

In Franklin's teaching, practice usurps the place of theory. His maxims, Twain observes, make only a "show of originality"; in fact, Franklin teaches a radical self-seeking which was platitudinous "as early as the dispersion from Babel."[28] Paralleling the "science of politics" as the Framers understood it, Franklin's doctrine promotes a method for controlling outward behavior, not the inward shaping of the soul. Franklin deprecated humility, for example, because it could not be learned behaviorally: after a few days of practice, Franklin said, he became proud of his humility, wittily implying that humility, if a virtue at all, is incapable of rational cultivation.[29] Twain, on the other hand, begins Wilson's education with a humiliation, prizing that egalitarian excellence of soul.

Moreover, Franklin's individualism led to a kind of tyranny over the self in the interest of socially defined success rather than the sort of self-government in which every part of the soul has its say. His nostrums, "calculated to inflict suffering on the rising generation," set terms on which boys know – or so Twain said – that success is not worth having. In this, Franklin was either a deceiver or self-deceived; an "adroit old adventurer," he claimed to be "fishing for lightning" when he wanted to fly his kite on the Sabbath, and got praised for Sabbath-breaking.[30] In Franklin's teaching, however, seriousness displaces playfulness, and with it, theoretic perspective on the self and society alike. By contrast, Pudd'nhead Wilson defines his science as an amusement, which of course it is, although its implications for political practice prove to be fateful. Letting Wilson's joke be taken seriously, Twain leaves him the fool's freedom to be playful about serious things, a liberty essential to a ruler's education.

Wilson's long exclusion may have made a more specifically political contribution to his education. Debarred from the practice of the law, he could pursue his chosen profession – to which he was determined to return – only through theoretical reflection. Earning a living by surveying and accounting, marking the extent of private estates and fortunes, it seems likely that Wilson would have felt as well as perceived the public nature of law. Similarly, the quantitative and technical character of his workaday occupations would have emphasized the qualitative and deliberative reasoning of the law. At any rate, Wilson came to understand that the law, a human art, must often proceed by indirections. "Adam was but human – this explains it all. He did not want the apple for the apple's sake – he only wanted it because it was forbidden. The mistake was in not forbidding the serpent; then he would have eaten the serpent" (6).[31]

Wilson began with "Scotch patience and pluck," but his long exile tested and strengthened those native virtues. Democratic politics is slow and necessarily tries the patience of natural aristocrats. *Pudd'n-head Wilson* is the *Pilgrim's Progress* of a political man, one who learns from experience the painful lesson of political practice: not to expect much, or very soon.

All of this political education is effective, however, only because Wilson stays in Dawson's Landing after his original failure. That he does so reflects his character, not his fate: college-bred and university-trained, David Wilson need not have endured humiliation in a small Missouri town. Sam Glover, judged a "perfect chucklehead" by Hannibal, went on to become a successful lawyer in St. Louis.[32] In Twain's story, however, Pudd'nhead Wilson sticks out his time in the wilderness.

Wilson *cares* about Dawson's Landing, and that affective bond to the community is a mark of his politicality. Wilson's amiable civility, his capacity for civic friendship, is one of his most admirable qualities. Out of friendship for Judge Driscoll, Wilson says, he would have kept Tom's case out of court had he known the circumstances, even though it was by defending Luigi that Wilson became a "launched and recognized lawyer" (63). Wilson seems to have assumed that the Judge knew of and permitted Tom's appeal to the law, and even though he found such agreement puzzling, he did not go out of his way to inquire about the Judge's knowledge and intent. That atypical incuriosity does not mean — as Eberhard Alsen argues — that Wilson was insincere in his proclaimed loyalty to Judge Driscoll (328). It shows only that the claims of civic friendship are limited. Always utilitarian in part, civic friendship is satisfied when the proprieties are observed, a standard Wilson more than meets.[33] No one doubts that Wilson would have kept the case out of court had the Judge's disapproval been clear and public, and this alone makes Wilson an exception to the ordinary rule — articulated at the beginning of chapter 8 — in which money prevails over friendship (33).[34] If compelled to choose, Wilson is willing to subordinate private interests to personal loyalties and civil decencies, a readiness which is at least the first step toward public virtue.[35]

However, this very political gift or quality leads Wilson, out of friendship, to lend support to a code of honor he despises. That questionable loyalty indicates how much democratic leaders need to be protected against their desire for the public's love and esteem.[36] Democratic rulers need critical perspective, the outsider's vision nurtured during Wilson's pilgrim years.[37] Even that distance, however, may not be enough. Up to a point, it is a ruler's virtue to do as Wilson does, to try to preserve a regime for which one feels a measure of disdain.[38] Natural nobility accommodates itself to democracy only when scorn and contempt, those aristocratic sentiments, are moderated by sympathy and compassion. But even natural aristocrats are too apt to find excuses for the publics and polities they love. There is also a point at which a regime, flawed in its first principles, becomes insupportable, when compromise is unworthy and when tenderness demeans rulers and ruled alike. In the great crises and founding moments of political life, natural aristocrats need the guidance and example of natural monarchs.[39]

Roxy, a woman and a black, is a memorial to Jefferson's omissions and the Framers' departures from the principle of equality. Even her name commemorates the faults of American political culture, since Twain was probably thinking of Plutarch's account, according to which Alexander – moved by a passion for Roxana – married her in order to gratify a conquered people and to show that, even in lust, he was ruled by law.[40] Recalling that ancient example, Roxy's name mocks white men in America.

Yet Roxy is also a queen, as Twain is at some pains to point out, with a natural majesty only imperfectly disguised by her surroundings (38, 43).[41] Twain makes Essex her lover rather than her owner, a less than subtle hint. Beyond such allusions, he tells us that although Roxy did not love Tom – who was not very loveable, after all – she was fond of him because "her nature needed someone to rule over, and he was better than nothing" (46).

Affected by the society in which she lives, Roxy accepts, along with much of its racism, the myth of blood descent, the idea that identity derives from the body.[42] Sensing her own regality, she invents a noble ancestry which is laughably false, a burlesque of American genealogizing (70). In fact, Roxy herself refutes the prevailing American notion of identity. Biologically, of course, it is absurd to classify Roxy as black: Twain makes clear that her race is defined politically – "the one sixteenth of her which was black out-voted the other fifteen parts" – a convention which makes sense only on the assumption that blacks are a physical aristocracy whose genes are entitled to overrule white majorities. Despite the fact that Roxy looks white, however, Twain's readers envision her as black. Her identity is established by her speech: she is heard before she is seen, and her appearance, at first jarring, tends to be gradually discounted in the reader's imagery. Speech, the most political of faculties, is second sight, our best guide to the soul. In political practice, however, speech is ordinarily subordinated to sight. The citizens of Dawson's Landing partly correct their mishearing of Wilson; distracted by race and gender, they remain deaf to Roxy's majesty.

Roxy is royal because her willingness to sacrifice is not limited to what she loves. It extends to what she has ceased to love, to the relationships and designs in which she had a part, a founder's sense of responsibility for the unlovely as well as the seemly.[43] Ruthless as well as magnanimous – for she is engaged in a kind of war – she is ready to kill her child to save him from being sold down the river, but she will not desert him, even in death.[44] And later, Roxy chooses to be sold back into slavery, a sacrifice beyond dying, to save her child. In the ruler's soul, faithfulness outranks both life and liberty.

Even her hubris is of royal proportions, although its form is characteristically American. Roxy justifies changing the babies by comparing herself to an English servant who, in like manner, made her son into a king. This reversal of fates, however, was meant to illustrate God's Free Grace; Roxy usurps God's role or, at least, claims to be acting as God's agent (15).[45]

Roxy's wisdom says otherwise. In a passage eventually omitted from *Pudd'nhead Wilson*, Roxy declares her disbelief in "special providences" – the doctrine of Grace applied to secular affairs – holding that this world obeys "well-regulated general laws." As she rebukes Jasper, the belief in "special providences" derives from the conceit that one is the center of and reason for a complex event. In the age-old human delusion, the individual imagines himself the "chief delight of God," exempt from the common fate (189–90).[46]

Believing that her son can be made the exception to the rule of slavery and racism, Roxy violates her own political sense of general law and common order. Slavery corrupts whites as surely as it deprives blacks: ironically, by making Tom the beneficiary of her version of special providence, Roxy damages his health and dooms his character (20–21).[47] From an evil like racism, "nobody can save his own self" by effort or fortune: the thing is a part of the regime as a whole. Whatever secular salvation there is must come through the laws of nature or political life, and it must begin with a recognition of dependence and community.

In America, however, the hope of elevating one's children, the dream of transfiguring opportunity, tempts even natural monarchs to brush aside that political understanding. Roxy's undoing is the result of her moment of private mastery and individual freedom.

Twain prefaced his "Whisper to the Reader" with a quotation from *Pudd'nhead Wilson's Calendar* praising the ass as "the choicest spirit among all the humbler animals" (1). This saying points toward the story, of course, because Wilson, like the ass, has his reputation "destroyed by ridicule." The aphorism also speaks to Twain's fundamental theme: it proclaims that the ass is noble, excellent among animals who are not inferior for being humble.[48]

The ass, no passive servant, has a sturdy will of its own, but is notable for its ability to bear great burdens. In that respect, it resembles the "load-bearing spirit," the first of the three metamorphoses in *Thus Spake Zarathustra*. Zarathustra teaches that "the beast of burden which renounces and is reverent," although admirable in its way, is no longer enough for the spirit: it must be transformed, through freedom and mastery, into the child, a new beginning and a creator of values. In *Pudd'nhead Wilson*, Roxy's attempt to bring about just these three metamorphoses ends disastrously, and the Ubermensch is parodied by Tom's shabby nihilism. Twain's human race is creature, not creator, noblest when, like the ass, it endures without being broken.[49]

The "Whisper" itself begins by referring to law, and to Twain's need to have his legal chapters revised by "a trained barrister – if that is what they are called." But, of course, Twain knew that American lawyers are not called barristers, and the term would be even less applicable to William Hicks. More important, the sentence referring to Hicks is a burlesque, long, convoluted and digressive, full of apparently irrelevant references to Florence in the age of Dante, calculated to amuse but also to alert.[50]

The sentence ends with a reference to a "historic" chestnut-cake stand which continues to sell the "same old cake" as it did in Dante's day, "just as light and good as it was then, too, and this is not flattery, far from it." Indeed not: since Beatrice allegedly used this cake to defend herself, it cannot have been very light. Implicitly, the chestnut cake being sold today is heavy or at least tough, but useful for defense, and Twain is offering a form of "old chestnut" to help his readers defend themselves.

Beatrice needed protection, Twain tells us, against outbreaks of party violence which might occur "before she got to school." Party rivalry is an element in *Pudd'nhead Wilson*, and it is at least one purpose of the tale to warn Americans of the limits of partisanship, at least until they have received an adequate political schooling.[51]

It was appropriate for Twain to draw Dante into his story. Noble both by birth and achievements, an aristocrat by convention and nature, Dante was caught up in and victimized by party strife. Dante's humanistic wisdom, better appreciated than Pudd'nhead Wilson's, was by itself not enough to earn him public office. He was elected through the guild of apothecaries and physicians, compelled to make some claim to craft and science, just as Wilson spent his outsider's years as an accountant and surveyor.[52] A reformer concerned to check commerce and to subordinate private interest to public principles, Dante associated with a party of new men, the Cerchi. In the event, however, his party proved to be preoccupied with property.[53] It is not hard to imagine Wilson suffering the same fate twice: because the

Democrats fell short of a principled opposition to slavery, Wilson – like Twain – might easily have made common cause with the Republicans, until that new party, too, showed itself to be the servant of property.

In the end, Dante was forced into exile. If the "senators and grandees" of his day approved of Dante at all, it was for his literary gifts, and Twain – in voluntary exile – was probably right to imagine them approving him as much and no more (2). Yet exile has its liberative side, as it had for Pudd'nhead Wilson: it sharpened Dante's critique of the city, and drew him, "a party by himself," into the politics of speech and theory. Dante turned to vulgar or common speech in the hope of reaching all citizens; that path, obviously, was the one Twain had chosen for himself.[54] Twain, however, lacked Dante's soaring confidence.[55]

American democracy, as Twain saw it, required rule in the high sense, a reweaving and not a patching. The defect was in the warp, the first principles of the culture. The concluding maxims from *Pudd'nhead Wilson's Calendar* speak to the point. "It is often the case," the first asserts, "that the man who cannot tell a lie thinks he is the best judge of one" (113). A very familiar association suggests that George Washington, a "man who cannot tell a lie," failed to detect some falsehood. The second saying remarks that it would have been more wonderful for Columbus to have missed America, and the accompanying drawing indicates the American lie: the Santa Maria is welcomed by a sign, "Lots Sold on Easy Terms." Exploitation precedes liberty: America is fundamentally a place in which to seek private fortune, where freedom and equality take second place at best.[56]

Any reformation requires unsettling Americans, shaking them – like Tom Driscoll – out of the complacent delusion that they have been born and remain free. Of course, this is a tall order, even though speech is far from impotent. Tom's example, moreover, indicates that such deracination is dangerous. Slowly and marginally, opinions alter character, but the effects of such change depend on original character and unpredictable circumstance (45). Theory's liberation from convention leads some human beings out of Egypt; others – most human beings at most times – it sends down the river. The risks may be even greater in America where the lies to be exposed – the republic's public principles – are the best things about America and Americans. Respecting the democratic decencies, Twain elected to write in soft disguises, hoping to move his readers to free themselves. The sovereign precept of democratic pedagogy is not force or reason, but beguilement.[57]

The vernacular, Dante wrote, is "the new light, the new sun which shall rise when the old one has set and shall illumine those who are in shadow and darkness."[58] Twain, on the other hand, had come to distrust modern efforts to enlighten "the person sitting in darkness."[59] He ends his "Whisper" celebrating ties to the past and praising his villa for its sunsets, its dreamlike and enchanting view of the coming of the darkness. On the evidence so far, we would be wise to follow Twain in cherishing that storyteller's twilight.

GEORGE E. MARCUS

"What did he reckon would become of the other half if he killed his half?"

Doubled, Divided, and Crossed Selves in *Pudd'nhead Wilson;* or, Mark Twain as Cultural Critic in His Own Times and Ours

I say two, because the state of my knowledge does not pass beyond that point. Others will follow, others will outstrip me on the same lines and I hazard the guess that man will be ultimately known for a mere polity of multifarious, incongruous and independent denizens. — DR. JEKYLL

Subjectivity and objectivity are affairs not of what an experience is aboriginally made of, but of its classification. — WILLIAM JAMES

Modernism had its own widening gyres and ruptures — ruptures enough, hollow men and waste lands, the smashing of every rooted assumption and literary guaranty — but one center did hold, one pledge stuck. This was the artist's pledge to the self. Joyce, Mann, Eliot, Proust, Conrad (even with his furies): they *knew.* And what they knew was that — though things fall apart — the artist is whole, consummate. At bottom, in the deepest brain, rested the supreme serenity and masterly confidence of the sovereign maker. — CYNTHIA OZICK

There has always been a genre of nonsense jokes or tales in American life, the inherent sense of which lies precisely in their subversion of what we hold dear or assume to be true and natural. If they were reflected upon, however, the dangerous and uncomfortable sense of such jokes would emerge — a fact that usually goes ignored in favor of their enjoyment as nonsense, as a zone of tolerated foolishness. For example, Twain obviously plucked the "half a dog" story from the everyday voices around him to draw attention to its sense.[1] By first denaturing the joke as a piece of mere folklore through exaggerating its nonsense in the passage where he introduces it (5), he then lets the whole story of *Pudd'nhead Wilson* that follows stand for the trenchant cultural criticism as the subversive sense that the joke makes. Most obviously, the townspeople's exaggerated response to newcomer David Wilson's nonsense joke fixes him as Pudd'nhead for decades – and presumably irrevocably – regardless of who he actually is or becomes subsequently, although the designation of Pudd'n-head for Wilson might be finally and ironically justified in terms of his failure to act upon his flawed but subversive insight about life in small-town America.

More subtly, the half a dog joke itself is a highly condensed text that comments upon the consequences of its telling for the teller Wilson in the local society of Dawson's Landing. As such, it incorporates two distinguishable but closely related themes that have become, in their variant expressions, the identifiable core of a tradition of American (and certainly, European) cultural criticism at least from the Gilded Age to the present. First, the joke (and the treatment of race in the novel) critiques the power of categories as essences or reifications in social life when they are really arbitrary conventions upheld by processes of coercion, sanction, and socialization. By treating the joke with seriousness rather than humor, the townspeople momentarily entertain the idea that a living dog can be so divided, and this so confuses their common sense that they immediately categorically fix the joke's teller as a fool, a label he cannot escape. By parallel, a dog cannot escape its categorization as a unified organism (as "man's best friend," the closest of the animals to humans), even in an act of comic imagination, and finally, and also by parallel, persons of diverse character and racial mixture cannot escape their black and white labellings under a regime of slavery. As a matter of ontology rather than ethics, the insistence on social categories in Western societies as a god-given, natural set of distinctions, rather than as a fuzzy, negotiated set, has led to the evils specifically targeted by cultural critics.

Second, this critical insight that society and social forms are constructed rather than given has been repeatedly brought to bear on the main ideological premise of bourgeois, middle-class life in the West – the priority and irreducibility of the autonomous individual as the meaningful, coherent actor in social life (of course, in Wilson's joke, the unity of the dog stands for the unity of the individual, any halving of which dangerously challenges order and sanity). Put together, these two themes of modern Euro-American cultural criticism in diverse ways have challenged the coherence of the self and personal identity which economic, political, and legal institutions assume, and on which cultural understandings of mental health, character, and personal virtue are established in everyday life.

My intention herein is to explore Mark Twain's skillful variant of this tradition of cultural criticism, on the threshold of modernist influence in American philosophy and literature of the later nineteenth century, and in conclusion, to comment on how Twain's critique of the person, self, and identity, as specifically developed in *Pudd'nhead Wilson*, would fare under the late-twentieth-century conditions of so-called postmodernism through which this critical tradition is still being debated and produced in American (and European) literature and social thought.[2] While I make no claims about Twain's actual association with or influence by any sort of intellectual movement such as modernism — in fact, it would be a mistake to do so — those who self-consciously have identified with modernism either in Twain's own time or later ought to embrace the craft he displays as culture critic in *Pudd'nhead Wilson*, among other works.

H. Stuart Hughes generally characterized late-nineteenth-century intellectual history as a revolt against positivism.[3] Accounting for emotion and the nonrational, probing the nature of consciousness and the concept of self — these were the puzzles that defined "a problematic of the times" for a wide spectrum of thinkers between the 1890s and the 1930s. In the American expression of this concern with the nature of consciousness and subjectivity, the work of Charles S. Peirce and William James stands out, the former trying to come to terms with the construction of meaning and the self as a social process of semiosis — communication through and within sign systems — the latter by the creation of an introspective psychology.

Writers of these decades shared the insight that consciousness or the self had no essential unity, an insight that was a direct and potentially subversive contradiction to the ideology of autonomous individualism that so pervaded the common sense and institutional discourses of Euro-American societies. Yet, this insight did not often lead to radical critique (as Nietzsche practiced, then, or as the "deconstruction of the self" has become radical chic across multiple genres, now). Instead, attempts to come to terms with this understanding of a less-than-whole, if not fragmented, self were hedged by conceptual accommodation, theoretical artifice, or by literary technique that willfully attempted to limit or reorder a potentially disorderly vision of the individual — for example, the ideal type of Weber (the forerunner in the social sciences of routinely dealing with the booming buzz of reality by modeling it); the therapeutic framing and rationale of Freud's construction of the unconscious; and William James's understanding of how the facts of an individual's life can be either radically diffused or unified by the mental acts of self-consciousness and reflexivity.

Relatedly, the burgeoning literary genre of autobiography during this period might have proved particularly subversive to hegemonic autonomous individualism (as it has always tended to be in women's autobiography, and as it more recently has generally become in autobiographical fiction),[4] since the hyperreflexivity that it entails might easily have led to an awareness of a thoroughly fictionalized self (and thus of alternative selves). Yet, as in philosophy and social theory, the radical potential of a fragmented self in autobiography was contained either by a limited set of techniques for representing fragmentation (more clearly exemplified in the novel, as we will see in a moment) or by acts of the will in imposing character upon the acknowledged fragments of one's life and affirming cultural models of the coherent, autonomous self as in *The Education of Henry Adams,* for example.

Amid this general intellectual environment of a strongly expressed, but contained critique of autonomous individualism, we find three tactics for representing less-than-whole selves in American novels of the later nineteenth century: those of divided, doubled, and crossed selves. The oldest tactic, and the one least challenging to autonomous individualism, is that of the divided self which concerns the development of techniques for representing consciousness in the realist novel. Fully rounded characters are developed by the exposure of their internal thought processes, prominently figured as internal voices speaking to oneself. These various techniques for developing complex representations of mind in the realist novel — what commonly came to be termed "psychological novels" — have been thoroughly discussed in Dorrit Cohn's *Transparent Minds* and Ann Banfield's *Unspeakable Sentences.*[5] While the self is divided and made complex in such novels, the fundamental coherence, autonomy, and boundedness of the self is not challenged.

The second and third tactics were more specifically common to certain authors of later-nineteenth-century American novels than was the longstanding tactic of the divided self; they were more sociological rather than psychological in orientation; and they were potentially much more subversive of the cultural construct of the coherent, autonomous self as the real, natural, irreducible unit of social life. The doubled self involved the creation of distinctly separate, dual selves out of one character, and demonstrated, in one sense, a very radical challenge to the idea than any self was monolithic, let alone coherent. However, in a more subtle sense, this tactic was very much in line with the construct of autonomous individualism, since it did, after all, preserve the construct of a sharply bounded, whole self, albeit as a doubling out of one. This tactic was expressed in the construct of the doppelganger, about which Robert Alter has provided an interesting discussion.[6] It is interesting that doppelgangers either in novels (see the words of Stevenson's Dr. Jekyll in the epigraph) or in the burgeoning interest in the psychopathology of dual personality during the later nineteenth century[7] were limited to two rather than many, thus distinguishing this tactic from the multiplicity of selves in the renewed interest in the phenomenon of "multiple personality" and the multiply fragmented self in literature and literary theory of the later twentieth century. Still, the nineteenth-century neatly cleaved or doubled self achieved through the tactic of the doppelganger does not really challenge the reader's common-sense cognition of a fundamental division of the world into sharply bounded characters, even though some of the characters as doubles might be bizarrely located within, or as a spirit familiar, external to a normal, common-sense individual.[8]

Disrupting the reader's common sense about the sharply bounded self, especially as a psychological myth and an arbitrary construction of social relationships, was profoundly achieved by the third tactic, that of creating crossed selves. The plots of novels based on this tactic involved the switching of identities among characters, by acts of deception, secrecy, or mistake. As in *Pudd'nhead Wilson*, the identities of two characters, unknown to themselves, are switched; each, at the same time, inhabits the social and intimate psychological persona of the other. It is the *simultaneity* of difference between the two selves involved, without any sense of clear boundaries between them, that makes this tactic more profoundly complex and subversive to the cultural construct of the coherent self than that of the doppelganger. As noted, the doppelganger doubles, creates a new bounded self in relation to an already existing one and thus merely reproduces an autonomous self, within or as familiar to another. Crossing selves thoroughly blurs boundaries of selves – both individuals whose identities are switched are ambiguously each other at the same time. The reader's attempt to keep sorting out who is who is defeated at every point by the complete merging of both selves in each character simultaneously.

Furthermore, this tactic is effective precisely because it works so insidiously on the cognitive response of the reader, whereas neither of the other two tactics so directly forces such a slightly irritating disruption of the habit of smooth reading. One is constantly prodded to remember who is who at any moment in the novel, to keep identities straight. This is very much how the rhetorical figure of chiasmus works. Chiasmus, literally meaning *crossing*, is the figure by which the order of words in one or two parallel clauses is inverted in the other. Such inversions produce a vertigo-like effect on the reader or listener that breaks the hold of cognitively powerful, taken-for-granted dichotomies. For example, in the hands of the anthropologist Marshall Sahlins, the chiasmus "the history of a structure and the structure of a history" is used to great effect to break the hold of the notion that structuralist and historical perspectives are categorically opposed—the frequent use of such crossings forces readers to entangle the notions of structure and history which they were likely to be in the habit of keeping apart and in opposition. Likewise, crossed selves as a tactic of plotting and character development in the nineteenth-century American novel were a powerful chiasmus-like mode for engaging the reader, even if through an unrelenting effect of slight cognitive imbalance, with the subversive truth of the arbitrariness of cultural categories and especially as they apply to a near sacred ideology in American life about autonomous individualism and the coherent self. The tactic of crossed selves "gets" at how this ideology operates in the cultural assumptions affecting habits of reading.

In *Pudd'nhead Wilson*, Mark Twain employs all three of the above tactics for critically representing the self against a culturally hegemonic ideology of autonomous individualism. However, because Twain's approach to consciousness was far more sociological than psychological (his sensibility, I believe, being comparable to that of the ethnographer who derives insights about mental phenomena from mores, social relationships, and cultural discourses rather than from postulates about the internal dynamics of individual minds), and because by the 1890s, he had become despairingly and radically critical of American (and human) society,[9] his craft as culture critic in *Pudd'nhead Wilson* depended less on the psychologistic and accommodating tactic of the divided self, and more on those of the doubled self and crossed selves, especially the latter. The divided self tactic of the psychological realist is apparent in Twain's treatment of Roxy, the most complexly developed person in a novel not very concerned with complexity of character; only with her is internal voice and a psychologically "real" divided self occasionally established.

With regard to the tactic of the doubled self, Twain repeatedly uses this technique of representing consciousness when he deals with "the other within," that is, racial identity as an intimate part of oneself portrayed as a dissociated alien body. For example, after the switch, Roxy becomes painfully aware that she is becoming a slave to her son, and a mother to her former master: "As she progressed with her practice, she was surprised to see how steadily and surely the awe which had kept her tongue reverent and her manner humble toward her young master was transferring itself to her speech and manner toward the usurper, and how similarly handy she was becoming in transferring her motherly curtness of speech and peremptoriness of manner to the unlucky heir of the ancient house of Driscoll" (16).

There is one self here, the self-conscious observant one, watching what the other doubled, disembodied social self is doing. This discrete doubling of selves is much like the effect of the schizophrenic's and literary modernist's hyperreflexivity that Louis A. Sass has noted,[10] and it appropriately makes the key critical point about how the compellingness of social categories like that of race on consciousness might be arbitrary and a matter of convention in origin, but in the realm of subjectivity, such categories can generate dissociation, and something very much like schizophrenic doubling – the self as observer observing itself – brought on by hyper-self-awareness.

In another example, just following the revelation about his true identity as a black, "Tom" literally experiences a doppelganger within:

For days he wandered in lonely places thinking, thinking, thinking – trying to get his bearings. It was new work. If he met a friend he found that the habit of a lifetime had in some mysterious way vanished – his arm hung limp instead of involuntarily extending the hand for a shake. It was the "nigger" in him asserting its humility, and he blushed and was abashed. And the "nigger" in him was surprised when the white friend put out his hand for a shake with him. He found the "nigger" in him involuntarily giving the road, on the sidewalk, to the white rowdy and loafer. When Rowena, the dearest thing his heart knew, the idol of his secret worship, invited him in, the "nigger" in him made an embarrassed excuse and was afraid to enter and sit with the dread white folks on equal terms. The "nigger" in him went shrinking and skulking here and there and yonder, and fancying it saw suspicion and maybe detection in all faces, tones and gestures. . . . (44–45)

Some paragraphs later, Twain resolves this doubled self state in Tom by the return of his "true," essential nasty character, and in this resolution we find a limitation on how far Twain wants to go, like most other critical thinkers and writers of his day, with the critique of the self (this observation is of course made from the vantage point of the late-twentieth-century state of critiques of the self; in the context of his own intellectual environment, as I have outlined, Twain was advanced in his criticism of autonomous individualism, but, not unsurprisingly, still very much a product of his time in firmly positing an underlying, essential character in each person that wills out). I will return to these crucial passages about Tom's revelation concerning his crossed selves and the portrayal of its effects on his consciousness, but for now, I merely want to emphasize the skill with which Twain used the specific tactic of the doubled self to demystify the essentialism of racial identity in a society where the operation of racial classification was overlaid upon a more basic ideology of autonomous individualism (race is correspondingly hard and fast in a society in which the individual self is hard and fast; cross-culturally, there is much variability as to the flexibility of racial identity depending in turn on the lability of the cultural construct of the self). Twain also used the doubled self tactic to demonstrate the confusions within the subjective realm of consciousness that this essentialized view of race can engender.

Finally, it is through the third tactic of crossed selves that Twain's cultural criticism is most skillfully developed in *Pudd'nhead Wilson*. This tactic, of course, is the plot device that structures the novel, and as I noted, was the most powerful critical tactic available because it cognitively engaged the reader through intentionally creating a persistent confusion of identities which the reader must constantly work at keeping straight, thus profoundly challenging conventional holistic views of characters and strictly bounded individuals and selves. Perhaps more than any other nineteenth-century American writer, Twain appreciated the special power of this tactic and used it repeatedly, nowhere as effectively as in *Pudd'nhead Wilson*.

Twain's critique of the conventional view of the self in American society is developed within the action of the novel. Because crossed selves or mistaken identity is the key tactic employed, those moments of revelation when articulated consciousness, of an individual character or of the community, comes to terms with this deception (more acutely, this subversion of culture) are the appropriate sites in the novel for elaborated attention and analysis. In reading and rereading the novel, I was struck by the centrality of the passage dealing with Tom's revelation about his true identity and his immediate reaction (44–46), the passage to which I have already referred but which I would like to discuss further in the following two sections, each devoted to a different dimension of this passage. First, this passage, in combination with some others, indicates much about Twain's specific critique of the American treatment of race, which I consider to be epiphenomenal or secondary in his concerns to the entwined critique of essentialized thinking about classifying others and the fundamental ideology of autonomous individualism in American culture, which is so antithetical to the "real" common-sense of what a moment's introspection would tell anyone about the complexity of self-consciousness. Race is merely an occasion, albeit a seminal one in American culture, for exploring the masked complexities of consciousness and self.

Second, I view the passage of Tom's discovery that he is a doubled self, and its immediate aftermath, in its most obvious sense as the key moment in the novel of personal revelation, and thus the key site of exposure and exploration of self-consciousness. Further, this moment can be juxtaposed with two subsequent key moments of revelation by others of the same instance of crossed selves at the heart of the novel's plot that bring it to rapid climax and conclusion: the scientific discovery of Tom's true identity through Wilson's detection by the evidence of fingerprints, and then the legal and public exposure of Tom's true identity in court. Revelation of an other than whole self at each of these levels – the personal, the scientific, and the legal – has different characteristics. At each level, to a different degree, subversion of fundamental cultural premises about the nature of reality and the self is a threat, and at each level, in different ways, the threat is resolved not by fundamental cultural change in perspectives on the self, but by its defeat. By juxtaposing the three contexts or moments of revelation of the central deception in the novel, we can see both Twain's development of cultural critique and also its eventual containment by the more powerful hegemonic processes that he puts into play at the end of the novel (the co-option of Wilson as mayor, and the reduction of self to property as an authoritative legal solution to a metaphoric "half a dog" problem and subversion of society). Finally, just as the telling of the "half a dog" story comments on what happens to those who tell it – they get bounded off and marginalized, or contained – so the telling of the tale of Pudd'nhead Wilson by Twain comments on the pessimistically viewed prospects his main reader-engaging tactic of crossed selves might have on permanently changing the deeply engrained cultural assumptions of his momentarily agitated readers about the autonomy and unity of self.

Twain's Concern with Race in His Critique of the American Bounded, Integrated Self

Race is such an integral theme of *Pudd'nhead Wilson* that it might seem wrongheaded, on first view, not to emphasize Twain's critical insights about it. The fact that I don't, but rather see race as a kind of allegorical vehicle for probing the injury generated by particular American habits of social classification, combined with the powerful cognitive hold of the unified self construct – that is, race as a story through which another more profound story of self can be told – is based on my sense of the incompleteness with which he treats this topic. True, there is much sharp critique of race in *Pudd'nhead Wilson*, which is not at all half-hearted and which has deserved the attention it has gotten in Twain scholarship, but it did not seem to me to be what the novel was centrally about, as it did not to other scholars, like a number of those whose early essays are reprinted in the Norton edition of *Pudd'nhead Wilson*. Like myself, they were moved to see another story to which Twain seemed more committed within the one about race – a story really about property, community, equality, or any of a number of the other terms through which the great themes of American history and culture have been conventionalized. What then might account in Twain's biography or in the novel itself for this recurrent sense among several critical readers that if his treatment of race in *Pudd'nhead Wilson* is not half-hearted, then at least it is half-committed, compared to the perceived power of other issues that Twain seems to be raising through the manifest racial issues in the plot?

One might argue (weakly I think) that Twain's full and committed treatment of race in American society was offered earlier in *Huckleberry Finn*, and that *Pudd'nhead Wilson* is merely a replaying of the theme, pervasive in the America that Twain knew and drew upon as a writer, as a vehicle for other concerns. All of Twain's fiction is richly multileveled, and my reading of *Huckleberry Finn* did not find a treatment of race that was any more committed than it seems to be in *Pudd'nhead Wilson*. Further, if race were to be considered Twain's central concern in *Pudd'nhead Wilson*, some scholars have questioned why, writing in the 1890s – during the post-Reconstruction period of visceral racism, and in the Southern states, of the evolution of Jim Crow legislation – Twain would situate his story in the antebellum period of slavery. This historic situating of the novel has been attributed to such factors as Twain's intense state of depression and despair in the 1890s, leading to his withdrawal from close attention to current affairs in favor of retrospection. Or, it has been seen merely as a skillful technique of displacement whereby the past is used to disarmingly comment on a problem that was still very much with the society of his times – and far more virulently, given Jim Crow laws. In line with my argument in this section that the story of race is perhaps the most salient phenomenon in American life for developing a critique of the self, I favor the view that the past regime of slavery was the most clearly defined and stark ground (*unlike* the present of the 1890s, in which virulent racism ironically clouded rather than reinstated the rigid social boundaries of the antebellum order) on which to situate a racially defined allegory of American commonsensical and categorical misunderstandings of the phenomenon of the self.

About the nature of racial identity itself within the regime of slavery, at least as he portrayed it in *Pudd'nhead Wilson*, I believe Twain was fundamentally ambivalent, and this ambivalence kept him away from the sort of fully committed treatment of it that a number of readers, including myself, have found lacking in *Pudd'nhead Wilson*, despite the story being so manifestly about race. The major feature of the novel which led me to this argument is the relative asymmetry in his treatment of Tom and Chambers. In the passage about the moment of revelation concerning crossed selves, on which I have focused, and in general character development, Tom gets the attention, and Chambers receives very little. Recall that although unsettled by the discovery that he is the black Chambers, Tom, raised as a white, soon recovers and is able to be his former self, but at the end of the novel, the white Chambers, raised as a slave, is shown to be clearly incapable of assuming the role that Tom had.

While Twain was certainly not a biological determinist about race (the tactic of crossed selves being the effective demonstration of his view about the arbitrary social construction of racial identity), in light of his choice to focus on Tom rather than Chambers, might he not then have been a cultural determinist, at least within the confines of *Pudd'nhead Wilson*? That is, black life under slavery was so injurious that it effaced normal human psychological and social capacities. The ambiguity in the novel, then, is, given that we know Tom so well, who is Chambers, or can he even be known in the same sense as can Tom? Twain's pushing of Chambers to the margins in favor of Tom will be relevant again when I discuss the limitations of Twain's critique of the self, in light of the state of that critique now, but in the context of race, it goes to the heart of his (and other contemporaneous liberal social critics') ambiguity about the effect of such a negative and oppressive social category for those on whom it is imposed. Contemporary readers might see this ambiguity in the context of modern debates in the history of slavery, the major divide being between an early writer like Stanley M. Elkins,[11] who emphasized the dehumanizing injuries of slavery, and since the 1960s, a whole tradition of scholarship pioneered by Eugene D. Genovese,[12] that has demonstrated the resistance, resources, and complexity of slaves and slave culture. In *Pudd'nhead Wilson*, at least, Twain seemed satisfied to take the dehumanizing view in his treatment (or lack thereof) of Chambers.

But then what of Roxy, the only fully and complexly developed character in the novel, for was she not a product of slavery just as Chambers was? This difference between Roxy and Chambers is indeed an inconsistency, one that reflects Twain's profound ambivalence about the extent of the transformative effects of imposed, but arbitrary social identities on the self. Perhaps this ambivalence is why he did not try for as consistent and committed a critique of race as the critique of the self that is achieved through the former.

Roxy is indeed a victim of a culture that sees others largely in racial terms, but through the beliefs she expresses about the racial determination of character – beliefs which Twain mercilessly satirizes – she simultaneously presents a distorted version of Twain's critique of the coherent self. To frame a critique in which he invests much validity within a piece of racial folklore that he devalues is another instance, I believe, of his complex and unresolved treatment of race in *Pudd'nhead Wilson*. Roxy's embedded discourse about how the self is composed concerns the character of Tom, her biological son, in relation to the mixed white and black descent in his pedigree. Of course, in a rigid system of social classification, predicated on race, where the categories of black and white do not account for the offspring of racially mixed parentage, such offspring stand as living contradictions to the rigidity of the system of racial categories. Inevitably in such societies, Creole identities and social strata evolve along with a complex folklore about the qualities and characters of persons based on the degree of black or white blood in their pedigrees.[13] Twain makes the most of this weak point of rigid systems of racial classification, by casting Roxy and Chambers as totally white in appearance, and as Creoles classed rigidly as blacks, or at least, classed with blacks as nonwhites (Twain does not go into the complexities of classification that American slave societies in fact evolved, in the face of an increasing Creole/mulatto population). The most obvious metaphorical referent for the "half a dog" story, then, is the internal racial division of persons of mixed blood, and the attribution, in folk belief, of a person's particular character to it. This is the internal doubling of the self, which comes to Tom's consciousness as a "doppelganger within" when his true identity is revealed to him.

Roxy's attachment to Tom is metaphorically expressed through the folklore of his racial pedigree. Her maternal tendency to overlook repeated evidence of his character flaws is rationalized by the high white blood which mostly composes him (43): "Dey ain't another nigger in dis town dat's as high-bawn as you is. Now, den, go 'long! En jes' you hold yo' head up as high as you want to – you has de right, en dat I kin swah." Yet, after several indications of his treachery and bad character, an exasperated Roxy admits that the modicum of black blood which actually composes Tom powerfully accounts for his basically flawed character:

It's de nigger in you, dat's what it is. Thirty-one parts o' you is white, en on'y one part nigger, en dat po' little one part is yo' *soul*. . . . What ever has 'come o' yo' Essex blood? Dat's what I can't understan'. En it ain't only jist Essex blood dat's in you, not by a long sight — 'deed it ain't! My great-great-great-gran'father en yo' great-great-great-great-gran'father was ole Cap'n John Smith, de highes' blood dat Ole Virginny ever turned out; en *his* great-great-gran'mother or somers along back dah, was Pocahontas de Injun queen, en her husbun' was a nigger king outen Africa — en yit here you is, a slinkin' outen a duel en disgracin' our whole line like a ornery low-down hound! Yes, it's de nigger in you! (70)

This fragment of spoken cultural ideology about race distortedly makes Twain's point about a strong belief in coherent self ("character") contradicted by a perception that the self is fragmented (the folklore of mixed descent in Roxy's comment). Roxy (and inevitably Twain, in contradiction to his own suspicion of such culturally relative constructs as character) insists on positing an essential character for Tom, even though he is the complex product of a racially diverse genealogy, standing for multiple identities with different cultural evaluations. While it is clear that Twain both satirizes and sees the tragedy of self-loathing in this folklore of mixed descent, he still uses it to stand for a kind of counter-discourse to that of the autonomous, unified self which is the main target of his cultural criticism. A racial ideology that is nonsense at one level (that is, incidentally, the same kind of nonsense that makes the "half a dog" story amusing) harbors the main line of critical sense that Twain wants to make.

Three Moments in the Aftermath of Revelation About the Crossing of Tom's and Chambers's Selves

At every point when the action of the novel brings to personal or collective consciousness the deception of crossed selves, a subversion of American commonsense about individualism and the nature of identity is threatened, presumably as strong as that which motivates Twain as author to orchestrate his critique within the story he creates. At each point, however, this danger of subversion and fundamental change in otherwise tacit cultural premises is averted or contained by processes that keep persons and communities blind and essentially true to their self-serving faith in the essences of various social categories. This repeated defeat of the subversive that might potentially have radically therapeutic effects on society casts a pessimistic pall over the novel; all is revealed, but nothing really changes. By parallel, at the level of authorial device and orchestration, Twain manifests the very same co-option and containment of subversive insight waged within himself. In a regress of dually fragmented selves, Wilson is ultimately Twain's double, who serves in Twain's own word not as a character, but as a "mechanism" — a kind of reflective panopticon standing for Twain within the novel itself. Wilson is drawn fully into the local society of Dawson's Landing without changing it, and Twain, on the verge of a completely radical deconstruction of the American self-construct, succumbs, like many other writers of his age, to imposing unity on a fragmented self by repeatedly attributing to his creations whole selves in the form of their base and natural characters, "character" being the key idiom of the autonomous, whole self of his time.

The first and most important moment of revelation is the personal one — when Tom learns that he is really Chambers. Very much like schizophrenic self-perception and the representation of the self in modernist writings,[14] in the immediate aftermath of revelation and both hyper and painfully aware of his dual identity, Tom sees himself as doubled with the racial doppelganger within gaining control over his former whole self, but only momentarily. He returns to his old (whole) self, as the threat of permanent doubling, brought on by hyper-self-consciousness, dissipates:

> For as much as a week after this, Tom imagined that his character had undergone a pretty radical change. But that was because he did not know himself.
> In several ways his opinions were totally changed, and would never go back to what they were before, but the main structure of his character was not changed, and could not be changed. . . . He dropped gradually back into his old frivolous and easy-going ways, and conditions of feeling, and manner of speech, and no familiar of his could have detected anything in him that differentiated him from the weak and careless Tom of other days. (45)

Not being a psychological novelist, Twain does not elaborate the mental processes by which Tom soon returns to his old self. The important point is that he does, and in his so doing, Twain posits an effective mechanism at the level of self-consciousness, without specifying it, that defeats a powerful sensation of doubled, fragmented self. What's more, in the aftermath of doubling, Twain seems to be positing a return to a truer, deeper character which is Tom's essence – one that has little to do with the social construction of selves through identities like race, class, and ethnicity. Rather than a thorough relativizing of any notion of an essential self or character as the consequence of the various tactics of decomposing the autonomous self that Twain so artfully employs, he seems to be yielding, at least in this crucial moment of self-revelation in the novel, to clinging to vestiges of notions of a unified self like other cultural critics of his age, who saw through the hegemonic American cultural premise of autonomous and essential individualism. At the most basic level of self-awareness, then, containment of a powerful insight about the decentered nature of the self occurs both for Tom and for Twain, orchestrated by the latter through the former.

The other two moments of revelation of the novel's secret of crossed selves are by Wilson's scientific detection (reflecting the reaction of "the rational" to the subversive confusion of selves perpetrated by Roxy) and by the legal system's handling of Tom-revealed-as-Chambers as a by-product of the climactic discovery of his murder of Judge Driscoll (reflecting the reaction of "the ethical" or "the just" to the confusion of selves). In neither instance, unlike that of the revelation at the level of self-consciousness, is the hegemonic ideology of the unified self very much threatened or even troubled, despite the exposure in plain and full view of the relativity, malleability, and divisibility of the integrated self. Finally, the order of society, as culturally constituted (by such notions as racial and individual essence), depends on the narrow vision of truth-seeking science and the "blindness" of justice, just as the repression of the sense in the "half a dog" story depends on the conventionalized acceptance of its telling either as enjoyable nonsense or idiocy.

The hubris of Wilson's self-presentation of his scientific ingenuity in the courtroom climax of the novel – the revelation of his own true identity to the community as scientific "magician," of which Roxy long suspected him in her early attribution of him as a witch (16) rather than pudd'nhead – focuses on his method or technique rather than on its outcome or the consequences of it for society: "For more than twenty years, I have amused my compulsory leisure with collecting these curious physical signatures in this town. . . . There is hardly a person in this room, white or black, whose natal signature I cannot produce, and not one of them can so disguise himself that I cannot pick him out from a multitude of his fellow creatures and unerringly identify him by his hands. And if he and I should live to be a hundred I could still do it!" (109).

Perhaps because of his marginalized, underdog role and his obvious intelligence, we had been thinking of Wilson as a particularly moral and progressive force in contrast to the town, but all the while, it seems, he merely wanted to be accepted by the townspeople, and in finally being so accepted, he provides new, powerful, and scientific means to feed their prejudices. In revealing his own true self to the community, just as he disentangles the crossing of selves at the root of the novel's mysteries, Wilson disappoints the reader. He is not the social progressive that we (mistakenly, it appears) associated with his intelligence. His prideful exposure of his own magic – the finger-printing as the effective proof of his intelligence – is the final move toward his acceptance by the community, and he turns out to be just as distasteful as they are. Science, as the certain way to truth, far from undermining the habit of rigid classification of others in American social life, linked to the ideology of autonomous individualism, reaffirms it in Wilson's hands. Wilson demonstrates with certainty that Tom is really Chambers the black slave. The way is cleared for a comfortable understanding of Tom's evil, revealed to the community at the same time – it *is* the nigger in him, but not in the ironic, partial way that Roxy attributed a flawed racial self to and within him, but in terms of the rigid black-and-white distinction among human beings that organizes American slave society. By science, Wilson shows that Tom – everyone – has a single, autonomous, unified, and racial true self, and his is black and evil. The half a dog has become whole again on several levels.

In being freed from the pudd'nhead designation in the town's judgment, then, Wilson perhaps becomes pudd'nhead in the judgment of the reader and in that of his creator. Recall that Twain disavows Wilson as a character, acknowledging him as a mere plot device. There is indeed some sort of ambivalence here on Twain's part, since Wilson seems so obviously his double as cultural critic within the action of the novel. It turns out badly for Wilson – the co-opted critic – from his creator's olympian perspective. One wonders how it turns out for the divided warring selves within Twain as they relate to the culturally hegemonic autonomy of self and the equal "reality" of a contradictory subversive insight, but in the locus of the author's self, no "realist" narrative is being written, and no resolution is necessary.

With Chambers/Tom returned to his true essential social identity and self as black slave, all that remains is for the court to dispose of him as one simultaneously judged as heinous criminal. Being a core institution of the culture, the legal system deals only in autonomous individuals, "but now a complication came up" (a final and particularly difficult return of the "half a dog" subversion that arises repeatedly in the novel, no matter how effectively it is repressed): "The Percy Driscoll estate was in such a crippled shape when its owner died that it could pay only sixty per cent of its great indebtedness, and was settled at that rate. But the creditors came forward, now, and complained that inasmuch as through an error for which *they* were in no way to blame the false heir was not inventoried at the time with the rest of the property, great wrong and loss had thereby been inflicted upon them. . . . Everybody granted that if 'Tom' were white and free it would be unquestionably right to punish him – it would be no loss to anybody; but to shut up a valuable slave for life – that was quite another matter. . . . As soon as the Governor understood the case, he pardoned Tom at once, and the creditors sold him down the river" (114).

It seems, then, that Tom/Chambers would simply not fit the autonomous, responsible self model of persons recognized by the law, and the one maneuver that might preserve the culture within the operations of the law was the extreme one, in all but slave societies, of giving priority to Tom/Chambers's dehumanized status as property. As property, easily represented by the flexible divisibility of money in terms of which it is valued, Tom/Chambers's stubbornly dualistic self, even *after* exposure of his one true self by Wilson's detection, could finally and definitively be dealt with in terms that culturally made sense. Then, only with reference to slaves, or persons as property, could the "half a dog" nonsense story finally make a distorted kind of sense to the society Twain has created.

Of course, there is one other remaining loose end that Twain chooses not to deal with – the reciprocal of Tom/Chambers's fate, that of Chambers/ Tom. He remains the one contradiction and living subversion of the whole self ideology that will not go away: "the real heir suddenly found himself rich and free, but in a most embarrassing situation. He could neither read nor write, and his speech was the basest dialect of the negro quarter. . . . Money and fine clothes could not mend these defects or cover them up . . . (114). As Wilson, the teller of the subversive tale, is marginalized by the community at the beginning of the novel, so the fate of Chambers/Tom, the loose end of Twain's story, is marginalized by Twain's choice in his own craft of storytelling and cultural criticism: "But we cannot follow his curious fate further – that would be a long story" (114). Indeed, Twain's choice not to deal in any detail with Chambers/Tom throughout the novel (one reason for which we have already speculated), and particularly, his choice not to elaborate on the unresolvedness of Chambers/Tom's situation, given the premises of his culture about the self, after he assumes his "true" identity, marks the limitation and containment of Twain's radical-seeming criticism of American cultural notions about autonomous individualism. The marginalization of Chambers/Tom's reciprocal in the novel, Tom/Chambers, even though Twain apparently saw the critical implications of the latter's story, kept Twain's critique of the self well within his times, rather than precociously linking it to the more complexly contemporary version of the same critique.

Twain as Cultural Critic of the Self in Light of the Postmodern Present

What if Twain had doubled the double he focused upon? That is, what if he had followed a strategy through the novel, awkward though it might have been for his storytelling, of treating Chambers/Tom with the equivalent emphasis that he treated Tom/Chambers? He might have achieved a thoroughly postmodernist work, in the contemporary sense.

Michael G. Kenny, who studied the forerunner phenomenon of multiple personality in the nineteenth century, and Robert Alter, who has written an essay on doubling in the nineteenth-century novel, both suggest that the fundamental difference between the critical perspective on the self then, in contrast to now, is that between a limitation to duality or doubling of the self and its multiplicity and fragmentation (e.g., recall the prescient statement of Stevenson's Dr. Jekyll, used as epigraph to this essay and as a conclusion to Alter's essay). That is, the force or amplitude of the critique of the self has increased in the twentieth century; this is indeed a case of the notion that increasing quantitative change induces at some point a qualitative change, the implication being that the later nineteenth-century critique of the self released from its dualist constraint becomes far more radical.

However one may judge the validity of this quantity-quality relationship as it applies to the critique of the self, I think the social condition that primarily accounts for the then-and-now difference in the way that this critique has been developed rests with a variant of the issue of dissemination, so powerfully evoked in the wordplay of Jacques Derrida. In Twain's time, both systems of social categorization and the conventions enacted to impose them as reality were assumed by writers, among others, to be effective and secure in their authority. In general, meanings were seen to be unproblematically imposed, for good or evil, on subjects through language, either in real-life communities on the order of Dawson's Landing, for example, or in works of the imagination, such as *Pudd'nhead Wilson* itself, by their authors. While questioning conventional meanings such as cultural common sense about race, the autonomous self, and the rigid nature of social labels, critical works of the time did not give up completely the notion that controlled coherent meanings could be imposed, especially by the author's control over his writing, as in Ozick's epigraph to this essay. The critical dualist tactics that I have described were indeed a challenge to the common sense of the coherent, bounded self as well as to ideologies of the reality and fixedness of social labels, but in their restraint (more so in the case of the tactics of the doubled and divided self than that of crossed selves), they were also accommodating the general notion that meanings were not radically nomadic or subject to seemingly infinite chains of association that, in the mode of Derrida, subversively challenged any attempt to finally establish an authoritative meaning or truth. Doubling, within a novel or between an author and his or her characters, was a partial strategy of dissemination in relation to the ideology of the self, which showed that the self could not easily be fixed monolithically, but ironically only by in turn authoritatively limiting the effect of the dualist critical weapon; conventional common sense might have to be overturned, but at the cost of reimposing the order of fixed meaning in critique. Doubling calls into question the integrity of that which is doubled, but not the integrity of its own stratagem.

Today, the faith in the authoritative fixing of meanings in society or in acts of writing is much less certain than it was in the later nineteenth century; to be sure, this loss of faith is the emblematic position of contemporary postmodernism, especially as it relates to representations of the self and self-enactments such as authorship. For example, with the penetration of electronic media, and the vast fashion-minded, commodified popular culture which it promotes into every household, into every brain in contemporary America, Dawson's Landing as described by Twain would ill-serve as the setting for a present critique of a much more fragmented self in the environment of seemingly uncontrollable (or at least not fully controllable) disseminations of meaning. The social order of Dawson's Landing of the 1830s and 1850s, under the regime of slavery, was even too severe for Twain's time of writing in the 1890s, but it was not far enough off that it could not serve as an allegory of his present.

In *Pudd'nhead Wilson*, Twain indeed hovers on the verge of a more radical critique of the self in contemporary terms, a critique that would depend on disseminating beyond given dualist tactics into a multiplicity of selves, thus fundamentally breaking with the authority of findable, certain truth and order, at least in some dimension, to which even the most acute of his fellow American cultural critics clung. Yet, Twain's flirting with multiplying selves, beyond doubles, in *Pudd'nhead Wilson* remains partial. There are two main indications of his move beyond doubling in the novel. One is the working into the main story of mistaken identities, the story of the twins. This move is not skillfully achieved, and it has long stood for Twain scholars as the sign of a flawed work, one that cannot be justified in any other way. I would suggest along the lines of the argument herein that the inclusion of the twins' story in *Pudd'nhead Wilson* is a gesture, a stretching, toward a more complex critique of the self that is unresolved and flawed precisely because, if fully achieved, it would have been far beyond the representational practices, the social conditions, and the cultural premises of the times. The twins plus mistaken identities assemble the elements of a postmodern tale — Twain has these instincts — but beyond the assembling nothing is done; thus stands both the willful perpetration and admission of a flawed work by Twain.

The other indication is Twain's primary use in constructing the plot of the crossed selves tactic, which I suggested was the most radical of the dualistic tactics of critique of his time since it cognitively engaged the reader by placing him or her off balance. Yet, Twain does not exploit the dimension of multiplicity which is inherent in this tactic and places it on the verge of contemporary critiques of the self. What is involved in the case of mistaken identities is really four identities negotiated simultaneously, not just two — that is, Tom, "Tom," Chambers, and "Chambers." Here, we would have had a dissemination of selves that would have required a radical nonpositing of essential character to any self (which, as we have seen, Twain does not refrain from in his treatment of Tom/Chambers). For Twain to have immersed himself in a larger field of dissemination he would have had to integrate into his narrative either the parallel situation of Chambers/Tom or the story of the twins, or both. Instead, he chose to elide the former and merely include the latter.

Perhaps. Twain's restraint from going beyond dualistic tactics of critique, even when he saw beyond them, can be simply attributed to the fact that he was more interested in being a storyteller than a literary experimenter. Like so much contemporary postmodern fiction,[15] an amplified version of *Pudd'nhead Wilson* with a plot constructed fully on a strategy of multiplicity of selves might have been judged unreadable by all but a rarified readership. Purely in terms of craft and an intended broad readership, to have toyed further with his insights would hardly have been worth the cost to Twain. "Half a dog," then, for him, was better than one, or fragments of one.

JOHN H. SCHAAR

Some of the Ways of Freedom in
Pudd'nhead Wilson

According to *The History of Brazos County, Texas,* by Elmer Grady Marshall, this county
was not a large slaveholding county compared to those in other Southern states. Of the
446 white people living here in 1850, 148 were black, all of whom were slaves.

I have some misgivings about this book by Mark Twain. I also
have some misgivings about our doings with the book, our mar-
shaling of so much intellectual artillery upon one small target. I
wish I didn't have these misgivings, because it is more agreeable to
praise than to bury either a book or a conference, but they are there,
and some of them must out. It's a mess, all right, both the book and
the world. The book, which is about a mess in the world, is a bit of
a mess in itself. Anyone who tries to clean up either the mess of the
book or the mess in the world with the help of the book will come
away messed-up, like Tarbaby.

That is surely true of everyone in the book who tries to clean up
the mess. What shall we make of Pudd'nhead Wilson, with his prying ways, his use of dirty fingers to trap dirty characters, his willingness to preside as mayor over a town whose citizens he knows to
be hypocrites and fools when they are not reprobates and criminals?
With his paraphernalia of detection, his concealed contempt for the
people around him, and his patient ambition for petty power, he
looks like an only slightly less shifty version of Simon Suggs, whose
motto was "it is good to be shifty in a new country." He foreshadows
J. Edgar Hoover, who also understood the value of a fingerprint, and
who expanded Wilson's pioneering efforts into a national industry.
The citizens of Dawson's Landing had better all buy gloves once
Wilson comes to power.

What about Roxy? We can sympathize with her commission of
one wrong in order to avert another, even though her act triggers the
sequence of squalid events that make up the book, culminating in

murder and the selling of her son into harshest slavery. Slavery is a greater wrong than any attempt on a slave's part to save her baby from slavery, even at the cost of condemning another's baby to the fate she spared her own. Still, this is no way to right the balance because in moral arithmetic, two wrongs don't make a right, even though they may make the adder feel good, at least in the short run. But when Roxy ascribes her son's bad conduct to his tainted blood – "It's de nigger in you"[1] – she adds her portion to the mess that is racism – and adds to it intellectually as well as morally, for she seems to invert the conventional relation or ratio between blood and behavior. That is, Tom has but half the portion of bad blood that Roxy has, so by racist logic his crimes should weigh only half as much as hers, whereas in fact they outweigh hers. In racist logic, blood will tell, but in Roxy's version of racist logic, the less the blood the more it will show. That is surely a bleak prospect on racial intermixture. But Roxy's ideas are hopelessly muddled. She attributes her own actions not to her blood but to her needs and condition. And in her fabricated genealogy, which traces her lineage through Captain John Smith and Pocahontas back to an African king, she is proud of her mixed ancestry and berates Tom for betraying its nobility – that is, for betraying his black origins.

The list goes on. It includes Percy Driscoll, F.F.V., who is so caught up in land speculations and lawsuits that he cannot see his own son, and his brother the Judge who stoops to chicanery in order to control a petty election. And what shall we make of the citizens of the town and the governor of the state, who, acknowledging the claims of Driscoll's creditors, cause Tom to be sold down the river into deepest slavery? The plague spreads with each effort to confine it.

Twain doesn't come away much better. There is no way to redeem his spattering the baleful word "nigger" all over the pages of this book. It is hard to excuse that in a book published in 1894 by an author as popular as Mark Twain, for his practice gives others license to the word. I am not sure the author is to be praised for his courage in treating the dangerous issue of miscegenation. In fact, he doesn't treat it: the miscegenation takes place off the pages of the book, outside the reader's experience. It is merely the act which winds up the book's machinery and sets it going. Besides, W. D. Howells had already treated the theme in *An Imperative Duty* of 1892, and his treatment is deeply imagined, brave, and richly textured. It still stands, I think, as the best exploration of the theme in our literature. Nor can much that is charitable be said about the way Mark Twain contrives one "funny" episode after another about things that are not funny at all. It is tasteless at best, morally coarse at worst, and makes a sprawl of the book besides, as the jokes get stretched past the breaking point. Furthermore, Mark Twain is the only great American author who tried to make (in *Tom Sawyer* and in *Huckleberry Finn,* as well as in this book) "Masters and Slaves" into a fun – let alone a funny – game. Real white American boys, unlike the fictional Tom Sawyer, stopped at "Cowboys and Indians." The childish thrill of replaying the conquest of the "Cruel Savage" did not extend, so far as I know, to making fun out of the enslavement of blacks. In this respect, at least, white popular culture has been superior to the Mark Twain who could, at his best, so humorously expose it, and, at his second-best, so bitterly condemn it, along with the rest of the whole "damned human race." So, the author doesn't help much in cleaning up the mess. Rather, the stains rub off the pages onto his snowy costume.

But what is the use of his line of inquiry? It's a waste of time to read books as though one were a censor charged with rendering a judgment: this one guilty, that one innocent; this one good, that one bad. Such judgmentalism is guided more by conceit than by humility and the readerly urge to expand understanding, and its fruits are little more than expressions of the tastes of the judge. This can be a hard temptation to resist for persons accustomed to giving grades, but resist we should, for yielding rarely brings any enlargement of pleasure and understanding, and usually produces something merely cranky. One doesn't have to read far into the critical literature on *Pudd'nhead* for cautionary examples. The warning signal is the expression "a close reading shows . . . ," or even "a close reading proves . . . ." What critic ever confessed to a shallow reading? A "close reading" shows – whatever is in the reader's mind. Thus, fictional works and characters, and their authors too, can be processed through some elaborate theoretical mill. Literary texts can be psychoanalyzed, contextualized, structuralized, semioticized, intertextualized, and postmodernized. They can be Marxed, Freuded, Foucaulted, Nietzsched, Derrida'd, Heideggered, and Bakhtined. The voice of the text is drowned out by the clanking of interpretive machinery. The eager student of literature is ground into the professional theoretician. Just as the Greek and Latin classics were once almost pulverized into syntax, scansion, and philology, so today the study of literature in universities is threatened by overtheorization and by the methodist passion that has wasted vast tracts of the social sciences. The text lies there, inert. The theoretician performs the autopsy.

Or, the text lies there, inert, weakened by neglect and by the negative judgments of common readers. Along comes the theoretician, bent on the alchemical feat of transmuting base metal into noble. Perhaps we are assaying something like that. *Pudd'nhead Wilson* is not among Mark Twain's most admired and loved works, and there are probably good reasons for that.

Critics can also give painstaking attention to fictional lives and worlds and be blind to their own households. There is a choice involved in giving professional care to literary texts, and there is no way to escape the contradiction implicit in that choice. In front of our very eyes, under our noses, there is a society: our own, the one we live in. Why should we spurn it, turn away from it, grant to artificial worlds the patience and devotion we deny to the life we share with our fellow citizens? No thinking critic can be unaware of this contradiction. Is criticism the child of remorse? Distressed by the shortcomings of our own society, we turn away from it and toward texts, seeking in them perhaps the same or worse shortcomings that we see in the society, or hoping to find explanations of why our society has the faults it has, or perhaps taking revenge against society by adulating the text.

How strange it begins to appear, this intense attention to fictional worlds. Yet, maybe not so strange after all. There are lively pleasures and strong advantages in talking about fictional characters. For one thing, such talk, done rightly, can lead to tenure. For another, fictional persons can't talk back, whereas if you talk about your children or your colleagues, you're likely to get some backtalk. Probing fictional lives can give some of the pleasures that prying into your neighbors' lives can give, but without the risks attached to the latter. Also, when the critic analyzes a fictional episode or character, there is no way the analysis can be proven wrong, and we all take satisfaction in being right. If an analysis of a real person is wrong, the error is likely to show up in your marriage or your bank account, your reputation or your comfort. Then too, a lot of fictional worlds and people are widely known, so talking about them can give persons who might be shy and lonely, and maybe a bit arrogant, something of the pleasures of real conversation with none of the inconveniences such as being interrupted or challenged.

These are lively pleasures. They do little harm. It would be churlish to deny them to those who enjoy them. But I am not sure what gain there is in such analyses; or, at least, I am pretty sure there is not much to be gained from deep analyses of the characters in this book. They are merely human – all too human, each one a mix of familiar ingredients in familiar proportions: moral blindness or coarseness; selfishness and self-delusion; vanity, ignorance, and cowardice; pretentious phoniness. They are largely creatures of the ordinary conventions and prejudices of their time and place, as imagined by Mark Twain, although, like most people, they are also capable of moments of honesty and insight. But, as many critics have pointed out, the characters in this book are not deeply imagined, not richly drawn. They are collections of themes or traits rather than individual human beings who are as they are, down to their shoelaces. They do not reward close attention. There is no more there than meets the eye. If the primary vocation of the novel since Richardson has been the exploration of the enigma – but not defeat – of the self, an exploration which has deepened ignorance as it has deepened knowledge, it cannot be said that this novel pursues that vocation at the highest level of achievement. Its way of "revealing" character is the (easy) way of unmasking. But when all the masks have been stripped away at the end, nothing more has been revealed than that masks are masks.[2]

Once you have said that the people of Dawson's Landing, like most people everywhere – when hastily observed, sketched from a distance – put more stock in their manners and prejudices than in their morals, you have said most of what there is to say about them. There is little to be gained in trying to say *everything* that might be said about them, or about any other characters real or fictional, for that matter. The inhabitants of Dawson's Landing are about as misguided as people anywhere else are. If there is a "failure" in the book, it lies in the author's unwillingness to give the slightest indication that any of the characters, while of course misguided, might be – just possible might be – redeemable. That is as much a failure of moral psychology and faith as of art. Not even the God of John Calvin damned the whole human race.

I have expressed these few misgivings about the book; try though I have, I cannot entirely convince myself that it merits so much attention. As a work of art, I am sure it does not rank with Twain's best. I am even inclined to believe, with Hershel Parker, that the book is all-but unreadable, that sense cannot be made out of it.[3] And as I continue to believe, with the Melville of "Hawthorne and His Mosses," that great art is "the Art of Telling the Truth," it is even more unsettling to conclude, as I tentatively have, that there is not much truth in this book – or, at least, that such truth as it offers is not of great depth. I know that no one will insist that everything Mark Twain ever wrote is gold, but still I worry that I may be suspected of weak loyalty and weaker judgment.

I shall not explore the beauties and the truths in Mark Twain's book. I shall do something else, something that perhaps does some violence to a work of fiction. I do it out of the naive conviction, a conviction which I'm sure many share with me, that one's reading, including one's reading of fiction, should help with one's thinking. I shall examine the book for what it can teach about the difficulties of thinking and feeling well and justly about two important topics of social thought. One topic is freedom: or, alternatively, because English speakers have a choice here, and one that usually costs little, the topic is liberty. The other is classification or categorization, the logics by which we gather human beings into groups and treat them as members of a set. The two topics are interconnected, for it is through social classifications that we define and assign rights and liberties.

There are gradations or degrees of freedom as there are of most things. Samuel Clemens surely knew that as well as anyone else, but Mark Twain came close to forgetting it in this book. The book opens with four or five paragraphs of description of Dawson's Landing as a snug and tidy place, contented, prosperous enough. And then the snake: "Dawson's Landing was a slave-holding town . . ." (4). The book closes with the words "sold him down the river" (115). The two expressions frame the action. What appears within the frame is a hell of captivity and enslavement, as composition almost without shading and degree. (And of course in life, and in the study of life, degree makes all the difference.) Freedom is the great prize, and no one wins it. Each character is trapped, confined in one or another cell of the universal prison house.

Roxy, born a slave, buys her freedom, only to lose her strength to the work on the riverboats and her small savings to a bank failure. Tom treacherously sells her down (not up) the river into harsher slavery. She escapes, and for a while extorts a living from her cowed son, but even that fails when he is exposed as a thief and murderer. At the end of the story, Roxy also is exposed as a criminal, and falls to her knees begging mercy from her God. Tom is sold down the river to satisfy the creditors of the bankrupt Driscoll estate.

Roxy switches the two infants in their cradles, so Tom, her son and born a slave, grows up free. But of course he is slave of his fears and his lusts, the passions which make of him a thief and killer and finally reduce him to the slave status of his birth. The real Tom, victim of the switch, grows up in the slave quarters, and although restored to legal freedom is unfit to live anywhere else. For him, legal freedom is a cruel mockery.

For one offhand remark, young David Wilson is reduced to Pudd'n-head and condemned to twenty years of isolation. He gains liberation of a sort by working a kind of magic trick – the fingerprint business and the courtroom spectacular – but in doing so accepts the code of the duel, the system of slavery, and the banal opinions of the ordinary folk of Dawson's Landing. He becomes mayor of a town whose popular politics are divided between the pro-rum brawlers and the anti-rum brawlers.

Wilson has had lots of practice in keeping his views to himself, although he finds some relief in his Calendar. It matters that Dawson's Landing is an *American* town, a town whose chief public ceremony is the Fourth of July, Independence Day. Pudd'nhead's Calendar for that date reads: "Statistics show that we lose more fools on this day than in all the other days of the year put together. This proves, by the number left in stock, that one Fourth of July per year is now inadequate, the country has grown so"(83).

If any motif can be said to dominate the Calendar entries, it is death-as-liberation. The tones of the entries range from grim to funny, but darkness pervades them all. Their deepest message is that death is the only relief for a species as wretched as the humans. Chapter 3: "Whoever has lived long enough to find out what life is, knows how deep a debt of gratitude we owe to Adam, the first great benefactor of our race. He brought death into the world" (12). Chapter 9: "Why is it that we rejoice at birth and grieve at a funeral? It is because we are not the person involved" (40). Chapter 10: "All say 'How hard it is that we have to die' – a strange complaint to come from the mouths of people who have had to live" (44).

The place in Mark Twain's work occupied by David Wilson is, I suppose, that of Tom Sawyer grown up: Tom Sawyer, Detective/ David Wilson, Detective. And Wilson's Dawson's Landing is Tom Sawyer's St. Petersburg is Samuel Clemens's Hannibal. But Tom is now grown up. Occasional spectacular effects are still possible (duels, brawls, courtroom pyrotechnics) along with zap-gadgets like the fingerprint trick, but they don't give much relief. He is a cold man, this Wilson, and he bears an implacable grudge – a grudge not just against a town which has cut him but an America which has failed, an America whose dream of freedom and dignity is an illusion; a grudge, finally, against life itself, against no longer being a boy but having to endure the failures and shams of grown-up life: "You have seen all of it that is worth staying for when the band and the gaudy officials have gone by" (84).

For all the main characters, then, freedom is the dream and bondage the reality. This book begins to look like a foretelling of the grim story of dozens of liberation movements in our own day. We have seen in Africa, Asia, and Latin America, as well as here at home, heroic struggles for liberation end in subjection little lighter and sometimes heavier than the subjection they struggled to overcome. *Pudd'nhead Wilson* is a gloomy guide to the politics of liberation. It teaches that the exodus from Egypt ends where it began.

Mark Twain's book was written in the early 1890s. By that time it was clear that only in legal form and not in social substance did the Civil War mark the dividing line between bondage and freedom in this country, just as in Clemens's life the war marked the line between carefree youth and the heavy burdens and problematic freedoms of adulthood.[4] By the mid 1890s, the Jim Crow system was solidly in place, capped by *Plessy v. Ferguson* (1896). Under that system, enforced by violence when necessary, the freed people were thrown back into a condition of servitude and exploitation little different in substance from that which they had known as slaves.

The book, then, reflects and foreshadows events in the real world, both then and later, and in this country as well as in others. By saying it that way, I mean to suggest some questions about the meaning of freedom, the idea of a free person. I mean to suggest some questions about America as well. For this is an American book, and that matters. For this was to be a country different from the old ones: "A new nation, conceived in liberty...."

What, then, is this liberty? And where? A few quotations, introduced now, but to be recalled later on:

"Every man is a cause, a country, and an age.... Nothing is at last sacred but the integrity of your own mind." — R. W. EMERSON, "Self-Reliance"

"Know all men by these presents, that I, Henry Thoreau, do not wish to be regarded as a member of any incorporated society which I have not joined." — H. D. THOREAU, "Civil Disobedience"

"The silver trump of freedom had roused my soul to eternal wakefulness. Freedom now appeared, to disappear no more forever. It was heard in every sound and in every thing.... I saw nothing without seeing it, I heard nothing without hearing it, and felt nothing without feeling it. It looked from every star, it smiled in every calm, breathed in every wind, and moved in every storm."

"They [the slaves] have been set free. This means only just this: they now work and hold their own products, and are assured of nothing but what they can earn.... The notion of civil liberty which we have inherited is that of a status created for the individual by laws and institutions, the effect of which is that each man is guaranteed the use of all his own power exclusively for his own welfare." — w. g. sumner, *What Social Classes Owe to Each Other*

Of all these authors, Frederick Douglass, a slave, knew best what he meant when he talked about "freedom": no more masters; no more slaves. He knew because his was a society of two distinct legal statuses, free and slave. The Old English word *free*, like its Latin counterpart *liber*, was a status word. It originally meant "not a slave," one who held the legal status of a freeman. In two-status societies, to call someone "free" was to point to that person's legal condition. You could determine whether a person was free, for example, by examining certain laws, looking at identifying marks such as brands or tattoos, inspecting commercial documents such as bills of sale, and so forth. The meaning of the term was fixed and accessible. Such societies had no need for elaborate philosophies, psychologies, and metaphysics of freedom. They had no need because the answer to the question, What *is* freedom? was easy to discover. It is we who live in societies where all adults have the same legal status who have the need for elaborate thought about the question. A quick survey of the library shelves will show how many have sought the answer. A little reading will show that there are many answers and little agreement among them. Further reading might lead to the disturbing conclusions that the answers supply information mostly about their authors, that "philosophies" or "theories" of freedom or liberty are best classified as polemics, and that the "meanings" of freedom and liberty, like the meanings of many important political words, can best be understood within a polemical context.[5]

The original "status sense" of freedom was extended easily and naturally to include other useful and related things. The freeman was a full member of the community, with all the rights and privileges of membership, which ordinarily included the right to participate in the conduct of public affairs.[6] The important point is that the statuses of slave and free were defined not by the presence or absence of various and shifting constraints and capacities whether "positive" or "negative," but by the possession or nonpossession of *rights.* Slaves whose masters were rich, generous, and humane might even be free to do or not to do many desirable things that freemen who were poor, old, or sick could not do. Hence, the freedoms of the slave might in fact be quite extensive. But whatever liberties slaves enjoyed were theirs not by right but at the pleasure of the master. Freemen's liberties, on the other hand, are theirs by right, and can be neither granted nor withdrawn at the pleasure of another.

So much is clear in the original definition of freedom, and this original definition is probably the only good definition of the word we have ever had — if one understands a "good" definition as having the properties of coherence, clarity, and determinateness.[7]

This "good" definition, by another easy process, soon acquired other components. We expect persons to behave in ways appropriate to their social station or status, almost to be or to embody the traits and qualities of character and conduct expected of their class or occupational grouping. Our professors should be learned, our soldiers brave, our priests pious. In this way, the word *free* soon became, and long remained, not only a name for a legal status, but also a short-hand expression for a set of virtues and character traits thought to be peculiarly appropriate to a person who occupies that status. Here, of course, the word will take on many of its dimensions by contrast to another family of character traits associated with the slave status. The freeman has a set of traits and virtues appropriate to his status; the slave another set appropriate to his status.

The freeman is his own man rather than another's. His liberties are his as of right. All of the character traits ascribed to the occupants of status stem from that root condition. Such a person need not study how to please other persons as a condition of his own well-being. Hence, free people can (should) be straightforward, self-confident, and substantially self-sufficient. People who are free do not flatter or cow to their superiors but are open and direct in all engagements. Secure in their status, knowing their own value, free persons need not be always calculating their own advantage, assessing every situation for what can be gained from it. Free people should have an easy and natural dignity of manner. They do not put on airs, make displays of vanity, or require that others show them exaggerated deference. Freemen are courageous and honorable. Their word is their bond. They take responsibility for what they do in the world, and feel shame when they fall short of the standard of conduct expected of them. That standard is a high one. The freemen is by no means, in Emerson's fine phrase, "as care-less as a boy who is sure of his supper."

If I get it right, these are the characteristic traits and virtues traditionally associated with free status. Everyone will recognize the (ideal) portrait, just as they recognize its opposite, the servile character.

The servile character lacks self-confidence and is incapable of self-direction. Such persons are as lacking in courage as they are in genuine pride and self-respect. Indeed, they have no genuine virtues but only counterfeits. They can be arrogant bullies when that is safe, and obsequious when that is advantageous or necessary. Servile persons live much in fear. They adapt to their dangerous condition by shrewdness and cunning, and by keeping a sharp lookout for every danger and opportunity. They are incapable of true generosity or magnanimity, incapable of disinterestedness too, because they care little for any interest other than their own. Their word is all but valueless. They have little sense of responsibility and less shame. Whatever they do that is not compelled by a superior is done at random, at the whim or opportunity of the moment.

Finally, free persons in the two-status societies had not only their characteristic traits and virtues but also a set of interests and occupations appropriate to their class. Free people do not do things mainly for gain or for expediency or out of necessity. Whatever they do of "necessity" they do in obedience to a standard freely chosen, an obligation freely accepted, not in response to a requirement externally imposed. Free people engage in activities that are agreeable and worthwhile in their own right, that call forth and encourage the style and virtues appropriate to freedom, and that gratify and earn the respect of others. They give themselves to causes other than their own. They cultivate the attitudes and activities that add to life what Burke called its "pleasing illusions" and its "unbought grace." They are amateurs of the arts and sciences and give themselves to activities which seem idle to the servile. In sum, they care for the liberal arts, the arts of leisure. Theirs is a liberal education, an education appropriate to free people.

The sketches are overdrawn; caricatures. Yes, but not entirely. We, inheritors of a tradition, speakers of English, are not at perfect liberty to add to or subtract from a word just as we wish. Our words come to us from elsewhere and with lives of their own. We of course choose the words we speak, but we are not free to use them any way at all, although we do have some leeway. The meaning of the conception *free man* is not entirely open, although it is not entirely closed either. On balance, it is probably more closed than open. If we stipulate meanings too arbitrary, too remote from remembered and established usage, our productions will be stillborn, will not have the breath of life. Or we can use words in ways that convict us of faithlessness or perverseness (*"Arbeit Mach Frei"*; "justice is the interest of the stronger"; "pacification"; "Long live Death!"). Words are condensations of experience, repositories of what a community has learned and done and come to believe over time. If we subtract essential components from a word and then employ the stripped-down version in new settings, we are likely to fall into confusion or even mindlessly commit monstrosities. Perhaps something like this has happened with *freedom* and *liberty*. We have extended free status to all but we have not carried along with that extension the older understanding that living a free life requires not just free status but the character, manner, and interests appropriate to that status. And so we have "democracy" but few citizens. And we wonder why. Or, as another example, a look at what we mean by *leisure* today or a look at the confusion and hypocrisy surrounding the idea of "liberal education" (i.e., the education appropriate to free persons) will show how far we have fallen from the older and fuller conception of the "freeman" and, perhaps, will show also how poorly equipped we are either for thinking about freedom or for living free lives.

The point is that the words *freedom* and *liberty* come to us full of meanings they acquired from their birthplaces in two-status societies. The words associate virtues and vices with social classes. There is much that is troubling about this: it stereotypes; it grinds down individuals into types; it works injustice on groups and individuals. But the process is not without some large advantages. Most important, the process inevitably produces thought, thought turning on the question, why should this group (or individual) be seen and treated *this* way, while that group (or individual) is seen and treated *that* way? Such thought can take a critical and challenging turn, and thus fuel claims and struggles for social change. C. S. Lewis's brilliant essay on freedom says much about how this dynamic works. Thus:

A word like nobility begins to take on its social-ethical meaning when it refers not simply to a man's status but to the manners and character which are thought to be appropriate to that status. But the mind cannot long consider these manners and that character without being forced on the reflection that they are sometimes lacking in those who are noble by status and sometimes present in those who are not. Thus from the very first the social-ethical meaning, merely by existing, is bound to separate itself from the status meaning. Accordingly, from Boethius down, it becomes a commonplace of European literature that true nobility is within, that *villanie,* not status, makes the villain, that there are "ungentle gentles" and that "gentle is as gentle does." The linguistic phenomenon we are considering is therefore quite as much an escape from, as an assertion of, that pride above and servility below, which in my opinion, should be called snobbery.[8]

Lewis's formulation goes far beyond a modest linguistic point. It also captures and condenses the "logic of liberty" in two-status societies. But that same logic of liberty is also the fulcrum of political-moral criticism in such societies *and* the engine of social change. The complexities come when the same logic is carried over into very different settings.

The planting and cultivation have been laborious. The harvest will be short work.

Pudd'nhead Wilson moves within the conceptual/social framework of a two-status society. It scores point after point by exposing the gap between what is expected of persons located at various points in the status order and what those persons actually are and do and want. It can score these points (that is, engage readers) because Mark Twain could confidently assume that his audience would hold many of the ideas I have sketched about the relations between individual character and social role. This elementary point could be demonstrated by examining each of the major characters in the book. I shall offer only a few illustrations. They will suggest, I think, that on this subject Mark Twain does not get much beyond what C. S. Lewis referred to as "commonplaces."

Take the gentlemen, the F.F.V. They should have the virtues of their class, but most of them, for the most part, do not. Twain gets a lot of mileage (reader interest and agreement) by pointing to the gap between the code and the "facts." The representatives of the leisure class, the free class, in this book have so little culture that they are impressed by the piano thumping of the Italian twins. With ignorant pride, Driscoll shows the twins the civic monuments of Dawson's Landing, as though they were glories on a par with those of Rome or Florence. The Driscoll family, far from being free of material concerns, is caught up in land speculation: the Judge is killed while worrying late at night over his account books; Tom is sold down the river to satisfy the claims of the Driscoll creditors. The members of the free class have of course sexually exploited the underlings. Twain especially gets a lot of mileage out of Tom, for Tom is a coward and a liar. That is, he violates the supreme principles of the freeman's code – courage and honor. Underlings love to hear such accounts, for anything that lowers the masters elevates them. And yet, Mark Twain makes the job too easy for himself. Whatever else Clemens/Twain might or might not have known, he had to know that the slaveholding aristocracy, the F.F.V., did not, as a class, lack courage and honor. They gave their blood and their treasure without stint in the Civil War. The individual failures were few, the general level of performance extraordinarily high. The mocking entry in Pudd'nhead's Calendar naming the flea as the paragon of courage looks cheap when set alongside that reality; and, perhaps, looks even cheaper when we try to imagine living in a world from which courage has fled.

Or, still staying with the gentry, look at the easy spot Mark Twain has with the duel episodes in this work. The duel is the product of aristocratic (timocratic) society, and as such is a ludicrous relic in a democratic society. The duel had its code, of course, and heavy elements of ceremony and ritual, of routine and predictable practices. But that is only the surface of the matter. The engine of the system was not a principle or a codified set of rules, but a *disposition*, a trained sense of liberty and honor. The formation of this disposition began very early in the gentleman's life and was powerfully supported by group customs. The disposition was manifest, visible, in the body, in posture and carriage; and it was resident in the consciousness as well, in frameworks of perception, thought, and judgment. The finished product was an agent, a person, who could engender the practices appropriate to liberty and honor, and only such practices, just as a native speaker of a natural language can engender appropriate utterances in the language without "knowing" (as a linguist might know) its formal logic.

All that is left of that old system in this book are its surfaces, and so it is easily mocked. Driscoll's "religion," the only one he knows, is the "code of honor," but it is a religion of external observances alone. The spirit is gone. Driscoll stoops to election fraud. He worries about his land speculations. He is willing to pay Tom to stay away from Dawson's Landing so that his mean ways will be hidden from the townsfolk. This man is no freer than any other character in the work. All he retains of the old ways of the free person is a few ritualized phrases and observances, so Mark Twain has an easy romp exposing him to ridicule.

But that romp diverts attention from the real question, which is the question of what honor – a commodity whose value is set by its scarcity – might mean in the society where all are said to be free and entitled to equal respect. In the two-status societies, where *some* were free, the meanings (experiences) of freedom and respect were clear. In the formally one-status societies, where *all* are said to be free and equal, the meanings of freedom and respect are opaque. It is easy to make fun of the survivals of a departed age, but there is little instruction in the sport. It is hard but valuable work to try to understand what freedom might mean in our age, the formally democratic age. *Pudd'nhead Wilson* does not help with that work.

The book exhibits the same logic in its treatment of the folks downstairs. Slaves are expected to have the servile characters appropriate to their status. Of course, some do and some don't. (As Lewis put it, this knowledge was a "commonplace" of European literature since Boethius.) This is no matter requiring deep thought. So Twain has his two Toms, and gets good service from them, but it is service of exactly the kind Lewis calls "commonplace." It is perfectly familiar; there is nothing deep in it.

Roxy is another stock figure, the one who partakes of both sets of status traits, each by turns, and mostly the worst of each. But that is exactly how the code reads on mulattoes or mixed-breeds. Commentators have wanted to see depth and richness in the figure of Roxy. She certainly is multidimensional when compared to many of Twain's characters, and especially his women, and yet her portrait is mainly drawn after the model of the mixed-status code. Her character is not much more complex than that; indeed, she comes perilously close to being the conventional figure of the mixed-breed.

Nor is the heredity-environment question probed deeply or worked through to anything like a satisfactory conclusion. The topic is run both ways in this book, at the author's convenience. Tom (i.e., Roxy's son) appears to be the inevitable bad product of his upbringing. Or is he? How much credence shall we give to that account of the matter? After all, many members of the free status in the Old South, and elsewhere too, were spoiled rotten as infants, yet grew into worthy adulthood. A pampered infancy is no predictor of a worthless maturity. Then maybe Tom's character is curdled by that drop of "Negro blood"? But that cannot be right either. The other Tom, pure in blood but raised among slaves, grows into the pure type ascribed to the servile class. But that's not true of Roxy, who is almost pure white in the blood sense, although raised a slave. In sum, the matter can be run in any direction, ending in muddle. That, I think, is the way this matter stands with most of us, so I do not mean to fault Mark Twain's account as falling short of the average. I only mean to say that there are no advances on that front in this book. Just the usual, confused commonplaces.

Look at the ordinary citizenry. Here too readers bring to the text a bundle of images and expectations inherited from times when citizenship was a limited and honored status, a status drawing its high value from its narrow base. We still are inclined to judge citizen conduct by that old and high standard, and of course the citizenry of Dawson's Landing falls abysmally short. They are little more than an ignorant, brawling rabble, moved by slogans and easily dazzled by showy tricks. But here too the analysis in the book hardly moves beyond the conventional aristocratic indictment of democracy.

By the time of *Pudd'nhead Wilson*, free status had become a general legal condition: no more masters and slaves; all are free. And yet the point of the book, the motif that gathers all its scattered parts, is that no one in this society is really free. I have suggested that any treatment so monolithic as that is grievously oversimplified: it does not honor degree, and in "real life" differences of degree make all the difference. Beyond that, I have suggested that Mark Twain's treatment of his theme rests on a foundation (of which I'm sure he was only partly aware) of ideas and values drawn from older social orders, social orders in which the meaning of freedom was clear because its opposite was clear. Perhaps that older understanding of the idea of a free person, as I sketched that idea above, was the correct one—perhaps even the only correct one. It is surely an attractive one, both for its content and for its conceptual coherence and clarity. Maybe the book could even be read as trying to recall us to that older ideal, but now under changed conditions.

But I doubt that. And I doubt that calling, even exhorting, is enough anyway, or even what is needed. What is needed is thinking that can help get us out of the muddle we are in about freedom. In turn, the initial focus of that thinking must be critical. It must focus on the main ideas of freedom currently operative in this society today, which are the same ones that were current in Twain's day.

I have tried to point to those operative ideas in my quotations from Emerson and Sumner. There are only two such core ideas, although each has many variations. The first is the idea of a free person as a universe, a self that is all. It is astonishingly boundless, oceanic. The other is the idea of the free person as the independent seeker of self-interest, owing nothing to others, and owed nothing in return. It is astonishingly narrow, solipsistic. Neither appreciates how much and in how many ways freedom is found in fellowship and membership, whereas the older conception of freedom was rich in that appreciation. In addition, neither of the two operative conceptions shows any appreciation of the follies and perversions which flow from the granting of civil liberties to all without an equal cultural emphasis on the development of civil (citizenly) manners and character among the bearers of those liberties. Again, the older conception was richest in its appreciation of that cultural task. One might suggest, in highly abbreviated form, that the critical task for thinking in this area today might be that of rounding out Emerson and Sumner with Aristotle and Tocqueville. Mark Twain's book does not help much with that critical task. Rather, it takes up a different task, one, I think, which is largely beside the point.

One more comment about the book. Many thoughtful people, watching the bloody march of the totalitarian and mobilized societies across the field of modern history, have learned to shy away from any but a very restricted concept of liberty. In politics, where power is at stake, muddled thinking is dangerous thinking. And we rightly worry that once we leave the safe harbor of a narrow concept of liberty we will go astray in a dangerous muddle of obscurity and imprecision. Do we (can we) really know what we are talking about when we talk about positive freedom, or public liberty, or true autonomy, and so on? Maybe not. Maybe there is no way out of the muddle. Maybe the "good definition" of liberty that Lincoln said this country was (even then) much in need of is unobtainable. Maybe the "new birth" of freedom he called for at Gettysburg cannot happen.

If that is so, our case is desperate. For this country, from the discovery, has always existed most intensely in its passion for and obsession with freedom; and, given the intensity of the obsession, existed most intensely also in the dreadful fear that the epochal opportunity of the discovery has been or will be lost forever. Highest hope, dashed, becomes deepest despair. I think that is what happened in Mark Twain's book. The last entry on Pudd'nhead Wilson's Calendar reads: "October 12, the Discovery. It was wonderful to find America, but it would have been more wonderful to miss it" (113). The illustration accompanying this entry shows Columbus's three ships standing just off shore. On the land may be seen a huge billboard saying: AMERICA — lots sold on easy terms. We cannot miss the duplicities of that "lots."

Somewhere in the middle ground between absolute hope and absolute despair we must continue to search for that new way or birth, that right understanding, of liberty. I surely do not claim to know the way, or even if there is one. I have only argued in this paper that Mark Twain's book, which is about liberty, does not, for reasons I have specified, give us much help toward the way. The way, surely, requires both choosing freedom for all and simultaneously cultivating civil manners and characters among all. No society known to me has done that.

Notes

Introduction

For their help in the development of this project, we thank Gabriel Brahm, Maggie Collins, and Thomas Thurston. We are also grateful to the Humanities Division at the University of California, Santa Cruz, for continued support.

1. See Hershel Parker, *Flawed Texts and Verbal Icons: Literary Authority in American Fiction* (Evanston, Ill.: Northwestern University Press, 1984), 142–44.

2. See James M. Cox, *Mark Twain: The Fate of Humor* (Princeton, N.J.: Princeton University Press, 1966).

3. Published in 1894, *Pudd'nhead Wilson* is set in a small Missouri town, Dawson's Landing, in the 1830s to 1850s. At the outset of the story, the mulatto slave Roxana (Roxy) – who is so white that she does not appear visibly black at all – gives birth to an equally white son named Valet de Chambre, or Chambers; his father, we later learn, was a leading citizen, Colonel Cecil Burleigh Essex, now dead. At the same time, Roxy's mistress, Mrs. Percy Northumberland Driscoll, gives birth to a son named Thomas à Beckett Driscoll, or Tom. She dies in childbirth. Roxy, recognizing a chance to free her son from slavery, switches the baby boys and no one notices. When Percy Driscoll dies, Roxy is set free; the false Tom is then raised by his uncle, Judge York Leicester Driscoll, with the false slave Chambers as his companion and servant.

The theme of doubles embodied in the two boys is compounded by a subplot concerning the visit to Dawson's Landing of twin Italian noblemen, Angelo and Luigi. In the original, separate short story – entitled "Those Extraordinary Twins" – they are Siamese twins, and Twain constructs comic adventures based on the fact that they have contrasting personalities and alternating control of their one pair of legs. Thus, one drinks and the other is a teetotaler; one is a coward and the other wishes to duel. When the twins are accused of kicking Tom Driscoll, the jury can reach no verdict as to who is guilty. When one is elected alderman, and the town government falls apart because both men must sit on the board, the townspeople end the stalemate by hanging the guilty "one" of the twins.

The twins are separated in *Pudd'nhead Wilson* except for fragments of the text where Twain forgot to pull them apart as he apparently wrote quickly and sloppily to put together a book for badly needed money. The fates of Tom Driscoll and the twins are entangled when their contest as candidates for political office leads to a duel – a duel in which Judge Driscoll must fulfill the honor of his cowardly nephew. Tom has grown up to be a scoundrel and a thief, perhaps because he is black, perhaps because he is simply bad, perhaps because of his aristocratic training. To pay his gambling debts, he disguises himself and commits robberies around the town. At last, he murders his uncle in the course of robbing him, using a knife that he has stolen from the Italian twins. Already accused of being secret assassins, they appear to be guilty of the murder.

The crime is solved by David (Pudd'nhead) Wilson. Having come to Dawson's Landing at the beginning of the story to practice law, Wilson has been branded a pudd'nhead and ostracized for some twenty years because of a joke he tells. Annoyed by a barking dog, Wilson says to a group of townspeople that he wishes he owned half the dog, so that he could kill his half. The crowd, unable to comprehend irony, deems him a complete fool. By the end of the book his standing has improved because he acts as a second for Luigi in the duel and with the judge's support successfully runs for mayor. The collection of fingerprints Wilson has made ever since his arrival – fingerprinting was new in the 1890s but anachronistic in the story – allows him both to discover that Tom is the murderer and, by comparison with early prints of the two boys, to reveal that Tom is in fact the "black" Chambers. Rather than being executed or imprisoned, Tom is sold down the river as valuable property; and Chambers, who has been raised a slave, is restored to his proper station in society, where he is pathetically out of place.

Pudd'nhead Wilson Revisited

1. Samuel Langhorne Clemens, *Pudd'nhead Wilson and Those Extraordinary Twins*, ed. Sidney E. Berger (New York: W. W. Norton, 1980), 169-70. Quotations from this edition are cited parenthetically in the text.

The Sense of Disorder in *Pudd'nhead Wilson*

I am grateful to Michael Cowan, Susan Gillman, and Scott Pugh for their valuable commentary on this essay.

1. Hershel Parker, *Flawed Texts and Verbal Icons: Literary Authority in American Fiction* (Evanston, Ill.: Northwestern University Press, 1984), 132, 136.

2. Parker, *Flawed Texts and Verbal Icons,* 145.

3. Parker's essay, "Exigencies of Composition and Publication: *Billy Budd, Sailor* and *Pudd'nhead Wilson,*" *Nineteenth-Century Fiction* 33 (1978), centers its criticism of *Pudd'nhead* on the failure of the ending. In emphasis and many details, this earlier work clearly anticipates *Flawed Texts and Verbal Icons.*

4. Evan Carton's brilliantly incisive "*Pudd'nhead Wilson* and the Fic-

tion of Law and Custom," in *American Realism, New Essays*, ed. Eric J. Sundquist (Baltimore: Johns Hopkins University Press, 1982), 82–94, is the most directly relevant of numerous examples that might be mentioned in this regard. I am in Carton's debt both for the reinforcing example of his general approach, and for confirmation in matters of detail.

5. Parker's allegations about Mark Twain's lying and shamelessness, often ventured in a tone of condescending familiarity, are scattered liberally through both essays on *Pudd'nhead*; see *Flawed Texts and Verbal Icons*, 117, 127, 130, 131, 132, 133, 135, 142, 144. As for his assault on the critics, a small sampling should suggest something of the energy and evident relish that Parker brings to his work: "However uncomfortable a bolus it proves, almost any ending can be swallowed by a modern critic determined to prove the unity of a novel" ("Exigencies of Composition and Publication," 133); "While the published *Pudd'nhead Wilson* is patently unreadable, anyone who knows literary critics will know that a simple fact like that has not deterred them from trying to read the book and bragging about having done so. . . . There is almost nothing so bad that you can't get one critic to praise it and another to praise the first one for having praised it" (*Flawed Texts and Verbal Icons*, 136, 138).

6. "Exigencies of Composition and Publication," 142.

7. Ibid., 141.

8. Ibid., 141.

9. Ibid., 139; *Flawed Texts and Verbal Icons*, 130–33. The letter to Hall is quoted by Parker from *Mark Twain's Letters to His Publishers, 1867–1894*, ed. Hamlin Hill (Berkeley: University of California Press, 1967), 354–56.

10. This is a radical condensation of major lines of argument in my book, *In Bad Faith: The Dynamics of Deception in Mark Twain's America* (Cambridge, Mass.: Harvard University Press, 1986).

11. In this multilayered array of conflicting drives to see and to be blind, Mark Twain's work displays some of the essential characteristics of what Fredric Jameson calls "mass culture." Not "empty distraction or 'mere' false consciousness," mass culture is defined as "transformational work on social and political anxieties and fantasies which must then have some effective presence in the mass cultural text in order subsequently to be 'managed' or repressed." Thus mass culture entertains "relations of repression with the fundamental social anxieties and concerns, hopes and blind spots, ideological antinomies and fantasies of disaster, which are their raw material." Such matters are addressed in mass culture, but then invariably repressed "by the narrative construction of imaginary resolutions and by the projection of an optical illusion of social harmony." "Reification and Utopia in Mass Culture," *Social Text* 1 (1979):141.

12. Parker, "Exigencies of Composition and Publication," 141.

13. My account of the development of the novel is based entirely on Parker.

14. Samuel Langhorne Clemens, *Pudd'nhead Wilson and Those Extraordinary Twins*, ed. Sidney E. Berger (New York: W.W. Norton, 1980), 119. Quotations from this edition are cited parenthetically in the text.

15. Mark Twain, *Adventures of Huckleberry Finn*, ed. Walter Blair and Victor Fischer (Berkeley: University of California Press, 1985), 362.

16. See the detailed analysis of the novel, with its interspersed commentary on audience response, in Robinson, *In Bad Faith*, 111–217.

17. The simultaneous assertion and cancellation of the same message is a phenomenon everywhere to be observed in Mark Twain's work, although nowhere with more penetrating cultural authority than in *Huckleberry Finn.* While *Pudd'nhead* is quite obviously to be compared with its great predecessor in this regard, the specific dynamics of its bad faith, as they are manifest in the history of its composition, are also analogous in fundamental ways with Mark Twain's late, now seldom read, "unfinished" works. I refer here to the likes of "Which Was It?" "The Stupendous Procession," the "Schoolhouse Hill" version of *The Mysterious Stranger,* and "The Secret History of Eddypus, the World-Empire," all of which rise to sharply critical perspectives on American race-slavery only to submerge them in their formal literary status as negligible fragments. *Pudd'nhead* falls into a very similar pattern. For in fostering the impression that it is two incompatible narratives, one imperfectly grafted onto the other, and in conferring a completeness on the mystery plot that is denied to Roxy's story, the novel invites the critical neglect of its most serious message. For a fuller discussion of Mark Twain's "unfinished" works, see Robinson, *In Bad Faith*, 217–22.

18. On dreams, see 104, 125, 158; on dogma and authority, see 9, 93, 134, 135, 161; the play of the language is everywhere.

19. Justin Kaplan, *Mr. Clemens and Mark Twain* (New York: Simon and Schuster, 1966), 340–41. Kaplan's account includes Mark Twain's extraordinary dream of a "negro wench" whose powerful appeal seemed to confirm his suspicions of psychic doubleness.

20. These passages appear on p. 191 of the Norton edition.

21. Parker, *Flawed Texts and Verbal Icons,* 143.

22. Ibid., 144–45.

23. Ibid., 129–30. It is equally clear, I think, that Mark Twain's uncertainty on this matter underwent no final clarification in the uneven course of composition and emendation that resulted in the published text. The suppressed passages of speculation on these questions are especially important here.

24. Parker, "Exigencies of Composition and Publication," 140.

25. James M. Cox, "*A Connecticut Yankee in King Arthur's Court:* The Machinery of Self-Preservation," in *Mark Twain: A Collection of Critical Essays,* ed. Henry Nash Smith (Englewood Cliffs, N.J.: Prentice-Hall, 1963), 128.

26. James E. Caron's penetrating essay, "Pudd'nhead Wilson's Calendar: Tall Tales and a Tragic Figure," *Nineteenth-Century Fiction* 36 (1982):452–70, parallels my own in its probing of Pudd'nhead's characterization, and in some aspects of its analysis of the social dynamics of Dawson's Landing. Caron's notion that "Slavery and aristocracy are like the preposterous con-

ceptions of the tall tale" (455) is especially rich in implication for the study of Mark Twain, but also casts useful light on Southwestern humor generally, not least as it surfaces in the works of William Faulkner.

Mark Twain and Homer Plessy

This essay originated in a conference on *Pudd'nhead Wilson* held at the University of California, Santa Cruz, in 1987, organized by Susan Gillman and Forrest Robinson. My arguments have been shaped by their papers, as well as by others presented at the conference, especially those of Michael Cowan, Myra Jehlen, Carolyn Porter, and Michael Rogin. I have also benefited from the advice of Martha Banta, Richard Bridgman, William Cain, Eric Cheyfitz, Frederick Crews, Robert Kaufman, Walter Benn Michaels, Wayne Mixon, Robert Post, and C. Vann Woodward.

1. Parenthetical page numbers refer to the Norton Critical Edition of *Pudd'nhead Wilson and Those Extraordinary Twins*, ed. Sidney E. Berger (New York: W.W. Norton, 1980).

2. Hershel Parker, *Flawed Texts and Verbal Icons: Literary Authority in American Fiction* (Evanston, Ill.: Northwestern University Press, 1984), 115–45.

3. George Walker, "The Real 'Coon' on the American Stage," quoted in Nathan Huggins, *Harlem Renaissance* (New York: Oxford University Press, 1971), 282.

4. On the cultural reunion of North and South see, for example, C. Vann Woodward, *Origins of the New South, 1877–1913* (Baton Rouge: Louisiana State University Press, 1951), 142–74; Paul H. Buck, *The Road to Reunion, 1865–1900* (Boston: Little, Brown, 1937), 209–35; Wayne Mixon, *Southern Writers and the New South Movement, 1865–1913* (Chapel Hill: University of North Carolina Press, 1980); and Rayford W. Logan, *The Betrayal of the Negro: From Rutherford B. Hayes to Woodrow Wilson* (1954, revised ed., New York: McMillan, 1965), 242–75; Albion Tourgée, "The South as a Field for Fiction," quoted in Woodward, *Origins of the New South*, 165.

5. See, for example, Justin Kaplan, *Mr. Clemens and Mark Twain* (New York: Simon and Schuster, 1966), 341–47; Arthur G. Pettit, *Mark Twain and the South* (Lexington: University of Kentucky Press, 1974), 141–72; Evan Carton, "*Pudd'nhead Wilson* and the Fiction of Law and Custom," in *American Realism: New Essays*, ed. Eric J. Sundquist (Baltimore: Johns Hopkins University Press, 1982), 82–94; and Susan K. Gillman and Robert L. Patten, "Dickens: Doubles:: Twain: Twins," *Nineteenth-Century Fiction* 39 (March 1985): 441–58.

6. My following account of *Plessy v. Ferguson* and its background relies primarily on the following sources: Otto H. Olsen, *The Thin Disguise: Plessy v. Ferguson, A Documentary Presentation* (New York: Humanities Press, 1967); Olsen, *The Carpetbagger's Crusade: A Life of Albion Winegar Tourgée* (Baltimore: Johns Hopkins, 1965), 312–31; C. Vann Woodward, "The National Decision Against Equality," in *American Counterpoint: Slavery and*

Racism in the North-South Dialogue (New York: Oxford University Press, 1971), 212–33; Richard Kluger, *Simple Justice: The History of Brown v. Board of Education and Black America's Struggle for Equality* (New York: Knopf, 1975), 51–83; Robert J. Harris, *The Quest for Equality: The Constitution, Congress, and the Supreme Court* (Baton Rouge: Louisiana State University Press, 1960), 82–108; Loren Miller, *The Petitioners: The Story of the Supreme Court of the United States and the Negro* (New York: Pantheon, 1966), 99–160; Leonard W. Levy and Harlan B. Phillips, "The *Roberts* Case: Source of the 'Separate but Equal' Doctrine," *American Historical Review* 56 (April 1951):510–18; Barton J. Bernstein, "Case Law in *Plessy v. Ferguson,*" *Journal of Negro History* 47 (July 1962):192–98; and Paul Oberst, "The Strange Career of *Plessy v. Ferguson,*" *15 Arizona Law Review* 389 (1973).

7. Charles Fenner, *Ex parte Homer A. Plessy,* 45 La. Ann. 80 (1893), reproduced in Olsen. *Thin Disguise,* 71–74; Fenner cites the Pennsylvania Supreme Court in *Westchester R.R. Co. v. Miles,* 55 Penn. St. 209 (1867), and Lemuel Shaw, *Roberts v. City of Boston,* 5 Cush. 198 (1849). For Shaw's decision in the Sims case, see *Thomas Sims's Case,* 61 Mass. 285 (1851).

8. Fenner, *Ex parte Homer A. Plessy,* in Olsen, *Thin Disguise,* 73; Woodward, "National Decision Against Equality," 229; Henry Billings Brown, *Plessy v. Ferguson,* 163 U.S. 537 (1896), reproduced in Olsen, *Thin Disguise,* 108–12.

9. Harris, *Quest for Equality,* 101; Miller, *Petitioners,* 106.

10. Frederick Douglass, quoted in Miller, *Petitioners,* 114.

11. Charles Sumner, quoted in Harris, *Quest for Equality,* 50–51; Joseph Bradley and John Marshall Harlan, *Civil Rights Cases* 109 U.S. 3 (1883), quoted in Harris, *Quest for Equality,* 87–91; Miller, *Petitioners,* 138–44; and Kluger, *Simple Justice,* 65–66.

12. Fenner, *Ex parte Homer A. Plessy,* in Olsen, *Thin Disguise,* 73; Morrison Waite, *United States v. Cruikshank,* 92 U.S. 554 (1875), in Harris, *Quest for Equality,* 85; Brown, *Plessy v. Ferguson,* in Olsen, *Thin Disguise,* 108–9.

13. Emma Lou Thornbrough, quoted in C. Vann Woodward, *The Strange Career of Jim Crow,* 2nd revised ed. (New York: Oxford University Press, 1966), 72.

14. John Marshall Harlan, *Plessy v. Ferguson,* in Olsen, *Thin Disguise,* 113–21. Harlan's position reverted toward Lemuel Shaw's in 1899, however, when he wrote the majority opinion in *Cumming v. Richmond County Board of Education,* 175 U.S. 528, which upheld separate but equal schools. Both an advocate of black rights, in most cases, and a conservative defender of property rights, Harlan betrayed an unusual mix of attitudes. Harlan's evolution, as Kluger points out, from a former slaveholder to a convert to the cause of civil rights is not entirely unlike Twain's response to childhood memories of slaveholding and postwar turmoil; it might be "traceable to the brutalities he saw inflicted upon Negroes in his native Kentucky during the post–Civil War years – beatings, lynchings, terror tactics beyond any conceivable justification." See Kluger, *Simple Justice,* 81.

15. Albion Tourgée, *Brief for Homer A. Plessy*, in Olsen, *Thin Disguise*, 80–103; Charles Sumner, *Roberts v. City of Boston*, reprinted as "Equality Before the Law," in *Complete Works*, vol. 3 (1900; reprint ed., New York: N.W. Ayer, 1969), 81.

16. Stanley P. Hirshson, *Farewell to the Bloody Shirt: Northern Republicans and the Southern Negro, 1877–1893* (Bloomington: Indiana University Press, 1962), 78–258, passim.

17. Joseph McKenna, *Williams v. Mississippi*, 170 U.S. 213 (1898), quoted in Kluger, *Simple Justice*, 67–68.

18. Mark Twain, "The United States of Lyncherdom," from *Europe and Elsewhere*, in *The Portable Mark Twain*, ed. Bernard DeVoto (New York: Viking, 1968), 586; Joel Williamson, *The Crucible of Race: Black-White Relations in the American South Since Emancipation* (New York: Oxford University Press, 1984), 318–19. See also George Fredrickson, *The Black Image in the White Mind: The Debate on Afro-American Character and Destiny, 1817–1914* (New York: Harper and Row, 1971), 256–82.

19. *Washington Post*, quoted in Logan, *Betrayal of the Negro*, 211; Albion Tourgée, *A Fool's Errand: A Novel of the South During Reconstruction* (New York: Harper and Row, 1966), 5–6.

20. Tourgée, *Brief for Homer A. Plessy*, in Olsen, *Thin Disguise*, 83, 97–98.

21. George Washington Cable, *The Negro Question: A Selection of Writings on Civil Rights in the South*, ed. Arlin Turner (New York: Somerset, 1958), 92; Williamson, *Crucible of Race*, 101; Pettit, *Mark Twain and the South*, 131–32.

22. Joel Williamson, *New People: Miscegenation and Mulattoes in the United States* (New York: Free Press, 1980), 101–3; Charles Dudley Warner, quoted in Olsen, *Thin Disguise*, 43–45.

23. Buck, *Road to Reunion*, 186–95; Logan, *Betrayal of the Negro*, 180–82; Booker T. Washington, *Up from Slavery*, in *Three Negro Classics* (New York: Avon, 1965), 149.

24. See John Higham, *Strangers in the Land: Patterns of American Nativism, 1860–1925* (1955; reprint ed., New York: MacMillan, 1963), 150–52; and Michael Rogin, "Francis Galton and Mark Twain: The Natal Autograph in *Pudd'nhead Wilson*" in this volume.

25. *Mark Twain-Howells Letters*, ed. Henry Nash Smith and William M. Gibson, 2 vols. (Cambridge, Mass.: Harvard University Press, 1960), 1:10–11; Sigmund Freud, "The Uncanny," in *Standard Edition of the Complete Psychological Works*, trans. and ed. James Strachey et al., 24 vols. (New York: W.W. Norton, 1976), 17:241.

26. Mark Twain, "Personal Habits of the Siamese Twins," in *Sketches, New and Old* (New York: Harper and Brothers, 1875), 273–79; see also Leslie Fiedler, *Freaks: Myths and Images of the Second Self* (New York: Simon and Schuster, 1978), 204–18.

27. John E. Coxe, "The New Orleans Mafia Incident," *Louisiana Historical Quarterly* 20 (October 1937):1066–1110; Maldwyn Allen Jones, *Ameri-*

can Immigration (Chicago: University of Chicago Press, 1960), 266; Higham, *Strangers in the Land,* 66, 90–92.

28. J. Alexander Karlin, "The Italo-American Incident of 1891 and the Road to Reunion," *Journal of Southern History* 8 (May 1942):242–46.

29. Pettit, *Mark Twain and the South,* 17; James M. Cox, *Mark Twain: The Fate of Humor* (Princeton: Princeton University Press, 1966), 232. See also Henry Nash Smith, *Mark Twain: The Development of a Writer* (Cambridge, Mass.: Harvard University Press, 1962), 174: "From the standpoint of imaginative coherence Judge York Leicester Driscoll is the father of Tom just as clearly as Roxy is his mother. But Mark Twain places the unmentionable fact of sexual intercourse between master and slave at two removes from the actual story – first by making Roxy, Tom's mother, the slave of the shadowy brother of Judge Driscoll at the time of Tom's birth; and then by the further precaution of creating an even more shadowy figure, Colonel Cecil Burleigh Essex, to be his father."

30. Thomas Nelson Page, "The Negro Question," in *The Old South: Essays Social and Political* (New York, 1892, repr. Westport, Conn.: Greenwood Press, 1970), 284.

Francis Galton and Mark Twain

1. Samuel Langhorne Clemens, *Pudd'nhead Wilson and Those Extraordinary Twins,* ed. Sidney E. Berger (New York: W.W. Norton, 1980), 154. Subsequent citations are by page number in the text. The criticism reprinted in the Norton Critical Edition (NCE) is cited in the following notes.

2. Hershel Parker, "*Pudd'nhead Wilson*: Jack-leg Author, Unreadable Text, and Sense-Making Critics," in *Flawed Texts and Verbal Icons: Literary Authority in American Fiction* (Evanston, Ill.: Northwestern University Press, 1984), 132.

3. Henry Nash Smith, "*Pudd'nhead Wilson* as Criticism of the Dominant Culture," NCE, 248; Parker, *Flawed Texts,* 123–25, 135; Edward Wagenknecht, "Development of Plot and Character in *Pudd'nhead Wilson,* NCE, 343; Arthur G. Pettit, "The Black and White Curse: *Pudd'nhead Wilson* and Miscegenation," NCE, 347–48. My thinking about the law, racial identity, and disguise in *Pudd'nhead Wilson* has also been influenced by Susan Gillman, *Dark Twins: Imposture and Identity in Mark Twain's America* (Chicago: University of Chicago Press, 1989).

4. Cf. Michael Paul Rogin, *Subversive Genealogy: The Politics and Art of Herman Melville* (New York: Knopf, 1983), 289–95.

5. Parker, *Flawed Texts and Verbal Icons,* 132.

6. James M. Cox, *Mark Twain: The Fate of Humor* (Princeton, N.J.: Princeton University Press, 1966), 227.

7. Cox, *Mark Twain,* 236; Barry Wood, "Narrative Action and Structural Symmetry in *Pudd'nhead Wilson,*" NCE, 379.

8. Leslie Fiedler, "As Free as Any Cretur . . . ," NCE, 224–25.

9. Cf. Karl Marx, "The Eighteenth Brumaire of Louis Bonaparte," in

Surveys from Exile, ed. David Fernbach (New York: Random House, 1974), 196; and Fredric Jameson, *The Political Unconscious: Narrative as a Socially Symbolic Act* (Ithaca, N.Y.: Cornell University Press, 1981).

10. Joel Williamson, *The Crucible of Race* (New York: Oxford University Press, 1984), 5–32, passim. The classic statement on Jim as mother in particular and on interracial male love in the West in general is Leslie Fiedler, *Love and Death in the American Novel* (New York: Scarborough House, 1960).

11. Williamson, *Crucible of Race,* 111–18, 184–88. Cf. also Lawrence Friedman, *The White Savage* (Englewood Cliffs, N.J.: Prentice-Hall, 1970).

12. Thomas Dixon, *The Leopard's Spots* (1902, repr. Ridgewood, N.J.: Irvington, 1967), 152, 161, 244. On Dixon, cf. Williamson, *Crucible of Race,* 158–76, and Michael Paul Rogin, "'The Sword Became a Flashing Vision': D.W. Griffith's *Birth of a Nation,*" *Representations* 9 (Winter 1985):150–95. On the lynching of Luigi, see Eric Sundquist's "Mark Twain and Homer Plessy" in this volume (pp. 66–69).

13. Pettit, "The Black and White Curse," NCE, 351n.; Arlin Turner, "Mark Twain and the South: *Pudd'nhead Wilson,*" NCE, 281.

14. Cf. Stanley Brodwin, "Blackness and the Adamic Myth in Mark Twain's *Pudd'nhead Wilson,*" NCE, 338–40.

15. Williamson, *Crucible of Race,* 184–85, 315–18.

16. Cf. Cox, *Mark Twain,* 237.

17. George M. Spangler, "*Pudd'nhead Wilson*: A Parable of Property," NCE, 295–303; Eberhard Alsen, "Pudd'nhead Wilson's Fight for Popularity and Power," NCE, 324–32.

18. Francis Galton, *Finger Prints* (1892, repr. New York: Da Capo, 1966), 2.

19. Galton, *Finger Prints,* 192–95; Daniel J. Kevles, *In the Name of Eugenics* (New York: Knopf, 1985), 1–76.

20. Kevles, *In the Name of Eugenics,* ix., 8–12, 76.

21. Ibid., 140, 281.

22. Ibid., 37, 57, 61; Williamson, *Crucible of Race,* 511–13; Michel Foucault, *The History of Sexuality,* vol. 1: An Introduction (New York: Random House, 1978), 124.

23. Galton, *Finger Prints,* 9.

24. Ibid., 1-2, 26. Cf. Gillman, *Dark Twins,* 88–91.

25. Cf. Marvin Fischer and Michael Elliot, "*Pudd'nhead Wilson*: Half a Dog Is Worse than None," NCE, 304–15; Cox, *Mark Twain,* 91–92, 235–36.

26. Gillman, *Dark Twins,* 93.

27. The last sentence paraphrases ibid., 73–74.

28. Parker, *Flawed Texts,* 123–25.

29. Cox, *Mark Twain,* 71.

30. Fiedler, "As Free," 226.

31. Cox, *Mark Twain,* 16.

32. Pettit, "The Black and White Curse," 355.

33. Ibid., 356–57.

34. Cox, *Mark Twain,* 227.

35. Ibid., 247-52. Cf. Gillman, *Dark Twins*, 77, 81-85, and Rogin, *Birth of a Nation*, 180-83.

36. Ibid., 102-3.

37. Clemens to Olivia L. Clemens, 12 January 1894, *The Love Letters of Mark Twain*, ed. Dixon Wecter (1949, repr. Hamden, Conn.: Greenwood Press, 1976), 291.

"Sure Identifiers"

1. Hjalmar Hjorth Boyesen, Review, *Cosmopolitan*. 18 (January 1895): 379.

2. Hershel Parker, *Flawed Texts and Verbal Icons: Literary Authority in American Fiction* (Evanston, Ill.: Northwestern University Press, 1984), 115-36. While Parker is patently wrong when he dismisses *Pudd'nhead Wilson* as "patently unreadable," he does pose a number of provocative questions about authorial intention and racial issues in the manuscript (see 142-44).

3. Even historically oriented literary critics like Arlin Turner ("Mark Twain and the South: An Affair of Love and Anger," *Southern Review* 4 [April 1968]:493-519) and Arthur Pettit (*Mark Twain and the South* [Lexington: University Press of Kentucky, 1974]) place Twain's dealings with the race question primarily in the context of literary history (the figure of the "tragic mulatto," for example, in Cable, Melville, Stowe, Howells) or of Clemens's own life (his Missouri background) and writings (notebook passages, autobiographical passages on race and sexuality).

4. The physiological differences between the two pairs of twins, the Italian and the Siamese, are telling: the Toccis shared one body, unlike Chang and Eng whose separate bodies, complete in themselves, were joined by a ligature. The crucial distinction is the shared body, which heightens the dilemma of the metaphysics of Siamese twinhood: whether the twins are individual or collective. For a late-nineteenth-century view, see *Scientific American* 65 (December 1891):374; for a modern view, see Stephen Jay Gould, "Living with Connections," in *The Flamingo's Smile: Reflections in Natural History* (New York: W.W. Norton, 1985), 64-77.

5. The terms in which I discuss these developments derive largely from George M. Fredrickson, *White Supremacy: A Comparative Study in American and South African History* (New York: Oxford University Press, 1981), 94-108, 129-35.

6. Joel Williamson, *New People: Miscegenation and Mulattoes in the United States* (New York: New York University Press, 1980), 24, 57-59.

7. On the legal problem of the slave's humanity, see Eugene D. Genovese, *Roll, Jordan, Roll: The World the Slaves Made* (New York: Random House, 1976), 28-37.

8. Fredrickson, *White Supremacy*, 133.

9. Samuel Langhorne Clemens, *Pudd'nhead Wilson and Those Extraordinary Twins*, ed. Sidney E. Berger (New York: W.W. Norton, 1980), 8-9.

10. On the "descent rule" or "rigorous ancestry principle," see Fredrickson, *White Supremacy,* 95–99, 129–30; see also 101–8 on the antebellum history of the legal color line. On "statutory homogenization," see Winthrop D. Jordan, *White Over Black: American Attitudes Toward the Negro, 1550–1812* (Greenville: University of North Carolina Press, 1968) 169.

11. Fredrickson, *White Supremacy,* 96; Jordan, *White Over Black*, 175, n. 84.

12. Leon Litwack argues that despite such legal erasure, on a more informal level, both before and after the Civil War, "whites made no attempt to deny the presence of a substantial mulatto population." The distorting combination of acknowledgment and denial is precisely what *Pudd'nhead Wilson* registers. See Litwack, *Been in the Storm So Long: The Aftermath of Slavery* (New York: Random House, 1980), 265–66.

13. John C. Hurd, *The Law of Freedom and Bondage in the United States,* 2 vols. (New York: D. Van Nostrand, 1858), 1:236.

14. Quoted in Williamson, *New People,* 66.

15. On Southern "muleology" and religious arguments about the South's defeat (including the passage in the letter from William Heyward to James Gregorie, 12 January 1868), see Williamson, *New People,* 73, 92, 96; on the etymology of "mulatto" and its cultural meanings, see Jordan, *White Over Black*, 168.

16. Jordan, *White Over Black,* 178.

17. George Washington Cable, "The Freedman's Case in Equity" and "The Silent South," in *The Negro Question: A Selection of Writings on Civil Rights in the South,* ed. Arlin Turner (New York: Somerset, 1958), 71, 85.

18. Edward S. Abdy, *Journal of a Residence and Tour in the United States,* 3 vols. (London, 1835), quoted in Leonard L. Richards, *Gentlemen of Property and Standing: Anti-Abolition Mobs in Jacksonian America* (New York: Oxford University Press, 1970), 42; Jefferson quoted in Ronald T. Takaki, *Iron Cages: Race and Culture in Nineteenth-Century America* (Seattle: University of Washington Press, 1979), 46, 49–50; Lincoln quoted in Henry Louis Gates, Jr., "Writing Race and the Difference It Makes," *Critical Inquiry ["Race," Writing, and Difference]* 12 (Autumn 1985):3.

19. Richards, *Gentlemen,* 45, 166.

20. Mary Boykin Chesnut, *A Diary from Dixie,* ed. Ben Ames Williams, (1949, repr. Cambridge: Harvard University Press, 1980), 21–22.

21. On race classification in Louisiana, see Virginia R. Dominguez, *White by Definition: Social Classification in Creole Louisiana* (New Brunswick: Rutgers University Press, 1986). On the "one-drop rule" in general, see Fredrickson, *White Supremacy,* 130.

22. Francis Galton, *Finger Prints* (1892, repr. New York: Da Capo, 1966), 12.

23. Samuel Clemens to William Dean Howells, 21 January 1879, in *Mark Twain–Howells Letters,* ed. Henry Nash Smith and William Gibson, 2 vols. (Cambridge: Harvard University Press, 1960), 1:246.

24. Conan Doyle, *The Complete Sherlock Holmes* (1930, repr. New York: Doubleday, 1960), 17.

25. Clemens, *Pudd'nhead Wilson*, 49.

26. Ibid., 119-20, 49.

27. Clemens to Fred J. Hall, 30 July 1893, in *Mark Twain's Letters to His Publishers*, ed. Hamlin Hill (Berkeley: University of California Press, 1967), 355.

28. Clemens to Miss Darrell, 23 February 1897, Typescript in Mark Twain Papers, Bancroft Library, University of California, Berkeley.

29. Galton, *Finger Prints*, 113, 167.

30. Ibid., 149.

31. Ibid., 2, 169.

32. Clemens, *Pudd'nhead Wilson*, 108.

33. Ibid., 109.

34. Ibid., 99.

35. Galton, *Finger Prints*, 151.

36. Clemens, *Pudd'nhead Wilson*, 112.

37. Galton, *Finger Prints*, 1-2, 20.

38. Clemens, *Pudd'nhead Wilson*, 115.

39. Clemens to Hall, 30 July 1893, in Hill, *Mark Twain's Letters to His Publishers*, 354-55.

40. Leslie Fiedler, "As Free as Any Cretur . . . ," in *Mark Twain: A Collection of Critical Essays*, ed. Henry Nash Smith (Englewood Cliffs, N.J.: Prentice-Hall, 1963), 138; see James Cox, *Mark Twain: The Fate of Humor* (Princeton: Princeton University Press, 1966), 323.

41. Clemens, *Pudd'nhead Wilson*, 45.

42. I am indebted to Leslie Fiedler's reading of the final Calendar entry as "a disconcerting ending for a detective story, which should have faith in all disclosures" ("As Free as Any Cretur . . . ," in *Collection of Critical Essays*, 138).

43. On the history of developments in anti-civil rights legislation following the Civil War, see Richard Bardolph, ed., *The Civil Rights Record: Black Americans and the Law, 1849-1970* (New York: Crowell, 1970), 58-72, 144-54.

The Ties that Bind

1. I use "sex" instead of "gender" in the title not to reject the argument that sexual identity is a social construction, but to sidestep it in order to evoke the material condition itself; the way sex is interpreted into gender being precisely the subject of this essay. I am aware that one view holds that no material condition as such exists, or none we can apprehend, so that the language of gender is all we know of sex and all we need to know. To this, my response is implicit in what follows, that gender, like any ideological construction, describes the interactions of several realities, at least one of which is not the creature of language but material – the world out there. Gender is all we know of sex, but not all we need to know. This essay also depicts the inadequacy of ideological knowledge.

2. Samuel Langhorne Clemens, *Pudd'nhead Wilson and Those Extraor-*

dinary Twins, ed. Signey E. Berger (New York: W.W. Norton, 1980), 114. Quotations from this edition are cited parenthetically in the text.

3. The first description of the two children distinguished only by the "soft muslin and . . . coral necklace" of one and the "coarse tow-linen shirt" of the other (9) recalls the similarly contrasting costumes of the Prince and the Pauper. In that story, however, the little pauper fulfills all sentimental expectations, and far from usurping the throne, returns it more secure to its rightful owner. Are there implications in the virtue of this poor boy, versus the vice of the black boy, for different authorial attitudes toward class and race?

4. Here I would mention specifically that portion of the literature that has reevaluated the sentimental tradition as a female, sometimes feminist, critique of the male ideology of the market. See especially Jane Tompkins, *Sensational Designs: The Cultural Work of American Fiction, 1790–1860* (New York: Oxford University Press, 1985) and Elizabeth Ammons, "Stowe's Dream of the Mother-Savior: *Uncle Tom's Cabin* and American Women Writers before the 1920s," in *New Essays on Uncle Tom's Cabin,* ed. Eric J. Sundquist (Cambridge: Cambridge University Press, 1986).

5. I have discussed this phenomenon more fully in an essay, "Archimedes and the Paradox of Feminist Criticism," *Signs* 6 (Winter 1981):575–601.

Roxana's Plot

1. For example, while calling Roxana Twain's "most fully realized female character," Arlin Turner argues that "through her, in the clearest instance in all his fiction," Twain "acknowledged sex to be an element in human relations." Frederick Anderson sees her as "Twain's most successful female protagonist," pairing her with the Aunt Rachel of "A True Story" to suggest that Twain apparently "required the distance provided by color to establish and sustain the vulgar quality of life in female character." One of the most impressive critiques of Twain's characterization of Roxana is also based on this assumption that her power is fueled by her sexuality. According to Arthur G. Pettit, it is Twain's ambivalence toward the powerfully sexual black woman of his imagination that accounts for Roxana's "bewildering" role changes from "black shrew" to "tragic mother figure." Twain "used blacks and mulattoes," Pettit argues, "to express sexual feelings that were prohibited by white standards of propriety," and Roxana's contradictory behavior reflects Twain's inability to cope with such feelings. Thus he "wound up with two Roxana's," Pettit suggests, a "near-white one, . . . and a much darker Roxana." See *Pudd'nhead Wilson and Those Extraordinary Twins,* ed. Sidney E. Berger (New York: W.W. Norton, 1980), 275, 285, 351–54.

2. See James M. Cox, "The Ironic Stranger," in Clemens, *Pudd'nhead Wilson,* 259–67. For a fuller version, see Cox's *Mark Twain: The Fate of Humor* (Princeton, N.J.: Princeton University Press, 1966), chap. 10, 222–46.

3. Cox, "The Ironic Stranger," 262.

4. Quotations from Spillers taken from lecture delivered at the University of California, Berkeley, November 1987. Twain explored the theme of the "tragic mulatto" more fully in the original manuscript of the novel before he separated the "tragedy" of *Pudd'nhead Wilson* from the "farce" called *Those Extraordinary Twins*. On these revisions, see Hershel Parker, *"Pudd'nhead Wilson*: Jack-leg Author, Unreadable Text, and Sense-Making Critics," in *Flawed Texts and Verbal Icons: Literary Authority in American Fiction* (Evanston, Ill.: Northwestern University Press, 1984), 115–46. Francis Harper's *Iola Leroy*, which appeared two years before Twain's novel, was the most contemporary of several fictional representations of the tragic mulatto. Critical assessments of this figure, and of the rich and heterogeneous tradition in which she or he functions, have proliferated in recent years. A beginning may be made with the following: Judith Berzon, *Neither White nor Black* (New York: New York University Press, 1978); Barbara Christian, *Black Women Novelists: The Making of a Tradition, 1892–1976* (Westport, Conn.: Greenwood Press, 1980); Hazel Carby, *Reconstructing Womanhood: The Emergence of the Afro-American Woman Novelist* (New York: Oxford University Press, 1987); Mary Helen Washington, *Invented Lives: Narratives of Black Women: 1860–1960* (New York: Doubleday, 1987).

5. Clemens, *Pudd'nhead Wilson*, 8–9. All further references are to this edition, and will be cited in the text.

6. *"Pudd'nhead Wilson* and the Fiction of Law and Custom," in *American Realism: New Essays*, ed. Eric Sundquist (Baltimore: Johns Hopkins University Press, 1982), 86.

7. See Clemens, *Pudd'nhead Wilson*, 244.

8. See Orlando Patterson, *Slavery and Social Death: A Comparative Study* (Cambridge, Mass.: Harvard University Press, 1982), esp. chap. 2, 35–76. In addition to Winthrop Jordan's *White over Black: American Attitudes Toward the Negro, 1550–1812* (Baltimore: Penguin, 1969), useful sources on the cultural, legal, and political contexts of miscegenation in the United States are Michael Grossberg, *Governing the Hearth: Law and the Family in Nineteenth Century America* (Chapel Hill: University of North Carolina Press, 1985), 136ff. and Marylynn Salmon, *Women and the Law of Property in Early America* (Chapel Hill: University of North Carolina Press, 1986), esp. 211ff.

9. The question of whether it must remain a secret to her son, once he is old enough to hear it, is begged by Twain's account of Tom's upbringing as a white master. But the question is answered differently by Faulkner in the story of Charles Bon. See *Absalom, Absalom!* (New York: Vintage, 1936).

10. See George M. Spangler, *"Pudd'nhead Wilson*: A Parable of Property," in *Pudd'nhead Wilson*, 295–303.

11. In fact, the collapse of difference between death and alienability has already been accomplished for her. When her efforts to exploit the exchangeability of death for alienability culminate in her own sale down the river, her experiences there can be read as narrativing the metaphorical relation be-

tween killing and selling, relocating it along a metonymic axis where her sale and her death threaten to achieve a cause-effect relationship.

Fatal Speculations

1. Samuel Langhorne Clemens, *Pudd'nhead Wilson and Those Extraordinary Twins*, ed. Sidney E. Berger (New York: W.W. Norton, 1980), 115. Quotations from this edition are cited parenthetically in the text.

2. See Arlin Turner, "Mark Twain and the South: *Pudd'nhead Wilson*," in the Norton Critical Edition, 282: "By 1894, the problems explored in *Pudd'nhead Wilson* had grown wearisome in the North as well as the South. More than a decade earlier the political decision had been made that the Southern states should solve the race problem without interference from the national government. As state laws were enacted in the early 1890s which decreed for the former slaves a segregated, non-voting status, no effective protest was voiced in either section. The public, valuing the peace which had been achieved, did not welcome disturbances, even in fiction. There is something of irony in that, by chance rather than intention, Mark Twain wrote his most perceptive and most impressive attack on racism and related doctrines at a time when his attack could stir no spark in the reading public." My argument, of course, attempts to lend Twain's "attack on racism and related doctrines" more relevance to late-nineteenth-century, industrial America, North and South.

3. The "p'fessor in a college" so reviled by Pap Finn in chapter 6 of the novel is particularly hateful to him because he can *vote* in "Ohio." Freedom and voting rights are very often linked by Twain, which is why vote-buying is such an immoral "speculation" for him.

4. Mark Twain and Charles Dudley Warner, *The Gilded Age: A Tale of Today* (New York: New American Library, 1969), 393–94. Quotations from this edition are cited parenthetically in the text as *GA*.

5. While working as a surveyor and investor in a speculative scheme to develop a small Missouri settlement in advance of the railroad, Philip Sterling visits the New York offices of the company to find out why no funds for the workers' salaries have been sent. By the time he leaves these "headquarters," he finds himself several thousands of dollars in debt and his workers considerably "overpaid." The "accounting" given him is a splendid parody of the rhetorical sophistry by which commerical America would give "objective" credibility to its speculative fictions.

6. See my discussion of Twain's representations of parents and children in *Through the Custom-House: Nineteenth-Century American Fiction and Modern Theory* (Baltimore: Johns Hopkins University Press, 1982), 161.

7. Dixon Wecter, *Sam Clemens of Hannibal* (Boston: Houghton Mifflin, 1952), 68–72.

8. Wecter, *Sam Clemens*, 72.

9. As quoted in ibid., 72.

10. If Percy and the Judge represent two "halves" of Judge John M. Clem-

ens, then David Wilson and Tom represent two "halves" of Twain's own personality. A psychoanalytical reading of *Pudd'nhead Wilson* that would elaborate the literary mechanisms by which Twain distances, represses, and still recognizes his kinship with these two corrupt characters would be most welcome and helpful.

11. Perry McCandless, *A History of Missouri,* vol. 2, *1820–1860* (Columbia: University of Missouri Press, 1972), 119.

12. McCandless, *A History,* 2:138.

13. Philip Sterling finally overcomes his "speculating instincts" by working hard and discovering shared labor with his workers in the coal mine he develops in the latter part of the narrative. Henry Brierly's financial and romantic "schemes" lure him into the clutches of Laura Hawkins, who uses him as an unwitting accessory in her murder of the lover who had betrayed her. Finally released from prison, Harry heads for San Francisco, apparently unregenerate, "to look after some government contracts in the harbor there" (*GA,* 346). The morality of Warner and Twain in *The Gilded Age* is heavy-handed and puritanical, but it provides a clear background for Twain's indictment of cancerous immorality of speculation in *Pudd'nhead Wilson.*

14. *The Autobiography of Mark Twain,* ed. Charles Neider (New York: Washington Square Press, 1961), 281.

15. Neider, *Autobiography,* 282. Of John Clemens's efforts to satisfy his creditors, Dixon Wecter writes in *Sam Clemens of Hannibal*: "The code of the Virginia gentleman permitted no other course to Mark Twain's father, and the pride which the son took in his father's stripping himself to satisfy all claims – beyond the call of duty, we are told, down to offering the forks and spoons, and every stick of furniture – presaged a similar act in Mark's life half a century later" (71).

16. Turner, "Mark Twain and the South," 280, makes a strong case for finding traces of Judge John Clemens in the characters of both Percy Driscoll and Judge Driscoll.

17. Tom's cowardice throughout *Pudd'nhead Wilson* often has been noted by critics. Tom's famous reflection in chapter 10 on his newly discovered identity as a black slave seems only to intensify that cowardice by adding self-contempt to the formula. Twain often noted that it was just this "slave-mentality" that was white America's worst sin against blacks. By the same token, Roxy's will, cleverness, and moral righteousness all seem to come from her general imitation of white customs and attitudes. As potentially racist as Twain's distinction between Tom and Roxy seems to be, it's fair to note that Twain gives us virtually no means for generalizing about the "essence" of the "Negro" in *Pudd'nhead Wilson.* As Roxy's fantastic family genealogy suggests, the "Essex blood" of which she is so proud is traceable ultimately to "Pocahontas de Injun queen, en her husbun' was a nigger king outen Africa" (70). In her own fictional origins – the ones that are finally the important ones for Twain's characters – Roxy rediscovers her strength, intelligence, and will in native American and African roots.

18. Michael Paul Rogin, *Subversive Genealogy: The Politics and Art of Herman Melville* (Berkeley: University of California Press, 1983), 73.

19. Rogin, *Subversive Genealogy,* 73.

20. See Frederick Anderson, "Mark Twain and the Writing of *Pudd'nhead Wilson,*" in the Norton Critical Edition: "Aspects of Pudd'nhead Wilson's character and career, specifically his barren law practice, are based on that of Mark Twain's brother Orion and the crushing failure he encountered in his attempt to practice that profession" (285). We might add the "crushing failures" that Orion's speculative and inventive schemes invariably encountered in his curious career. The character Washington Hawkins in *The Gilded Age,* chief victim of Colonel Sellers's fantastic schemes, is clearly modeled after Orion Clemens.

21. George M. Spangler, "*Pudd'nhead Wilson*: A Parable of Property," Norton Critical Edition, 303.

22. The anonymous reviewer of *Pudd'nhead Wilson* in *The Athenaeum* (January 19, 1895), reprinted in the Norton Critical Edition, 216, complains: "Why drag in, for example, all the business about the election, which is quite irrelevant? and the Twins altogether seem to have very little *raison d'etre* in the book." It is fair to say that these are old complaints that have not been sufficiently answered by modern critics of the novel.

"By Right of the White Election"

1. Page references in the text are to the Norton Critical Edition of *Pudd'nhead Wilson and Those Extraordinary Twins,* ed. Sidney E. Berger (New York: W. W. Norton, 1980).

2. Stanley Brodwin, "Blackness and the Adamic Myth in Mark Twain's *Pudd'nhead Wilson,*" *Texas Studies in Literature and Language* 15 (Spring 1973):167–68. In a series of articles, Brodwin has argued for the centrality of theological speculation in Twain's thought and writing. See, for example, "The Humor of the Absurd: Mark Twain's Adamic Diaries," *Criticism* 14 (Winter 1972):49–64; "Mark Twain's Masks of Satan: The Final Phase," *American Literature* 45 (May 1973):206–27; "The Theology of Mark Twain: Banished Adam and the Bible," *Mississippi Quarterly* 29 (Spring 1976): 167–89; and "Mark Twain in the Pulpit: The Theological Comedy of *Huckleberry Finn,*" in *One Hundred Years of "Huckleberry Finn": The Boy, His Book, and American Culture,* ed., Robert Sattelmeyer and J. Donald Crowley (Columbia: University of Missouri Press, 1985), 371–85.

3. Brodwin, "Blackness and the Adamic Myth," 169.

4. John Carlos Rowe, *Through the Custom-House: Nineteenth-Century Fiction and Modern Theory* (Baltimore: Johns Hopkins Press, 1982), 167. Rowe's emphasis is on the way the text "historicizes" and thus relativizes the religious and philosophical ideals that prop up the power structure of Dawson's Landing. I am more inclined to see historicization itself as a secular "faith" to whose truth-value Twain is not fully prepared to commit himself.

5. Quoted in Svend Petersen, ed., *Mark Twain and the Government* (Caldwell, Idaho: Caxton Printers, 1960), 43.

6. It is perfectly possible of course, as Hershel Parker would argue, that this "dangling" plot reflects the haste and carelessness of a "jack-leg" novelist more than crafted thematics. However, it seems equally plausible to find such a truncation part of a larger inconclusiveness that I am arguing is central to the themes of both *Those Extraordinary Twins* and *Pudd'nhead Wilson*. See Parker, *Flawed Texts and Verbal Icons: Literary Authority in American Fiction* (Evanston, Ill.: Northwestern University Press, 1984), 115–45.

7. My argument here is considerably indebted to Lawrence W. Levine's *Black Culture and Black Consciousness: Afro-American Folk Thought from Slavery to Freedom* (New York: Oxford University Press, 1977), especially chapter 1, which stresses slaves' creative and strategically effective adaptation of Christian beliefs and imagery to their own harsh situation.

8. For a useful overview of evangelical Protestant belief in the antebellum West, see Sydney E. Ahlstrom's magisterial *A Religious History of the American People* (New Haven, Conn.: Yale University Press, 1972), especially chapters 27–29. My discussion necessarily rides roughshod over Ahlstrom's sensitive explication of the often-subtle theological discriminations made by the intellectual leaders of the Old Northwest's major denominations, including the three – Presbyterian, Methodist, and Baptist – that appear in *Pudd'nhead Wilson* and *Those Extraordinary Twins*. Ahlstrom himself notes that, from the perspective of the ordinary members of these denominations' congregations, many of these subtleties tended to disappear into a common set of notions revolving around the sovereignty of God and the depravity – but savability – of humanity.

9. Ahlstrom stresses the widespread importance of "Arminianism set on fire" to evangelical Protestantism in the Old Northwest, and of its intertwining with more traditional Calvinist notions. As he observes of frontier Methodism, however, "Arminianism . . . meant not an optimistic view of human nature . . . but a reinterpretation of the strict Calvinistic understanding of atonement, grace, and the sanctifying work of the Holy Spirit" (*A Religious History*, 438).

10. Levine, *Black Culture and Black Consciousness*, 39.

11. Several critics have noted a passage deleted by Twain from the novel in which Roxy attacks her black friend Jasper's defense of "special providences" by asserting her own belief in "a body of well regulated laws." I believe it plausible to argue that Twain deleted this passage because it would have dramatically contradicted the line of argument that Roxy takes in the baby-switching episode. Far from turning her into a Deist, he keeps her leaning toward Calvinism and even, as I suggest, Antinomianism.

12. A usefully succinct discussion of Antinomianism, and its relationship to Arminianism, can be found in Edmund Morgan, *The Puritan Dilemma: The Story of John Winthrop* (Boston: Little, Brown, 1958), 136–40. Historians of nineteenth-century Protestantism rarely mark the continuing, if faint,

presence of Antinomianism; but I believe it plausible to suggest resonances between such a dark theology and Twain's own increasingly pessimistic and even nihilistic meditations.

13. See Robinson's essay in this volume, as well as the equally provocative exploration of such tensions by most of the other contributors.

14. A partly farcical, partly probing meditation on the epistemological problematics of salvation is manifest in *Those Extraordinary Twins* in the baptism of Angelo/Luigi. The man of true faith cannot be baptised without the simultaneous immersion of his free-thinking brother. Is Luigi damning himself by what might be considered a blasphemous act? Does the act in fact irresistibly save him? Or is the only consequence for him a bad cold? Conceivably, a soul, either light or dark, can never rid itself of its opposing twin, and the religious consequences may thus be constantly and unavoidably contested.

Pudd'nhead Wilson on Democratic Governance

1. Eberhard Alsen, "Pudd'nhead Wilson's Fight for Popularity and Power," in *Pudd'nhead Wilson and Those Extraordinary Twins*, ed. Sidney E. Berger (New York: W. W. Norton, 1980), 331–32. Quotations from this edition are cited parenthetically in the text. It is always wise to assume that Twain is up to something, that he *has* a design, often a very subtle one. Humor — especially in the form of story-telling — is a duplicitous and crafted art, and Twain took pains to prepare his effects, as much a showman as Hank Morgan in *Connecticut Yankee*, but more conscious of the human limitations of his audience. And Twain, who told us that he "always preached," kept his mind's eye on the great issues of human life. *The Autobiography of Mark Twain*, ed. Charles Neider (New York: Harper, 1959), 273.

2. Richard P. McCormick, *The Second American Party System* (Chapel Hill: University of North Carolina Press, 1966).

3. It also parallels Twain's early life. Born the son of a Whig judge very much like Judge Driscoll, reared in a Whig community during the age of Jackson but then apprenticed to a Democratic newspaper, Twain, as Cox observes, was "reborn" as Mark Twain one month after the Emancipation Proclamation. James M. Cox, *Mark Twain: The Fate of Humor* (Princeton, N.J.: Princeton University Press, 1966), 4–5; Dixon Wecter, *Sam Clemens of Hannibal* (Boston: Houghton Mifflin, 1952), 78, 110–11, 124, 201.

4. Robert Regan, *Unpromising Heroes: Mark Twain and His Characters* (Berkeley: University of California Press, 1966), 240–41; Harvey C. Mansfield, Jr., *Statesmanship and Party Government* (Chicago: University of Chicago Press, 1965), 198–200.

5. Alexis de Tocqueville, *Democracry in America* (New York: Schocken, 1961), 1:176–82.

6. In fact, according to Aristotle, elections which turn on the virtue of those chosen — rather than their birth or wealth — deserve to be called "aristocratic" because they select rulers thought to be the best. *Politics*, 1293b10–11;

compare Tocqueville, *Democracy in America*, 1:34–36. Apparently, Twain approved the idea of an American Hall of Fame because turn-of-the-century Americans, drowning in a "tide of glory and affluence," needed to be reminded of the nature of republican nobility. Henry Nash Smith and William Gibson, eds., *The Twain-Howells Letters* (Cambridge: Harvard University Press, 1960), 2:729. See also Twain's comparison of the examples set by George Washington and General Frederick Funston, "A Defence of General Funston," in *Mark Twain on the Damned Human Race*, ed. Janet Welt Smith (New York: Hill and Wang, 1962), 82–94.

7. *The Writings of Thomas Jefferson*, ed. A. E. Bergh (Washington, D.C.: Thomas Jefferson Memorial Association, 1907) 13:396ff.

8. Jefferson, *Writings*, 11:244–45, see also 11:192 and 14:197; John Chester Miller, *The Wolf by the Ears* (New York: Free Press, 1977), 46–50; on women, see Linda Kerber, *Women of the Republic: Intellect and Ideology in Revolutionary America* (Chapel Hill: University of North Carolina Press, 1980).

9. After all, Roxy's "six generations of white blood" testify to an apparently untroubled tradition of doing as one pleases while disclaiming responsibility, at least so long as the victim is black and female.

10. Dawson's Landing, founded in 1780, dates from the years between the Declaration and the Constitution.

11. Ronald Reagan's distaste for "government" and his preference for heroic individuals, while peculiarly cinematic, stands in the same tradition. Garry Wills, "A Fantasy Breeds a Scandal," *Newsweek*, December 29, 1986, 22–23.

12. Tom's indifference to questions of honor and his straightforward materialism only voice a scapegraced version of the acquisitive tradition in which he has been brought up, just as Jim Fiske's high capitalist mot, "Nothing is lost save honor," descends from the Framers' gentlemanly commercialism. Tom lacks the Judge's generosity, no small difference, but Tom's vice – gambling – is of the same quality as respectable speculation: "OCTOBER: this is one of the particularly dangerous months to speculate in stocks in. The others are July, January, September, April, November, May, March, June, December, August, and February" (61); see also George Spangler, "A Parable of Property," *PW*, 298.

13. The term *granfalloon*, of course, is borrowed from Kurt Vonnegut's *Cat's Cradle* and refers to any "proud and meaningless association of human beings." Kurt Vonnegut, *Wampeters, Foma and Granfalloons* (New York: Delta, 1974), xv.

14. The fact that the Cappellos are Florentine is an echo of Twain's "Whisper to the Reader," especially since the hint of the family's Imperial connections – they fled to Germany – implies that they are modern Ghibellines.

15. The "sole surviving member of the Freethinker's Society," Wilson is the heir to Jefferson's science, but not to his Virginia gentility. Cox, *Mark Twain*, 244.

16. Of course, in this respect, Enlightenment theorizing also lowered the

standard of critical judgment, turning away from the best regime in favor of the practicable regime, building on the foundation of modern political philosophy laid down in the fifteenth chapter of *The Prince*.

17. This carries to a revealing, farcical extreme Locke's argument in *Essay Concerning Human Understanding*, Book II, chap. xxvii, sec. 19.

18. Charles Neider, ed., *The Complete Short Stories of Mark Twain* (Garden City, N.Y.: Doubleday, 1957), 588.

19. Compare Twain's comments to Elinor Glyn in *The Autobiography of Mark Twain*, ed. Neider, 355.

20. Mark Twain, *Joan of Arc* (New York: Harper, 1926), 245.

21. *Republic*, 334a–b.

22. Cox, *Mark Twain*, 234–35.

23. Ibid., 235; this parallels the discovery in *Huckleberry Finn* that Jim is not a slave at all.

24. Ibid., 92, 238. Notably, in his essay "The Late Ben Franklin," Twain begins by reformulating one of Poor Richard's adages in the style of *Pudd'nhead Wilson's Calendar*: "Never put off till tomorrow what you can do day after tomorrow just as well." *Sketches New and Old* (Hartford: American Book Company, 1899), 211.

25. Alsen, "Pudd'nhead Wilson's Fight for Popularity and Power," 325.

26. Jay B. Hubbell, *The South in American Literature* (Durham, N.C.: Duke University Press, 1954), 835.

27. Twain, "The Late Ben Franklin," 214.

28. Ibid., As Cox comments, in Franklin's *Autobiography*, Franklin's own life virtually displaces the American Revolution. Cox, *Mark Twain*, 93.

29. *The Autobiography of Benjamin Franklin* (New York: Heritage, 1951), 118–19. Franklin did not include humility in his original list of the virtues, adding it later only at the suggestion of a Quaker acquaintance.

30. Twain, "The Late Ben Franklin," 211, 213.

31. Twain would have agreed with Holmes's observation that the law "cannot be dealt with as if it contained only the axioms and corollaries of a book of mathematics." Oliver Wendell Holmes, Jr., *The Common Law* (Boston: Little, Brown, 1881), 1.

32. Wecter, *Sam Clemens*, 164–65. Twain concluded that it is easier for a fool to succeed in the law than in any other profession. This emphasizes that Twain, contriving to have Wilson thought a fool, also denies him a fool's success.

33. Aristotle, *Nichomachean Ethics*, 1159b29–31, 1164b30–31.

34. Ibid., 1162b34–1163a2.

35. Aristotle, *Eudemian Ethics*, 1234b; Kurt Riezler, *Man, Mutable and Immutable* (Chicago: Henry Regnery, 1950), 193. All friendships, Aristotle argues, aim at equality (*Nichomachean Ethics* 1158b25–33); in the same way, all political equality aims at at least a kind of friendship.

36. For example, Wilson's sociability – and doubtless, his desire to impress his hearers – leads him to reveal his secret scheme for catching the

murderer in a conversation which includes Tom. His sociophilia dooms his plan; in this respect, he is truly a pudd'nhead (65, 77); on the general point, see Plato, *Gorgias,* 481 D–E and J. B. Salter, "The Pattern of Politics," *Journal of Politics* 1 (1939):265.

37. That Wilson puts the obligations of friendship above the hope of honor is a protection against the appeals of popularity as well as the lures of interest. It also suggests a proper order of priorities (Nichomachean Ethics, 1159a13–27).

38. Cox, *Mark Twain,* 245–46.

39. Plutarch, *Moralia,* 827b9–c9.

40. Plutarch, *Lives of the Noble Grecians and Romans* (New York: Modern Library, n.d.), 835. Another likely source is Montesquieu's *Persian Letters*: in the last letter, Roxana, who has chosen suicide, proudly proclaims that she has deceived her husband: "How could you have imagined that I existed only to adore your caprices . . . ? No: I have lived in slavery, but I have always been free. I reformed your laws by those of nature, and my spirit has always held to its independence." Letter CLXI, G. Healy trans. (Indianapolis: Bobbs Merrill, 1964), 172. Smith and Gibson's suggestion that Roxy's name derives from Defoe via Howells is plausible, but much less apposite, *Twain-Howells Letters,* 2:536–37.

41. Cox, *Mark Twain,* 231.

42. For example, see Locke, *Essay Concerning Human Understanding,* Book II, chap. xvii, sec. 6.

43. Of course, she will more readily sacrifice for what she loves, and her coming to love Tom again is probably a precondition for her highest sacrifice (80).

44. It is worth noting that, for Roxy, involuntary separation, not slavery itself, is the supreme indignity.

45. F. R. Leavis, "Mark Twain's Neglected Classic: The Moral Astringency of Pudd'nhead Wilson," *PW,* 241.

46. Smith, ed., *Mark Twain on the Damned Human Race,* 68. In his putative special providence, Jasper won freedom by stopping a runaway coach on a narrow road by a precipice, saving a mother and daughter. The scene begs to be compared with Oedipus' meeting with Laius, and I think that Twain was playing with the idea of Jasper as anti-Oedipus, one who saves women rather than slaying men, perhaps because he is more aware of human duties than of violated rights or dignities. It might also be worthwhile to compare Roxy, willing to kill herself and her child in order to spare him separation and indignity, with Jocasta who allows her child to be sent away, even though she may have conspired with the shepherd to save his life. And Wilson, who teaches by an appeal to sight, is less grand a prophet than blind Tereisias, but he brings a gentler doom.

47. Even the most decent whites were prone to the damning "lie of silent assertion," the pretense which allowed them to ignore the monstrous injustice of slavery. Charles Neider, ed., *Complete Humorous Sketches and Tales of Mark Twain* (Garden City, N.Y.: Doubleday, 1961), 672–73.

48. It is only a little less evident that women and blacks have also had their reputations "destroyed by ridicule."

49. Friedrich Nietzsche, *Thus Spake Zarathustra*, 1st English translation (New York and London: Macmillan, 1896), chap. 1. In 1907 Twain claimed that he had not read Nietzsche, "or any other philosopher," because he knew that philosophy has not a "single original thought" and that everything important can be learned through introspection. Frederick Anderson, ed., *A Pen Warmed Up in Hell* (New York: Harper and Row, 1972), 176. Yet this assertion amounts to a stunning rebuke to Nietzsche, because it denies creativity and affirms human equality in a fairly radical way. Moreover, Twain went on to claim enough familiarity with Nietzsche's doctrine to know that Nietzsche was scoffed at by thousands who shared his beliefs. Twain's denial is also undermined by the fact that he certainly had read philosophically inclined thinkers like Carlyle and Heine, and he mentions Aristotle from time to time. Because Parts 1 and 2 of *Zarathustra* were completed in 1883, it is at least possible that Twain had read or knew of the work. That Nietzsche admired Twain makes this even more plausible. Stanley Hubbard, *Nietzsche und Emerson* (Basel: Verlag fur Rechts u. Gesellschaft, 1958), 10. And a reference to Zarathustra would account for Twain's ironic comment that "instead of feeling complimented when we are called an ass, we are left in doubt." Common usage, of course, involves no such ambiguity, but Nietzsche does have mixed feelings about the camel and the load-bearing spirit.

50. Compare the famous "esophagus" sentence in "A Double-Barreled Detective Story," in *Complete Short Stories*, ed. Neider, 436–38.

51. On Twain's views of party, see A. B. Paine, ed., *The Autobiography of Mark Twain* (New York: Harper, 1924), 2:13–21 and "Skeleton Plan of a Proposal for a Casting Vote Party," in *Complete Essays of Mark Twain*, ed. Charles Neider (Garden City: Doubleday, 1963), 647–50.

52. Michele Barbi, *The Life of Dante*, trans. Paul G. Ruggiers (Berkeley: University of California Press, 1954), 11.

53. Barbi, *Life of Dante*, 119–20; on Dante's political teaching, see Joan Ferrante, *The Political Vision of the Divine Comedy* (Princeton, N.J.: Princeton University Press, 1984), 3, 42–43, and Ernest L. Fortin, *Dissidence et philosophie au moyen age* (Montreal: Bellarmin, 1981).

54. Barbi, *Life of Dante*, 17, 44–45.

55. For example, see Ferrante, *Political Vision*, 196–97, 251–52.

56. George M. Spangler, "A Parable of Property," *PW*, 295–303. On George Washington, see also *Complete Humorous Sketches and Tales*, ed. Neider, 676–77. The American ideal of independence, Twain was to say later, is itself a lie, perhaps the most important of the deceptions that Washington failed to discern. By thinking of liberty and independence as natural—that is, biological—principles, Americans mislead themselves and ignore the social and psychological foundations of a self-ruled soul. *Autobiography of Mark Twain*, ed. Paine, 2:8.

57. According to the *Calendar*, had Eve eaten the "true Southern water-

melon," she would not have repented (66). But Eve does not repent, except by claiming that she was "beguiled," (*Genesis* 3:13). Because the watermelon, for Twain, often symbolized politically unappreciated wisdom, he may have meant to imply that Eve, properly "watermeloned," would have been *so* beguiled as to take responsibility for her own acts. *Complete Short Stories*, ed. Neider, 403–4; *Autobiography*, ed. Neider, 370; see also *Autobiography*, ed. Paine., 2:283–85.

58. Cited in Barbi, *Life of Dante*, 47, from *Convivio*, I:xiii:12. Zarathustra, too, proclaimed the coming of a "great noontide." *Thus Spake Zarathustra*, chap. 80.

59. *Complete Essays of Mark Twain*, ed. Neider, 282–96.

"What did he reckon would become of the other half if he killed his half?"

1. For much of his material, Twain drew upon a skill of direct participant observation at the grass-roots level of American life that any ethnographer or folklorist would both admire and envy. The "half a dog" story seems obviously to be this kind of material, but instead of its accurate representation within its social contexts of telling and reception, which would be the folklorist's or ethnographer's interest in it, Twain molds it to his own storytelling purposes. James M. Cox, who also focused a *Pudd'nhead Wilson* essay on the "half a dog" story ("The Ironic Stranger," reprinted in *Pudd'nhead Wilson and Those Extraordinary Twins*, ed. Sidney E. Berger, [New York: W.W. Norton, 1980]; quotations from this edition are cited parenthetically in the text), noted (264) the earlier observation of Jay Hubbell (*The South in American Literature* [Durham, N.C.: Duke University Press, 1954]) that indeed the "half a dog" story was a part of regional culture, but unlike Twain's use of it, it would have been received as a genre nonsense story which listeners would find amusing, rather than confounding.

2. Cross-cultural and ethnographic concerns with the self, personhood, and the cultural expression of the emotions have enjoyed a revival in anthropology that is generating a vigorous literature. For an understanding of this revival, presently common to a number of disciplines, see Thomas C. Heller, et al., eds., *Reconstructing Individualism: Autonomy, Individuality, and the Self in Western Thought* (Stanford, Calif: Stanford University Press, 1986); in the context of anthropology's particular variant of a response to postmodernist conditions of knowledge, see George Marcus and Michael M. J. Fischer, *Anthropology as Cultural Critique: an Experimental Moment in the Human Sciences* (Chicago: University of Chicago Press, 1986). For an interesting set of essays that trace the anthropological study of the self back to the seminal essay by Marcel Mauss, see Michael Carrithers et al., eds., *The Category of Person: Anthropology, Philosophy, History* (New York: Cambridge University Press, 1985). For exemplary studies in the revival, see, for example, Michelle Z. Rosaldo, *Knowledge and Passion: Ilongot Notions of Self and Social Life* (New York: Cambridge University

Press, 1980); and Michael G. Kenny, *The Passion of Ansel Bourne: Multiple Personality in American Culture* (Washington, D. C.: Smithsonian Institution Press, 1986).

3. H. Stuart Hughes, *Consciousness and Society: The Reorientation of European Social Thought* (Cambridge, Mass.: Harvard University Press, 1958).

4. Of course, everything said herein about the nineteenth-century critique of the American self is heavily gender inflected from the male perspective. Scholarship on nineteenth-century women's autobiography and literature, for example, suggests that a contemporaneous feminine critique of the self, if given the same attention, would have been far more radical, twentieth-century in style, and less ambivalent about not clinging to hegemonic individualism than was the cultural criticism of their male counterparts. For some treatment of women's autobiography, see Paul John Eakin, *Fictions in Autobiography: Studies in the Art of Self-Invention* (Princeton, N.J.: Princeton University Press, 1985); also, see him for an excellent statement of the inherently subversive nature of autobiography (but which may not always be exploited), in relation to rigid ideologies of the coherent self.

5. Dorrit Cohn, *Transparent Minds* (Princeton, N.J.: Princeton University Press, 1978); Ann Banfield, *Unspeakable Sentences* (Boston: Routledge and Kegan Paul, 1982).

6. Robert Alter, "Playing Host to the *Doppelganger*," *Times Literary Supplement*, October 24, 1986, p. 1190.

7. See Kenny, *The Passion of Ansel Bourne.*

8. Spiritualism and an interest in extrasensory phenomena were legitimate aspects of the formation of a scientific psychology in late-nineteenth-century America (see Kenny), as they were in literature. The creation of doubles as doppelgangers was thus not a completely figurative move by critics of the autonomous self in a society in which the belief in spirits was widespread.

9. Justin Kaplan, *Mr. Clemens and Mark Twain, a Biography* (New York: Simon and Schuster, 1966).

10. Louis A. Sass, "Introspection, Schizophrenia, and the Fragmentation of Self," *Representations* 19 (Summer 1987):1–34.

11. Stanley M. Elkins, *Slavery: A Problem in American Institutional and Intellectual Life* (Chicago: University of Chicago Press, 1959).

12. Eugene D. Genovese, *The Political Economy of Slavery: Studies in the Economy and Society of the Slave South* (New York: Vintage Books, 1965).

13. For a brilliant historical and ethnographic study of such a system in Louisiana from legal institutions to grass-roots culture, see Virginia R. Dominguez, *White by Definition: Social Classification in Creole Louisiana* (New Brunswick, N.J.: Rutgers University Press, 1986).

14. Sass, "Introspection, Schizophrenia."

15. See Christine Brooke-Rose's "The Dissolution of Character in the Novel," in Heller et al., eds., *Reconstructing Individualism*, 184–96.

Some of the Ways of Freedom in *Pudd'nhead Wilson*

This chapter was prepared for a conference; I have made revisions in points of detail, but the tone and direction of the original are unaltered.

1. Samuel Langhorne Clemens, *Pudd'nhead Wilson and Those Extraordinary Twins*, ed. Sidney E. Berger (New York: W.W. Norton, 1980), 70. Quotations from this edition are cited parenthetically in the text.

2. To say that the novelists' exploration of the self, of identity, has deepened ignorance as it has deepened knowledge is not to say that the exploration has ended in failure. Far from it. How much we have learned about identity from Proust, Joyce, James, Kafka! It is an immense intellectual achievement, as splendid as any of the triumphs of science. And to say that the great novelists have explored the enigma of the self is not to say that they have pursued an illusion, or have discovered that identity is an illusion. That is the "discovery" trumpeted by so much contemporary literary (and social) theory. An enigma is not an illusion. I think much of the current theoretical buzz about the "disappearance of the subject" and the "illusion of identity" is based, unknowingly, on the hapless idea that if an identity is not like an atom then it is not real. Novelists, unlike theorists, have been happily immune to the Cartesian syndrome.

3. Hershel Parker, *Flawed Texts and Verbal Icons: Literary Authority in American Fiction* (Evanston, Ill.: Northwestern University Press, 1984).

4. Clemens himself, along with a few other swaggerers, had roved about for a time in the early stages of the war looking for some Yankees to fight. He soon abandoned the field and became secretary to his brother, who had been appointed governor of Nevada Territory by Lincoln. Clemens was not eager to recall these facts later on.

5. I am saying something close to what I think Hannah Arendt meant when she reminded us that "philosophies" of freedom appear after freedom-as-action has disappeared, and what Orlando Patterson meant when he said that the idea of liberty, every bit as much as sugar or indigo, was a product of slave society. See Arendt, "What Is Freedom?" in *Between Past and Future* (New York: Viking, 1961), 143–73; and Patterson, *Slavery and Social Death* (Cambridge, Mass: Harvard University Press, 1982), esp. 340–42.

6. C. S. Lewis says that in the ancient world, freedom could mean simply citizenship. See his *Studies in Words* (Cambridge: Cambridge University Press, 1961), 125.

7. So when Lincoln said in 1863 at the Baltimore Sanitary Fair that "the world has never had a good definition of freedom," he was wrong. The world has had *one* "good" definition of freedom.

8. Lewis, *Studies in Words*, 22.

About the Contributors

Michael Cowan is Professor of Literature and American Studies at the University of California, Santa Cruz. He is the author of *City of the West: Emerson, America, and Urban Metaphor* and essays on American cultural theory, urban American literature, and writers from Emerson to Faulkner and Mailer.

James M. Cox has retired from Dartmouth College and has returned to the house and farm where he was born and raised. He is the author of *Mark Twain: The Fate of Humor, Recovering Literature's Lost Ground: Essays in American Autobiography*, and many essays on writers ranging from Stowe, Hawthorne, and Henry Adams to Ring Lardner, Faulkner, and Hemingway.

Susan Gillman teaches at the University of California, Santa Cruz. She is the author of *Dark Twins: Imposture and Identity in Mark Twain's America.*

Myra Jehlen teaches at the University of Pennsylvania. She has recently published *American Incarnation: The Individual, The Nation and the Continent.*

Wilson Carey McWilliams is Professor of Political Science at Rutgers University. He is the author of *The Idea of Fraternity in America* and other works on American politics and political thought.

George E. Marcus is Professor and Chair, Department of Anthropology at Rice University. He is co-author with Michael Fischer of *Anthropology as Cultural Critique: An Experimental Moment in the Human Sciences;* co-editor with James Clifford of *Writing Culture: The Poetics and Politics of Ethnography*; and inaugural editor of the journal *Cultural Anthropology.*

Carolyn Porter teaches at the University of California, Berkeley. She is the author of a forthcoming study of Melville and of *Seeing and*

Being: The Plight of the Participant Observer in Emerson, James, Adams, and Faulkner.

Forrest G. Robinson teaches American Literature and American Studies at the University of California, Santa Cruz. He has written books on Sir Philip Sidney, Wallace Stegner, and Mark Twain, and articles on a wide range of English and American subjects. He is currently at work on a biography of Henry A. Murray, the eminent American personality theorist and Melville scholar.

Michael Rogin teaches Political Science at the University of California, Berkeley. His most recent books are *Ronald Reagan, the Movie and Other Episodes in Political Demonology* and *Subversive Genealogy: The Politics and Art of Herman Melville.*

John Carlos Rowe teaches the literature and culture of the United States and critical theory at the University of California, Irvine. His most recent book is *At Emerson's Tomb: The Politics of American Modernism.*

John H. Schaar is Professor of Politics in the University of California, Santa Cruz. He is the author of *Loyalty in America, Escape from Authority,* and *Legitimacy in the Modern State.*

Eric J. Sundquist is Professor of English at the University of California, Los Angeles. He is the author of the recent *Faulkner: The House Divided* and the editor of *Frederick Douglass: New Literary and Historical Essays.*

Index

Adams, John, 178
Adventures of Huckleberry Finn, The
  (Twain), xix, 8, 11, 27, 50, 141, 153,
  165, 168; bad faith in, 25–26, 29,
  232 n.17; parent-child bond in, 142;
  slavery in, 5–7, 75–76, 199, 213;
  social change in, 138
Adventures of Tom Sawyer, The
  (Twain), 25, 168, 213, 217
Africa, 20, 93; South Africa, 91
Ahlstrom, Sydney E., 246 n.8
Alsen, Eberhard, 184
Alter, Robert, 193–94, 207
Antinomianism, 168, 172–76
Aristocracy, 19, 178–81, 184, 224
Aristotle, 226
Arminianism, 168–76
Autobiography, 192–93

Bad faith, 22–45, 172; in *Huckleberry
  Finn*, 25–26, 29, 232 n.17; in *Tom
  Sawyer*, 25
Banfield, Ann, 193
Beecher, Lyman, 93
Beloved (Morrison), 134
"Benito Cereno" (Melville), 52
Berger, Sidney E., viii
Billy Budd (Melville), 74
Birth of a Nation, The (film), 49
Blacks. *See* Mulatto (es); Race;
  Slavery
Blaine, James, 68
Boyeson, Hjalmar Hjorth, 86, 88
Bradley, Joseph, 55
Brodwin, Stanley, 156, 174
Brown, Henry Billings, 52–57, 61,
  62
Brown v. Board of Education, 53,
  60
Bunker, Chang and Eng, 14, 67
Burke, Edmund, 221
Burt, Cyril, 79

Cable, George Washington, 49, 60–62,
  72, 92–95
Calvinism, 168–73, 176
Capitalism. *See* Market economy
Carton, Evan, 1, 126
Century Magazine, 61, 88
Cerchi, 187
Chang and Eng, 14, 67
Chase, Richard, 126
Chesnut, Mary Boykin, 94
Chiasmus, 194–95
Civil Rights Cases, 54–55, 57, 61
Civil War, U.S., 2, 4, 7, 78, 138, 141,
  223; and freedom, 13, 218; and mis-
  cegenation, 67, 90, 92, 94; and
  Plessy v. Ferguson, 52–53
Clansman, The (Dixon), 49, 76–77
Clemens, Jane, 144, 145
Clemens, John Marshall, 70, 77, 144,
  145, 147
Clemens, Olivia, 82
Clemens, Orion, 144, 245 n.20
Clemens, Samuel. *See* Twain, Mark
Cohn, Dorrit, 193
Columbus, Christopher, 20, 227
Conan Doyle, Arthur, 95–96
Confidence-Man, The (Melville), 175
*Connecticut Yankee in King Arthur's
  Court, A* (Twain), 20, 27, 138
Consciousness, 192–93. *See also*
  Identity
Constitution, U.S., 178; Thirteenth
  Amendment, 52; Fourteenth Amend-
  ment, 52–56, 92–93, 102–3; Fifteenth
  Amendment, 54, 92–93, 102–3
Cotton Centennial Exposition, 62
Cowan, Michael, xiv
Cox, James M., viii, x–xi, xvii, 44, 70,
  81, 85, 102, 121–22, 124, 135
Creoles, 201
Crossed selves, 193–98, 200, 202, 208,
  209

Dante, 12, 187–89
Death, 166–67, 217; slavery as, 126–29, 133–34
Democracy, 13, 25, 222, 224, 225; question of who should rule, 177–89. *See also* Freedom
Democratic party, 177, 187–88
Derrida, Jacques, 207, 208
Desdunes, Daniel, 51
Detective, in fiction, 95–97
Dickinson, Emily, 176
Divided self, 193–95, 208
Dixon, Thomas, 49, 76–77
Doppelganger, 193–94, 196, 201, 203
Doubling, 46, 142, 190–210; and bad faith, in social order, 32–44; and guilt of blackness, 73–74, 84; in *Huckleberry Finn*, 6; as literary device, 193–94; and national racial policy, 50–51, 61–69; and Poe, 10; of will, 11–13. *See also* Crossed selves; Divided self; Identity
Douglass, Frederick, 54, 219
Dred Scott v. Sandford, 54, 55, 57, 138
Duality. *See* Doubling
Dueling, 224

Education of Henry Adams, The (Adams), 193
Edwards, Jonathan, 169
Election(s), 157–64, 167–70, 175–76, 178. *See also* Democracy
Elkins, Stanley M., 200
Emancipation Proclamation, 4, 138
Emerson, Ralph Waldo, 218, 220, 226
Enlightenment, 2, 180
Eugenics, 19, 63, 78–80

"Facts Concerning the Recent Carnival of Crime in Connecticut, The" (Twain), 166
Fatout, Paul, 4
Faulkner, William, 84, 86
Fenner, Charles, 52, 54, 62
Fiedler, Leslie, 75, 82, 102
Fingerprinting, 13, 15, 157, 182, 211, 217; and bad faith, 37–39; and race-sex paradigms, 118–20; and racial identity, 18–20, 63, 78–81, 84–85, 95–102, 126, 128, 182; and revelation of fragmented self, 198, 204–5; and speculative economy, 141, 150–52; and theology, 172. *See also* Identity

Finger Prints (Galton), 19, 63, 78–80, 97–100
First Families of Virginia (F.F.V.), 79–80, 142–43, 153, 179–80, 223–24
Fitter Family Contests, 80
Flaubert, Gustave, 114
Following the Equator (Twain), 20
Fool's Errand, A (Tourgée), 59
Foucault, Michel, 80
Franklin, Benjamin, 7, 81, 106, 169, 182–83
Fredrickson, George, 2, 89, 91, 94
"Freedman's Case in Equity, The" (Cable), 61, 72
Freedom, 4–5, 20–21, 216–27; in *Huckleberry Finn*, 5–7; slavery versus, 1–21, 177–89, 216–19. *See also* Democracy
Freud, Sigmund, 65, 192

Galton, Sir Francis, 19, 63, 78–80, 95–100, 103
Gender. *See* Sex (gender)
Genovese, Eugene D., 200
Gilded Age, The (Twain and Warner), 137, 139–41, 144–47, 149–52, 154
Gillman, Susan, xii, 81
Glover, Sam, 184
Go Down, Moses (Faulkner), 84
Grady, Henry, W., 62
Grant, Ulysses S., 2
Griffith, D. W., 49

Hall, Fred J., 24, 97
Harlan, John Marshall, 53, 55, 57, 60, 70, 72
Harris, Joel Chandler, 49
Harris, Robert, 53
Hawthorne, Nathaniel, 8
"Hawthorne and His Mosses" (Melville), 215
Heredity, 41, 63, 74, 95, 99; and character, 18–19, 41, 74; Galton's views on, 19, 79–80; and miscegenation, 92. *See also* Fingerprinting
Hicks, William, 12, 187
Higham, John, 68
Holmes, Sherlock, 95–96
Hoover, J. Edgar, 211
Howells, William Dean, 4, 49, 65, 83, 212
Hubbell, Jay, 182
Huckleberry Finn (Twain). See *Adventures of Huckleberry Finn, The* (Twain)

Hughes, H. Stuart, 192
Hutchinson, Anne, 171–72

Identity, 50, 70, 90, 185, 190–210, 254 n.2; and bad faith, 35; constructed nature of, 103–4; and fingerprinting, 19–20, 63, 78–81, 84–85, 97, 128, 204–5; of slaves, 128–29; of Twain, 3–5, 7. *See also* Fingerprinting; Race
Imitation, theme of, 48–49, 64–66, 69–71, 126–27, 133, 146
Immigration, 47, 63, 67–69, 149, 154
Imperative Duty, An (Howells), 212
Imperialism, 2, 20
Indians, American, 2
IQ test, 79
Italian immigrants, 66–69

Jackson, Andrew, 145, 177
James, Henry, 9, 21
James, William, 190, 192
Jameson, Fredric, 231 n.11
Jefferson, Thomas, 2, 93, 178–80, 185
Jehlin, Myra, vii, xiii
Jensen, Arthur, 79
Jezebel, black, 123, 124
Jim Crow laws. *See* Law(s)
Jordan, Winthrop, 91–93

Kansas-Nebraska Act, 177
Kenny, Michael G., 207
Kipling, Rudyard, 103
Ku Klux Klan, 49

Latin America, 91
Law(s), 11, 12, 14, 35, 177, 179, 187; and bad faith, 35, 39; and custom, fictions of, 38–39, 43, 46, 47, 90, 101–2, 124, 128, 142; Jim Crow, after Reconstruction, 46–72, 87–88, 102–3, 108–9, 135, 199, 218. *See also* Constitution, U.S.; Supreme Court, U.S.
Leavis, F. R., 7–8
Leopard's Spots, The (Dixon), 76–77
Levine, Lawrence, 170
Lewis, C. S., 222–23, 225
Liberty. *See* Freedom
Life on the Mississippi (Twain), 19, 138–39
Lincoln, Abraham, 2, 4, 93, 227
Louisiana, segregation law in, 47, 51–52, 56, 60
Lynchings, 58–59, 68–69, 76–77, 88, 135

McKenna, Joseph, 58
McWilliams, Wilson Carey, xiv–xv
Mafia, 68
Mammy, black, 123, 124, 133
Manifest Destiny, 139, 149
Marcus, George E., xv
Market economy: maternal economy versus, 113–14; racial identity in, 127–28; speculation and slavery in, 137–54
Mark Twain's Autobiography (Twain), 137, 144–45
Marshall, Elmer Grady, 211
Martinet, Louis A., 51
Massachusetts, segregation law in, 52–53
Mass culture, 231 n.11
Matrilineal descent, 129–30, 135
Melville, Herman, 52, 74, 175, 215
Miller, Loren, 54
Mind, as "meaning-seeking faculty," 40
Minstrel show, 48–49
Miscegenation, 50, 74, 90–91, 122, 142, 143; fear of, 35, 46, 61–67, 76–79, 83–84, 87–95; as literary theme, 212; and matrilineal descent, 129–30; and speculative economy, 139–40. *See also* Mulatto(es)
Montesquieu, 250 n.40
Morrison, Toni, 134
Mulatto(es), 73–74, 88; and descent rule, 90–91; and Jim Crow laws, 51–52, 58, 60–67, 70, 72; and miscegenation, 35, 91; and slavery, 88–89; stereotype of, 77, 83–85, 225; tragic, 123–24. *See also* Miscegenation
Multiple personality, 194, 207

National Civil Rights Association (NCRA), 60
New Orleans, 62, 67–68
New South, The (Grady), 62
Nietzsche, Friedrich, 186–87, 192
Notes on the State of Virginia (Jefferson), 2, 93
Novels, fragmented self in, 193–95

Old South myth, 49, 57–59, 72
"Old Times on the Mississippi" (Twain), 138, 147
Original sin, 156
O'Sullivan, John L., 149
Ozick, Cynthia, 190, 208

Page, Thomas Nelson, 49, 72
Palmistry, 19, 80, 83, 102, 150, 153.
    See also Fingerprinting
Panic: of 1837, 145, 147; of 1893, 7,
    147
Parker, Hershel, xvi, 8, 22–24, 26,
    39–41, 46, 87, 215
Patterson, Orlando, 126, 127, 134
Peirce, Charles S., 192
"Personal Habits of the Siamese
    Twins" (Twain), 67
Pettit, Arthur, G., 241 n.1
Pinchback, P. B. S., 51
Plessy, Homer. See *Plessy v. Ferguson*
Plessy v. Ferguson, 46–72, 102, 135,
    218
Plutarch, 185
Poe, Edgar Allan, 10
Poor Richard's Almanac (Franklin),
    81, 182
Porter, Carolyn, xiii
Positivism, 192
Postmodernism, literary, 192, 207–10
Prince and the Pauper, The (Twain),
    14, 27, 138
Property: and aristocracy, 179; slaves
    as, 127–30, 137–38, 206
Psychological novels, 193
Pudd'nhead Wilson. See *Tragedy of
    Pudd'nhead Wilson and the Com-
    edy of Those Extraordinary Twins,
    The* (Twain)
Puritans, 2, 169, 172

Race: contradictory dynamics of,
    1–21; and descent rule, 47, 91–92,
    94, 185, 212; and fingerprinting,
    78–81, 84–85, 95–102; and guilt,
    73–85; post-Reconstruction laws on,
    46–72, 87–88, 102–3, 108–9, 135,
    199, 218; and sex, interaction be-
    tween, 105–20; as social construc-
    tion, 86–104, 191, 196. *See also*
    Miscegenation; Mulatto(es); Slavery
Rader, Ralph W., 40
Rape, 76–78
Reconstruction, 78, 108, 138; Jim
    Crow laws after, 46–72, 87–88,
    102–3, 108–9, 135, 199, 218; and
    miscegenation, 92–94
Regan, Robert, 177
Religion, 155–76, 224. *See also* An-
    tinomianism; Arminianism,
    Calvinism

Republican party, 58, 188
Richards, Leonard L., 93
Rights, and freedom, 219
Roberts v. the City of Boston, 52–53,
    57
Robinson, Forrest G., xi, 172
Rogin, Michael, xii, 19, 149
Roughing It (Twain), 65, 83
Rowe, John Carlos, xiii–xiv, 157

Sahlins, Marshall, 195
Sass, Louis A., 196
Saving, in theology, 157, 164–67,
    170
Schaar, John H., xv–xvi
Schizophrenia, 196, 203
Science, 172; and racial
    characteristics, 79–81; and
    speculative economy, 150–52. *See
    also* Fingerprinting; Heredity
Segregation law: in Louisiana, 47,
    51–52, 56, 60; in Massachusetts,
    52–53
Self. *See* Crossed selves; Divided self;
    Identity
Separate but equal doctrine. See
    Plessy v. Ferguson
Sex (gender), 178–79, 253 n.4;
    disguises of, 90; and oedipal pat-
    tern, 121–22; and race, interaction
    of, 105–20. *See also* Women
Sexuality: black, threat of, 35, 65,
    76–78, 83–84; of Roxana, 121, 123;
    and tragic mulatta, 123, 124. *See
    also* Miscegenation
Shakespeare, William, 181
Shaw, Lemuel, 52, 53, 55, 57
Siamese twins, 18; Chang and Eng,
    14, 67; race and slavery as, 1–2; in
    Those Extraordinary Twins, 9, 11,
    14, 65–67, 87, 88; Tocci brothers,
    66–67, 87
Silent South, The (Cable), 61
Sims, Charles, 52
Slaughterhouse Cases, 53–54, 56
Slavery, 94, 96; and bad faith, 22–45;
    and doubled self, 195–202, 208; and
    freedom, opposition between, 1–21,
    177–89, 216–19; in *Huckleberry
    Finn*, 5–7, 75–76, 199, 213; mulatto,
    88–89; reinvention of, 55, 57, 60, 63,
    66; and relation between race and
    sex, 106–10, 114, 115; Roxana's plot
    and system of, 121–36; and "selling

down the river," 126–27, 164–65, 174; and speculative economy, 137–54; and theological politics, 155–76. *See also* Race
Smith, Henry Nash, 16, 73
South Africa, 91
"South as a Field for Fiction, The" (Tourgée), 49
Southern Horror: Lynch Law in All Its Phases (pamphlet), 58
Spangler, George, 127, 150
Spanish-American War, 68–69
"Specie Circular," 145
Speculative economy, 137–54
Spillers, Hortense, 123
Stevenson, Robert Louis, 38, 190
Stout, Ira, 145
Stowe, Harriet Beecher, 107, 165
Strange Case of Dr. Jekyll and Mr. Hyde, The (Stevenson), 38, 190
Study in Scarlet, A (Conan Doyle), 95
Sumner, Charles, 52, 55, 57
Sumner, William Graham, 53, 218–19, 226
Sundquist, Eric, xi–xii
Supreme Court, U.S., 49–50, 102; and *Plessy v. Ferguson*, 50–61, 68, 102

Taney, Roger B., 54
Thoreau, Henry David, 218
Those Extraordinary Twins (Twain). See *Tragedy of Pudd'nhead Wilson and the Comedy of Those Extraordinary Twins, The* (Twain)
Thus Spake Zarathustra (Nietzsche) 186–87
Tillman, Benjamin, 68
Tocci brothers, 66–67, 87
Tocqueville, Alexis de, 226
Tom Sawyer (Twain). See *Adventures of Tom Sawyer, The* (Twain)
Tourgée, Albion, 49, 59, 72; and *Plessy v. Fergusson*, 51–52, 57, 59–61, 63
Tragedy of Pudd'nhead Wilson and the Comedy of Those Extraordinary Twins, The (Twain): bad faith in, 22–45; Boyesen on, 86; "Calendar," 81, 102, 154, 169, 170, 172, 174, 179–80, 182, 188, 217, 223; contradictory dynamics of race in, 1–21; criteria for racial identity in, 86–104; on democratic governance, 177–89; and freedom con-

cept, 216–18, 223–27; guilt and race in, 73–85; incoherence of, 22–45, 211–15; and minstrel show, 48–49; personal identity concept in, 190–210; and *Plessy v. Ferguson*, 46–72; relation between race and sex paradigms in, 105–20; Roxana's plot and slavery system in, 121–36; and speculative economy, 137–54; theological politics in, 155–76; "Whisper to the Reader," 12–13, 23, 69, 186–89
Transparent Minds (Cohn), 193
Turner, Arlin, 243 n.2
Turner, Frederick Jackson, 75
Turner, Victor, 159
Twain, Mark: business career of, 147; childhood of, 144–45; disorder in style of, 22–23; on Franklin, 182–83; identity of, 3–5, 7; sexual dream of, 65, 83–84; on writing of *Pudd'nhead Wilson*, 8–11, 13, 27–28, 96, 102
Twins: fingerprinting of, 98; scientific study of, 19, 79. *See also* Doubling; Siamese twins

Uncle Tom's Cabin (Stowe), 107, 165
United States v. Cruikshank, 54–57
United States v. Harris, 54, 57
United States v. Reese, 54
Unspeakable Sentences (Banfield), 193

"Villagers, The" (Twain), 144–45
Virginia. *See* First Families of Virginia (F.F.V.)

Waite, Morrison, 55
Walker, George, 48
Warner, Charles Dudley, 62, 63; *The Gilded Age*, 137, 139–41, 144–47, 149–52, 154
Washington, Booker T., 62–63
Washington, George, 188
Weber, Max, 192
Webster and Company, 147
Wecter, Dixon, 145
Wells, Ida B., 58
West Indies, 84, 91
White, Deborah, 123
Wigglesworth, Michael, 169
Will, 9–14

Williamson, Joel, 59, 62, 76, 78, 88–89
Williams v. Mississippi, 58
"William Wilson" (Poe), 10
Winthrop, John, 169, 171–72
Women: and miscegenation, 94; status of, 178–79; white, sexual assault on, 78. *See also* Sex (gender)
Woodward, C. Vann, 53

Yale University, 110, 146
"Young America," 149